TITANS OF INDUSTRIAL AGRICULTURE

One Planet

Sikina Jinnah and Simon Nicholson, series editors

Peter Dauvergne, *AI in the Wild: Sustainability in the Age of Artificial Intelligence*

Vincent Ialenti, *Deep Time Reckoning: How Future Thinking Can Help Earth Now*

Maria Ivanova, *The Untold Story of the World's Leading Environmental Institution: UNEP at Fifty*

Peter Friederici, *Beyond Climate Breakdown: Envisioning New Stories of Radical Hope*

Jennifer Clapp, *Titans of Industrial Agriculture: How a Few Giant Corporations Came to Dominate the Farm Sector and Why It Matters*

TITANS OF INDUSTRIAL AGRICULTURE

HOW A FEW GIANT CORPORATIONS CAME TO
DOMINATE THE FARM SECTOR AND WHY
IT MATTERS

JENNIFER CLAPP

THE MIT PRESS   CAMBRIDGE, MASSACHUSETTS   LONDON, ENGLAND

© 2025 Massachusetts Institute of Technology

All rights reserved. No part of this book may be used to train artificial intelligence systems or reproduced in any form by any electronic or mechanical means (including photocopying, recording, or information storage and retrieval) without permission in writing from the publisher.

The MIT Press would like to thank the anonymous peer reviewers who provided comments on drafts of this book. The generous work of academic experts is essential for establishing the authority and quality of our publications. We acknowledge with gratitude the contributions of these otherwise uncredited readers.

This book was set in Stone Serif and Avenir LT Std by Westchester Publishing Services. Printed and bound in the United States of America.

Library of Congress Cataloging-in-Publication Data

Names: Clapp, Jennifer, 1963– author.
Title: Titans of industrial agriculture : how a few giant corporations came to dominate the farm sector and why it matters / Jennifer Clapp
Other titles: One planet (MIT Press)
Description: Cambridge, Massachusetts : The MIT Press, [2025] | Series: One planet | Includes bibliographical references and index
Identifiers: LCCN 2024019109 (print) | LCCN 2024019110 (ebook) | ISBN 9780262551700 (paperback) | ISBN 9780262382342 (epub) | ISBN 9780262382359 (pdf)
Subjects: LCSH: Agricultural industries—Mergers. | Agriculture—Economic aspects. | Consolidation and merger of corporations.
Classification: LCC HD9000.5 .C546 2025 (print) | LCC HD9000.5 (ebook) | DDC 338.1/9—dc23/eng/20240923
LC record available at https://lccn.loc.gov/2024019109
LC ebook record available at https://lccn.loc.gov/2024019110

10 9 8 7 6 5 4 3 2 1

publication supported by a grant from
The Community Foundation for Greater New Haven
as part of the *Urban Haven Project*

CONTENTS

SERIES FOREWORD ix
PREFACE xi
LIST OF ABBREVIATIONS xvii

1 INTRODUCTION 1

I THE INITIAL RISE TO CORPORATE BIGNESS IN THE AGRICULTURAL INPUTS INDUSTRY

2 FARM MACHINERY 27
3 FERTILIZERS 59
4 SEEDS 87
5 PESTICIDES 113

II CONSOLIDATION AND EXPANSION FROM THE MID-TWENTIETH CENTURY

6 LOCK-IN AND SHIP OUT 139
7 MERGERS OF DISTRESS IN FARM MACHINERY AND FERTILIZERS 163
8 MERGERS OF OPPORTUNITY IN SEEDS AND PESTICIDES 191

III TWENTY-FIRST-CENTURY MEGAMERGERS AND THEIR CONSEQUENCES

9 DRIVERS OF RECENT AGRIBUSINESS MEGAMERGERS 221
10 THE POWER TO SHAPE MARKETS 245
11 THE POWER TO SHAPE TECHNOLOGY 269
12 THE POWER TO SHAPE POLICY AND GOVERNANCE 293

IV CONCLUSION

13 THE UNCERTAIN PATH AHEAD 321

NOTES 341
REFERENCES 373
INDEX 423

SERIES FOREWORD

This is at once an odd and exhilarating time to be alive. Our species, *Homo sapiens*, has had roughly 350,000 years on the planet. For most of that time our ancestors barely registered as a quiet voice in a teeming chorus. No more. Now, a human cacophony threatens the ecological foundations upon which all life rests, even as technological wonders point the way toward accelerating expansion. We find ourselves at a moment of reckoning. The next handful of decades will determine whether humanity has the capacity, will, and wisdom to manufacture forms of collective life compatible with long-term ecological realities, or whether, instead, there is an expiration date on the grand human experiment.

The One Planet book series has been created to showcase insightful, hope-fueled accounts of the planetary condition and the social and political features upon which that condition now depends. Most environmental books are shackled by a pessimistic reading of the present moment or by academic conventions that stifle a writer's voice. We have asked One Planet authors to produce a different kind of scholarship. This series is designed to give established and emerging authors a chance to put their best, most astute ideas on display. These are works crafted to show a new path through the complex and overwhelming subject matters that characterize life on our New Earth.

The books in this series are not formulaic. Nor are they Pollyannaish. The hope we have asked for from our authors comes not from overly optimistic accounts of ways forward, but rather from hard-headed and clear-eyed accounts of the actions we need to take in the face of sometimes overwhelming odds. One Planet books are unified by deep scholarly engagement brought to life through vivid writing by authors freed to write from the heart.

Thanks to our friends at the MIT Press, especially to Beth Clevenger, for guiding the One Planet series into existence, and to the contributing authors for their extraordinary work. The authors, the Press, and we, the series editors, invite engagement. The best books do more than convey interesting ideas: they spark interesting conversations. Please write to us to let us know how you are using One Planet books or to tell us about the kinds of themes you would like to see the series address.

Finally, our thanks to you for picking up and diving into this book. We hope that you find it a useful addition to your own thinking about life on our One Planet.

Sikina Jinnah and Simon Nicholson

PREFACE

My daily walk to work takes me down a short, one-block street called Sunshine Avenue. The street is poorly maintained, rarely has cars on it, and is filled with potholes. One side of the street has no sidewalk and is flanked by a gravel parking lot and a grassy field at the back of a retirement complex that I walk through to get to campus every day.

After several months of research for this book, I was surprised to read that the very first line of an article on the rivalry between different harvester companies in the 1930s mentioned Waterloo, Ontario, the town where I live. At first, I found it odd that a medium-sized Canadian city played a role in the story I was researching on the history of the big, multinational agricultural input companies. The article highlighted how the Waterloo Manufacturing Company, which produced threshers and farm engines beginning in the 1850s, partnered with H. V. McKay Company of Australia in 1930 to make a self-propelled combine harvester, known as the Sunshine Waterloo combine. The abandoned site down the road was where the Sunshine Waterloo factory once stood.

What happened to the factory? Ironically, the firm barely produced the combine harvesters it was built to manufacture. The Great Depression of the early 1930s meant that farmers did not have the funds to buy expensive harvesting machines. Smaller farm machinery firms were also up against the huge North American manufacturers like International

Harvester, which held over 80 percent of the tractor market in the United States at the time, and Massey-Harris, the dominant Canadian firm at the time. Those larger firms enjoyed a range of market, technology, and policy advantages not readily available to smaller firms. The Sunshine Waterloo manufacturing plant only narrowly avoided closure by diversifying out of farm equipment into other products, such as automotive parts, bicycles, roller skates, and baby carriages. A handful of the Sunshine Waterloo combines were sold on consignment for farmers farther west in the Canadian Prairies, but the plant never mass-manufactured them. By 1934 the Waterloo Manufacturing Company pulled out of the venture to focus on other industrial products like boilers and engines, and several years later, after the outbreak of World War II, the company started manufacturing armaments to stay afloat.

The Sunshine Waterloo Company never went back to making farm machinery and was eventually sold along with H. V. McKay in the 1950s to what by then was Massey Ferguson (the product of another merger between farm equipment firms). While there were a number of intervening factors, the Sunshine Waterloo Company simply could not compete with the big farm equipment firms that dominated the increasingly global market. Instead, it got swallowed by one of them. The factory was eventually demolished in 1994 when Massey Ferguson was bought by AGCO, now one of the four largest farm equipment firms in the world.

This account of a smaller firm succumbing to the power of a larger dominant firm in the agricultural inputs sector is not unique. There are likely hundreds of abandoned industrial sites scattered around the world that used to produce farm equipment a century or two ago. And it's not just farm machinery that has seen this pattern of big overtaking small. In seeds, fertilizers, and agrochemicals, it is a similar story. Today, just a handful of giant transnational corporations dominate all of these markets. This book is about what has driven that pattern of growing corporate concentration and bigness in agricultural inputs and why it matters.

This story is one with many fascinating details about the people, technologies, policies, and broader market dynamics in the farm machinery, fertilizer, seeds, and pesticides industries. Because it seems a shame to leave out these details, the result is a longer book than I initially intended to write. But I have tried to write each chapter in a way that it can stand

PREFACE

alone to some extent, such that readers can pick and choose which chapters might interest them the most. Readers should, however, be sure to start with the introduction, which sets the scene by describing the core arguments of the book as a whole.

I should also comment on the approach I take in this book in light of the goals of the book series in which it appears. I believe that the kind of hope this series seeks to instill depends on a deep and sober understanding of the complexities of our current predicament. In my view, that requires an appreciation of history. Specifically, in the case of this book, it means a close and detailed study of the origins of corporate dominance within industrial agriculture, as well as the challenges it presents. Only from that historical foundation is it possible to chart a hopeful course forward.

This project would not have been possible without help and support from many. I am grateful to the Social Sciences and Humanities Research Council of Canada for a grant that supported this work (grant 435-0664-2020). I am also very appreciative of the Canada Research Chairs program and the Faculty of Environment at the University of Waterloo for invaluable research support. I am deeply grateful for the generosity of the Killam Trusts. My 2020 Killam Research Fellowship, now known as the Dorothy Killam Fellowship, provided me with the invaluable gift of time to focus on research and writing. I am also grateful to the Rockefeller Foundation's Bellagio Center Residency Program, from which I benefited in November 2019, just as I was getting this project off the ground. The focused time I had in Bellagio was vital for shaping the project, and I gained many insights from interactions with the other residents. I also extend my thanks to Beth Clevenger at the MIT Press for her interest in this project, as well as to Simon Nicholson and Sikina Jinnah for their enthusiasm to have the book reside in their MIT book series. I am also grateful to Anthony Zannino and Judith Feldmann for their work in shepherding this book through the publication process. And I am thankful to three anonymous referees who provided invaluable comments on an earlier draft of the manuscript.

I gained important insights from many people who kindly offered their time to engage with me on this topic while I was working on this book. Some offered to read all or parts of the manuscript when I was in the process of writing it. Others spoke to me at length about the topic. Some shared vital information that was not easy to access. They provided enormously helpful feedback and perspective that deeply enriched the analysis. I am deeply indebted to Molly Anderson, Hilde Bjørkhaug, Jostein Brobakk, Mary Clock, Andrea Collins, Emile Frison, Keith Fuglie, Shane Hamilton, Angela Hilmi, Phil Howard, Claire Kelloway, Bob Leibenluft, James MacDonald, Sarah J. Martin, Nora McKeon, Philip McMichael, Sofía Monsalve Suárez, Pat Mooney, Maren Oelbermann, Raj Patel, Helena Shilomboleni, Matt Stoller, Mohammad Torshizi, Anders Wästfelt, and Kate Weaver. A number of current and past students also provided outstanding assistance with research and graphics as well as collaboration on related projects, including Taarini Chopra, Kestrel DeMarco, Rebecca Dragusin, Zachary Grant, James Hannay, Indra Noyes, Jenna Phillips, Sarah Louise Ruder, and Rachael Vriezen. I am indebted to a number of librarians and archivists who helped me find specific documents as I researched this topic, including at the FAO Archives and Library, the University of

0.1 Sunshine Waterloo Combine Thresher. *Source*: The Ellis Little Local History Room, Waterloo Public Library.

Waterloo, the Waterloo Public Library, the McLean County Museum of History, and the Vintage Machinery website.

I thank my children, Zoë and Nels Helleiner, for their patience, especially during the pandemic, when I found endless ways to share my excitement about the history of tractors, fertilizers, seeds, and pesticides during dinner conversations. I am grateful to the companionship of my cat, who patiently sat beside me for many hours as I wrote this book and urged me to take occasional breaks. My most special thanks go to my partner, Eric Helleiner, for his willingness to listen to me as I worked out how to approach this topic and formulate my arguments. I could not have completed this work without his love and support. Finally, this book is dedicated to my parents, Jack and Judy Clapp, who taught me the importance of history and the value of critical thinking.

LIST OF ABBREVIATIONS

AAA	Agricultural Adjustment Act
ABC	American Agribusiness Council
AFBF	American Farm Bureau Foundation
BASF	Badische Anilin & Soda-Fabrik
BIO	Biotechnology Industry Organization
Bt	*Bacillus thuringiensis*
CEMA	Comité Européen des Groupements de Constructeurs du Machinisme Agricole
CFS	UN Committee on World Food Security
CGIAR	Consultative Group on International Agricultural Research
CIMMYT	Mexican Maize and Wheat Improvement Centre
CLI	CropLife International
CR4	four-firm concentration ratio
CSIPM	Civil Society and Indigenous Peoples' Mechanism
CSR	corporate social responsibility
DOJ	US Department of Justice
EPA	US Environmental Protection Agency
ESG	environmental, social, and governance
EULA	end-user license agreement
F2F	farm to fork
FAO	Food and Agriculture Organization of the United Nations

FBN	Farmers Business Network
FDI	foreign direct investment
FI	Fertilizer Institute
FIFRA	Federal Insecticide, Fungicide, and Rodenticide Act
FNRL	Fixed Nitrogen Research Laboratory
FTC	Federal Trade Commission
GM	genetically modified
HYV	high-yielding variety
IARC	International Agency for Research on Cancer
ICI	Imperial Chemical Industries
ICP	Industry Cooperative Program (FAO)
IFA	International Fertilizer Association
IFDC	International Fertilizer Development Center
IP	intellectual property
IRRI	International Rice Research Institute
ITC	International Trade Commission
LISA	low-input sustainable agriculture
MAP	Mexican Agricultural Program
MNC	multinational corporation
MOU	memorandum of understanding
NCGA	National Corn Growers Association
NGO	nongovernmental organization
NPK	Nitrogen, phosphorus, and potassium
PAN	Pesticide Action Network
PCS	Potash Corporation of Saskatchewan
PEA	Phosphate Export Association
PPP	public-private partnership
PVPA	Plant Variety Protection Act
R2R	right to repair
SDGs	sustainable development goals
TRIPS	trade-related intellectual property rights
TVA	Tennessee Valley Authority
UAN	urea ammonium nitrate
UCC	Union Carbide Corporation
UNFSS	UN Food Systems Summit

UPOV	Union for the Protection of New Plant Varieties
USDA	US Department of Agriculture
WEF	World Economic Forum
WHO	World Health Organization
WTO	World Trade Organization

1
INTRODUCTION

The agricultural inputs industry is big business. Every year, farmers around the world spend hundreds of billions of dollars on farm machinery, fertilizers, seeds, and pesticides. Although agricultural inputs are a huge sector of the global economy, a relatively small number of very large transnational corporations collectively command the lion's share of the market. For the world's farmers, the names of these firms are all too familiar. In agricultural seeds and pesticides, they are Bayer, Corteva, Syngenta Group, and BASF. The household names in farm machinery—such as tractors and combine harvesters—are John Deere, CNH Industrial, AGCO, and Kubota. And when farmers need fertilizer, they are often buying from big global firms: Nutrien, Mosaic, Yara, and CF Industries. Of course, other large firms in these sectors are also vying for market share, but these are by far the biggest ones.

It is remarkable that the sector looks the way it does today—with only a handful of global firms providing such a large share of world's farm inputs—considering that just a few hundred years ago, agricultural inputs were not usually widespread market commodities. Farmers typically saved their own seeds to plant the next season; used available waste materials and crop rotations to ensure that plants received sufficient nutrients; intercropped plants to keep pests at bay; and used hand or horse-drawn implements that they could craft themselves to till the soil and harvest crops. No doubt there was some local commercial trade in some of these farm inputs dating back even further than a few centuries ago, but as late as the mid-nineteenth century, agricultural inputs were not very commodified and certainly not dominated by transnational corporations.

This book explains how we got from there to here. In other words, it outlines how the agricultural inputs sector came to be dominated by just a few gigantic agribusiness firms—the titans of industrial agriculture. It begins by showing how the roots of today's giant agribusiness firms in fact run deep. Already by the early twentieth century, some parts of the sector—especially farm machinery—were controlled by just a few massive firms. By the mid-twentieth century, this was true of the entire sector, including not just farm machinery but also fertilizers, seeds, and pesticides. Each of these four industries has a specific history, from initial widespread commodification in the early to mid-1800s to dominance by just a few very large firms by the early to mid-1900s. Tracing these separate trajectories, however, reveals that they share some broad similarities. The firms that rose to the top benefited from distinct market, technology, and policy advantages that enabled them to gain power and wealth.

Once these firms became large and dominant, they leveraged various dimensions of their power and wealth to shape markets, technological innovation, and government policy processes in ways that enabled them to grow even bigger as they acquired their rivals, even as they often changed names while undergoing consolidation. In short, bigness soon begot more bigness, and the power of the big players became increasingly entrenched and globalized. Over the past century, the sector was restructured over and again, but always with just a few firms taking a commanding lead over the others. In the past fifty years, the seed and agrochemical pesticide industries—once entirely separate sets of firms—combined into one set of firms that sold both products, tethering together seeds and agrochemicals with agricultural biotechnology, which modified seeds to work with specific chemical herbicides. The fertilizer and farm machinery sectors also saw major consolidation, which dramatically reduced the field of firms to a handful in each sector that dominated globally by the turn of the twenty-first century. As this consolidation continued apace, farmers became locked into industrial production systems that made them increasingly dependent on the large agricultural input firms.

In 1999, US Secretary of Agriculture Dan Glickman expressed his concern about farmers' loss of power in relation to the large agricultural companies: "There's a fear this will turn into 14th-century feudalism. Those farmers will become serfs. We're not there yet, but it may be coming."[1]

Many would say we are already there. The Big Ag companies that dominate the inputs sector have grown even bigger in the decades since Glickman's observation, with the latest major restructuring taking place since 2015. The most recent round of mergers reduced the number of dominant players in the seed and agrochemical pesticide industry from six to just four. It also saw two of the major fertilizer firms combine forces and integrate activities not just horizontally across the main nutrient inputs of nitrogen, phosphate, and potash, but also vertically along the supply chain from production to retail. At the same time, all the major firms in the agricultural inputs sector began a flurry of acquisitions of smaller technology firms to place themselves in the race for digital or biological dominance in agriculture—or both.

The complex history that generated today's concentration in the agricultural inputs sector is frequently obscured from view and replaced by a much simpler explanation often promoted by the leading firms themselves. According to that version of history, today's large and dominant firms were able to rise above the rest simply because they were more efficient and more successful at innovating in ways that made them market leaders. This efficiency of large firms in concentrated markets, the argument goes, translates into lower prices and better products for their customers.[2] Ed Breen, CEO of DuPont, exemplified this view when Dow and DuPont announced their merger in 2015. The merger resulted in the creation of three new firms, including Corteva Agriscience, a new giant agricultural input firm, which Breen declared "will be able to allocate capital more effectively, apply its powerful innovation more productively, and extend its value-added products and solutions to more customers worldwide."[3]

A deeper historical look at the drivers behind the rise of corporate concentration and bigness in the agricultural inputs industry exposes this "bigger is always better" narrative for what it really is: a myth. There were in fact multiple factors that encouraged consolidation, including direct support from governments, technological lock-ins, and preferential access to financial capital. This closer read of history shows that in line with studies of other sectors such as automobiles, airlines, and pharmaceuticals, the dominant firms did not become big and dominant by simply being "better" at what they do.[4] Over and again, these other kinds of factors enabled the lead firms to extend their dominance by merging with or acquiring their rivals while discouraging competition from would-be challengers.

Why does it matter how these firms got so big and powerful? If large companies in the sector are able to deliver productivity-enhancing inputs, and farmers continue to buy them, then perhaps bigness is not an issue. That is what the giant firms want us to believe. They point to increased agricultural productivity under the corporate-dominated industrial agricultural model as evidence of the benefits of bigness. These firms often portray themselves as the only actors capable of ensuring sufficient food production to "feed the world." When Bayer announced its acquisition of Monsanto in 2016, its CEO at the time, Werner Baumann, stressed this approach: "This combination is going to create a global leader in agriculture and realise the shared vision of an enhanced agriculture offering that is ultimately going to deliver earlier access to better solutions for growers, so that they can help contribute to closing the gap between supply and demand that is unfolding with an ever growing population in the world."[5]

The notion that we need industrial inputs from the Big Ag firms to ensure global food supply has long been a powerful narrative. That view, which draws on what many analysts deem to be flawed neo-Malthusian thinking, extends far beyond corporate headquarters and into policymaking arenas.[6] Indeed, the issue of corporate dominance in food systems barely registered at the 2021 UN Food Systems Summit, which was tasked with finding "game-changing solutions" to transform food systems to make them more equitable and sustainable. This lack of attention to corporate dominance sits in sharp contrast to growing civil society and antitrust movements that have focused on this very problem.[7]

The rise of corporate power in the sector matters because it has enormous implications for the future of food systems.[8] Most directly, the titans of industrial agriculture exercise their power to shape markets in ways that weaken competition and reduce choice. They also direct innovation in ways that prioritize profits over the public interest. And they exert political influence over policy processes in ways that advance their interests while undermining democratic participation. More broadly, the rise of just a handful of powerful firms selling farm machinery, fertilizers, seeds, and pesticides cannot be easily separated from the transformation of agriculture into a large-scale industrial activity, which has generated enormous social and ecological consequences that threaten the planet and the future of food systems. The model of agriculture that these firms developed and have refined over the past two centuries has become locked in, such that shifting away from it is especially challenging, despite the growing awareness of the need for food systems transformations to address the social and ecological impacts of the industrial model.

Concerns about corporate concentration today extend well beyond the agricultural inputs sector. For example, we have heard a lot in recent years about the concentrated power of the Big Tech firms, which are often put in a longer historical context of corporate dominance in other sectors, such as oil and railways.[9] Until recently, there has been much less attention paid to the power of big, concentrated firms in the agricultural sector within this broader discourse on corporate power. And there has been even less attention paid to the long history of the dominant firms in the sector. The long view of corporate dominance in the agricultural inputs sector that I take in this book is important because today's agribusiness titans have an extensive lineage back to some of the original firms in the sector, from which we can learn a great deal about the nature and dynamics of corporate power more generally.

I was motivated to focus on bigness in the agricultural inputs sector after reading *Other People's Money and How the Bankers Use It* (1914), by Louis Brandeis, US Supreme Court justice and critic of large corporations and their power. In this short but powerful work, he wrote: "Size, we are told, is not a crime. But size may, at least, become noxious by reason of the means through which it was attained or the uses to which it is put. And it is size obtained by combination, instead of natural growth, which has contributed so largely to our financial concentration."[10] For Brandeis, the concentration of wealth went hand in hand with the concentration of power and political influence, which ultimately undermined democratic institutions. He is widely quoted as saying, "We must make our choice. We may have democracy, or we may have wealth concentrated in the hands of a few, but we cannot have both."[11]

Brandeis sought to understand how concentrated market structures emerged. He stressed that this understanding must come not from theorizing, but from detailed study of the experiences of the firms involved, especially as they rose to power in the late nineteenth and early twentieth centuries—a period of expanding industrial capitalism. Brandeis emphasized that monopolies were not "natural," nor were they simply the result of the superiority or greater efficiency of certain firms over others. Rather, he believed that the suppression of competition was due to either "ruthless processes" or "improper use of inordinate wealth and power."[12] My aim in this book is to investigate the details of how this process unfolded in the agricultural inputs sector.

In tracing the rise of corporate dominance across four agricultural input industries, this book chronicles many stories that are punctuated with fascinating characters and complex dynamics. Because this is a long book, I provide next in this chapter a brief overview of the key themes that emerged from the analysis. I advance three broad points. First, I show that dominant agribusiness firms over the past two centuries benefited from market advantages, technological change, and state support within the wider economy in ways that enabled them to expand and capture commanding market shares. Second, I explain how those firms, once big, actively used their already advantaged position to exercise influence over those same market, technology, and policy contexts in ways that enabled them to extend their dominance. Third, I make the case that there are extensive costs to having just a few large firms dominating the agricultural inputs industry, including the immediate costs of concentration and the exercise of corporate power, as well as the wider costs of the industrial agricultural model developed and promoted by those same firms.

HOW THE AGRICULTURAL INPUT FIRMS GOT SO BIG

Throughout this book, I explain how the dominant firms in the farm machinery, fertilizer, seeds, and pesticides industries grew so big and powerful in the first place and how they continued to get bigger. It is important to pause briefly here to define what I mean by *big*. Although there are numerous works on the question of corporate dominance in the economy more broadly, *bigness* is difficult to define in specific, numerical terms. What may be considered "big" differs by sector, and there are data gaps and weaknesses that make exact measurement tricky. Most analysts consider big firms to be those that lead in what economists call oligopolistic markets, where just a handful of firms hold a significant share of a market. These firms are often easy to spot, even if it is hard to measure them precisely.[13] Usually such corporations are found within markets where the top four firms control 40 percent or more of the market. The 40 percent threshold for this four-firm concentration ratio (often called the CR4 for short) is a general one; beyond this threshold, economists believe that competition is likely to be weakened.[14] The emphasis in this book is not on measuring precise concentration ratios in the input industries, but rather on the idea that a small number of firms can dominate markets by making up a large share of the market and that this market domination has important implications.

Critical analysts argue that the top agricultural input firms are large and powerful today because of the unequal dynamics generated by industrial capitalism—especially the drive on the part of firms for profit accumulation. This process was turbocharged by the rise of neoliberalism in the 1980s, as states implemented hands-off regulatory processes that put businesses in the driver's seat. These forces are indeed important and inform this analysis. At the same time, it is also instructive to disentangle the key constituent aspects of these broader dynamics of capitalism, including the way in which the drive for profits in the marketplace intersects with government policies and technological change. What I found is that dominant firms in the sector had distinct advantages along each of these dimensions that allowed them to climb to the top of the market, typically by acquiring other firms until they had amassed a significant market share. Echoing Brandeis's findings from a century earlier, being "better" or "more efficient" was not a predominant force. I next outline the importance of the market, technology, and policy factors that benefitted the dominant firms. I separate them into three distinct categories to highlight the conceptual framework being employed for this analysis, but in practice, the ways in which these factors encouraged bigness in the sector are often deeply entwined with one another.

MARKET AND FINANCIAL DYNAMICS

Economic explanations for corporate bigness usually focus on some element of market dynamics. "Economies of scale," commonly cited, occur when average costs of production fall as output is increased. In other words, as firms expand their scale of production, they can often benefit from lower costs per item they produce, making them more efficient. Economies of scale have indeed been important to some extent as the agricultural input industries have grown in size. Many of the early firms in this sector were established at the same time that national and regional markets were emerging in the late 1800s in the United States, Canada, and Europe, with new transportation technologies such as railways enabling those firms to produce goods on a larger scale for wider markets.[15] As markets became more globalized after World War II, firms that were already set up with large-scale production had an advantage in reaching worldwide markets. Although economies of scale can explain bigness to some extent, the concept also has limits. As firms get larger, they can actually encounter "diseconomies of scale," whereby they get so big that they become inefficient.[16]

Privileged access to capital has favored certain firms and enabled them to become large through mergers and acquisitions of their rivals. Firms in sectors that are highly concentrated can access funds for such deals by coordinating implicitly or explicitly with other large firms to fix higher prices or by participating in cartels to manage prices and supply, practices that dissuade competitors from entering the market.[17] Firms across all of the agricultural input industries have a long history of engaging in such practices, even though many of those activities have long been forbidden by state competition policies.

The largest firms also typically have cozy relationships with financiers and wealthy investors, who encourage merger deals as a way to achieve higher earnings on their investments. To meet investor demands for higher returns, many firms have ramped up their pursuit of mergers and acquisitions, especially in response to agricultural boom-and-bust cycles that create market opportunities. In boom times, when agricultural prices are rising, there can be mergers that try to capitalize on expanding demand as well as new opportunities that may arise from technological developments. In down times, when agricultural prices are falling, financial investors typically encourage firms to join efforts to save costs and achieve "synergies"—a euphemism for cutting jobs and combining research and development efforts. Investor pressure for consolidation has become more pronounced since the 1970s, when a broader shift toward the prioritization of "shareholder value" meant that the primary role of firms was increasingly seen to be delivering value to shareholders rather than serving the needs of society.[18] Consolidation, in other words, means more market share, which translates into higher profits and more income for investors. Dominant firms' privileged access to finance creates further barriers to entry that make it difficult for other firms to enter the market because they cannot match such levels of investment.

All of these market factors have been important in helping to explain concentration and consolidation in the agricultural inputs sector, as will become clear in the following chapters. Mass manufacturing in large factories that began in the latter part of the nineteenth century brought down average costs for the production of farm equipment and tractors in the United States, for example, enabling those firms with patent protection to capture large portions of an expanding market and earn huge profits. Firms across all four inputs have engaged in extensive mergers and acquisitions in concert with wealthy financiers and investors for well over a century, as exemplified by the 1902 megamerger that brought together seven farm equipment manufacturers under one new firm that suddenly commanded 85 percent of the US tractor market. Firms in the input industries also have a long history of engaging in the formation of cartels, some of which still exist today in the fertilizer industry.

TECHNOLOGICAL CHANGE

Technology also plays a role in explaining the rise of corporate bigness. Firms with pioneering entrepreneurs and inventors are often at the cutting edge of technological changes that can transform markets in ways that give the first movers distinct advantages in the market.[19] When first movers have intellectual property protection over their inventions, such as patents or trade secrets, they are well placed to make enormous profits if those technologies are widely adopted. Firms that control existing assets that are suddenly deemed important or useful to new production processes can also benefit. These factors were important across the agricultural input industries, as the firms that rose to the top of their sectors by the mid-twentieth century often were in positions to capitalize on new technologies and new uses for existing materials to drive profits and command market share.

Technological change can also alter the structure of an industry in ways that encourage corporate mergers.[20] Just as fossil energy in the form of coal and then petroleum gave rise to large-scale manufacturing firms, it also encouraged the industrialization of agriculture.[21] The invention of techniques to synthesize nitrogen-rich ammonia in the early twentieth century, for example, created entirely new dynamics in the fertilizer industry that shifted its focus from guano trading firms to chemical companies, very few of which initially had access to the new process. Technological complementarities within and across the agricultural inputs sectors also mattered, such as the development in the 1990s of genetically modified (GM) seeds that work with specific herbicides, which encouraged consolidation among top firms in the seed and agrochemical industries.

Related to these dynamics are technological lock-ins, which have benefited larger firms. As a technology becomes dominant and widely adopted, the benefits accruing to its users and to its producers tend to increase. Firms that produce dominant technologies often benefit from network effects, including increased sales as the number of users of that technology grows as well as sales of complementary products that are linked to the original technology, which tend to lock in users to certain technological pathways. Sectors with locked-in technologies tend to be more oligopolistic, especially when there are significant barriers to entry for newcomer firms.[22] These dynamics are prominent today in debates over the power of Big Tech firms, but they also have long-standing relevance to the rise of bigness in the agricultural input sector.

The protection of intellectual property (IP), through patents or trade secrets, was a vital factor in the early development of the seeds, agrochemicals, fertilizer, and farm machinery sectors. Those industries experienced breakthrough innovations such as the hybridization of seeds, the development of synthetic pesticides using organic chemistry, nitrogen synthesis, and new machinery designs and features that benefited the first movers. Lock-ins also developed across all four inputs, especially as machinery, fertilizers, seeds, and agrochemicals were increasingly developed by firms to work together in farm fields. This planned lock-in reinforced the use of all of these inputs through industrial farming practices that were subsequently globalized under the Green Revolution after World War II.

POLICY CONTEXT

Various government policies and regulations have long played critical roles in shaping the rise of the big agricultural input companies. Laws protecting IP enable inventors to claim exclusive rights to their innovations. Patent protection, for example, gives firms a temporary legal monopoly over their intellectual property for a specific period, typically around twenty years. States typically support this kind of IP protection to encourage innovation. Some analysts contend that the largest and most profitable firms today are those that control the most valuable portfolios of IP rights, which generate large cash flows that they can use to buy up would-be competitors.[23] IP protection has been especially important in the rise to bigness of the firms in the agricultural input industries, which has given those firms first-mover advantages.

A great deal has been written more broadly—from both critical and mainstream perspectives—about the ways in which firms have benefited from state policies that have championed their industries through subsidies, access to state-sponsored R&D funding, and other policies and regulations that favor certain products and industries. Across all the agricultural input industries, state support was extremely important in building up the sector, and some firms benefited handsomely. The US government, for example, provided the bulk of the basic research that supported seed hybridization, from which just a few firms with privileged access to key seed varieties and breeding processes benefited.[24] State-funded research and development also benefited large firms in both the fertilizer and agrochemicals industries.

Weak and uneven competition policies (referred to as "antitrust" in the United States) also played a significant role in the rise of big firms in the agricultural inputs sector. The 1890 Sherman Act in the United States, as outlined by the US Federal Trade Commission, prohibits "every contract, combination, or conspiracy in restraint of trade" and any "monopolization, attempted monopolization, or conspiracy or combination to monopolize."[25] In other words, it outlaws collusion and monopolization. The United States passed subsequent rules to strengthen competition laws by the mid-twentieth century. The 1914 Clayton Act, for example, prohibits activities that weaken competition, such as mergers that result in less competitive markets, the tying or bundling of related products, predatory pricing (charging low prices to drive out competition and then raising them), and interlocking directorships where individuals sit on the boards of competing companies.[26] Although other countries also put competition policies in place—such as Canada's Anti-Combines Act of 1889, which predates the Sherman Act—there is no global agreement on competition policy, and the rules across jurisdictions vary.

The robustness with which competition authorities have enforced laws has varied over time. The United States strictly enforced antitrust laws in the early part of the twentieth century, for example, a key factor in the trust-busting that dismantled large firms that tended toward monopoly. Standard Oil, for example, which controlled not only the oil market but also the oil trading infrastructure, was broken up in 1911. These laws were also instrumental in several big antitrust cases against firms in the farm machinery, fertilizer, and agrochemical sectors in the early twentieth century. But as the ideology of neoliberalism rose in the 1970s and 1980s, antitrust laws were interpreted in new ways that allowed more corporate consolidation to occur. Mergers across all the agricultural input industries since 2015 have been in part linked to this weakening of antitrust rules, with many countries following the US lead since the 1980s in watering down how antitrust rules are applied.[27]

EXTENDING BIGNESS: THE EXERCISE OF CORPORATE POWER AND ITS CONSEQUENCES

In addition to explaining how the agribusiness titans grew so big over the past century and a half, this book explains how their bigness enabled them to shape the very same market, technology, and policy contexts in ways that extended their dominance. In practice, these various kinds of power are entangled with one another. For example, the power to shape markets often derives from the power to influence policy and vice versa, and dominance in the marketplace can privilege certain technologies over others. When firms adopt certain kinds of practices, it is a sign that they are seeking to exercise their power to strengthen their position in the market.

POWER TO SHAPE MARKETS

Large and dominant firms have the ability to shape the contours of the marketplace. Economists call this market power, and it refers to the capacity to raise prices above competitive levels by controlling key aspects of the market, resulting in excess profits.[28] Market power helps explain both how firms can raise funds to get big and how they can stay big. Large and dominant firms can extend their market power by taking actions that reduce competition, such as by erecting barriers that dissuade entry into the market for other firms. The larger the share firms have in the market, especially in highly concentrated sectors, the more capacity those firms have to exercise market power. Although formal collusion among firms to raise prices is technically illegal under competition policies, it becomes increasingly easy for dominant firms in highly concentrated sectors to tacitly follow price increases of other top firms without hurting sales.[29]

These kinds of practices have been common in the agricultural inputs sector. For example, the dominant firms have been able to push up prices well beyond their costs of production, especially for products with few competitors, such as GM seeds, without fear of losing markets. Similarly, farmers have long been suspicious that fertilizer firms have curtailed production and elevated prices in times of rising crop prices as a way to capture excess profits. Firms in the sector have also erected barriers to entry, as we have seen with firms acquiring numerous patents for a certain type of product—such as genome-edited crops—that allows them to act as a gatekeeper for certain technologies. Firms also engage in vertical integration across inputs sectors, such as the merging of production, mixing, and retail in the fertilizers sector, which makes it difficult for newer firms to compete. All of these strategies reinforce the concentrated nature of the inputs markets in ways that give these firms additional power to shape the terms of the market in ways that expand their ability to raise profits and thereby accumulate more capital.

POWER TO SHAPE TECHNOLOGY

Firms at the top of concentrated sectors also have enormous power to shape technology and innovation pathways in ways that serve their own interests. This kind of technology power is an aspect of corporate power that I would argue, along with international relations scholar Robert Falkner,[30] deserves more attention in the literature and in competition policies. It is related to what international political economy expert Susan Strange called "knowledge power"—the power to access and use knowledge in ways that advance one's interests, such as shaping the direction of technological innovation to create or extend a market advantage.[31]

Economists recognize that firm size can affect innovation, although whether larger or smaller firms have more innovation capacity is subject to debate. It comes down to differing views on incentives. On one hand, because of their access to greater amounts of capital, larger firms have more funds to invest in R&D. On the other hand, why would a monopolist invest in innovation if it did not need to do so to continue to sell its products? There is an emerging middle ground position in this debate that recognizes that large firms may indeed lead in spurring some innovation, but beyond a certain point, the innovation intensity of large firms declines.[32] This insight is important for understanding the technology power of large and dominant firms in the agricultural inputs sector because it indicates that they have the power to both encourage *and* stifle innovation to suit their priorities.

The dominant firms also have the capacity to spend large amounts on what might be seen as defensive R&D rather than innovation that breaks new ground and establishes better ways to do things. That is, they may be spending on research for innovation, but their efforts on this front focus on ways to shore up markets for their existing products, especially as patents for particular products expire, rather than investing in novel ideas that are likely to lead to transformative breakthroughs.[33] Whether the dominant firms focus on novel or defensive innovation, economist Mordecai Kurz notes that in the absence of strong public policy to regulate market power, "innovators are able to drive out competitors and turn a small initial competitive advantage into a sprawling monopoly."[34]

The exercise of technology power has long been extensive in the agricultural inputs industry and is accentuated by the fact that corporate R&D

in the agricultural inputs sector now outpaces all public sector agricultural R&D. Although investment in R&D in the combined seed and agrochemical industry initially increased following the corporate mergers and acquisitions of the 1990s, by the early 2000s, that innovation had already begun to decline.[35] Moreover, the innovation in which those firms invested overwhelmingly focused on genetically modifying seeds to work with existing products, such as glyphosate-based herbicides, which increased chemical sales, rather than new seed traits that would have been useful for farmers, such as higher-yielding and drought-resistant varieties. Similarly, firms in the sector are now investing in digital and biological technologies, also with a view to extending the use of existing herbicides.

POWER TO SHAPE POLICY AND GOVERNANCE

Large firms have the power to shape the direction of policy and regulations that affect their businesses. In the agricultural inputs sector, they have long used this power to press for rules that enable them to expand their businesses. They do this through multiple strategies that are outlined in the literature on the different dimensions of corporate political power—some of which are more visible than others.[36]

One of the more visible and direct ways that agribusiness firms have attempted to shape policies is by lobbying policymakers. When firms lobby, either individually or through industry associations in which they are members, they are attempting to directly influence the behavior of another actor to generate certain outcomes. Agribusiness firms can also have somewhat direct influence over policy by nominating private sector executives for government regulatory positions and then rehiring those executives when their time in government has ended, in what is often termed the revolving door. Firms can also access direct channels of influence over policy through their engagement in public-private partnerships with governments or international organizations.[37]

The big firms in the agricultural inputs industry also can influence policy in less direct and sometimes less visible ways. They can leverage their structural position in the marketplace to set regulatory agendas and benefit from policy advantages. Governments, for example, often pursue policies that serve the interests of large and powerful firms even in the absence of those firms expressing their preferences via lobbying. They do this simply because those firms provide jobs and tax revenue and governments do not want them to relocate. Firms also set agendas by establishing voluntary industry codes of conduct, thus shaping the broader context of policymaking, including in ways that make those rules de facto conditions for operation for smaller firms, which can make it difficult for the latter to compete.[38] Agribusiness firms also actively use other indirect strategies to influence the discourses and narratives that are the backdrop to the broader policy context. Dominant firms can shape ideas that influence the public's reception of their businesses by engaging in public debates, sponsorship of scientific studies, corporate advertising, and other forms of public messaging.[39]

When large firms are able to exercise these kinds of power, they undermine processes for democratic participation in the policymaking process. As the following chapters outline, the big agricultural input firms have actively sought to influence government policies since the 1800s. They have spent hundreds of millions of dollars to lobby governments, sponsored scientific studies on agrochemicals in a bid to influence regulatory decisions, engaged in partnerships and multistakeholder initiatives in the agricultural sector, and pushed voluntary industry measures as a means to dissuade governments from pursuing stricter regulations.

THE BROADER COSTS OF CORPORATE CONCENTRATION AND POWER IN THE FOOD SYSTEM

Corporate concentration in the agricultural inputs industry matters in multiple ways. The analysis in this book notes the extensive costs to having just a few large firms dominating in a concentrated agricultural inputs industry. These costs arise because the dominant firms have exerted their power for nearly two centuries in ways that support their business model, which is based on a continuation of industrial agricultural production methods.

The firms in the agricultural input industries claim that bigness enables them to deliver better products that will increase farmer profits. But the pricing and innovation implications of concentration noted above bring these claims into question. Critics have long insisted that the various dimensions of power at the disposal of the agribusiness titans result in greater inequities. Farmer livelihoods are at risk from growing corporate concentration and power in the food system, which directly affects their production costs. Especially vulnerable to these effects are the nearly 600 million small-scale farming households around the world that produce a significant proportion of the world's food. Small-scale enterprises that seek to provide alternative inputs to farmers also face huge obstacles to entering the market and are disadvantaged in terms of access to funding for research and development. As a result, farmers have fewer input choices available to them. And if these effects result in an increase in production costs for farmers, it can push up food prices.

There are also massive implications that arise from the broader development and spread of the industrial agricultural inputs that have been delivered by large, concentrated firms. The introduction and evolution of the industrial model of agricultural production were intimately shaped by the large agribusiness firms in the farm machinery, fertilizer, seeds, and agrochemicals industries since at least the mid-1800s. From their earliest days, the industrial versions of these inputs have been critiqued for their enormous social and ecological consequences, although critics' voices were often drowned out by promoters of those technologies.

The social costs of the industrial agricultural model go beyond the impacts of higher prices. The diffusion of farm machinery on a wide scale has long been associated with rising concentration in landholdings and displacement. In most industrialized countries and increasingly in less industrialized countries, average farm sizes have grown as the number of farms and farmers have been declining. This process began as early as the mid-1800s with the initial adoption of industrial farm tools such as steel plows and mechanical reapers, which enabled settlers in North America to move westward and clear new lands, displacing Indigenous peoples from their lands. There is also a long history of racial discrimination and harsh working conditions, including forced labor, associated with the fertilizer sector.

The advent of tractors and modern inputs in the early twentieth century accelerated the concentration of landholdings and displacement. As tractor use expanded in the early 1900s, many farmers sought to increase the size of their farms. Farming larger tracts of land lowered the cost per acre of operating farm machinery and increased revenue, making the adoption of other inputs such as synthetic fertilizers, hybrid seeds, and pesticides more affordable. Poorer farmers and those who did not own farmland, including many Black farmers who rented farmland or worked as sharecroppers on others' land, were displaced in this farmland consolidation process. These social costs of the rise of the corporate-led industrial agricultural model have long been overshadowed by narratives of the necessity of industrial inputs to "feed the world." It is important not only to recognize this history of the early development of industrial farm inputs and its human costs, but also to address the injustices that took place in the name of the industrial farming model that powerful corporations today work so hard to uphold.

The industrial agricultural model supported by large input companies also has widespread ecological and health costs, many of which have been increasingly recognized as the model has emerged and evolved. Soil fertility was a major issue of concern in the mid-1800s, and it was a key factor in the drive to find artificial fertilizers to counter soil deficiencies. But by the early twentieth century, there were concerns about the impact of overplowing and the use of synthetic fertilizers on soil quality. In addition, land clearing for large-scale industrial monoculture farming has raised concerns about biodiversity loss for at least a century.

The industrial model of agriculture is widely associated with increased emissions of greenhouse gases, not just from the fossil fuels needed to propel machinery on the farm but also from plowing soil that releases carbon and because pesticides and artificial fertilizers are petroleum-based products. These latter two inputs are also responsible for significant chemical runoff, resulting in pollution that is a threat to human and animal health and ecosystems. Additionally, as weeds become more resistant to the application of widely used herbicides, the big corporations are rolling out or reviving even more toxic chemicals to address the problem. Early environmental and health critics of industrial agriculture such as Rachel Carson were often harshly critiqued by the large corporate players. The big firms claimed that these critics had limited scientific expertise and were overstating the problems. However, large corporate firms in the sector are now increasingly being forced to acknowledge and respond to these environmental concerns, even as they continue to fight for regulatory processes to approve of the very products that have caused those problems.

Of course, many factors contribute to the social and ecological problems generated by industrial agriculture. But a deeper historical analysis reveals that it is impossible to disentangle the large and dominant firms that shape the markets, technologies, and policies that underpin the industrial agricultural model from the many problems associated with that model. The extraordinary power that firms in the sector have in shaping markets, technological pathways, and policy frameworks is deepening the lock-in of the industrial agriculture, which presents an enormous challenge to the project of food systems transformation. Instead, the large, powerful firms are advocating for what they call "transformation," but which many critics say is really just a set of minor tweaks to the industrial farming model that continues to deliver excessive profits and control to the existing big firms within the system.[40]

The political power and actions of the large industrial input firms also illuminate the ways in which democratic participation in the policymaking process is being undermined by those dominant firms. As fewer, larger firms preside atop the sector, their voices become amplified because there are fewer well-funded actors vying for the ear of policymakers. And as these firms increase their presence in other policymaking forums, including multistakeholder initiatives in the field of food systems governance, they are crowding out the voices of farmers, civil society, environmental organizations, and marginalized people whose lives have been profoundly affected by the large-scale industrial agriculture advocated by powerful firms.

APPROACH AND CONTRIBUTIONS

The analysis that underpins this work is guided by several broader conceptual frameworks grounded in diverse literatures. I employ international political economist Susan Strange's approach of focusing on changing dynamics among state policies, markets, and technological developments as key to understanding shifting power relationships in the global economy.[41] I also draw on insights from the international political economy and environment literature, which examines the relationship between

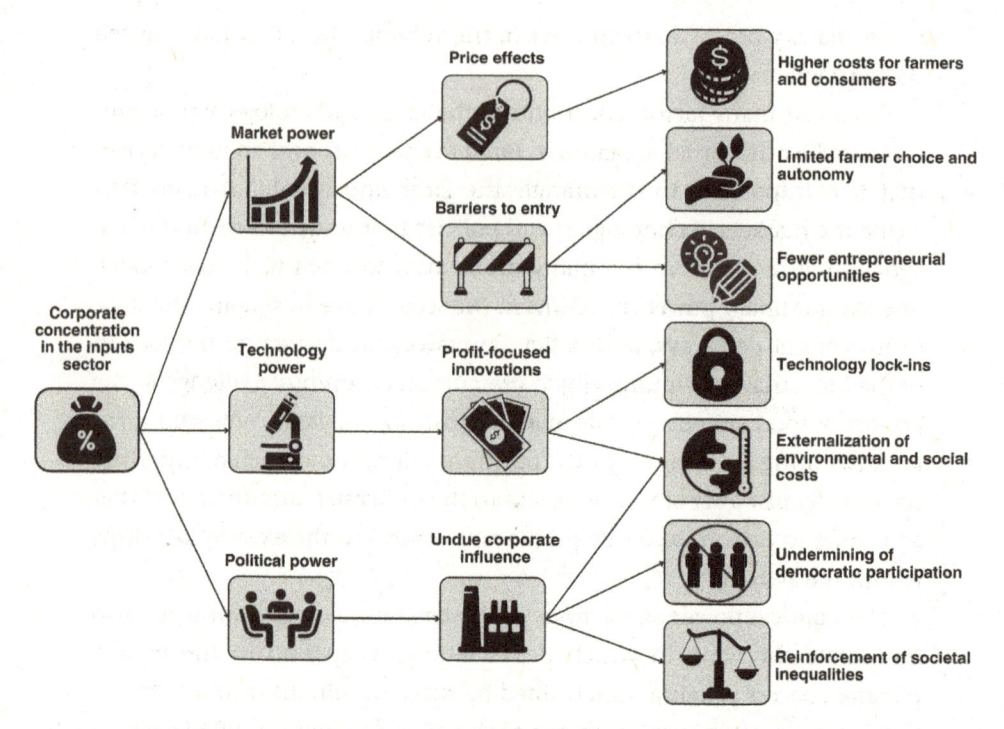

1.1 How corporate concentration can affect food systems. Image by author.

broad structural trends in the global economy, including technological change and the exercise of corporate power, and the environment.[42] Ideas from the science and technology studies literature on technological lock-ins and path dependencies are also relevant, helping to explain the interplay of scientific advances, economic dynamics, and institutions in shaping new technological paradigms.[43]

Any project with problem-driven research questions is necessarily interdisciplinary. In the course of research for this book, I drew on a wide range of literatures that touched on my research questions, albeit from vastly different angles. These literatures included the fields of food studies, agricultural history, business, economics, political science, environmental studies, and more. I also drew on some primary data, including databases of corporate financial statements and lobby registers, as well as the historical archives of the Food and Agriculture Organization (FAO) of the United Nations and several local libraries. At times, it was overwhelming to take in information from these various quarters, but doing so was essential to get the big picture across the four input industries and to understand the range of forces affecting change and consolidation in the sector over the past two hundred years, as well as the wider impacts. I hope I have done justice to these bodies of work in putting this story together.

This book seeks to advance the literature in several ways. First, it contributes to current debates about the rise of corporate concentration and power and its influence on the wider political economy and the role of competition and antitrust policies in addressing it. As noted earlier, much of the attention in recent work on this theme has focused on consequences of the ascent of the Big Tech firms, but this pattern has long affected a range of sectors.[44] This study shows that patterns of corporate concentration and power in the agricultural inputs sector have deep roots that date back to at least the mid-1800s. In fact, many of the dominant firms in the market today can trace their lineage to the earliest firms in the sector, showing that their dominance has been in place for well over a century. This long historical trajectory of the dominant agribusiness firms offers a unique insight into not only how they attained power in the first place, but also how they have been able to remain large and dominant in the contemporary era. The lessons from the agricultural inputs sector thus have relevance for our understanding of the dynamics of corporate concentration and power more generally.

Second, this book also contributes to the literature on the historical evolution of industrial agriculture and the role of corporations within it. It is the first work to take a deep historical look at the rise and evolution of all four of the main agricultural input industries—farm machinery, fertilizer, pesticides, and seeds—in an integrative fashion. There are, of course, a number of excellent historical studies of agricultural inputs, and that work was deeply informative to my own research.[45] However, most of that previous literature focuses on one or perhaps two of the input sectors rather than the full suite. Examining the rise of the lead firms across all four inputs in tandem through a long historical time frame shows that the reasons for corporate dominance and power, although somewhat specific to each input sector, also are similar in other respects. In particular, it highlights the importance of market, technology, and policy contexts to the rise of bigness in all these industries, as well as the similarities in the ways they exert influence over those same contexts to stay big. This integrative approach also reveals interconnections and technological lock-ins across the sectors that have contributed to the endurance of both the industrial agricultural model and the dominance of the leading firms that have promoted it, despite the known costs of this approach.

Third, this book contributes to the food studies literature as well as broader debates over the transformation agenda of food systems. Although there is wide agreement on the costs of the industrial agricultural model and the need to make food systems more equitable, healthy, and sustainable, there remains sharp disagreement over the direction of that transformation and the appropriate role of agrifood corporations. These divisions were on full display at the 2021 UN Food Systems Summit.[46] The corporate-driven vision—to further embrace the latest technological advances to reduce the worst impacts of industrial agriculture—is increasingly being challenged by an alternative perspective that seeks a complete transformation away from the industrial model that does not rely on industrial inputs. The historical and integrative approach of this book shows that the evolution of the industrial model of agriculture has long been shaped by a small set of dominant firms, making it difficult to disentangle the firms that promote that model from its wider consequences. It also reveals that concerns about the wider costs of the industrial agricultural inputs are long-standing. These insights suggest that any agenda for food systems transformation must squarely address the question of corporate power and its consequences. I see this work as complementing what some call the "corporate food regime"—the notion that corporations and financial actors have hegemonic influence over the governance of the global food trade, especially since the rise of neoliberal capitalism in the 1980s.[47] This book is focused on the historical trajectory of the firms that shaped agricultural production methods rather than the norms governing food trade, although of course the two intersect in important ways.

BRIEF PLAN OF THE BOOK

This book is organized chronologically as well as thematically. Part I focuses on the early development of industrial agricultural inputs and how they became concentrated industries. Chapters 2 through 5 provide an overview of how each of the four main agricultural inputs—farm machinery (chapter 2), fertilizers (chapter 3), seeds (chapter 4), and pesticides (chapter 5)—rose from their initial widespread commodification in the 1800s to corporate dominance and control by the early to mid-twentieth century.

Part II of the book focuses on the consolidation and expansion of the industrial agricultural model and the firms that spawned it from the mid-twentieth century. Chapter 6 reflects on the ways in which this corporate-led industrial agricultural model became locked in and globalized, despite its known consequences, including by large corporate players and through the Green Revolution. Chapter 7 provides an overview of the consolidation of the farm machinery and fertilizer industries that took place in the second half of the twentieth century. Chapter 8 examines the merging of the pesticide and seed industries into one set of firms that specializes in both products starting in the 1970s.

Part III examines the drivers and consequences of the most recent round of consolidation in the agricultural inputs sector. Chapter 9 outlines the main drivers of the megamergers across the sector after 2015, highlighting the deepening role of financial factors as well as new technological developments, including the rise of digital farming and genome editing, in encouraging consolidation. Chapters 10 to 12 focus on concerns about the exercise of power by the dominant firms in the sector following the most recent mergers, examining their ability to shape markets (chapter 10), the technological context (chapter 11), and policy and governance (chapter 12).

In the concluding part, chapter 13 reflects on broader lessons and the potential pathways that lie ahead on this issue. Based on the book's analysis, the chapter charts out the public policy responses that might be able to effectively counter corporate dominance in the sector. The chapter also discusses several movements that are currently pushing for reforms to address corporate power in the agricultural input industries. These include calls from various quarters within civil society to replace the current system with agricultural models that sit in opposition to industrial agriculture, especially agroecology, which embeds deep ecological principles as well as more equitable and participatory governance systems in the agricultural system. There is also a growing movement of antitrust reformers who are pushing to strengthen competition rules in the face of growing corporate power in a digital age. These antitrust reformers have identified agriculture as a key area where corporations have extraordinary power. Whether these diverse movements can effect change in the sector is not yet clear.

A FEW CAVEATS

It is important to note several caveats to this work. Much of the analysis in part I, which focuses on the rise and exercise of power of the large agricultural input firms, draws on examples from North America and Europe, where these firms initially rose to dominance. Later parts of this work discuss implications of the power of these firms in less industrialized country contexts as well, but there are still many examples from North America and Europe, where data were more easily available to me as a researcher based in Canada. If I had more time and space, I would have liked to have gone into more detail to understand better how the power of the agribusiness titans plays out in different developing country contexts. Many of the examples of agricultural inputs are those developed for use with industrially grown commodity grain crops like maize, wheat, and soy—the main crops for which many of the industrial inputs were initially developed. These same inputs are, of course, used in the production of other food and industrial crops, but I chose to keep the focus mainly on commodity grain crops to keep the research scope manageable. And while this book focuses specifically on agricultural inputs, other parts of agrifood supply chains, where similar dynamics are at play, are also highly concentrated. I hope that this book provides a framework for future work that understands corporate power and lock-ins in these other contexts.

I
THE INITIAL RISE TO CORPORATE BIGNESS IN THE AGRICULTURAL INPUTS INDUSTRY

2

FARM MACHINERY

In the 1860s, US farmers were up in arms about the dominance of the Big Tech firms of their day: harvesting machinery companies. Although at that time harvesting machines had been on the market for only a few decades, they had fundamentally changed farming practices in North America. The fact that just a few companies held patents for harvesters and other farm machinery meant that farmers' livelihoods depended on the firms that produced them. The emergence and transformation of the farm machinery industry into a highly concentrated sector dominated by a handful of firms occurred at a lightning-fast pace. Historically, farm implements such as scythes for harvesting crops and plows for turning the soil were typically either fashioned by farmers themselves or produced and traded by local toolmakers, most often on a small scale within local or regional markets. This model of production enabled toolmakers to stylize their wares to specific soil conditions and crops grown in those regions. The age of more modern, industrially made farm equipment dates only from the mid-nineteenth century. Gasoline-powered tractors have been produced only since the early twentieth century.

This chapter shows that the rapid transformation of the farm machinery sector was the product of a combination of several key shifts that began around the early to mid-1800s. Major technological innovations dramatically reorganized the production of goods more broadly along a large-scale industrial model. The firms that came to dominate the market entered the sector just as the Industrial Revolution in North America was accelerating and were able to benefit from large-scale standardized industrial production processes. The firms that entered this sector early also benefited from broader market dynamics, in particular the rise of a national market in both the United States and Canada, which developed with the advancement of the railways into western regions of both countries throughout the latter part of the 1800s. Railway expansion fueled demand for mechanical farm equipment that enabled farmers to grow more grain to reach distant markets. Early firms also benefited from privileged access to finance, making it possible for them to acquire rivals and to sell their equipment to farmers on terms of credit, securing more sales. Governments provided intellectual property protection with patents, which provided first-mover advantages in the marketplace for firms holding those patents. In some cases, national tariff policies also worked in firms' favor. Once these firms gained substantial size and market share, they frequently used different aspects of their power to persuade politicians to make policy decisions that reinforced their place in the market.

MECHANICAL REAPERS

The mechanization of crop harvesting marked a significant moment in the industrialization of agriculture. Cyrus H. McCormick is often credited with inventing the mechanical reaper, or harvesting machine, in 1831, although others at the time also devised similar types of machines to harvest crops. Some fifty-eight different mechanical reapers were in fact invented between 1786 and 1831 across England, the United States, France, and Germany. This included a machine invented by Patrick Bell in Scotland in 1828, which was never patented. In the United States, William Manning patented a machine that was similar to Bell's in in 1831, and Obed Hussey patented a reaper machine in 1833.[1] McCormick gets much of the attention in the origin story of mechanical reapers because his firm ended up being among the most successful in the following century and also because his family built up his legend as the true inventor of the harvesting machine in the years after his death.[2]

McCormick's reaper was an idea that built on his father's failed efforts in the 1820s to devise a mechanical harvesting machine. Working to construct his mechanical reaper with the assistance of one of the family's slaves, Jo Anderson, Cyrus H. McCormick first publicly demonstrated his machine's capacity to cut wheat cleanly and efficiently at his family's Virginia farm. Fabricated of cast iron, the first McCormick mechanical reaper required one person to operate a rake to push the wheat off the board of the machine and one or more people to direct the horse or horses. The machine could harvest far more acres in a single day than a farmer and hired labor could achieve manually. Because labor was generally in short supply in North America at the time, particularly in the midwestern grain-growing regions, the mechanical reaper became popular as the technology spread.[3]

Although others invented and even patented similar machines, McCormick's mechanical reaper was the first to meet wide success and market dominance. McCormick waited until 1834 to patent his reaper design as he worked on improvements after the initial demonstrations. His interest in securing a patent was sparked by a realization that Hussey was producing and marketing his own mechanical reaper shortly after patenting it. McCormick felt that the idea had originally been his, and the episode sparked a deep rivalry between the two men. McCormick began to produce his mechanical harvesters for commercial sale in 1840, working on a small scale in his family's workshop in Virginia. He sold only seven reapers in 1842 but gradually increased production in the following years as sales grew to about fifty reapers in 1844. In 1845, McCormick filed for a patent on some of the improvements he made to his machine in the intervening years. For most of the 1840s, McCormick and Hussey were the main producers of harvesting machines, largely due to their patent protection.

Most of McCormick's mechanical reapers built between 1845 and 1848 were produced by licensee firms that paid for the right to produce them using the patented technology. McCormick moved to Chicago in 1847 to establish the McCormick Harvesting Machine Company, with the intent of producing the machines himself. He also sought to be closer to where the market for mechanical reapers was expanding in the western plains of North America where labor was scarce. The relocation to the US Midwest turned out to be important for the growth of the firm. McCormick built his own industrial factory to produce the machines in mass quantities, now out of steel and based on standardized parts, just as industrial factory production for a range of goods expanded rapidly in the United States. By 1848, the firm was already marketing the McCormick harvesting machine in European markets in addition to targeting US markets. The firm was family owned and managed, with McCormick's brothers and other relatives in key management and sales positions.

When McCormick's original patent expired in 1848, he applied for an extension, but was met with fierce resistance from licensee firms and farmers. The US Patent and Trademark Office did not grant the extension, stressing that the technology was too important and that there were questions about its originality, given that other patents for similar machines predated McCormick's patent.[4] After McCormick's original reaper patent expired, a number of new firms came onto the scene in the latter half of the century to capitalize on the rising demand for mechanical harvesters. By 1850, for example, there were approximately thirty companies producing mechanical harvesting machines in the United States. Despite not having extended patent protection for its original machine, the McCormick Harvesting Machine Company still overshadowed its rivals. Because McCormick had quickly scaled up to mass production at his Chicago plant, he was able to produce and sell as many reapers as his competitors combined throughout the 1850s.[5] He also pursued patents on some of the improvements to his machines, which gave him an edge over his competitors, who would have to pay fees for a license to use those technological advancements in their own harvesters. Through hundreds of lawsuits and countersuits, McCormick vigorously sought enforcement of these patent protections and remuneration from licensees who wished to use his technological ideas.

This era also saw the rise of "patent pools," whereby several firms would work together to buy up all patents related to a particular feature of a machine or invention, effectively monopolizing the patent protection, and then force all others to pay steep fees to use that technology under license. Firms in the pool would often aggressively sue in court firms that did not pay the royalties for the use of the patented features.[6] Dominant firms that were first movers in the sector often had an advantage in these situations. Such was the case with technologies for grain binding techniques in later harvesters. McCormick, for example, teamed up with Marquis L. Gorham to buy up a suite of patents related to binder technologies for reapers, and then he charged other manufacturers steep fees to incorporate that feature into their own machines. These tactics also forced a particular binder technological pathway that benefited the holders of the patents while disadvantaging smaller firms and other techniques. These practices also encouraged the largest firms to establish engineering departments to develop patentable technologies and gain patent advantages over other firms.[7]

McCormick was able to establish dominance in other ways too. His firm developed a specific model of sales and distribution that has since become standard for many farm inputs businesses. Based in Chicago, the firm was especially well situated to take advantage of the expansion of the railways to move its products to newly settled farmlands to the West.[8] McCormick's firm also developed a unique distribution system that contracted local sales and service agents, who were tasked with demonstrating the machinery and taking sales orders on commission. The firm offered its customers credit for their farm machinery purchases, which was especially important because the machines were expensive. The firm gave farmers several years to pay the full amount of their purchase, although with a rate of interest sometimes as high as 10 percent.[9] Credit was a key marketing hook for McCormick because it attracted customers who did not have the capital up front to make such a large purchase. The local McCormick agents also served as suppliers of spare parts, which had become standardized with large-scale factory production. Initially, Cyrus H. McCormick enlisted cousins and even his grandchildren, as well as others close to the family, to serve as local dealers—basically, people he felt he could trust—sending them to live in smaller towns across the US Midwest to fulfill these functions for the firm. The dealer agents were typically contracted to deal exclusively for McCormick's firm, making it harder for smaller firms without an established distribution and sales infrastructure to enter the market.

Throughout the latter part of the nineteenth century, McCormick was widely viewed in the media as a greedy monopolist, similar to the way the media reports on the CEOs of Big Tech companies today—with both fascination and indignation for their monopolization of important technologies that have become entrenched in daily life. When McCormick sought a renewal of one of his patents in 1861, for example, several editorials published in the *New York Times* decried how he used his position of privilege to push for special treatment in his patent case, even seeking the help of Congress to oversee the request. He was accused of effectively stealing from farmers with his patent protection on harvesting machinery, which made him millions of dollars, and he was viewed as being out of touch with the majority of Americans, who were hard-working farmers. One editorial emotionally declared:

A powerful combination of capital and talent is at work at Washington, endeavoring to procure an extension of the reaping machine patent of Cyrus H. McCormick. This measure is one directly affecting the agriculturalists of the entire country, who number four-fifths of its population. The patentee, it is notorious, has made a colossal fortune by means of the exclusive right to his invention guaranteed to him by the Government during a specified term,—and he comes now to ask an extension of his monopoly for another seven years. The fact that he is already in the field for an extension, although his patent does not expire until October next, gives good ground for the suspicion that he relies for success upon something else than the merits of his case.[10]

Some of the other reaper firms saw how McCormick's distribution and sales model enabled the firm to quickly develop a commanding dominance in the market, and they subsequently copied it, establishing their own exclusive dealerships. However, even as this sales model gave the harvesting machinery companies more direct access to their markets, the extension of credit to farmers for a period of up to four years was an expensive proposition for firms. Sales expenses, including credit services, made up 30 to 40 percent of the costs incurred by these firms, in part because some farmers failed to repay their loans. The model also resulted in a huge amount of financial capital tied up in warehouses, branch houses, and their staff.[11] Such a system of sales—with exclusive dealerships—meant that many small towns had only a few brands of modern harvesting machines available to them. This arrangement gave the larger firms a huge advantage over smaller firms because they could more easily afford to establish local dealerships once they built up a sizable customer base.[12]

PLOWS

The modern plow business developed on a similar timeline as the harvesting machinery industry. Although implements to till soil have been used for thousands of years, and the ancestors of more modern plows have been around for over a thousand years, it was not until the early to mid-1800s that they became significantly improved, with better finishing and new materials, particularly polished iron and steel. At first, town blacksmiths made improved plows for local markets, but by the end of the nineteenth century, there were massive plow-making factories akin to the operations of the harvesting machinery companies. Although there were many locally based plow manufacturers in North America by the mid-1800s, offering a variety of designs, the case of John Deere is instructive in understanding the broad development of the industry into large industrial firms. Because Deere & Company emerged as one of the leading farm machinery firms by the early twentieth century, a focus on its development also reveals some of the key features that enabled certain firms in the sector to become large and dominant.

In 1836, during difficult economic times, John Deere moved from Vermont to Illinois to escape prosecution for failing to pay his debts. He quickly gained a reputation for making high-quality plows and other farm implements in his blacksmith shop in Grand Detour, Illinois, and later in Moline, Illinois. By the end of the century, Deere & Company was one of the largest plow manufacturers in the United States. John Deere was likely not the first person to fashion a plow out of steel (although he is often credited as such), but he was able to adapt ideas from others and was excellent at his craft.[13] The moist, sticky, highly fertile soils in Illinois did not adhere to Deere's polished iron moldboard plow with its steel ploughshare, as it did with other plows made from wood or unpolished iron. This feature made Deere's implement hugely popular with farmers because it saved them the time it took to constantly stop and scrape soil from the plow.

As in the case of the McCormick Harvesting Machine Company, Deere & Company was a family business. John Deere eventually passed the leadership of the firm on to his son Charles, who developed the marketing aspect of the firm by the latter part of the 1800s. In its early days, the firm employed traveling agents dispatched directly from Moline, who sold implements to local dealers such as hardware stores throughout the Midwestern United States. But after the Civil War (1861–1865), the firm developed a series of branch houses linked to the main headquarters. These branch houses, which served as regional hubs that stored plows in warehouses and supplied local dealers, were joint ventures between Deere and other operators and investors, and thus they were linked to the firm but also had a measure of independence. The firm also instituted a credit payment system that was not dissimilar to McCormick's system, which enabled farmers to pay for their purchases over several years, with interest. By using these tactics, Deere & Company became a large enterprise that was a formidable foe to other plow companies in North America.

Additional firms that emerged in this era came to be important players in the sector, including the Moline Plow Company. Other prominent firms included the Oliver Chilled Plow Works, so named for its founder, James Oliver, and the way the steel was cooled, which gave it extra strength. Jerome I. Case founded the J. I. Case Threshing Machine Company in Wisconsin in 1842, which produced machinery for processing harvested grain. Case also established a separate firm in the 1870s, the J. I. Case Plow Works. Patents were important for the plow sector, but perhaps not as important as in the mechanical reaper industry. Manufacturing quality was relatively more important in the plow industry because plows were less complex to design and produce compared to reapers. Thus, multiple firms were able to compete in the plow industry in the latter part of the nineteenth century.

THE GRANGE MOVEMENT PUSHES BACK

The Grange, formally known as the Order of the Patrons of Husbandry, formed in the United States in 1867 as a populist movement that fought the monopolies that farmers considered harmful to their livelihoods, including powerful farm equipment firms. The movement accelerated following a serious financial crisis that began in Europe and spread to North America, known as the Panic of 1873, which triggered a long period of economic depression. The economic turndown was especially hard on the US farming sector, as it led to lower prices, which added to existing problems that had reduced production, such as pest infestations that ravaged crops and soil exhaustion from monocultural production. During the depression of the 1870s, farmers felt squeezed by both lower crop prices and high prices for farm equipment sold exclusively by a concentrated group of firms. They were also aggrieved that they were reliant on railways to transport their crops, which had high freight charges because the key rail lines were monopolized by just a few dominant firms. Farmers also had become more indebted in this period. Many had mortgaged their farms, in part because increased mechanization was costly and also because they sought to improve efficiencies by expanding their farms.

Inspired by the ideas of the eighteenth-century physiocrats, the Grangers saw land as the source of all value and wealth and disdained wealth generated by merchant exchange.[14] The Grangers harshly critiqued farm equipment manufacturers for their "insatiable greed" and their control of patents, which gave them monopoly power over certain machinery designs.[15] The Grangers also complained about the sales and distribution model of the large firms, which they saw as transferring an undue portion of their hard-earned money to local sales agents, whom they saw as opportunistic middlemen whose services were not necessary. The Grange movement gained popular support in this period, as farmers believed that they had lost political clout after the Civil War because of rising urbanization and industrialization, which they felt eroded their position in society.[16] According to Edward Martin, an analyst of the movement who sympathized with the Grangers, "It has long been evident to earnest thinkers that the farmers of the United States are the most cruelly oppressed class of our community."[17]

To address their situation, the Grangers devised several plans. One was to try to purchase farm equipment at wholesale prices directly from manufacturers to cut out the dealer fees. Although direct purchase would not necessarily weaken the power of the dominant farm equipment manufacturing firms, it would enable farmers to obtain equipment at lower prices, reducing their debt burden. Cyrus H. McCormick was willing to engage with the request of the Grangers for direct sales from his company without involving agents, but these purchases would have to be on his terms. Specifically, he made it clear that purchasers would have to pay cash and would have to buy enough machinery to make these sales worth his while.[18] The plow manufacturers were less cooperative. The Northwestern Plow Manufacturers Association met in 1873 to discuss the request for direct sales, but nineteen manufacturers, including Deere & Co., agreed that they would not sell direct to Granger organizations at below retail prices or without their agents being involved.[19] The plow manufacturers eventually indicated that some agents might sell to farmer organizations at a discount if farmers paid for their equipment in cash. These offers from the large firms were not satisfactory to the Grangers, although they were able to buy direct from some of the smaller farm equipment manufacturing companies.

The Grangers' second strategy was to set up cooperative business ventures to begin manufacturing plows and harvesting machines themselves. They saw this approach as being more likely to "smash" the harvester and plow "rings" that they so despised. They managed to establish some manufacturing facilities in several midwestern states, and in some cases they were able to produce plows and harvesters that they could sell to members of the Grange for half to two-thirds of the retail prices of the largest manufacturers.[20] In Iowa, for example, the Grange purchased a small harvester factory that enabled them to produce approximately 250 harvesting machines at prices much lower than the list price.[21] In some cases, the Grange organizations purchased licenses that granted them the rights to produce patented farm machinery, although the designs for which they were able to acquire licenses typically lacked the latest features from the largest firms. However, the Grangers were generally short of financial capital, and some of their manufacturing facilities failed. By 1875, the Grange largely abandoned the idea of manufacturing their own agricultural equipment.[22]

Several factors disadvantaged the Grange movement's cooperative efforts relative to the larger firms, which had acquired considerable power to keep new competitors at bay. For example, the Grangers sold their manufactured products at prices close to the cost of production, but the large firms were able to withstand this price competition due to their superior access to capital. The Grangers also had more difficulty providing services for repairs and provision of spare parts, aspects that the large firms had already established through their sales and distribution networks. They also lacked capacity to sell their machinery on credit, which the large firms had normalized for sales of their commercial products. In the few instances where the Grangers did lend farmers the funds to purchase the equipment, they found that they lacked the capacity to handle bad debts, which again the larger firms could withstand because of their stronger financial position.

The Grange movement dwindled rapidly in the late 1870s as it became apparent that newcomer cooperative businesses were up against the enormous power of the established equipment firms. The local Grange houses did not want to be held responsible for the debts of failed manufacturing ventures, and so they quickly wound down their operations. Despite its failure to succeed in their quest to confront the power of the dominant companies in the sector, the Grange did provide some benefits and relief to farmers through the sales of less expensive equipment, and it did pressure the large firms to temporarily lower their prices.[23]

HARVESTER WARS AND MEGAMERGERS

Bitter rivalries characterized the harvesting machine industry in North America in the final decades of the nineteenth century. New competitors began to appear in the sector in the late 1800s. Deering Harvester Co., for example, became one of McCormick's biggest challengers just a few decades after entering the business in 1870. Although the Grangers had trouble vying for markets with the big players, William Deering entered the field with some advantages. He had sharp business management skills and experience in large-scale industrial production—and, more important, he had access to capital. His firm was licensed to produce the Marsh Harvester, which it did at a large scale. Deering's firm also manufactured a harvester that incorporated a twine binder for bundling the harvested grain that he licensed from inventor John Appleby. The twine binder was an improvement on McCormick's wire binder, which was known to leave small pieces of metal in fields and in cattle feed. Deering also made vertical investments in related sectors, such as twine and steel production, which reduced his production costs. By the 1880s, the Deering Harvester

Co. was able to cut into some of McCormick's markets enough that it hurt. Upon Cyrus H. McCormick's death in 1884, his son Cyrus, Jr. took over leadership of the firm and continued the rivalry with Deering and other firms in the sector.

With multiple manufacturers of farm machinery all angling for the same customers, many of the companies increasingly relied on their sales agents to pressure farmers into purchasing machines they likely did not need and could not afford. With sales costs on average making up over a third of the operating costs of the companies, the farm machinery firms were highly incentivized to make ever more sales to justify that cost. At the same time, labor unions were being established and demanding better working conditions and more pay at those firms. As a result, the harvester firms, some of the largest employers in the country, faced rising costs. The McCormick Harvesting Machine Company, for example, cut wages at its manufacturing plant in the mid-1880s, which sparked a bitter dispute between management and labor. The firm also fired some workers and replaced them with expensive automated machinery, but the investment was wasted due to the poor quality of the automation compared to skilled labor.[24]

The antagonism that characterized the sector in the late 1880s to the early 1900s—during which the larger firms became increasingly distrustful of each other—is often referred to as the "Harvester Wars." This was a period of slower growth in the market, as the North American frontier had become increasingly settled and demand for farm equipment began to stabilize. Despite tense relations among the leading firms, there were some initial efforts among them to collude to fix prices to make up for weaker sales volumes. However, in the absence of a formal agreement among the firms to cut back on production, the price-fixing initiatives failed to come to fruition.

The failure of the firms at the top of the market to collaborate with one another in a cartel-like agreement led to a different solution: consolidation. The first effort to combine the firms into a single company was envisioned as a massive merger comprising over half the firms in the industry, although it ultimately failed because no banker would fund the colossal deal. According to business historian Helen Kramer:

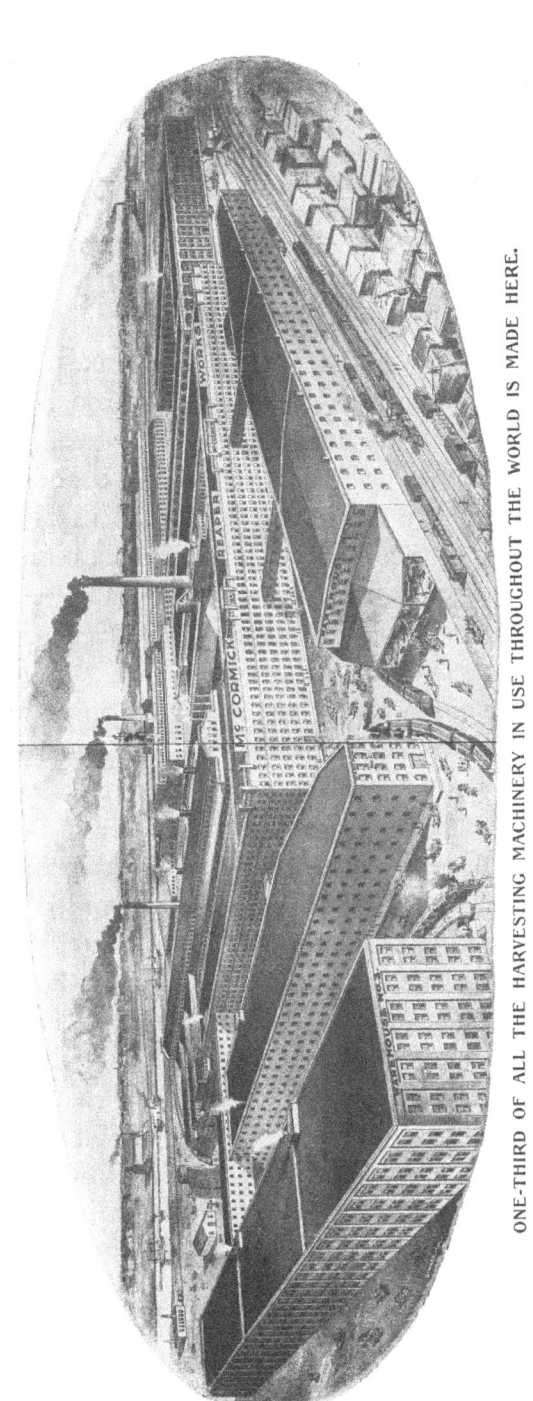

2.1 McCormick Harvesting Machine Co., factory view, 1896. *Source:* Courtesy of Vintage Machinery, www.vintagemachinery.org.

In December, 1890, a projected combination of eighteen concerns was incorporated in the form of a trust as the American Harvester Company, but had collapsed by January, 1891. The six largest firms had set the terms of incorporation, intending to purchase the plants of twelve smaller companies and to close some of them, thus restraining output. Properties were accepted without appraisal at inflated valuations and it soon became apparent that the new company would not have any working capital. Since there was also no plan of operation, it is not surprising that the manufacturers could not interest bankers in financing the project.[25]

Throughout the 1890s, the Harvester Wars continued, and the battle took a growing toll on firms' profitability. In this context, some of the large firms turned to foreign markets in an effort to expand sales to cover their costs. As indicated in figure 2.1, in 1896 the McCormick Harvesting Machine Co. bragged in its catalog that its Chicago factory supplied one-third of all harvesting machinery used in the world. Deering also sought other ways to reduce costs, going so far as to invest in the intermediate industries that provided the raw materials for production, purchasing a steel mill as well as interests in timber and iron ore.[26] Toward the end of the 1890s, talks resumed between Deering and McCormick, both eager to end the costly battle and expand their sales. Merger talks continued over the course of several years. William Deering was keen to retire from the business, and the McCormick family was interested in Deering's vertical integration with the raw materials needed for harvester production, although they were concerned that he was asking for too much money to conclude the deal. By 1900, prices for iron and steel rose sharply, in part due to the consolidation of the US steel industry—itself undergoing an extensive amalgamation that resulted in the US Steel Corporation in 1901, which at the time was the largest steel manufacturer and the largest firm in the world. Higher steel costs further pushed the merger of the harvester firms. Deering was interested in merging all the US harvester manufacturers in a massive megamerger. The firm's lawyer advised that the courts would likely not approve a merger that stifled competition completely via monopoly, given the passage of the Sherman Antitrust Act in 1890.[27]

Finally, in 1902, George Perkins of J. P. Morgan, one of the most prominent and powerful financial firms in the United States at the time, brokered a merger deal that brought together McCormick, Deering, and three smaller firms—Plano, Wisconsin, and Warder, Bushnell and Glessner—to form a massive new firm they called International Harvester Company. The new firm controlled 85 percent of the US domestic market for harvesters and maintained Deering's vertically integrated elements.[28] Although the deal squelched competition by combining the main firms in the sector into one corporation, Perkins advised that it was unlikely the new firm would be in violation of antitrust law since it did not include all the firms in the sector.[29]

In the next year, International Harvester bought up three other smaller firms in the industry. However, the firm kept its purchase of two of those firms under wraps. They continued to operate ostensibly as independent manufacturing companies, appearing to compete with International Harvester but in fact were controlled by it.[30] The manufacturing plants of these two firms were subsequently abandoned by International Harvester, leading the US Bureau of Corporations to conclude that the only purpose of the acquisitions was to eliminate competition.[31] Labor historian Robert Ozanne colorfully described it in this way: "If ever a corporation was 'born in sin' from the standpoint of the Sherman Antitrust Act, it was International Harvester corporation. At birth in 1902 it produced 85 percent of the nation's grain-harvesting machinery. Thereafter it continued a program of acquisition so vigorous that by 1907 there remained no semblance of competition."[32]

The deal that Perkins brokered established a voting trust that was shared by the McCormick family, the Deering family, and J. P. Morgan. This decision-making structure remained in place for a period of ten years while the firm integrated the various firms under the International Harvester banner. The firm became a publicly traded corporation listed on the New York Stock Exchange in 1902. Most of the shares, however, were still held by the McCormick and Deering families, with nearly 43 percent belonging to the former and nearly 35 percent to the latter. Approximately 5 percent of the shares were purchased by John D. Rockefeller, father-in-law of Cyrus H. McCormick's son, Harold, who was married to Rockefeller's daughter, Edith. Rockefeller was an enormously powerful industrialist who founded the Standard Oil Company, itself a massive petroleum trust that was subsequently dissolved in 1911 for violating antitrust laws.[33] By 1904, the McCormick and the Rockefeller families owned just over half of the shares of the newly formed firm. In that period, the firm took extensive loans from John D. Rockefeller, often in the millions of dollars.[34]

The merger that created International Harvester occurred while major mergers were also taking place in other sectors in the United States, such as oil and steel, in a period often referred to as the gilded age. This new era of corporate consolidation at the start of the twentieth century sparked widespread concern over the large trusts that dominated the economy because of their ability to set high prices and erect barriers that made it harder for smaller firms to enter the market.[35] The merging firms in the agricultural machinery sector defended consolidation as reducing costs for farmers. They claimed that in a context of rising costs of both labor and materials, without savings from the consolidation of the sales and distribution functions of the firm, they would have to charge farmers even higher prices. They also defended mergers as necessary to expand their sales more effectively into foreign markets to save domestic manufacturing jobs. But rather than generating cost savings for farmers, the prices of farm machinery produced by International Harvester actually rose following the merger, even as the combination of the firms reduced marketing costs. When the ten-year period set out by Perkins ended, the McCormick family, in conjunction with the Rockefellers, gained complete control of the company.[36]

As in the harvester sector, the plow industry saw significant consolidation in the late 1800s and early 1900s. Deere & Co. twice flirted with a major merger with other firms, once between 1889 and 1891, when a British financial syndicate sought to purchase the firm along with two other major US plow firms, and again between 1899 and 1901, though neither deal materialized. In the latter case, Deere & Co. was in active negotiations with nineteen other US plow manufacturers, with financial backing from the Equitable and Mutual life insurance companies. The plan was to develop a massive "plow trust" with a commanding market share by forming the American Plow Company, an idea that mirrored the formation of International Harvester in the same period.[37] Although these massive merger deals in the plow sector ultimately fell through, the fact that they were seriously attempted demonstrates the extent to which the firms at the time felt that the main way to survive was to acquire their rivals in order to dominate the marketplace.

CANADIAN CONCENTRATION

As competition heated up in the United States in the latter part of the nineteenth century, the farm machinery sector became larger and more concentrated in Canada as well. In this period, the Massey-Harris Company emerged as the largest and most dominant farm machinery firm in the country, rivaling the US producers in both Canadian and global markets. The firm was the product of a merger in the early 1890s between the Massey and Harris farm implement firms along with several other smaller firms.

Daniel Massey Jr. established a farm implement company in Ontario in 1847, the same year that the government imposed a 10 percent tariff on imported farm implements, which was progressively raised to nearly 15 percent by 1854.[38] Rather than develop its own innovations, the firm purchased licenses for US-designed farm implements, effectively benefiting from the fact that if those same machines were produced in the United States for export to Canada, then still a British colony, importers would face a stiff tariff charge. The Massey Manufacturing Company, soon taken over by Massey's son, Hart, sometimes modified the design of the machinery to better suit conditions in Canada and aimed to be the first firm to produce new US designs for the Canadian market.[39] As in the case of the United States, the development of railways in Canada in the latter part of the nineteenth century provided the firm with more reliable transit for both the acquisition of raw materials and the sale of its implements to wider markets in the West. Massey's biggest rival, A. Harris, Son and Company Limited, established in 1857, was also based in Ontario, and the two firms competed for farm machinery sales in that market.

Both Massey and Harris benefited from Canadian trade agreements. The 1854 Canadian-American Reciprocity Treaty offered free trade in primary goods, such as lumber and steel, while maintaining tariffs ranging from 15 to 20 percent on manufactured goods. The tariff on agricultural machinery reached 20 percent by 1858. Free trade within the British Empire enabled Canadian firms to import superior-quality British iron and steel at a better price than was available in North America.[40] As a result, these firms had the best of both worlds: they could import raw materials without tariff charges, and they were protected by steep tariffs placed on competing foreign machinery imports. The reciprocity agreement ended in 1866, but by this time these firms had already established themselves as market leaders in Canada.

Over this period, Massey also established distribution and marketing channels much like those McCormick was using in the United States , which included sales and service agents in local markets as well as the extension of credit with three-year payment plans. Massey also began to focus on foreign markets in the late 1860s. It was at that time cheaper to export harvesters to Europe and beyond than it was to transit machinery to the Canadian West, where the prairie lands were being settled by European immigrants. Because foreign manufacturers lagged behind those in North America with respect to the development of farm machinery, the firm found a ready market abroad, especially in Europe. Massey also exported to other regions, including Asia, Africa, and South America, as well as most British colonies, including Australia.

In 1879, Canada implemented the National Policy that sought to protect domestic industry by imposing a 35 percent tariff on some imports, this time on both raw materials and manufactured goods, including farm machinery. This period saw more intense competition between domestic farm implement manufacturers, and as in the United States at the same time, there was a saturation of the domestic market with the slowing of new settlements. There were thus similar pressures for consolidation in the Canadian market, and Massey and Harris merged in 1891, becoming Massey-Harris Limited. The firm then quickly acquired other smaller firms in the early 1890s, eventually controlling around 60 percent of the domestic market for farm implements. Massey-Harris effectively offered a full line of farm equipment beginning in 1894, including both harvesters and plows. In this period of consolidation, the number of domestic farm implement manufacturers declined from several hundred in the 1870s to just 114 by 1900. Massey-Harris also was able to negotiate with the government of Canada in 1894 to secure a 99 percent rebate on the tariff it paid on the raw materials that it imported from the United States for machines that were destined for export, a remarkable feat that helped the firm to secure its export markets.[41]

Although the US firms were not initially concerned about markets in Canada given their smaller size, both Deere & Co. and International Harvester made investments to produce their products in Canada in the early 1900s. That move enabled them to scale the tariff wall and meet some of the demand from the western provinces for the larger US machine models, as farms in the Prairie provinces were much larger than those in Ontario.

TRACTORS PROMPT FURTHER RIVALRY AND CONSOLIDATION

Although they were technically producing separate types of farm implements, International Harvester and Deere & Co. saw themselves as archrivals by the early twentieth century. Within the space of a few decades, further consolidation in the farm machinery sector brought these firms into direct competition with one another in the United States. In the decade after Charles Deere's death in 1908, Deere & Co. acquired eight smaller firms that produced a range of farm implements, as well as wagons, effectively achieving Deere's dream of consolidation.[42] Additionally, although both Deere and International Harvester had toyed with producing the products in which the other specialized since the late 1800s—that is, International Harvester looked into producing plows, and Deere looked into producing harvesting machinery—by 1918 both firms had fully moved into producing a full line of equipment, which now included a new technology: gasoline-powered tractors.

There were distinct advantages for full-line farm equipment firms that helped to reinforce their dominance in the market. These firms had more even earnings throughout the year because they sold tillage implements in the spring and harvesting machinery in the fall. They also typically forced dealers to sign exclusive contracts, stipulating, for example, that if they wanted to sell the firm's harvesting equipment, they would also have to carry the firm's plowing equipment and not the plows of another company, and vice versa.[43] These practices made it very difficult for smaller firms producing specialized implements to break into the market.

The tractors and self-propelled combine harvesters that came onto the market in the early decades of the twentieth century cemented the full-line approach. These innovations transformed the farm machinery sector and set off another wave of consolidation that concentrated power among the firms at the top. Most of the innovations in farm machinery in the latter part of the 1800s were improvements on earlier inventions, such as the mechanical harvester and the steel plow. But gasoline engine tractors marked a dramatic change in the dynamics of the sector, ushering in a second major technology-induced transformation of both farming and the farm machinery sector in the space of one hundred years. Although steam tractors had been around since the 1860s, they were large, heavy machines that were useful only for plowing fields on very large farms or for powering stationary threshing work. The innovation of the internal combustion engine was borrowed from the automobile industry rather than being a product of the big agricultural machinery firms. The earliest gasoline tractors emerged in the 1890s, although they were not produced in large quantities until the end of the first decade of the twentieth century. By 1910, there were dozens of firms producing tractors, and by 1916 some two hundred tractor models on the market.[44]

The big firms, such as International Harvester, Deere, and Massey-Harris, were somewhat slow to begin producing tractors, although they eventually dominated that market by the late 1920s despite not being the original source of this disruptive innovation. The J. I. Case Threshing Machine Company produced tractors as early as 1893, building on its experience producing steam and then gasoline engines for its threshing machines. International Harvester was one of the first of the big firms to begin making tractors. The firm started production in 1906 and almost immediately became the largest tractor supplier in the US market.[45] By 1909, International Harvester was the fourth largest firm in the United States overall; only US Steel, Standard Oil, and US Tobacco were larger.[46] Deere experimented with tractor production in the 1910s but entered into the business in earnest only after buying the Iowa-based Waterloo Gasoline Engine Company in 1918 and taking over production of the latter's Waterloo Boy brand of tractors. Massey-Harris purchased the J. I. Case Plow Works in 1927, which had earlier developed the capacity to produce tractors. At that time, Massey-Harris sold the name rights of J. I. Case to the J. I. Case Threshing Machine Company, finally ending the confusion arising from two firms having virtually the same name.

In this period, only a few of the newcomer firms in the farm machinery business were able to compete with the large full-line companies. Allis-Chalmers Company, formed in the early 1900s as a merger between two machinery firms that dated back to the mid-1800s, built on its expertise in engines to produce tractors in 1914. It steadily acquired other farm machinery firms to become a full-line firm able to compete with the larger players.[47] The Allis-Chalmers story is unusual, as this firm entered the farm machinery market by producing tractors first and then added other implements, eventually gaining a significant market share in the industry.

The Ford Motor Company was another newcomer to the industry with its launch of the Fordson tractor in 1917. Ford represented an important source of competition for the larger farm machinery firms, in large part due to the firm's reputation in the automobile sector for providing quality cars for average people at low prices. The company wanted to build the Model T equivalent for farm vehicles, and along these lines, the Fordson tractor was smaller and much less expensive than the other tractors on the market. The Fordson was an overnight success, as its price—under $1,000—was much lower than what the other manufacturers were charging—around $1,200 to $2,000. Ford even managed to arrange distribution of the Fordson through the US government wartime channels for $750 per tractor. The firm profited handsomely from this deal, especially because its production costs were just over $500 per tractor, and with direct sales to farmers, Ford did not have to pay commissions to dealers.[48] By 1920, one in three tractors sold in the United States was a Fordson, though Ford did not adopt the same credit system for its sales operation as the other firms, instead relying on farmers to get loans from commercial banks to finance their purchases.[49]

Although the Fordson sold well in its early years, it became clear that Ford was not interested in becoming a full-line firm, instead preferring to contract with implement makers to design and sell machinery specifically intended for use with the Fordson tractor. The Fordson had some weaknesses, namely its light frame, which made it weaker than its competitors and prone to flipping over and causing harm to its operator. It also faced steep competition from the established full-line firms that produced stronger machines with more uses. Given the tough market for these machines in North America, Ford exited the US tractor market in 1928, although it continued to produce tractors in Europe where the demand for smaller tractors was higher.

In 1929, the year after Ford exited the market for tractors in the United States, International Harvester accounted for 59.9 percent of all-purpose tractor sales in the US domestic market, whereas Deere held 21.1 percent of the market. The seven largest firms at that time controlled 96.3 percent of the tractor market. In that same year, two merger deals were completed. The first created the Oliver Farm Equipment Company by combining the Oliver Chilled Plow Works with three other firms, including manufacturers of tractors, seeding equipment, and threshing machinery, to form a full-line corporation. The other merger created Minneapolis-Moline, bringing together the Moline Plow Company with several threshing machinery and tractor firms. Market share in the overall farm equipment market in the United States that year was more evenly distributed than in the market for tractors, with approximately 28 percent for International Harvester, 12 percent for Deere, 5 percent for Oliver, 4 percent for J. I. Case, 2.5 percent for Minneapolis-Moline, and 2 percent for both Allis-Chalmers and Massey-Harris.[50] These figures for the US market do not include foreign sales, which were significant for both International Harvester and Massey-Harris.

Tractor sales were slow in the first decade of the twentieth century as the new technology was being introduced, but picked up during World War I. Between 1910 and 1920, the number of tractors in use on farms in the United States grew from around 1,000 to 246,000 and then to 1 million by 1929 and 4.5 million by 1960.[51] As more farmers shifted to using tractors, the need to purchase new plows and reapers to pull behind the machines was a major boon for the firms. A growing proportion of tractor sales took place among the full-line firms, as they sold implements and tractors that were meant to be used together. But as the newer full-line companies emerged, their sales shares also increased, reducing some of the concentration at the top of the industry. International Harvester's market share of farm machinery fell to around 23 percent in 1948, whereas Deere's increased to around 15 percent, and the others each held between 4 percent and 10 percent of the market.[52]

The early decades of the twentieth century also saw the rise of the combine harvester machine, which integrated reaping and threshing tasks. Although versions of the combine harvester were invented alongside the mechanical reaper in the 1830s and 1840s in various countries, including Scotland, Australia, and the United States, the machines were large and required a team of multiple—often twenty or more—horses to pull them. These machines became functional enough for widespread use only in the twentieth century because they incorporated internal combustion engines. It was not until around 1920 that combine harvesters could be used effectively in fields at an affordable price.[53]

THE INTERNATIONAL HARVESTER ANTITRUST CASE

Throughout the early decades of the twentieth century, International Harvester was dogged by accusations of violating US antitrust laws. The grounds for these accusations were evident in many aspects of the firm's operations. Several of its directors also sat on the board of US Steel, another major trust, in what is referred to as an interlocking directorship, linking the two firms and their business interests. In addition, J. D. Rockefeller, who was head of the Standard Oil trust, owned a significant number of shares in International Harvester, and the firm also had established relationships with other trusts, including the coal trust, the railroad trust, and the banking trust. The firm used these connections—the type that Brandeis warned were deeply problematic because they dampened competition—to obtain rebates on its materials purchases, secure low prices on raw materials, and access credit.[54] A report of Deputy Attorney General Burdette Townsend, who was charged in 1908 with investigating the firm on behalf of the US Department of Justice, called these intertwined—yet practically "invisible" — connections with other trusts "murderous to the competitors of the International Harvester Co."[55] The report also outlined how the firm charged higher prices in the US domestic market than it did to foreign buyers, and it revealed that the firm put political pressure on legislators to lower its tax bills.[56]

Townsend's damning report was suppressed by President Theodore Roosevelt, who had tight linkages with and financial support from both

J. P. Morgan and International Harvester. Roosevelt cast himself as a trust buster early in his presidency, but he apparently promised George Perkins in 1907 that he would not pursue an antitrust case against International Harvester.[57] Townsend's report came to light only after Roosevelt left office and the US Department of Justice brought a suit against the firm in 1912. A 1913 US Bureau of Corporations report on International Harvester stated, "There is no doubt that the principal motive for the formation of the International Harvester Co. was to eliminate competition and to secure a dominant position in the trade. This was also the salient fact of the transaction. The purpose of reducing costs and expenses by organizing a single great concern from several large ones was a secondary motive."[58] The report further stressed that the firm used its dominant position to elevate prices, noting that "even on the basis of the company's own statements the rate of return on investment in the monopolistic lines is at least from two to three times as great as on some lines in which it meets active competition."[59] The report also called out the firm for other offenses, including forcing its dealers into exclusive clauses that suppressed competition, hiding its ownership of other firms, and leveraging privileged access to capital from its financial connections to J. P. Morgan and J. D. Rockefeller to provide advantages in scale, provision of credit, and support of its dealer network.[60]

It was in this period that the McCormick family sought to resurrect the historical narrative about the elder McCormick as the true inventor of the mechanical reaper in a bid to build a public relations campaign to fight accusations of violations of US antitrust laws and to burnish the firm's reputation. The family even went so far as to lobby the US Treasury Office to have Cyrus H. McCormick's image printed on US national currency to honor him as a hero to farmers. But the firm's competitors objected, and the currency plan never came to fruition.[61]

The outcome of the US government suit against International Harvester, like many other antitrust cases, was complex. In 1914, the courts ruled that the firm was in violation of the Sherman Act and ordered it to dissolve and separate fully into at least three equal but distinct corporations. International Harvester appealed the ruling, but the results were inconclusive, and the resolution was delayed until the end of World War I, which the United States had since entered. The firm and the US

Department of Justice eventually agreed to a consent decree in 1918 with several stipulations, including a reduction in the number of dealers to just one per town, which would end the practice of selling the Deering and McCormick lines—which were still sold as separate brands—at separate dealerships. International Harvester was also required to sell off several of its product lines and their associated manufacturing plants.[62]

By the early 1920s, however, continuing concerns about competition in the sector prompted the US Department of Justice to demand further measures to restore competition. A government commission recommended the separation of the McCormick and Deering firms, but the Department of Justice (DOJ) lost this case in court. The government appealed the case to the US Supreme Court but again lost the case. The Court ruled that competition had been sufficiently restored, as indicated by International Harvester's declining share of the market relative to the early 1900s. The ruling from that case had important implications for future antitrust cases, as it included a line that is now often quoted in defense of large firms that the law "does not make the mere size of a corporation, however impressive, or the existence of unexerted power on its part, an offense, when unaccompanied by unlawful conduct in the exercise of its power."[63]

SOCIAL AND ECOLOGICAL CONSEQUENCES OF FARM MACHINERY

The costs associated with the technologies these developed and sold by the farm machinery firms were increasingly recognized in public discourse. The Grangers' accusations of market abuses, which were echoed by the US Department of Justice in the International Harvester antitrust case, highlighted the extent to which farmers faced higher prices and less choice in the highly concentrated sector than they would in a more competitive market. There were also wider social and ecological costs of the growing adoption of farm machinery that deserve consideration. The major firms in the sector played a key role in disseminating these technologies, although they were largely able to avoid being held responsible for those wider costs due to the complexity of the forces that led to the widespread adoption of their products.

By the early twentieth century, the debate regarding the social consequences of farm mechanization in North America had become robust. There was disagreement on the relative costs to farmers of adopting machinery versus maintaining livestock as their main source of power and traction on the farm.[64] A farmer's decision to purchase a tractor involved not just consideration of the price of the machinery but also other factors. Promoters of tractors stressed their superior draft power, which saved labor. They pointed out that replacing horses with tractors meant that farmers would no longer need to set aside fields to grow feed, maintain separate buildings to house their livestock, or pay laborers to care for the animals, all resulting in cost and production efficiencies.

Advocates of tractors also suggested that their benefits extended to all members of farm families. One analyst noted that women and children would have more idle time to enjoy "the leisure and culture products" that had become more available in broader society at the time.[65] And some observers argued that combine harvesters benefited farm families because they could handle the harvest themselves without the need to hire migrant labor. Cyrus McCormick, grandson of Cyrus H. McCormick, wrote in 1931: "Farm wives and daughters prepared huge tables and nerved themselves for hot hours of cooking for a swarm of hungry men; and they warned one another to be prepared to stay safe indoors at night." By contrast, he noted of the combine harvester:

Acre after acre the machine devours, thirty or forty before evening if the field is large enough; and when night comes, it is ready to move to the next field and do its work over again. As yet the combine has not learned to take mother's place as a home-maker; but she no longer has to labor through the night as well, in order that an imported army of harvest hands may eat. The harvester-thresher and the tractor, mightiest of the tools of power farming, have done as much for her, it seems, as for any other.[66]

Defenders of horses stressed that tractor advocates overstated their capacities and failed to note their costs. Switching to tractors meant the purchase of new implements such as plows, as the ones designed for use with horse traction were not compatible with tractors.[67] One horse advocate noted around 1920, already alluding to lock-in dynamics, "We believe all tractors are bad, only some are worse than others. When it comes down to actual facts in dollars and cents, we believe that any farmer who disposes of his horses and intends to do all of his farmwork with tractors, will eventually 'hit the rocks,' and that he is only working for the man who sells the tractors, for as soon as he had made enough wheat or other farm products to pay for his tractor, it will be necessary for him to purchase another."[68] Horse advocates at the time saw themselves as defending a way of life, with the livelihoods of many—including those who cared for the animals, made harnesses and other equipment, and attended to their veterinary care needs—all on the line.

The advocates of farm machinery largely prevailed in this debate, however, as tractor adoption continued apace in the following decades. This process sped up during World War I, as both horses and hired farm labor were in short supply. Farmers also increasingly saw it as their patriotic duty to acquire a tractor to increase food production to support the war effort.[69] As women increasingly performed more field tasks on the farm during the war, they found tractors easier to operate than horse-drawn equipment. A number of economic studies sprang up at the time to explain tractor diffusion based on these various comparative costs and considerations.[70]

The growing adoption of farm machinery, especially tractors in the early decades of the twentieth century, is widely associated with the displacement of farm laborers, sharecroppers, and tenants from farmlands.[71] The displacement and marginalization of these groups, who worked the land but did not own it, were often people of color or people who had few means. In her 1940 book, *Why Farmers Are Poor*, political economist Anna Rochester made a direct link between tractors and growing poverty: "Uncounted thousands have been driven off the land. Tractors are obliterating the boundaries of little sharecropper plots in some of the older cotton regions, tossing families from the poverty of extreme exploitation into the worse destitution of complete unemployment."[72] Those who were displaced typically migrated to poorer farms without machinery or to cities. Because many of the displaced people had less access to education, they often remained poor and lacked resources to establish their own farms.[73] In this way, tractors served as a barrier to their success as farmers in their own right.

Concurrent with labor displacement was a growing concentration in agricultural landholdings and a shrinking number of farms. It is well documented that to make their farm machinery purchases "efficient," farmers felt compelled to increase the size of their farming operations to reduce the marginal cost of farm machinery per unit of land, especially because farm machinery was so expensive. Many farmers went into debt to purchase both tractors and more land, finding themselves highly leveraged and much more vulnerable to fluctuations in production due to weather variability and other factors.[74] Some analysts at the time noted that farmers who had superior business skills, which made them "a desirable credit risk," were the ones who could gain financing to expand, whereas others who were less skilled in this respect were the ones to sell their land and leave farming.[75] In the United States, for example, the farm population declined by 25 percent between 1920 and 1945.[76]

These dynamics also worked to the detriment of Black farmers in the United States, many of whom became sharecroppers after the Civil War, farming on land owned by others. The number of Black farmers in the United States began to decline after 1920, just as tractor ownership began to rise.[77] There was widespread concern during the Great Depression about how farm mechanization generated enormous economic inequities, which were made worse by the fact that there were not sufficient employment opportunities in cities to absorb the excess labor, all of which contributed to racial tensions.[78] A 1940 US government report acknowledged the uneven social consequences of farm labor displacement due to farm mechanization, stressing, "Some labor supplanted by technological progress continues to be absorbed by reemployment as in the past, to be sure, but by no means does it take place in the rapid, semi-automatic manner of former years.... It is for this reason that consideration needs to be given to measures of a remedial nature—to seek thereby to reduce the impact and to cushion the effect of these changes upon the disadvantaged groups."[79]

The adoption of tractors also had economic repercussions for farmers who did stay on the land and oversaw ever larger farm operations. Although wealthier farmers typically were the first to adopt mechanization, those same farmers also faced increased debt loads and thus were encouraged to orient their operations toward more commercial farming to repay their loans. As such, those farmers became more exposed to business cycles and government policies. This process, as one analyst at the time noted, led to a "subsequent loss of traditional self-sufficiency and autonomy" on the part of farmers.[80] These dynamics took hold even as mechanization resulted in greater food production than was generally demanded in the economy. Indeed, by the 1930s there was serious overproduction of food in the United States, which resulted in weaker prices that ultimately hurt farm incomes. One farmer at the time captured the broad sentiment about this phenomenon: "Tractors cause the over production ... and it encourages corporation farming, which is a great drawback for agriculture. It crowds the small farmer and the beginner out of the game."[81]

The widespread use of plows across the North American Midwest raised concerns regarding soil structure and fertility by the mid-1800s. Although settled agriculture and the use of plows has been associated with soil erosion and fertility loss for thousands of years, the more modern iron- and steel-tipped plows have been specifically associated with its acceleration in North America.[82] The clearing of land with modern moldboard plows cannot be separated from the broader forces that encouraged the widespread use of this technology in the first place. These dynamics include colonial expansion and settlement by people of European origin, who violently displaced Indigenous peoples from their traditional lands, as well as the growth of a worldwide market for crops, such as wheat, that encouraged that expansion of European settlement in the Americas.[83] Volatile commodity prices also influenced farming patterns, as farmers often sought to increase production to maintain their incomes when prices fell. The corporations that provided industrially manufactured plows thus profited from a wide set of dynamics that created demand for their products. Although there is scant literature that explicitly places specific farm machinery firms within these broader considerations, the fact that they were the main providers of the technologies that facilitated these dynamics, and that they were direct beneficiaries of them, warrants more scrutiny.

Polished iron and steel moldboard plows contributed to soil degradation in several ways. These tools cut deep into the soil and turned it over, fracturing it and causing tillage erosion by moving soil from one part of the field to another, especially on slopes. Once disturbed in this way, soils were at increased risk of further erosion from water and wind.

Cutting into the soil also killed beneficial life forms in the soil, such as earthworms, fungi, and other living organisms, thus reducing the soil's structure and fertility. Extensive tillage also decreased soil organic matter, even as it temporarily raised mineralization of key nutrients that could boost soil fertility. As soil scientist Rattan Lal and colleagues explain, "While plowing improved soil fertility and agronomic productivity, it set in motion a long-term trend of decline in soil structure and increase in susceptibility to crusting, compaction and erosion."[84]

Indeed, the disturbance of soil and destruction of soil organic matter from excessive plowing on fragile prairie grasslands has been widely linked to the 1930s Dust Bowl, which resulted in massive soil storms that persisted for a decade. The storms were so severe that they resulted in the loss of some 350 million tons of topsoil that was carried as far away as Chicago and New York.[85] The use of tractors and heavy machinery such as combines also contributed to soil compaction. Edward H. Faulkner lamented in his popular 1943 book, *Ploughman's Folly*, "We have equipped our farmers with a greater tonnage of machinery per man than any other nation. Our agricultural population has proceeded to use that machinery to the end of destroying the soil in less time than any other people has been known to do in recorded history. This is hardly a record to be proud of."[86] Faulkner received scathing reviews of his book in journals such as *Nature* for not being sufficiently science based, because it pushed back against the dominant perspective that plowing was necessary to maintain agricultural production.[87] However, the idea of conserving soil by dramatically reducing tillage became widely accepted in subsequent years.

CONCLUSION

As this chapter has shown, the dominant farm machinery firms benefited from numerous market, technology, and policy factors that enabled them to grow big and command significant market share. These factors overlapped in practice, giving the first-mover firms a major lead over others. Patents on their products enabled them to control technologies, while some, such as McCormick, pursued aggressive lawsuits to gain access to royalties from those using their innovations. The dominant firms also had privileged access to financial capital from powerful investors, which enabled them to engage in merger and acquisition deals to overtake their rivals and develop sophisticated dealer-network and credit operations that locked farmers in as customers. They also benefited from technological complementarities that enabled them to develop into full-line firms. These strategies made it harder for newcomer firms to break into the market. Once they became big firms, the market leaders were able to exercise the various forms of power available to dominant firms, such as engaging collusion to fix prices and pressuring political figures to be lenient when they got caught. Although these firms were able benefit from economies of scale from mass production, other factors were equally, if not more, important.

Meanwhile, the broader social and ecological consequences of the growth of the farm machinery sector—with just a few firms at the helm—were massive. They included the displacement of marginalized populations—Indigenous peoples whose lands were confiscated as settlers of European descent moved west in North America in the mid- to late 1800s, followed by the displacement of poor and Black farmers as tractor use and farm consolidation accelerated. Farmers who remained on their farms typically incurred higher debt loads and faced lower commodity prices due to overproduction, which resulted in large part from mechanization and the rise of other inputs to be discussed in the following chapters. Furthermore, soil degradation typically followed from greater use of both steel plows and heavy farm machinery. Although these consequences were noted by some critics at the time, the promoters of farm machinery appeared to win the day as farmers became locked into the use of heavy machines.

3
FERTILIZERS

The top fertilizer firms in the United States were handed numerous indictments for market abuses in the early decades of the twentieth century, following a dizzying set of mergers and acquisitions that significantly consolidated the sector. In the space of about seventy years, the commercial fertilizer industry not only emerged but also had become highly concentrated. The sector has long been characterized by organized cooperation among the top firms to shape the contours of both national and international fertilizer markets.

The fertilizer sector has a complex history, in part because of the wide variety of materials that can be used to boost plant productivity and also because it is only in the past several hundred years that fertilizers have even been viewed as commercial commodities. From Neolithic times, farmers have applied various substances to soils, such as animal and human manures, waste, and wood ash, to improve plant growth. Other practices were also common, such as cultivating leguminous plants alongside or prior to the planting of other crops. Typically, these practices were used within closed ecological systems that used local wastes from animals and human settlements to enrich agricultural fields within the same region.[1] The rise of the commercial fertilizer industry was shaped by advances in scientific understandings of the nutrient needs of plants, the availability (and associated geopolitics) of key fertilizer resources, and breakthroughs in chemical processes over the course of the nineteenth and early twentieth centuries. As was the case for farm machinery, the sector experienced major technological transformations and became highly concentrated over a relatively short period of time.

The top firms in the sector achieved dominance through several strategies, including capitalizing on economies of scale for mined and synthetically produced fertilizer inputs that require large-scale capital inputs. Firms also engaged in rampant collusion and established cartels with other large firms in the sector at both the national and international levels. This collaboration among firms enabled them to control both production and prices, which effectively dissuaded new entrants or required them to take part in these arrangements. Fertilizer firms also benefited extensively from government support with respect to mineral exploration and mining, as well as the production of synthetic nitrogen, the latter especially because of its strategic military importance.

THE EMERGENCE OF A COMMERCIAL FERTILIZER INDUSTRY

Although they have long been used in agriculture, fertilizers became increasingly commercialized from the early nineteenth century onward. This period saw the rise of the global agricultural commodity trade as well as the expansion of settler colonialism that resulted in lands being cleared for cultivation to serve the growing global demand for key agricultural crops. A rising focus on commodity crop production in this era also encouraged more intensive farming practices as farmers specialized in crops with high export and trade value, such as cotton, tobacco, corn, and wheat, often growing these crops in monoculture patterns year after year. Tilling fields to prepare them for planting also degraded soil structure and killed living organisms, which reduced soil fertility, resulting in progressively lower crop yields that became evident to farmers who were seeking to maximize their production for commercial trade.

The processes of urbanization and enclosure of farmland across Europe and North America also affected soil productivity. As urbanization accelerated in the eighteenth and nineteenth centuries and lands became increasingly privately owned, populations and the wastes associated with them were less evenly distributed across the land. Urbanization also meant a move away from mixed farming, as the production of animals for meat became increasingly separated from commodity crop production, especially with the rise of the large-scale livestock industry in the mid-nineteenth century that served growing urban populations. These changes in land use broke the cycle of human and animal wastes returning nutrients to the soil in the same region where crops were produced.

By growing crops intensively in sparsely populated rural areas, farmers were essentially "mining" nutrients stored in the soil from past forest ecosystems, but they were not able to return nutrients to that soil easily.[2] The spread of urbanization meant that the problem of declining soil fertility increasingly affected all parts of the world. The issue became a focus of particular concern in Europe and North America in the early to mid-1800s. By the late 1800s, with the gradual closing of the agricultural frontier in North America, the use of fertilizers was widely seen as essential for agricultural intensification because extensification (i.e., expanding land areas under cultivation) was no longer possible.[3]

Rising concern about the loss of soil fertility created a context ripe for the development of the commercial fertilizer industry. Leading theories about soil fertility at the time influenced the shape of the industry in its early days. The dominant humus theory, for example, stressed the importance of maintaining soil organic matter, leading some commercial fertilizer operations to collect and distribute human solid and liquid wastes from urbanized centers—euphemistically dubbed "night soil"—back to rural areas. For example, "poudrette," a fertilizer first developed in France and produced commercially in the United States from the late 1830s, was a mixture of urban night soil and deodorizing substances.[4] The logistics of such efforts were challenging, however, given the distances between burgeoning urban areas and remote rural agricultural regions.

Phosphorus-rich bone-based fertilizer (bonemeal) was also used from the early 1800s, with animal bones typically ground into a powder or burned to ash to enable easier absorption of their nutrients into the soil. There are even widespread reports, noted in the press at the time, that the bones of fallen soldiers were raided from European battlefields in the 1810s, including at Leipzig and Waterloo, and shipped to Britain to be ground for sale as agricultural fertilizer. For example, an 1822 *London Observer* article noted, "It is certainly a singular fact, that Great Britain should have sent out multitudes of soldiers to fight the battles of this country upon the continent of Europe, and should then import the bones as an article of commerce to fatten her soil!"[5] Discarded animal parts from slaughterhouses, including dried blood and offal (internal organs), were also sold as fertilizing agents to enrich soils.[6] These early responses to declining soil fertility essentially commodified a variety of waste materials for soil enrichment.

In the mid-1800s, the work of the German chemist Justus von Liebig was instrumental in shaping scientific understandings of the nutrient needs of plants, and his ideas triggered important changes in the approach to soil fertilization on farms, which reshaped the commercial fertilizer industry. Liebig's widely read 1840 book, *Chemistry in Its Application to Agriculture and Physiology*, critiqued the prevailing humus theory and its focus on the quality of organic materials in topsoil.[7] Although organic material applied to the soil did help boost its fertility, there was until that point little understanding of why that was the case. Liebig's work outlined, in a scientific fashion, the chemical relationship of plants, soil, and the atmosphere, providing new insights into the elements needed for plant growth. Healthy plants, he argued, required specific mineral nutrients—namely, trace inorganic elements of nitrogen (N), phosphorus (P), and potassium (K). The implication was that crops absorbed these nutrients from the soil as they grew, weakening the ability of the soil to support further plant growth in successive growing seasons unless these nutrients were replenished.

Although he critiqued humus theory, Liebig still advocated for the recycling of wastes back into soils in the most efficient way possible. As such, he decried Britain's looting of far-flung foreign battlefields for bones and lamented the loss of human wastes from farm fields, which were being flushed down sewers in cities. Nonetheless, he argued that the recycling of wastes alone was not sufficient to ensure soil fertility over the longer term. The removal of crops that had absorbed the soil's nutrients, and the sale of those crops to distant markets, meant a loss of the necessary trace elements in crop-growing locations that would never fully be replaced in a natural manner.[8] Liebig argued that if soil fertility was to be restored, these specific nutrients needed to be explicitly replaced through better soil management, including the application of specific materials, or amendments, containing the elements of nitrogen, phosphorus, and potassium.[9] In his work, Liebig stressed that those nutrients that were least available would be depleted first, and that nitrogen, followed by phosphorus and then potassium, were the most important to add back into the soil.[10] Liebig also noted that the application of sulfuric acid to bones would create superphosphates, which were rich in phosphorus and more readily taken up by plants than untreated ground bones.

Liebig's ideas were revolutionary and opened the way to thinking about soil fertility mainly in terms of its chemical components in relation to plants rather than the factors that affect the physical quality of soils, such as the presence of organic matter. This approach implied that it was not just possible, but also desirable, to replace soil nutrients from other sources of N, P, and K, beyond the local recycling of waste that had been practiced historically. This realization prompted wider consideration of materials that could be sourced from outside local regions and applied to soils.[11] A regular application of externally sourced fertilizers to restore soil fertility could enable farmers to practice continuous cultivation of crops rather than engaging in crop rotations and fallow systems to promote fertility, which were viewed as less productive practices at the time. Although the specifics of some of Liebig's ideas have been critiqued as incorrect (and he is widely recognized to have been a shameless self-promoter of his ideas and inventions), his focus on the need to supplement soils with the three crucial nutrients—what some term the "NPK mentality"—had a lasting impact on the development of the fertilizer industry.[12]

NITROGEN FROM SOUTH AMERICA: GUANO AND SODIUM NITRATE

Liebig's work coincided with scientific experiments by others on the impact of guano—the dung of seabirds, specifically from the Chincha Islands of Peru—as a fertilizing agent. The potential of guano to enhance plant growth had been known for centuries. Biologist Walter Goldberg notes, "The value of bird poo as fertilizer was no secret to the peoples of Peru. They had been applying it to their crops for more than 1000 years and protected the birds under penalty of death for disturbing or killing them."[13] Although guano was known in Peru as a valuable substance for growing healthier crops, Liebig's work gave scientific credence to the idea of using Peruvian guano as a commercial fertilizer because it contained a high percentage of both nitrogen and phosphorus.

These developments led to the blossoming of the international guano trade and further development of the commercial fertilizer industry. Giant deposits of guano, which had been accumulating for thousands of years on the Chincha Islands, were hundreds of feet deep. Foreign commercial interests swooped into Peru in the 1840s to arrange the extraction of guano for export, primarily to markets in Britain and North America. These operations were gruesome and exploitative. Foreign firms engaged in practices such as the use of African slave labor (until Peru abolished slavery in 1855) and the transport of indentured laborers from China, who were brought in to do the dirty, smelly, and backbreaking work of mining the substance.

Workers were often tricked into taking up the work under false pretenses and were transported to Peru on ships under horrible conditions. Many died en route. Those who survived the journey to the mines faced years of servitude under unsafe working conditions with few, if any, rights. Many of the workers committed suicide.[14] An 1855 article in the *New York Times* described the harsh conditions of the workers in vivid terms: "Peru, by falsehood and fraud, has obtained Coolies from China to labor in her guano fields. Under a scorching tropical sun, doomed to severest toil seven days in the week, the cruel lash quivering in their bleeding, shrinking flesh, whenever from failing health or exhausted strength they lag in their tasks, furnished with poor and scanty fare, and breathing in a poisonous atmosphere, imagination can scarcely paint elsewhere so miserable an existence."[15]

The Peruvian government, keen to ensure a stream of revenue from the trade, nationalized its guano reserves in 1842, effectively giving the state a monopoly over guano production within its territory. The government arranged for private firms, mainly based in Britain, to have exclusive rights to handle the extraction and export of the substance. In exchange, the British trading firms provided large financial loans to the government of Peru, effectively providing the latter with easy access to credit that it could not otherwise obtain. The Peruvian government received half of all the proceeds from the guano trade, which accounted for most of its foreign exchange earnings and from which it repaid the loans from the trading companies. As of 1847, Antony Gibbs and Sons of London became the exclusive merchants of the guano trade for Britain and North America, whereas the European trade was controlled by Dreyfus Frères & Cie, a French trading house.[16]

The monopolies established by these exclusive arrangements made both the guano trading firms and the Peruvian government extremely wealthy. The European guano traders typically exported the substance to exclusive domestic agents in importing countries who handled local sales, and these agents essentially had a lock on the local trade. In the United States, for example, several dry goods merchants served as the exclusive agents of Gibbs and Sons in the mid-1840s. Some of these dealers also sold farm implements and seeds, and similar to the marketing arrangements for farm machinery, they often offered credit to farmers for purchases of farm inputs, including fertilizer.[17]

Although imported guano was relatively inexpensive initially for farmers to purchase, its rising popularity as a fertilizer in the mid-1800s—in what some historians have called a "guano mania"—led to higher and more volatile prices that affected farmers' costs of production.[18] The importation of Peruvian guano was widely seen as a progressive farming practice and was extensively promoted in the agricultural journals of the era. But farmers became irritated by Peru's "guano monopoly" once prices began to rise. Bird droppings from other sources, including from islands off the coasts of Africa, Europe, and the Caribbean, were exported to Europe and the United States to meet the surging demand for guano. However, these alternative bird dungs were widely viewed to be inferior to Peruvian-sourced guano because they had lower nitrogen content, although they did have high levels of phosphorus. There were also widespread cases of fraud in the guano trade. Some sellers tried to trick unsuspecting farmers by claiming their fertilizer products contained genuine Peruvian guano, but in fact they sold sacks of sand with the feces of other animals mixed in.[19] This development gives new insight into the phrase "useless sack of shit."

The volatility in price and the uncertainty of supply in this period prompted the US government to adopt the Guano Islands Act in 1856.

The act was strongly supported by private firms seeking to discover new sources of guano and therefore break into the market and challenge the supremacy of the British merchants. The American merchant firms included the American Guano Company, the US Guano Company, and the Oceanic Phosphate Company of San Francisco. The Guano Islands Act legalized and encouraged the appropriation of any unoccupied guano islands by US citizens, so long as they were not already claimed by another government. Claimants simply had to prove that an unoccupied island had exploitable guano deposits to declare it US territory. Dozens of Pacific islands were claimed under the act, although the quality of guano was not as high as Peruvian sources due to different climatic conditions and different kinds of fish and birds in these locations, which led to different chemical makeup of the bird dungs. The claims on these islands often resulted in diplomatic conflicts with other countries that had also laid claim to the territories, although some of the small islands claimed under the act remain US territories to this day.[20]

Although the accumulations of guano on the Chincha Islands were hundreds of feet deep, the Peruvian islands were relatively small, and by the mid- to late 1870s, the deposits were nearly completely depleted. As guano supplies dwindled, attention turned to other high-nitrogen content substances that could serve as substitutes for guano. One of most promising candidates was sodium nitrate, also referred to as Chile saltpeter, which had been discovered in the Atacama desert, the dry Pacific coastal region of what were at the time the regions of Tarapacá in Peru and Antofagasta in Bolivia. Many countries sought to import nitrates not just because they were a source of nitrogen for fertilizers, but also because they were key ingredients for making bombs and other munitions. Thus, sodium nitrate had a dual purpose as a fertilizer and in military applications.

The sodium nitrate mines in these regions of South America had extensive financial backing from British financial investors who sought to profit from the trade. In the case of the Tarapacá mines in Peru, Antony Gibbs and Sons—the same firm that dominated the Peruvian guano trade—was a partial owner of the Tarapacá Nitrate Company. In Antofagasta, Bolivia, William Gibbs and Company—the Chilean branch of the firm Antony Gibbs and Sons—partnered with wealthy Chilean investors, including a number of powerful politicians, to form the Antofagasta Nitrate and Railroad Company.[21]

In the mid-1870s, in the midst of a global economic downturn that saw agricultural and other commodity prices fall, Peru moved to monopolize its sodium nitrate mines in Tarapacá by expropriating the assets of the operations' financial investors. At the same time, Bolivia sought to raise the tax on its sodium nitrate exports from the Antofagasta mines in a bid to increase its revenues from the trade. This latter move threatened Chile's interests in the nitrate trade and sparked the 1879–1884 War of the Pacific, sometimes referred to as the Nitrate War, in which Peru and Bolivia allied against Chile's attempts to annex the territories of Antofagasta and Tarapacá. Chile, which had financial backing from Britain in its war efforts, was victorious in the conflict and took control of the sodium nitrate fields from both Peru and Bolivia, effectively giving the country a monopoly on sodium nitrate production and trade.[22]

While the war was still being fought, Thomas North, a British nitrate mine operator and trader based in Peru, bought up certificates of ownership for a significant number of the nitrate mines that were originally located in Peru. He secured the ownership of these mines at deeply discounted prices because their value was uncertain due to the conflict. This purchase enabled him to benefit from Chile's decree near the end of the war that it would respect ownership certificates for the former Peruvian mines in order to get them back up and running as soon as possible. North then returned to Britain in 1882 to secure financial investment to operate these mines. He was notorious for talking up the price of the shares in his firms well beyond their actual value and then selling them at inflated prices to investors who were eager to get in on a rising market. By 1890, North had founded or cofounded an astonishing seventeen out of twenty-three British companies involved in the nitrate trade.[23] The control of the nitrate trade by British firms rose from around 13 percent when the mines were part of Peru to 70 percent by 1890, when they were under Chilean jurisdiction.[24] Thomas North's role was central to the British corporate dominance in this sector, and his commanding control of the trade earned him the nickname "The Nitrate King."[25]

With its monopoly on the trade, the government of Chile imposed duties on nitrate exports at 30 to 70 percent of the selling price, earning over $1 billion in duties from nitrate exports between 1880 and 1930.[26] Chile was able to exact these exorbitant rates due to high demand, especially from the United States and Britain, which were reliant on imports of Chilean nitrates for fertilizer and munitions up to World War I. Nitrate producers in Chile also established a series of cartels, referred to as "combinations," to restrict production levels and manage prices, especially when demand dropped due to agricultural market conditions. These cartel arrangements, which were established over the course of the 1880s and early 1900s, typically involved foreign—mainly British—firms with financial interests in the nitrate mines. North headed up a "triple syndicate," or cartel, involving nitrate mining firms, nitrate railways, and banks in London. Chile's government kept a close watch over these combinations, in particular to prevent North's "Nitrate Ring" from wresting power and revenue from the government. The combinations were also often beset by internal rivalries among the participating firms.[27] The rise of synthetic nitrogen production from the early 1900s led to a dwindling sodium nitrate trade, as well as an end to the combinations that controlled that trade.

PHOSPHORUS, POTASSIUM, AND THE GERMAN POTASH SYNDICATE

From the 1860s to the 1880s, new ways of obtaining phosphorus were discovered or exploited, which also shaped the development of the fertilizer industry. Superphosphates were increasingly being produced from the application of sulfuric acid to bone material, following advice from Liebig's earlier writings. From the late 1870s through the 1890s, the bones that lay scattered across the North American Great Plains from the vast number of bison that were hunted and killed between the 1860s and 1880s were collected by both settlers and Indigenous people and sold to bone traders, who then sold them to refineries that served several industries, including the fertilizer industry. Cities across the US and Canadian plains accumulated massive piles of bones that were shipped east for processing. These bones were ground into a powder and sold as "bone ash," "buffalo bone meal," and even by one dealer as "homestead guano."[28] Bones were also sourced from the massive slaughterhouses that were becoming increasingly industrialized in this period in the US Midwest. Several meat-packing plants, such as Swift and Armour in the United States, established fertilizer divisions because of the availability of nitrates from animal wastes and phosphorus from bone waste. Bone charcoal, the material left after bones were burned in the process of sugar refining, was also used to produce superphosphates.[29]

Phosphate rock deposits were discovered in the United States in the latter part of the nineteenth century, including in the Carolinas, Georgia, and Florida, as well as in what was then French North Africa (now Tunisia and Algeria), Morocco, the Western Sahara, and several islands in the South Pacific, including Nauru and Christmas Island. These new sources of phosphorus gradually replaced bones in the production of superphosphates and gave rise to a host of new fertilizer companies based on phosphate mining. Initially, these mines required large amounts of manual labor, and as with guano mining, the work was backbreaking and treacherous.

Similar to guano extraction, much of the labor used in these phosphorus mines was racialized, coerced, and poorly paid. In the United States, for example, firms such as the Charleston Mining and Manufacturing Company raised capital to mine phosphates after the Civil War, which created a phosphate boom in South Carolina from the late 1860s through the 1880s. These firms primarily recruited former enslaved people—Black freedmen—to carry out the difficult and dangerous work. Immigrants and convicts were also conscripted as laborers in these mines. These workers were often paid below subsistence wages and were housed in company villages where they became indebted to company stores. Workers were harshly disciplined if they pushed back against their ill treatment. Similarly racialized labor regimes were instituted in the phosphate mines in North Africa and in the Pacific, often supported by government policies that restricted land and resource rights. Such practices prevented marginalized populations from accessing the means to pursue other livelihoods.[30] Later, these deposits were mined in large-scale industrial operations using heavy equipment powered by fossil fuels.

Until the 1860s, most of the potassium used as fertilizer was sourced from potash, a substance produced from the leaching of ashes from burning biomass in water to produce lye, which could then be heated to produce a solid that was rich in potassium. In fact, the origin of the word *potash* comes from this early process of ashes leached in a pot and then heated. Potash was produced as early as the seventeenth century by burning potassium-rich plants, including sea kelp in northern Europe and the barilla plant in the Mediterranean region. Potash derived from the leaching of ashes was used as a fertilizer and in certain industrial processes, such as making soap, gunpowder, and glass. This synthesized potash substance took considerable effort to produce. It was typically made by small-scale operations in regions that had access to the biomass resources—such as forests—that could be burned to produce ash, primarily in Europe, North America, and Russia.[31]

Despite the effort needed to produce it, enough potash was generated by this method that it was traded internationally. However, as forest resources that could be harvested for wood ash production dwindled in North America and Russia with clearing for settlement and to feed timber markets, the cost of producing potash by this method increased. The discovery of natural underground deposits of potash salts in Germany in the 1850s transformed potash production into large-scale mining operations. These salts were a highly soluble form of potassium that was ideal for use as a fertilizer, sparking major changes in fertilizer production and eventually leading to its control by a few large corporations. At that time, and for the next fifty years, Germany held a monopoly on this source of potash, which it began to export to other countries in the 1860s.

In the decades in which Germany had a monopoly on potash salts, the fertilizer sector both expanded and saw major corporate concentration, especially because the underground deposits could be exploited on a large industrial scale. With all of the effective (known) supply of potash salts located in one country, some of the original German potash mine operations, which had strong ties to the German government, sought to control supply and prices. Their desire to control supply was heightened after early overproduction of the mined potash led to a crash in prices, which drove some firms out of business. The response to this market volatility was the formation of the German potash syndicate, a cartel of the potash mining and manufacturing firms. The potash manufacturing firms produced concentrated potash salts for the export market, with the most important market outside Germany being US fertilizer firms. The potash syndicate arranged various agreements among German potash interests to set production quotas and fix prices between the 1870s and 1910, with higher prices being charged for exports than for domestic use.[32]

The German potash syndicate worked through exclusive dealers in the United States and later established its own agency in New York in the 1890s to represent its members in this market, which accounted for nearly half of its exports. The American fertilizer firms purchased the imported German potash to mix with other minerals, namely phosphates produced domestically and either guano from Peru or nitrates imported from Chile to provide farmers with a product that mixed N, P, and K in formulations that provided all three nutrients in appropriate amounts for different soil conditions. This type of mixing of N, P, and K was becoming standard practice in the fertilizer industry.

CORPORATE CONSOLIDATION

As US phosphate deposits were being discovered toward the end of the nineteenth century, a number of smaller fertilizer firms engaged in mergers and acquisitions to create several giant firms serving the North American market. In 1893, on the tail end of a decades-long economic downturn, the American Agricultural Chemical Company was formed out of a merger of sixteen smaller fertilizer firms based in the northern and eastern states. Within a few decades, the firm had acquired dozens more smaller fertilizer companies. The Virginia-Carolina Chemical Company was formed in 1895 as the product of a merger of over thirty companies based in the southern states that were either mixed-fertilizer firms or producers of raw materials for fertilizers. Within a few years of their formation, these firms began to invest in acquiring phosphate mines. In 1909, after several previous failed attempts, a third major firm emerged, the International Agricultural Corporation, as the result of a massive merger combining many of the remaining independent US fertilizer firms. By 1914, the Virginia-Carolina Chemical Company had expanded further, acquiring an additional forty-five to fifty firms in the fertilizer manufacturing and distribution businesses.[33] The result was a massive consolidation of the industry to just a few dominant firms.

The fertilizer mergers around the turn of the century reflected firms' defensive efforts to control the limited natural resources that were the key ingredients for mixed fertilizers at a time when prices for some of those resources, particularly phosphates, were falling due to newly discovered sources of phosphate rock in North America, North Africa, and on several Pacific islands. In this period, other large producers linked to slaughterhouses, such as Swift and Co. and Armour, also purchased other fertilizer firms to expand their operations. For example, Armour Fertilizer Works acquired control some twenty-seven subsidiary firms through a series of joint stockholding arrangements. By 1914, just six large firms dominated the US mixed fertilizer market: Virginia-Carolina, American Agricultural Chemical Company, Armour, International Agricultural Corporation, the F. S. Royster Guano Company, and Swift and Company. These six firms controlled 55 percent of the US fertilizer market in 1913, with the largest two commanding just over 34 percent and the largest four nearly 50 percent.[34] These same six firms maintained their market dominance until at least 1950.

In this period of consolidation, the US Department of Justice conducted numerous investigations of the fertilizer industry similar to its investigations of the farm machinery sector. In 1906, for example, the Virginia-Carolina Chemical Company and over fifty other fertilizer firms were handed indictments for violating the Sherman Antitrust Act, specifically for price fixing and the suppression of competition in the industry. However, the US government lost the case in 1908. Other antitrust cases against fertilizer companies were brought forward from the 1920s to the 1950s, for restraining competition and fixing prices, and fines were administered against the offending firms.[35]

The mergers of the American firms also appear to have improved their bargaining power with the German potash syndicate. In the first decade of the twentieth century, two American firms, the Virginia-Carolina Chemical Company and the International Agricultural Corporation, purchased significant shares in several of the German potash mining firms, in both cases gaining effective control over them and negotiating sales at discounted prices. In response to rising German concern about American capital edging in on its "natural monopoly" over potash, the market power of the German syndicate was reinforced by the 1910 German Potash Law, which placed the German government firmly in control of the potash market. It invalidated the American contracts and imposed a surcharge on the importing firms, and it strictly regulated exports.[36]

In 1911, the US government reacted to the German government's seizure of the potash market with congressional approval for funding for potash exploration within the United States. Through these government-sponsored efforts, minor deposits of potash salts were found in several states, including Texas, Nebraska, and New Mexico. A number of firms, such as the Potash Company of America, emerged to capitalize on these deposits, although it was difficult to achieve full-scale production at that time. Other countries also scrambled to step up exploration for potash deposits or to devise alternate means of producing potash, including Spain, Brazil, and Britain, among others.[37]

These efforts intensified during World War I, when Germany's exports of potash were cut off from the rest of the world. In the United States, some firms in California began producing potash by burning kelp, which is rich in potassium, while others used distillery wastes as raw materials for potash production.[38] The various sources of US-produced potash during the war made up around one-fifth of its previous imports of potash.[39] The German potash monopoly was finally broken after World War I, when Germany lost the region of Alsace to France, where additional potash-rich deposits were discovered in the early 1860s, and which had seen increased production in the early 1900s. Further new sources of potash were found in other regions, including the United States, as well as Spain and Russia. In response, Germany actively reduced the number of its active potash mines to quell concerns of overproduction, which had pushed prices down. Germany also sought to form potash cartels with France in the 1920s and with Russia and Spain in the 1930s.[40]

US firms did not join the formal international cartel arrangements, in part because the country was not a large producer of potash, but also due to fears of being in contravention of US antitrust laws. However, in 1918, given that the rampant cartel activity involving other countries was affecting the global export market, the US government passed the Webb-Pomerene Act, which granted an exception from antitrust rules to certain mineral export associations, provided their activities did not distort domestic markets.[41] It was not long before US phosphate producers, some of the largest in the world, formed such associations. In 1919, the phosphate firms that made up the bulk of US phosphate exports formed the Phosphate Export Association (PEA) to manage their collective interests. The PEA set fixed prices for the export of phosphate rock and strictly monitored its members to ensure compliance. In the early 1930s, the PEA entered into multiple international cartel agreements with firms in other producing regions, including in North Africa, France, Japan, and the Pacific Islands.[42]

SYNTHETIC NITROGEN: A GAME CHANGER

A major shift in the dynamics of the fertilizer industry came with the development of new chemical processes that enabled the production of synthetic nitrogen in the early decades of the twentieth century. Although there was abundant nitrogen gas in the earth's atmosphere, it was difficult to convert it into a physical form that could be applied to soil for use by plants. Scientists had been experimenting with methods to synthesize nitrogen from the atmosphere into a physical form since before 1800, but it was not until the early 1900s that nitrogen synthesis became viable on a large commercial scale. The efforts to develop these processes in this period were largely driven by importing countries' desires to be freed from Chile's monopoly on sodium nitrate.

Several processes for synthesizing nitrogen were developed in Europe in the early 1900s. The Frank-Caro cyanamide process, developed by German chemists Adolph Frank and Nikoderm Caro just before 1900, was the first to be widely used, including by firms in Germany, Italy, Norway, and other European countries.[43] The Frank-Caro process was also employed in Canada by the large US chemical firm American Cyanamid. The firm established a plant on the Canadian side of Niagara Falls in 1909 to take advantage of the inexpensive hydroelectric power that was necessary in large quantities for the nitrogen synthesis process to be economically viable. The cyanamide process produced calcium cyanamide, a black substance that can be used as a fertilizer. American Cyanamid aimed to use the Canadian plant to illustrate to US regulators and investors the benefits of constructing a large plant in the United States using the same process.[44]

The Birkeland Eyde process, first developed in 1905 by Norwegian scientists Kristian Birkeland and Sam Eyde, used Norway's abundant hydroelectric power to create an electric arc for the synthesis of nitrogen in the form of nitric acid. Birkeland and Eyde founded the firm Norsk Hydro (the forerunner of today's fertilizer giant Yara) to produce nitrogen-based fertilizer using this process. Although the firm's electric arc process worked, it was eventually deemed to be inefficient compared to other processes because it required large amounts of electricity from hydropower, and other forms of energy, particularly fossil fuels, were becoming more widely available. The firm was funded by foreign shareholders, including the French bank Paribas, which had a controlling ownership share until World War II, as well as German capital in the late 1920s (see below). In the postwar era, the dominant shareholder in the firm was the Norwegian government.[45]

Although these earlier processes for synthesizing nitrogen worked in a technical sense, the Haber-Bosch process was widely viewed as the most efficient in terms of energy use, as it used natural gas rather than hydropower, and it subsequently became the dominant means of synthesizing nitrogen. In 1909, German chemist Fritz Haber invented a process to convert the nitrogen in the atmosphere into ammonia by creating a reaction with hydrogen under high pressure and temperatures. Haber's work was financed by Badische Anilin & Soda-Fabrik (BASF), a large German chemical and dye company, that at the time was the largest chemical firm in the world. By 1913, Haber's process was being used on a large commercial scale under the direction of BASF's Carl Bosch.[46] The result was what is today referred to as the Haber-Bosch process of ammonia synthesis. Ammonia is high in nitrogen content and is still widely used for commercial fertilizer production. Both Haber and Bosch were awarded Nobel prizes in chemistry for their work associated with this process (Haber's prize, awarded in 1918, was highly controversial because of his later work developing chemical weapons that Germany deployed during World War I resulting in thousands of deaths).[47]

Nitrogen synthesis was extremely important for several reasons. First, it meant that countries that were able to synthetically produce nitrogen-containing compounds—ammonia, calcium cyanamide, or nitric acid—did not have to rely on Chile for imports of nitrates for the production of either munitions or fertilizers. With the Haber-Bosch process becoming available just before World War I, Germany was able to access this important munition ingredient despite its inability to import Chilean nitrate during the war. The war also made it impossible for other countries to replicate the nitrogen synthesis using the Haber-Bosch process because BASF did not share the details of the process or license its use to any foreign producers. The firm, in effect, monopolized not only the know-how but also the production of ammonia using the Haber-Bosch process.[48] Germany's nitrogen production was so valuable that at the end of World War I, it shipped nitrogen-rich ammonia as part of its reparation payments to the Allies.[49] The connection between national security and the fertilizer industry was especially strong during the war. For example, an executive from the Armour Fertilizer Works was made the head of the chemical division of the American War Industries Board. US purchases of nitrates throughout the war were managed by DuPont, the US chemical firm W. R. Grace & Co., and Antony Gibbs and Co.[50]

Clearly falling behind Germany in the development of important chemical processes such as nitrogen synthesis, the US government attempted to address this gap with the passage of the National Defense Act of 1916. The act supported the development of processes for nitrogen synthesis, which could be used for munitions in times of war and as fertilizers in times of peace, as a kind of "swords to ploughshares" effort.[51] Under this act, the US government invested in the construction of several nitrogen synthesis plants in Alabama, located at Muscle Shoals, to take advantage of a dam and the hydropower available at that location.[52] Although there was frenzied construction on the plants throughout the war, they were completed only in 1918, just prior to the war's end. One of these plants attempted to copy the Haber-Bosch process, while the other used the cyanamide process that had been successfully implemented at the American Cyanamid plant at Niagara Falls. But whereas the Canadian plant successfully produced calcium cyanamide as a commercial fertilizer (among other products) and operated until 1992, the US plants never viably produced nitrogen and were essentially abandoned at the end of the war, sitting idle for more than a decade.

The efforts to produce synthetic nitrogen outside of Germany were not just a response to the war blockades. The company that held the patent for the Haber-Bosch process, BASF, remained reluctant to sell licenses for access to the process to other companies, even after the war ended. Instead, the firm guarded its monopoly on the process, especially for nitrogen-based fertilizer production. This reluctance on BASF's part prompted a number of countries to undertake research to replicate the Haber-Bosch process of ammonia synthesis or develop alternative methods in the interwar period. For example, firms in Italy and Japan experimented with the cyanamide process, whereas the British chemical firm Brunner, Mond and Company and several French firms made progress with other methods of ammonia manufacture.[53] The United States established the Fixed Nitrogen Research Laboratory (FNRL) in 1919 to further research nitrogen capture, and the US government specifically sought to stimulate private industry's entry into the sector.[54]

Mastering nitrogen synthesis remained a key goal of the US government in the interwar years, and although military demands for nitrogen were its initial impetus, it soon shifted to fertilizer research in the 1920s. The FNRL, for example, was moved from the War Department to the US Department of Agriculture in 1921, and the government devoted significant research and development resources to the effort to develop more efficient and effective fertilizers. There were expectations on the part of the farming community that the government facilities would produce fertilizers for subsidized distribution directly to farmers, who had faced shortages during World War I because most of the imported sodium nitrate was directed toward munitions rather than fertilizer. Congress actively debated whether the government should produce fertilizer at the Muscle Shoals plants or whether it should lease the facilities to private firms.[55]

The National Fertilizer Association, an industry group, lobbied strongly against the idea of the federal government taking a strong role in fertilizer production, which it saw as a direct threat to the interests of private industry. In fact, the FNRL had a cozy relationship with American chemical firms, much to the annoyance of farmers. By 1925, the FNRL had developed a modified version of the Haber-Bosch process of ammonia synthesis, but while farmers requested direct access to government-produced fertilizers, the FNRL focused its attention on serving chemical companies. It shared its research insights liberally with private firms in ways that gave the latter extensive benefits in advancing their business interests in nitrogen-based chemical production, including advice on the construction of commercial nitrogen synthesis plants for fertilizer manufacture.

MORE CONSOLIDATION AND CARTELS

Perhaps more important than the FNRL work in establishing nitrogen synthesis on a large commercial scale in the United States was the work of private sector firms that encouraged corporate consolidation. Several firms produced synthetic nitrogen using a variety of processes—some with information and advice obtained from the FNRL and others through licensing arrangements with European firms. The largest producers of synthetic nitrogen in this period were Allied Chemical and Dye—formed as a result of a 1920 merger of six chemical firms including Solvay Process and General Chemical—and DuPont.[56] Allied Chemical and Dye used methods similar to the Haber-Bosch process, which it gained after discussions with Brunner, Mond and Company. In the late 1920s, DuPont obtained licenses for nitrogen synthesis processes necessary for large-scale production both directly from European start-up firms as well as through aggressive patent litigation against other US firms. These moves enabled it to acquire a number of firms that increased both its size and its capacity for synthetic nitrogen production. DuPont and Allied, including the latter's subsidiary Barrett Company, became huge producers of ammonia-based N fertilizers in the United States, with Allied accounting for 60 percent and DuPont for 40 percent of US synthetic ammonia production by the mid-1930s. This ramping up of capacity enabled the United States to become a global leader in nitrogen production.[57]

Consolidation also took place among the European chemical firms that were producing synthetic nitrogen. In 1925, a massive merger of six major German chemical firms, including BASF, Bayer, Hoescht, and Agfa, formed IG Farben, a new behemoth in the sector.[58] Imperial Chemical Industries (ICI) was formed out of the 1926 merger of Brunner, Mond and Company, the United Alkali Company, Nobel Industries, and the British Dyestuffs Corporation. ICI became a major fertilizer producer in the United Kingdom in 1920 after Brunner, Mond purchased Billingham

Works, a facility established by the UK government in 1918 to produce nitrates for war munitions.[59] The formation of IG Farben and ICI was widely seen to be a European response to the development of consolidated corporate trusts in the United States in the early decades of the twentieth century, in particular the "powder trust"—which produced explosives—controlled by DuPont.[60]

Less than a decade after the end of World War I, these giant producers of synthetic nitrogen began to worry about overcapacity and downward pressure on prices because of the growing number of plants around the world that had adopted one process or another to produce it. By 1930, an international nitrogen cartel had formed to control supply and prices. Often referred to as the DEN cartel, it included firms from Germany, England, and Norway. The German participant in the cartel was Stickstoff-Syndikat, the fertilizer subsidiary of IG Farben, whereas the British participant was ICI and the Norwegian participant was Norsk Hydro.[61] By the late 1920s, IG Farben owned a significant share of Norsk Hydro (in addition to the French financial interests noted above). Under this arrangement, IG Farben shared information that enabled Norsk Hydro to switch from the Birkeland-Eyde process to the Haber-Bosch process in return for carving up export markets between the firms.[62]

The international nitrogen cartel widened to include other European manufacturers of cyanamide throughout the 1920s. The US firms formally remained outside the cartel, as was initially the case with international potash and phosphorus cartels. Their distance from the cartel was partly because the US firms were not yet major producers of synthetic nitrogen on the same scale as the European firms and also because it might be perceived as illegal under the country's antitrust laws.[63] Despite US firms not being formal cartel participants, in the mid-1930s the US Department of Justice conducted a thorough investigation of market practices in the fertilizer industry. In 1939, a grand jury handed down five indictments to US nitrogen-producing firms—specifically Allied, Barrett Company, and DuPont—for cooperating with the international nitrogen cartel in ways that harmed the domestic market. This cooperation included engagement in price-fixing arrangements with foreign firms in Germany and Britain. These charges were eventually settled by consent decrees whereby the firms agreed not to engage in conspiratorial action.[64]

In the interwar decades, other countries, such as Japan, gained the technology to synthesize nitrogen. Japan, for example, became a major producer of calcium cyanamide for fertilizer use at several of its large conglomerate firms known as zaibatsu—large, vertically integrated firms that emerged in Japan in the nineteenth century and were controlled by powerful families. The zaibatsu had tight relationships among themselves through joint holding companies, interlocking directorships, and shared stock ownership, and they had enormous financial power through privileged access to bank credit.[65] These firms—including Mitsui, Mitsubishi, Kawasaki, and Sumimoto—operated much like a cartel in the Japanese fertilizer market. When fertilizer prices fell in 1930, the Japanese firms formed an agreement to sharply reduce production. They also convinced the government to pass laws favorable to their interests. The zaibatsu firms eventually joined the international nitrogen cartel in the mid-1930s, and the arrangement remained in place until the start of World War II in 1939.[66]

In North America, the US government retooled the Muscle Shoals nitrogen plants for experimental phosphate fertilizer production and research during the Great Depression of the 1930s as part of the Tennessee Valley Authority (TVA) development project. The project conducted fertilizer research, engaged in demonstration and education, and distributed fertilizers as a form of development assistance to the poorer parts of the country, including the Tennessee Valley, which had low-quality soil and weak economic growth. Public sector research and development into fertilizers as part of the TVA initiative was significant. The government shifted the emphasis of its fertilizer research from nitrates to phosphates—research that also assisted private firms—although it did continue some nitrogen synthesis research that was used during World War II.[67] The distribution of fertilizers by the TVA was a point of contention for the private fertilizer industry, which saw it as a threat to their business.[68] In Canada, the Consolidated Mining and Smelting Company of Canada began to produce nitrogen fertilizer in the 1930s, and it also mined phosphates and some potash, with operations across Canada and the United States. The firm changed its name to Cominco Fertilizer in the 1960s.

After World War II, the Allied countries required Germany to relinquish its patents, including for the Haber-Bosch process, and the technical details were made freely available to the Allies.[69] IG Farben was also broken up into a number of firms at that time—including BASF, Bayer, and Hoechst. Additionally, although the Allies attempted to break up the zaibatsu in 1945, this dissolution was never completed. The large zaibatsu firms in Japan continued to produce fertilizer, but they did not become dominant global players.

The mining of several new discoveries of potash also shaped the sector in the early postwar years. The former Soviet Union discovered potash-magnesium salts in the 1920s and began to develop its industry in the 1950s. By the 1960s, production increased, and the state-owned firm (known today as Uralkali) became a major exporter, controlling some 20 percent of the world's potash reserves.[70]

Canada also became a major producer of potash after high-quality deposits of the mineral were discovered in Saskatchewan in 1943. Although Saskatchewan possesses some 50 percent of the world's known potash reserves, it took decades for these reserves to be successfully mined due to technical extraction problems stemming from water seepage and the depths of the deposits. By the 1960s, a number of mining operations had started production in Canada, mainly subsidiaries of or joint ventures with US-based multinational firms. Over 90 percent of Canadian potash was exported in the early days of these operations. The United States purchased some two-thirds of the exported Canadian potash, which accounted for around 40 percent of the global potash trade.[71] In 1970, the Canadian government established an export marketing agency, Canpotex, effectively a cartel, and required all of the firms that exported Canadian potash to become members, enabling the government to collect taxes on their exports. By 1975, the provincial government of Saskatchewan had acquired 50 percent of the province's potash industry and established the Potash Corporation of Saskatchewan as a publicly owned firm.

SOCIAL AND ECOLOGICAL CONCERNS ASSOCIATED WITH COMMERCIAL FERTILIZERS

Enormous social costs were associated with the early fertilizer industry, including the horrific conditions faced by workers in the guano and phosphate mines. Although some observers at the time raised these costs, they were often overshadowed by the broad sentiment that fertilizer was necessary to provide a wider social good: ensuring greater crop yields and food security. In this sense, the large firms and merchants that came to dominate the early fertilizer industry were able to externalize those social costs. It was easier for them to do so when the realities of the mining operations were being experienced halfway around the world, and farmers in the Americas and in Europe, the largest customers of guano and phosphate, were desperate to replenish the fertility of their soil.

The advent of synthetic nitrogen fertilizer—for the countries that managed to produce it—was hailed as a way for states to ensure their own food security without having to rely on foreign sources of nitrogen. With this shift, as well as the mechanization of mining phosphates and potash, the labor regimes supporting the fertilizer industry also shifted. The use of nitrogen-based fertilizers rose dramatically in the countries that had the capacity to develop methods to produce them. The use of synthetic fertilizers, especially during wartimes, was widely considered to be essential and even the patriotic thing to do, because it resulted in higher crop yields and a reduction in reliance on imported food.[72] Public concern about the industry in various countries at the time was mainly focused on the price of fertilizers and control—by dominant firms or by states—over the use of the technology to produce it.

Although much of the public discourse on synthetic fertilizers in the early twentieth century praised them as essential to ensure national security by improving crop yields, some critiques did emerge on ecological grounds, especially after World War I. In his widely read 1935 book, *Deserts on the March*, referencing the 1930s dustbowl in the United States, American ecologist Paul Sears expressed alarm about the pace at which the fertility of US farmland was being depleted and made "unfit" for agriculture due to forest clearing and overcultivation. Beyond the need to maintain chemical elements in the soil, he emphasized the need to "safeguard the texture of soil and to maintain its integrity as a biological milieu." He stressed, "To mine the soil persistently and trust to heavy doses of chemical fertilizer when it becomes exhausted is to disregard the plain and explicit warning of nature." Sears saw humans as destroying the delicate natural balance of soils and warned that "there is no magic which will undo the mischief" that humans had wrought on the land.[73]

Sir Albert Howard, a prominent British agricultural scientist and advocate of natural farming methods, was also highly skeptical of synthetic fertilizers, which he saw as causing damage to crops. In his view, soils required humus to restore fertility and to protect crops from diseases.[74] "Artificials," as Howard termed synthetic fertilizers, killed living organisms in the soil, including the earthworms that play a crucial role in composting organic matter in soils. He was deeply skeptical of Liebig's critique of humus theory that gave rise to the growing demand for synthetic fertilizer. Howard also foreshadowed lock-ins across the inputs, seeing growing artificial fertilizer use as a product of "the imperative demands made on the farmer by the invention of machinery."[75] Perturbed that the "NPK mentality" had infiltrated universities and governments, especially during the world wars, when the use of artificial fertilizers was pushed by governments as a moral imperative, Howard called out the British Ministry of Agriculture's corporate ties, which he said effectively made its officials "salesmen of the contents of the fertilizer bag" when they subsidized farmers' purchase of synthetic fertilizers.[76]

In his 1946 book, *The War in the Soil*, Howard explicitly connected these problems to corporate power and to the rise of industrial agriculture that profited from what he saw as a technology that damaged ecosystem health: "The war in the soil is the result of a conflict between the birthright of humanity—fresh food from fertile soil—and the profits of a section of Big Business in the shape of the manufacturers of artificial fertilizers and their satellite companies who produce poison sprays to protect crops from pests and who prepare the various remedies for the diseases of live stock and mankind."[77] Howard's critiques of artificial fertilizers were shared by other leading thinkers in the organic agriculture movements in the United Kingdom and in Germany at the time, which were concerned that the application of synthetic fertilizers disrupted the metabolism of plants and the chemical balance of soil, which ultimately harmed plants.[78]

These critiques of synthetic fertilizers sparked highly polarized debates over organic versus conventional farming in the 1930s and 1940s. The proponents of synthetic nitrogen defended it as being effectively no different from nitrogen derived from organic materials from the plant's perspective, and claimed that the organic movement was spreading misinformation.[79] However, since that time, interest in organic farming has grown, particularly as more information has become available about the full range of ecological costs associated with synthetic fertilizers, including not just the problems pointed out by its early critics, but also as nitrogen pollution, greenhouse gas emissions, and energy use, discussed more fully in later chapters.

CONCLUSION

The commercial fertilizer industry has long been dominated by just a few firms, including in the nineteenth century, when the international guano, nitrate, phosphorus, and potash trades were first established. By the mid-twentieth century, the fertilizer industry was highly concentrated, both within regions and on an international scale. In the United States, just six firms dominated the sector from the early 1900s until the late 1950s. Internationally, IG Farben (which included BASF), Norsk Hydro, and ICI dominated production in Europe by the interwar period, with Japanese zaibatsu firms acting as significant players in the Asian fertilizer markets. These firms came to be large and dominant through their access to certain benefits across the nitrogen, phosphate, and potash markets. These benefits included corporate and government control over geographically specific and limited national resources and know-how, which encouraged the industry to engage in collusive and cartel-like behavior to control production and fix prices—including on an international scale—from very early on. Governments also provided support to the sector through research and subsidies, especially for nitrogen, which was important for military security reasons.

The huge capital outlays necessary for mining and nitrogen synthesis processes did result in some economies-of-scale advantages for the large firms that came to dominate, but they also created huge barriers to entry for other firms, cementing just a few firms at the top of the sector for long periods of time. Far from simply being "better" at fertilizer production, these firms had specific advantages that enabled them to escape from normal competitive market structures and instead operate in ways that extracted maximum profits, often with the explicit support of governments.

The consequences of the commercial fertilizer industry for social and ecological systems were dramatic and far-reaching, but only some of the costs were recognized at the time that these developments unfolded. The human costs of guano, nitrate, and phosphate mining were decried by some, but their distance from the point of consumption mitigated calls to address the abysmal working conditions of laborers. The ecological costs were also only partially recognized prior to the mid-twentieth century. There was some concern as synthetic nitrogen and mined fertilizers were being rolled out that artificial amendments were damaging to soil structure and were causing harm to living organisms, while at the same time they were lining the pockets of the fertilizer industry. Although the Haber-Bosch process of nitrogen synthesis consumed huge amounts of natural gas, the climate costs of fertilizer production became widely known only in the latter part of the 1900s.

4

SEEDS

In the 1930s, as hybrid seeds increasingly made their way into farmers' fields in the United States, just four firms controlled the vast majority of that market. The breakthrough technology of hybridization played an important role in ending the traditional role of farmers in selecting seeds at harvesttime to save for use in subsequent planting seasons. This shift was dramatic and swift. For millennia, farmers have made an enormous contribution to crop improvement through their careful observation and selection of seeds with desirable traits. The natural reproducibility of seeds meant that they did not readily develop into commercial market goods—at least not in a widespread way—until the past two centuries.[1] Rather than purchase seeds, migrants often brought seeds with them to new lands to ensure their own food security and preferences. The European settlers to the Americas, for example, brought seeds with them to safeguard their traditional crops, as did Africans who were forcibly taken to be traded into slavery in the Americas.[2]

Although some commercial seed companies existed as early as the mid-1700s, a substantial private sector seed industry did not develop until the mid- to late 1800s. It was not until the 1930s, with the advent of hybridization, that farmers in North America and Europe began to become reliant on that industry to supply the bulk of their seeds. Hybridization opened the door for a more commercialized and concentrated seed industry. Hybrid seeds, even though they were not patentable at that time, had to be produced every year, giving the companies that developed them a steady market. This feature meant that hybrids had a kind of built-in intellectual property protection provided the combination of plant genetic material behind them was kept secret. A small group of private sector firms benefited from key advantages for hybrid seed development: access to capital for research and development as well as privileged access to germplasm (seeds, plants, and plant parts used in crop breeding), including that developed by the US government in its public sector breeding program. This select group of firms was able to exploit the natural intellectual property protection of those seeds to their advantage. By the end of the 1930s, the four private seed companies had come to dominate the hybrid seed market and were on the verge of becoming the biggest seed companies in the world.

GOVERNMENT SEED ACQUISITION, DISTRIBUTION, AND RESEARCH

Although farmers have long been able to rely on themselves and their local communities to improve and obtain seed, some governments—especially those with strong naval capacities—actively worked to acquire seeds from other parts of the world in an attempt to grow those plants domestically or to control their production and trade.[3] Christopher Columbus, for example, brought maize seeds to Europe that he collected during his explorations in the Americas in the late 1400s, which were subsequently traded to distant ports, including China.[4] The seeds Columbus took from North America were acquired from Indigenous peoples, who cultivated and selected countless locally adapted and distinct varieties of maize, an important part of their diet, over thousands of years.

Government efforts to acquire seeds on a global scale were institutionalized in the mid-nineteenth century. Britain collected plants from other countries, often as part of colonial initiatives, many of which were planted to keep a living stock at Kew Gardens, west of London, which became a national botanical garden in 1840. Similarly, the Jardin des Plantes in Paris, first established as a royal garden for medicinal plants, housed a wide variety of plants collected from around the world, attracting botanical scientists who conducted research on-site.[5] The US government also worked with its consulates abroad and the US Navy throughout the early nineteenth century under the Patent Office Division of Agriculture to encourage the collection of foreign seeds to be sent back to the United States to be adapted for domestic planting as the country expanded westward. The Patent Office later arranged formal exchanges of plant germplasm with foreign governments. Plants were introduced into the United States in these ways from all parts of the world: Asia, Africa, South America, and Europe. The passage of the Morrill Act in the United States in 1862 created the Department of Agriculture, which was charged with continuing this work of collection and diffusion of plant material, including seeds.[6]

Some of these plant genetic acquisitions made their way into an early emergent commercial seed trade. One of the world's first commercial seed firms was the family-owned firm Vilmorin, established in Paris in 1743. Vilmorin sold a wide range of seeds, including for wheat, vegetables, and flowers, many of them based on varieties that came from other countries around the world. By the 1800s, the firm sold its seeds globally, including to Germany and the United States. Following the lead of the Jardin des Plantes in its scientific work, the company undertook plant breeding research, in particular under Louis de Vilmorin and then his son, Henry de Vilmorin, from the 1840s to the 1890s. By the mid-1800s, the firm was known as one of the world's most important seed companies for its leading research in plant genetics.[7]

The commercial seed market developed more slowly in North America, and although there is record of a seed company in Philadelphia in the 1780s that focused on vegetable and flower seeds, very few private seed companies were in operation before the mid- to late 1800s.[8] A likely reason for the comparatively slow development of a private seed industry in the United States was the government practice of distributing free seeds to its citizens from the 1830s. The government mailed packets of seeds, formally distributed by its elected members of Congress, to citizens who requested them. These seeds included those that were obtained abroad in a bid to encourage farmers to experiment with new crops with the hope that some would prove useful as export crops or would reduce the country's reliance on imports. The free seeds provided by the government were meant to focus on new varieties of plants that were not yet widely available to farmers, which enabled the government to use farmers' fields as sites of crop experimentation. However, seeds already in common use were also often distributed by these means.[9]

Rural sociologist Jack Kloppenburg outlined in his seminal book, *First the Seed*, the controversy that emerged in the United States as early as the 1850s over whether the government should be giving away seeds for free. In 1883, thirty-four private seed companies, claiming that free seed distribution undermined the viability of an emerging private seed sector, met to establish a lobby group, the American Seed Trade Association. This group subsequently pressed the secretary of agriculture, J. Sterling Morton, to scale back the US seed distribution program. Morton was sympathetic to the group's concerns, but his efforts met with congressional resistance due to the popularity of the program from which members of Congress directly benefited. Morton's attempt to end the free distribution backfired, and as Kloppenburg notes, "In 1897 the volume of seed distributed reached an all-time record of 22,195,381 packages. Because each package contained five packets of different varieties, the government actually sent out over 1.1 *billion* seed packets."[10]

In the latter part of the nineteenth century, the United States also established land-grant colleges with the passage of the Morrill Acts of 1862 and 1890, which granted land to the states that they could then sell to raise funds to establish colleges that would provide practical education, including in agriculture.[11] The 1887 Hatch Act extended this mission by establishing agricultural experiment stations at the land grant colleges. These stations conducted research into soil fertility and crop improvement, including seed selection and testing, and shared that information with farmers in the region. Experiment stations in several US states not only conducted research into improved seed stock but also sold that seed to farmers.[12] Through these various efforts—seed collection and distribution and the establishment of crop research and experimentation—the US government played a strong role in directing the development of that country's agricultural sector, which had significance for global agricultural development.

EMERGENCE OF A COMMERCIAL SEED INDUSTRY

Although the government led in the areas of seed acquisition, distribution, and agricultural research, a private seed industry eventually developed in the United States by the 1850s. The industry grew in subsequent decades, years when farming was becoming progressively more mechanized and commercialized. Private seed companies—many of them owned by farmers who grew the seed stock themselves—typically reproduced and sold seed that government researchers developed, using selection methods developed under state-sponsored research. These firms usually sold their seeds through catalogs or traveling salesmen. Farmers occasionally bought additional seed from these companies to acquire new seed stock when switching into the production of new crops or varieties or to mix with their own self-saved seed to ensure purity of the seed. Many of the commercial seed salesman, however, misled farmers with false claims about the purity and traits of their seed or sold farmers seed that was contaminated with debris and weeds.[13]

From the early 1900s, state agricultural experiment stations took on the role of certifying seed to ensure its varietal purity and its germinating qualities and published the results along with those who were selling them. The US Department of Agriculture (USDA) encouraged farmers to purchase only certified seed to protect themselves from untrustworthy salesmen. The government also stressed to farmers that buying rather than self-saving seeds could cut their expenses of selecting and saving seeds. Farm publications at the time pressed on both farmers and seed dealers the importance of quality seed. The certification of seed opened opportunities for private seed firms, which could sell their seed at a premium price if it was certified as being a quality product, and they contracted with farmers who specialized in seed growing to produce them.[14] By the 1920s, several hundred seed companies were in business, although most of these sold horticultural crop seeds rather than field crop seeds.[15]

The Funk Brothers Seed Company was one of these early commercial seed enterprises. The firm was established in 1901 in Illinois by Eugene Funk, who had visited the Vilmorin Seed Farm outside Paris on his studies in Europe as a young man. Funk returned to Illinois excited to start his own seed company on a similar model.[16] Both his father and grandfather were highly active politicians in Illinois, and the Funk family had come to acquire some 25,000 acres of land since settling in the state in 1824. With over a dozen of his siblings and cousins, Eugene Funk established the firm, and they all agreed to combine their resources, including capital and use of their lands for seed production. With corn as a major crop in Illinois, Funk immediately set out to gather as many corn samples as he could from across the country and to learn as much as possible about corn breeding. By 1905, Funk Brothers claimed to be "the largest seed corn growers in the world."[17]

These developments in the seed industry coincided with several other big changes that fundamentally altered the nature of farming: improvements in reaper and plow technologies, consolidation in landholdings into larger farms, an increase in the use of commercial fertilizers, growing urbanization, and the expansion of transportation networks. All of these changes made agriculture much more market focused and trade oriented, even before modern seed varieties like hybrids came on the scene. Britain's repeal of the Corn Laws in 1846, for example, along with the extension of the railways connecting different parts of the United States and Canada in the latter part of the 1800s, meant more opportunities for North American farmers to market agricultural commodities abroad. These changes further encouraged specialization of production and the use of machinery.

There was also a high demand for corn (maize) in the US Midwest, especially from the rapidly expanding livestock industry that was trying to keep up with growing meat purchases from burgeoning urban centers like New York.[18] Together, these changes cemented the trend toward more specialized and commercialized agriculture in the United States. According to agricultural policy analyst Carey Fowler, "By the late 1800s farming had become a business for most. Farmers had either become entrepreneurs or they had gotten out of farming."[19] Seed saving among farmers declined in this context, especially because the practice became more challenging as farms grew larger and became more specialized. Buying seeds rather than saving them became increasingly convenient for many farmers, and private sector seed companies, encouraged by the US government through its research and certification activities, stepped in to fill that role.

THE QUEST FOR CORN IMPROVEMENT THROUGH BREEDING

The growing commercialization and specialization of agriculture fueled interest in enhancing corn yields and the emerging field of plant breeding. "Corn shows" emerged in the United States from the late 1800s in the Midwest and offered farmers an opportunity to showcase their best varieties and encouraged them to strive to improve the crop through better seed selection. These competitions awarded prizes based on the evaluation of a sample of ten ears of corn submitted by entrants. The corn "show cards" listed the key attributes on which the ears would be judged, typically including appearance and uniformity, on the assumption that good-looking corn would lead to a better overall crop. Strikingly missing from the early corn show cards was evaluation of the yield of the corn.[20] These shows encouraged farmers to choose varieties to plant each season based on the show card attributes, but the result was not an increase in yield. Critics of the corn shows began to point out this weakness, with a prominent skeptic being Henry A. Wallace, who advocated for the institution of "yield tests" rather than appearance-based corn shows.

It is worth taking a closer look at Wallace and his family at this juncture, since they played a large role in shaping corn breeding in the United States and the commercialization of hybrid seeds. Wallace, who later had a major political career including as US secretary of agriculture and then as vice president under President Franklin D. Roosevelt, had been captivated by plant breeding—corn in particular—from a young age. As a boy, he was fascinated with plants and learned a great deal about botany from a family friend, George Washington Carver, a son of African American enslaved people who had become a student at Iowa State in the 1890s where Henry C. Wallace (Henry A. Wallace's father) was a student and then a professor.[21] The younger Wallace devoted most of his time as a young man to the effort of improving corn breeding and recognized even as a teenager that the prettiest ears of corn were not necessarily the most productive ones.[22]

The Wallace family was prominent in both Iowa and nationally in the late nineteenth and early twentieth centuries for their agricultural expertise. The first Henry Wallace (Henry C. Wallace's father and Henry A. Wallace's grandfather), also known as "Uncle Henry," founded *Wallaces'*

Farmer, a popular agricultural newspaper published in Des Moines, Iowa, from the 1890s. Uncle Henry's son, Henry C. Wallace, taught dairying at Iowa State and served as associate editor at the family newspaper and then succeeded his father as editor on the latter's death in 1916. Henry C. Wallace was tapped to serve as US Secretary of Agriculture in 1921, a position he held until his death in office in 1924.

Henry A. Wallace came by his agricultural and political interests from his family's deep engagement in both arenas. He took over as editor of *Wallaces' Farmer* from 1921 to 1933, until he was tapped to serve as secretary of agriculture (1933–1940), eventually becoming vice president (1941–1944) and secretary of commerce (1945–1946). In 1926, before his political career began, Henry A. Wallace founded the Hi-Bred Corn Company, the first seed company to be established specifically to breed and sell hybrid corn.

As corn shows in the United States gained in popularity in the first decade of the twentieth century, there were important breakthroughs in plant breeding, including with respect to corn. The rediscovery of Gregor Mendel's earlier scientific work on pea plants that laid out the laws of genetic inheritance had an enormous influence on efforts to develop hybrid corn. Mendel's work, which had been published in the 1860s, was not taken up by the scientific community until the early 1900s, when it sparked major new thinking on plant breeding and crop improvement.[23] Previously, plant breeders experimented with hybridization by simple crossing of different plant varieties. Mendel's work led them specifically down the path of more careful crossing of inbred lines, which gave the offspring improved vigor, or hardiness, over the parent lines. Early work conducted by US plant scientists Edward East and George Shull in 1907 and 1908 was important in advancing understandings of genetic inheritance in corn. But the private seed industry did not deem their work to be useful because the parent lines to produce the hybrids did not yield enough seeds, making the process of hybridization by this method difficult to achieve on a large scale. As a result, there was a widespread view at that time that it was unlikely that hybrid vigor would have much commercial value.[24]

One of East's students, Donald Jones, nevertheless continued to experiment with hybridization research. In 1918, while working as a government plant breeder at the Connecticut agricultural experiment station, he tried what has come to be known as double cross hybridization. This method involved crossing two pairs of inbred parent lines in two stages—effectively combining four different pure inbred lines by first combining two sets of pure inbred parents to produce offspring and then crossing the two offspring with each other. Double cross hybridization led to better results in terms of yield increases of the resultant seeds, although it was finicky work and only a small slice of the crosses—perhaps only 1 in 1,000—would lead to more vigorous plants that could potentially have higher yields. Moreover, even if strong hybrid vigor was established in some double cross hybrids, the offspring of those hybrids (that is, if the seeds were simply saved and planted in the next season) would produce much lower yields. This meant that new seed had to be produced from the inbred lines each season if the vigor was to be maintained in farmers' fields. Clearly this method of corn breeding was highly impractical for the average farmer to experiment with and produce hybrid seeds on their own farms.[25]

These various qualifications to the potential of hybrid corn led many to question its practicality as a viable seed breeding method. However, the fact that new hybrid seeds needed to be produced every year did open the door to commercial possibilities, which some seed companies and scientists fully recognized at the time.[26] Specifically, if breeders could develop unique inbred parent lines or could use different inbred lines obtained from government-sponsored agricultural research stations and combine them to develop new breeds without revealing the parentage of those breeds, it would be nearly impossible for others to replicate them. Such an approach would enable the firms to produce seeds that offered hybrid vigor that would need to be purchased fresh each year.

Although US patent laws at that time did not allow for the patenting of plant varieties that reproduced sexually (as is the case with maize), the advent of hybrids offered a degree of in-built intellectual property protection if managed carefully. In joint work published in 1919, East and Jones openly recognized this feature of hybridization: "It is not a method that will interest most farmers, but it is something that may easily be taken up by seedsmen; in fact, it is the first time in agricultural history that a seedsman is enabled to gain the full benefit from a desirable origination of his own or something that he has purchased.... The utilization of first generation hybrids enables the originator to keep the parental types and give out only the crossed seeds, which are less valuable for continued propagation."[27]

THE IMPACT OF HYBRIDIZATION ON THE US SEED INDUSTRY

In the next decade and a half, these developments fundamentally transformed the US commercial seed industry in a direction that favored corporate expansion and concentration. The prospect of charging higher prices for seeds, partly to recoup the cost of research and development and partly as a reward for inventiveness, was an attractive enticement for those companies. Four seed firms took the lead in the development of hybrid seeds, and those same firms subsequently came to dominate the US hybrid seed market, and eventually the global crop seed market.

The Funk Brothers Seed Company was one of the few commercial seed firms that employed professional agronomists to undertake breeding work from the early 1900s, inspired by similar efforts Funk had witnessed at Vilmorin. The breeding work at Funk Brothers focused on developing high-oil and high-protein corn varieties as well as hybridization.[28] Eugene Funk realized that he would need access to a laboratory to do testing and proposed to fund the establishment of a laboratory at Illinois Wesleyan University in 1902 in exchange for chemical analysis work on the firm's corn. He also kept up with the latest developments in the hybridization of corn and corresponded with George Shull in 1914, who encouraged him to continue with his single cross hybridization experiments. Funk was ultimately disappointed in his results, however.[29]

Funk Brothers employed plant breeding specialist Jim Holbert in 1915, who had worked summers for the firm in previous years when he was a university student. Holbert was given free rein to develop further hybridization research at the firm, something Eugene Funk himself lacked time to do while he was running the firm. By 1918, Holbert had completed a large inventory of potential germplasm for developing parent lines for hybrids. It was a massive job. He examined millions of corn plants in the field and selected several thousand ears with the best traits for experimentation that came from multiple varieties. After germination tests from his selection, Holbert determined that just a dozen ears—fewer than 1 percent of his original selections—were suitable for the development of hybrid parent lines.

Funk, who by this time held important positions in various agricultural associations at the national and state levels, was called to Washington, DC, in 1916 to take up a special wartime assignment with the USDA. While there, Funk fought for and won a special appropriation from Congress to establish an additional half-dozen experimental field stations in the corn belt to examine issues such as crop diseases that were plaguing the region. The first of these field stations was established on the property of Funk Farms near Bloomington, Illinois, and Eugene Funk "loaned" Jim Holbert to the USDA to direct the station's work.[30]

The establishment of the USDA experimental research station at Funk Farms took place at exactly the same time that Edward Jones had developed the double cross hybridization method at the Connecticut agricultural research station, and Holbert undertook experiments using this method for the USDA at Funk Farms. Holbert played a central role in the development of commercial hybrid seeds because in his USDA role, he was mandated to collect and openly share plant genetic material for experimentation. He was in an awkward position, given his close relationship to Funk Brothers, which wanted to keep the genetic material for the inbred parent lines secret.[31]

Holbert did meet with others researching hybridization of corn over the twenty years he worked for the USDA at the Funk Farms experiment station. In this role, he exchanged ideas and plant germplasm—specifically inbred parent lines of corn for hybridization experiments—with other individuals who were central in establishing what became the other three major hybrid seed companies: Henry A. Wallace of the Hi-Bred Corn Company, Charlie Gunn of the DeKalb Agricultural Association, and Lester Pfister of the Pfister Hybrid Corn Company. Historian Richard Crabb emphasized the significance of Holbert's interactions with these individuals: "The techniques these men learned in their visits to Bloomington, the inbreds given to them from the Federal Field Station, and the enthusiasm for the possibilities of this new kind of corn imparted to them by Jim Holbert constituted the greatest single force in the hybrid-corn movement during the twenties and early thirties when the question of having hybrid corn in our time was hanging precariously in the balance."[32]

Indeed, these interactions were instrumental in the establishment of additional hybrid seed companies. Henry A. Wallace established the Hi-Bred Corn Company in 1926 (renamed Pioneer Hi-Bred Corn Company in 1935). As noted earlier, Wallace experimented with single cross hybrids as a young man. He closely followed the news of the successful double cross hybridization performed by Jones, and using this method, Wallace produced his own hybrids that performed well in yield test competitions in Iowa. Wallace came to view the development of hybrids as too complex for farmers to perform on their own fields, which prompted him to start the firm. His wife, Ilo, who had received an inheritance from her family, invested in the company and became the firm's largest shareholder. He also benefited from access to land purchased by his father for seed production. Henry A. Wallace continued to edit *Wallaces' Farmer* while running the company and liberally filled the editorial pages of the newspaper with articles extolling the virtues of hybrid seeds. He also used his position of prominence as a major national magazine editor and the fact that he traveled widely in this role, to collect germplasm from all parts of the country, including from government experiment stations. It was in this context that he met with Jim Holbert to exchange ideas at the Funk Farms experiment station. Wallace also maintained close contact with both East and Jones in this period.[33]

The DeKalb Agricultural Association started as a cooperative venture among farmers in DeKalb County, Illinois. The association provided advice to farmers on matters such as soil fertility and seeds and eventually started a commercial seed business given the high demand for improved seeds from its members. DeKalb began research work into hybrid corn in the early 1920s, after Henry C. Wallace visited the association in 1923, while he was secretary of agriculture, to deliver a speech to the group. Charlie Gunn, who directed the seed breeding research at the DeKalb Agricultural Association, met with Wallace, who impressed on him that the double cross hybridization method of corn improvement held the most promise for commercial development. Gunn was inspired to undertake research on this method of hybridization and began this work in 1925, although his initial research was carried out in secret in order to ensure it would not meet the disapproval of the DeKalb board. In keeping his research under wraps, he sought to develop a first-mover advantage in the northern Illinois seed market.[34] DeKalb's research made use of inbred parent lines obtained from Holbert at the Funk Farms USDA experiment station and mixed those lines with the association's own inbred lines that were developed by Gunn for the specific climate and soils of the region. DeKalb brought its first hybrids to market in 1934 and went big in terms of market reach in the corn belt region, launching the DeKalb Hybrid Seed Company in 1938 as a research arm of the firm.[35]

The Pfister Hybrid Corn Company, the fourth large hybrid seed firm to develop in this period, was established by Lester Pfister, a farmer with no formal education in plant breeding. Although he dropped out of school after the eighth grade, he enthusiastically experimented with corn breeding in the 1920s.[36] Pfister had also been inspired to undertake hybridization experiments after meeting with Henry A. Wallace, and he also met and exchanged ideas, as well as germplasm, with Jim Holbert. Pfister's hybrids included inbred lines he developed himself from a variety of corn he encountered when he was hired to make detailed reports on the proving plots for a corn test competition, which is where he first met Henry A. Wallace. The variety that changed Pfister's fortunes was Krug Corn grown by George Krug, a farmer from Illinois who had won the competition for which Pfister was providing detailed reports. Pfister used Krug Corn to develop a highly successful hybrid variety that gave greater yields. Pfister shared this germplasm with Holbert, who subsequently included it in US government–developed hybrid varieties. Pfister's firm saw great success as a result, and he gained fame in the media for his dramatic rags-to-riches story.[37]

THE ROLE OF THE PUBLIC SECTOR

As research on hybrids by private actors was accelerating in the 1920s, the US government, which had until that point continued to support corn improvement research focused on natural selection methods, shifted its efforts to focus more on developing hybrids. In 1925, it halted its natural varietal selection and testing experiments.[38]

These developments began to take place while Henry C. Wallace was the Secretary of Agriculture in the early 1920s. Before his official appointment was publicly announced, he suggested that his son, Henry A., visit the USDA while he was on a business trip in Washington, DC, in order to provide his opinion to his father on the department's corn improvement work. Henry A. met with the head of corn improvement research within USDA, C. P. Hartley, who had earlier experimented with inbreeding methods of corn improvement but determined that it was a dead end. However, one of Hartley's staff, F. D. Richey, who had experimented with the method on his own and had a more positive outlook about the prospects for hybrid corn, impressed the younger Wallace, which he subsequently reported to his father. In early 1922, Richey replaced Hartley as the agronomist in charge of corn research at the USDA and quickly shifted USDA resources from efforts to improve open-pollinated varieties to hybridization.[39]

US public sector research into inbred hybrid corn seed varieties in the 1920s had an enormous impact on the development of the hybrid seed industry in ways that directly benefited the early private sector hybrid seed companies. Increased USDA funding for research initiatives in the 1920s supported Richey's initiatives to expand hybrid corn breeding research at the state experiment stations. Initially this research was undertaken on the assumption that farmers would grow their own hybrid seeds using publicly developed inbred lines, an effort some farmers did in fact take up, but this was far from the norm. At the same time, the four dominant commercial seed companies also benefited enormously from free access to publicly developed inbred parent lines. Because Jim Holbert had close relationships with all the key players in the dominant companies, these firms had especially easy access not just to superior germplasm but also the latest breeding techniques that were being developed by public sector seed breeders.[40]

The fact that these four firms had already conducted some of their own research and development, including the development of some parent lines, meant that they had a considerable first-mover advantage in using these methods. This head start was important because it could take a decade or more to develop a well-performing hybrid variety.[41] These firms were also able to develop varieties that others could not replicate because it included some of their own parent lines, which were kept secret, or "closed pedigree," whereas other seed companies focused on reproducing "open pedigree" hybrid varieties developed and made openly available by the public sector. These four firms had the capital, research facilities, intellectual property, and time advantage over others to develop their own inbred lines that gave them a market edge. Although there was no patent protection at the time for open pollinated plant varieties, these firms used the justification of "trade secrets" to not publish the parentage of their hybrid varieties.[42] USDA research scientist Jorge Fernandez-Cornejo explains, "As long as the lineage of a company's hybrid remained unknown to competitors or farmers, the company continued to hold a unique and marketable product until an even better hybrid was developed."[43]

THE PROMOTION AND ADOPTION OF HYBRIDS

Hybrid seeds were not an overnight success, in either productivity or commercial terms. Farmers were reluctant to adopt hybrid seeds because they were more costly, often two to four times as expensive as open-pollinated seed varieties.[44] It is important to recall at this point that the 1920s were difficult years for farmers in North America. Many were deep in debt, having purchased farm equipment and land during a period of high commodity prices during World War I. But the end of the war saw sharp declines in commodity prices that put many farmers in a precarious situation exacerbated by the Great Depression that took hold in the 1930s.

Between 1933 and 1945, hybrid corn went from making up 0.4 percent of the US corn acreage to 90 percent of the acreage, a remarkable increase that many promoters of hybrids attribute to their superior yield performance. The yield improvements of the early hybrids in the late 1920s and early 1930s, however, were hardly overwhelming compared to seeds improved through careful selection. According to agricultural historian Deborah Fitzgerald, hybrids averaged about six bushels more per acre than the average yields of traditional seeds, while well-selected open-pollinated seeds could achieve ten bushels more per acre.[45] These results were a product of the fact that open pollinated varieties were adapted to specific local conditions. Hybrids, however, were often more standardized and yield tested in their breeding grounds but subject to uneven performance when tried in individual farmer fields.[46]

So why did hybrid seeds eventually become so dominant if they were not overwhelmingly better than open pollinated varieties? There is no one causal explanation, but rather a combination of factors that contributed to the adoption of hybrids, which ultimately enabled the dominant firms in the sector to become more powerful as demand for their products grew.

The seed companies themselves launched aggressive marketing campaigns for their hybrid seeds in the early 1930s. All four of the major hybrid seed companies built their distribution networks on the extension-agent model of the USDA and marketed their seed as being of high quality.[47] Funk Brothers and Pioneer Hi-Bred offered special deals to farmers who were willing to try hybrids by offering free seeds so that farmers could compare the yields of the new seeds to their traditional seeds. Pioneer Hi-Bred, for example, would select one farmer per region and give them enough free hybrid seed to plant half of their acreage. In return, that farmer agreed to share half the proceeds of any additional production with the firm.[48] Pioneer Hi-Bred also charged high prices to portray hybrids as having superior quality. It sponsored 4H clubs, churches, and other local groups within farming communities to build brand loyalty and appear local rather than as a distant large company. It also advertised in a way that tried to create a romantic vision of farmers' identity and placed the firm within that image to further cement loyalty to the brand.[49]

Similarly, Funk Brothers launched a huge public relations campaign to promote hybrids and gave away small quantities of hybrid seeds for free, explicitly directing its advertising to younger farmers. The firm also encouraged farmers to report back on their experiments with hybrids as a way for the firm to collect data that would feed back into its breeding programs.[50] Funk Brothers marketed its "G" hybrids specifically as top-quality products. The use of letters in the varieties was a distinct marketing tactic. Most farm publications published yields of different seed varieties but published only the breed numbers rather than the firm names so as not to associate hybrids with specific brands. But Funk Brothers used letters to get around this problem, as a Funk Brothers pamphlet makes clear, "Using the B or G before the numbers made it likely that publications would print these letters with the numbers and farmers would soon associate them with Funk. It happened that hybrids in the G series were better in performance than those in the B series, so G was selected as a prefix for each number and was incorporated into the company logo."[51]

The ecological and technological contexts also affected the pace of hybrid adoption. North America faced severe droughts in 1934 and again in 1936 that hit the US Midwest particularly hard, wiping out much of the crop in the corn belt. The farmers who had experimented with hybrids found that they had stronger stalks and were better able than the open pollinated varieties to survive the extreme dry weather. The droughts also led to a scarcity of seed, because in many locations, the corn crop was completely decimated, and farmers were not able to save their own seeds. They had to purchase them for the following season, and many opted for hybrids after seeing that they had survived severe conditions.[52]

A key reason that farmers took up hybrids is their lock-in with other agricultural technologies that were dominant or becoming dominant at the same time (discussed more fully in chapter 6). Because hybrids had thicker and stiffer stalks and were bred to have the ears of corn appear at the same height on the stalk, they worked better with mechanical pickers. In fact, it was much more difficult to harvest hybrids by hand because of the effort required to remove the ears. Using a mechanical picker on nonhybrid corn was also a mess because if any plants lodged or fell over, those ears could not be picked up by the machine.[53] Farmers who had already made a capital investment in mechanization were thus more likely to adopt hybrid corn. Hybrid corn also worked well with additional fertilizers, again because of the thicker and stiffer stalks, which meant that the plants were less likely to lodge as they grew taller, as would happen with increased fertilizer use on traditional varieties. The stronger stalks could also resist pests more easily, a key consideration given growing infestations of fields with the European corn borer in North America in the 1920s.[54]

The policy context in which farmers made planting decisions was also extremely important in explaining hybrid adoption. The US government passed the Agricultural Adjustment Act (AAA) in 1933, shortly after Henry A. Wallace assumed the role of secretary of agriculture. The act, part of Roosevelt's New Deal policies, authorized the payment of subsidies to farmers on the condition that they voluntarily limit the acreage they planted, as a means to counter the overproduction that was dragging down crop prices.[55] In this context, farmers were interested in receiving the subsidies, but because the limits were on acreage planted and not overall production levels, they were motivated to find ways to increase yields on the lands they did cultivate and were willing to experiment with risky technologies if it meant a chance at a higher income.[56]

The US government also took a more direct role in promoting the adoption of hybrids. In 1936, as corn farmers were facing harsh conditions due to drought and depressed farm prices, Henry A. Wallace used his position of Secretary of Agriculture to openly promote hybrids in the USDA's 1936 *Yearbook of Agriculture*.[57] This move was a departure from past annual reports, which normally provided, as Wallace himself notes in the foreword, "brief summaries of miscellaneous new developments in agriculture." He went on to stress that "this year it is devoted to exploring a single subject—the creative development of new forms of life through plant and animal breeding. The material is the outcome of a survey of superior germ plasm made by the Committee on Genetics. What this superior germ plasm is and how it is used constitute a story of surpassing importance to the modern world."[58]

That Wallace used his official position in the US government to promote a technology being advanced by a firm in which he maintained financial interests was incredible. As economic historian Richard Sutch points out, "By today's standards, the glaring conflict of interest between Wallace's financial interest in the Pioneer Hi-Bred Company and the use of the government agency he controlled to advertise and advocate his product would be outrageous."[59] The fact that the USDA signaled to farmers that it was putting its full weight behind hybrids sent a powerful message.

Once hybrids became entrenched in the US context in the 1930s, Canadian farmers began to experiment with them. From the late 1930s, Ontario farmers imported government-bred Wisconsin varieties that were developed for similar agroecological conditions. The export of the government varieties from Wisconsin was halted in 1940, but Ontario government programs worked to cross the US varieties with other Canadian varieties. At approximately the same time, each of the four big seed companies began to export their varieties to Canada, and throughout the early 1940s, each also began production of hybrid seeds in Canada, mainly in Ontario.[60] Commercial hybrid seeds were not widely adopted in Europe until the 1940s. Although there was some research into hybrids in Europe in the 1930s, this work was disrupted by World War II. The UN Relief and

Reconstruction Agency encouraged research into hybrid maize, and the Marshall Plan provided funding after the war. This work was eventually turned over to the UN's Food and Agriculture Organization in the 1950s. As in the Canadian context, it was difficult to rely on direct transfers of US hybrid seeds because they needed to be bred for specific agroecological contexts. Russia also began to import and experiment with hybrid seeds in the 1950s.[61]

THE SHIFT FROM PUBLIC TO PRIVATE SEED RESEARCH AND DEVELOPMENT

After the early private hybrid seed companies had achieved some success, there was a burst in the establishment of new seed companies, with about 150 start-up hybrid seed companies being established in the 1930s. Many of these firms were family owned, operating on a small scale, and most were never formally incorporated. Around forty of the existing seed companies also began to produce hybrid seeds. The vast majority of the new start-ups and the existing seed companies that moved into hybrid seed production at this time did not conduct their own research and development, however. Instead, they simply reproduced either government-developed hybrids or those developed by Funk Brothers, Pioneer Hi-Bred, Pfister, or DeKalb. These four firms controlled a commanding share of the US seed market by the late 1930s.[62]

Hybrid corn seed research had already begun to shift from the public to the private sector by the mid-1930s. The close collaboration between a small group of plant breeders from private seed companies and government researchers that was prevalent in the 1920s came to an end as companies became more secretive about their breeding programs. The USDA agricultural experiment station on Funk Farms was closed in 1937, and Jim Holbert went back to working for the Funk Brothers Seed Company, becoming a vice president in charge of research.[63] In making his move back into the private sector, he brought with him a wealth of experience and contacts from his research work with the government, which he then deployed on behalf of Funk Brothers.

The USDA still conducted research into hybrids and developed varieties for distribution throughout the 1930s. The in-bred parent lines were still used by the private seed companies to produce their hybrids, and the publicly developed hybrid varieties were reproduced by the smaller seed companies. But there was growing pressure by the larger private seed companies to change the nature of public research away from the development and testing of hybrid varieties to focus more on developing the inbred lines. In other words, they wanted the public sector researchers to focus more on fundamental research and to leave the applied, or commercially relevant, research to the private sector. Their rationale was that public duplication of research efforts that also attract private investment was a waste of public resources. This pressure paid off: the number of hybrid varieties released by state agricultural experiment stations declined in the 1940s, and by the early 1950s, Iowa and Illinois, home to all four of the large seed companies, stopped producing inbred lines altogether.[64]

The shift toward private sector seed research presented a decided disadvantage to the smaller seed companies, which relied on reproduction of the publicly released varieties that came out of public sector seed breeding programs. If a firm did not have the capital resources for R&D on a similar scale to the big four firms, there was little chance that they could compete. In practice, if they were not already contracted to produce the seed varieties of the four major firms, many of these smaller companies and individual seed-growing farmers began to do so as new publicly released varieties became less available, which further strengthened the market power of the dominant firms. As Kloppenburg explains, "This simply underlines the fact that the dominance of the industry by capital has less to do with economies of scale or production considerations than with access to research."[65]

SOCIAL AND ECOLOGICAL CONSEQUENCES

The advent of a commercial seed industry, especially the development of hybrid seeds after the 1920s, had enormous social and ecological consequences. In North America, the early seed industry itself was built on access to germplasm and knowledge of how to cultivate it that was originally taken from Indigenous peoples. The cultivation of maize was an activity traditionally undertaken by women in many Indigenous societies in North America, grown in mounds with beans and squash. Many Indigenous peoples were still cultivating maize until the early to mid-1800s, when they were dispossessed of their land by war and continuous settlement westward by people of European descent who colonized North America. At this time, Iroquois women, for example, faced pressure to step down from farming and hand that activity over to men.[66] The activities of cultivation, seed selection, and seed saving were then shifted from being primarily female activities to male activities, and then to activities undertaken primarily by white male settlers. The free distribution of seeds in the United States in the mid- to late 1800s played a role in encouraging westward settlement, which further displaced Indigenous peoples from the best agricultural lands to those that were not as productive. It also led to the widespread conversion of farming from diverse fields to monocultures.

The advent of hybrids caused further disruption. The fact that hybrid seeds could not be saved and replanted with the same results as in their first season marked a major change in agricultural practices and had huge economic consequences for farmers, who became locked into purchasing seeds each season. Fitzgerald puts it bluntly: "Farmers accustomed to selecting their corn over the years to create a strain suited to their own farm conditions were shocked to discover that saving and planting hybrid seed resulted in distinct decreases in yield the second year."[67] Higher prices for hybrid maize seed meant farmers' expenses rose considerably for this important input, a cost that was amplified because now they had to purchase new seed every year. The price of hybrid seed in 1936, for example, was approximately double the cost of open pollinated seeds.[68] The seed companies claimed that hybrid seeds were worth the extra cost because they resulted in higher yields, but that was not always the case, and when it was, it was often the result of applying more fertilizer, an increased expense for farmers. Moreover, farmer revenue depends on prevailing prices, which fluctuate due to weather and wider economic conditions. In short, farmers found themselves paying higher prices for seeds and needing to purchase more fertilizer, but with uncertain returns.

The adoption of hybrid seeds also meant that farmers no longer had the same role they once did in seed selection and improvement. Seed companies actively discouraged farmers from saving their own seeds, making the claim that hybrids were of superior quality. This break in farmers' roles in seed breeding led to a huge loss of knowledge. Fowler notes, "The advance of genetics created a wall between farmer and scientist which could not easily be scaled."[69] Analysts refer to this process as agricultural deskilling, whereby specialized knowledge is "usurped or discarded" and the power and leverage that the knowledge provided are dissipated.[70] Fitzgerald points out that farmers knew which traditional seeds grew well in their fields and could predict a seed's performance based on its appearance. But with the introduction of hybrids, it was virtually impossible to discern this information from the appearance of the seed. Moreover, with the need to purchase new seed every year, farmers were removed from their ongoing experimentation in crop improvement, reorienting their incentives toward annual seed purchases and away from longer-term interest in crop seed development.[71]

The seed companies producing the hybrids that farmers were adopting saw farmers' own traditional varieties as essential to the development of those seeds. These firms used publicly bred seeds in their hybrid development, which were products based on farmers' own experimentation and crosses of different varieties and freely donated. Their seeds in turn were acquired from Indigenous peoples, also without compensation. The dominant firms, using this germplasm they freely acquired, presented hybrids as the product of specialized "science" that was far beyond the capacity of farmers to understand.

Hybrids also brought ecological concerns. As they were increasingly taken up by farmers throughout the 1930s, plant breeders became increasingly worried about the implications of hybrids for plant genetic diversity. As early as the mid-1930s, just as hybrid seeds were becoming more popular in the United States, plant scientists stressed that plant breeding programs to develop hybrids required diverse varieties of older, non-hybrid strains, which they warned could become extinct if not protected.[72] Even before hybrid crop seeds came on the scene, there was worry about "improved" varieties displacing the diversity of indigenous plant varieties as early as the 1890s.[73]

In response to these growing concerns, there were multiple efforts to preserve diverse plant germplasm and make it available for future plant breeding. In the early 1940s, the Rockefeller Foundation began to collect both indigenous and "pioneer" open-pollinated varieties of maize when it began its program of corn improvement in Mexico, originally intending it as a source of plant germplasm for maize improvement in that country.[74] The rapid adoption of hybrid corn in the United States sparked concern that a similar pattern could happen in Mexico, the center of origin of maize, which could have worldwide consequences as varieties that underwent thousands of years of evolution and selection by farmers could be lost.[75] Paul Manglesdorf, a Harvard University botanist and maize seed breeder who also served as a consultant to the Rockefeller Foundation, was clear on this point in a 1951 article published in *Scientific American*:

> The almost universal use of hybrid corn in the U.S., and the prospective wide adoption of it in other parts of the world, is not without its dangers. Chief among these is that farmers as a rule are no longer growing the open-pollinated varieties. These varieties, from which all inbred strains are ultimately derived, may therefore become extinct. Already more than 99 per cent of the corn acreage in several of the Corn Belt states is in hybrid corn; in Iowa it is 100 per cent hybrid. The loss of the original source of breeding material would mean not only that improvement of the present strains would be restricted but that new types of hybrid corn could not be developed to cope with new diseases or insect pests suddenly become rampant. Our corn would also lose the ability to adapt to climatic changes. Open-pollinated varieties of corn, in which cross-pollination is the rule, are admirably contrived for maintaining genetic plasticity and would be capable of surviving rather drastic changes in the environment. Hybrid corn, a small, highly selected sample of the original genetic diversity, has lost this capability.[76]

In the United States, the Committee on Preservation of Indigenous Strains of Maize (also referred to as the Maize Committee) formed in 1951 under the auspices of the National Academy of Sciences of the National Research Council. J. Allen Clark, the chair of that committee, noted, "In view of the rapid increase in the growing of hybrid corns in the United States and of the apparent value of the Mexican collection for producing new hybrids, the importance of keeping these collections viable and of preserving the pioneer open-pollinated corns of the United States was obvious."[77] The Maize Committee, which included a representative from Pioneer Hi-Bred, worked with the Rockefeller Foundation to establish seed centers in several Latin American countries, including Mexico, Colombia, and Brazil, with the USDA establishing a seed center along similar lines in Ames, Iowa. Some twelve thousand varieties of maize were collected for preservation at these regional seed centers to be made available for future breeding programs.[78] Agricultural historian Helen Curry notes that these efforts were a direct product of advances in plant breeding and the widespread adoption of hybrids.[79]

These concerns about biodiversity loss, however, were not at the time viewed as a reason to move away from hybridization. Rather, hybridization was widely viewed as the only path forward, but one that came with a responsibility to protect plant germplasm to maintain the viability of future breeding programs for crop improvement.

CONCLUSION

As earlier research has shown, the development of hybrid seeds through state-sponsored research basically eliminated barriers to the penetration of capital into agriculture, allowing the private sector to develop a major seed industry.[80] This chapter outlines how it is that just a small handful of firms that rose to the top of the seed industry were able to grow to be far and away larger than the rest, primarily by capitalizing on key market, technology, and policy advantages. They had privileged access to government-supported research and development into the hybridization of seeds, as well as privileged access to capital, which allowed them to appropriate public research and mix it with their own in ways that gave them intellectual property protection that was not easy for latecomers to replicate. The position of a key researcher able to move through the revolving door of public and private research settings who interacted with all of the key seed firms gave those firms an unusual ability to access the latest research through intellectual and corporate networks. Once they positioned themselves as leaders, these firms used trade secrets to bolster the barriers to others, while also benefiting from government policies, including via a major conflict of interest on Henry A. Wallace's part, which promoted the widespread adoption of hybrid seeds. The ways in which hybrids interfaced with other technologies, like fertilizers and machinery, also lent advantages to the top firms.

Almost from the start, farmers and researchers raised major concerns about the consequences of widespread adoption of hybrid seed varieties. Not only were farmers and Indigenous people now cut out of research and development activities around seeds—being effectively deskilled—but the costs of seeds as an input rose considerably, increasing farmers' debt and dependence on large firms for their livelihoods. The ecological costs were also evident, as there was growing awareness of the implications of hybrid development on agrobiodiversity. While the concern initially lay with the potential disappearance of the very germplasm needed to develop further hybrid seeds, the wider costs of lost biodiversity for small-scale and Indigenous farmers has only grown in subsequent decades.

5
PESTICIDES

The discovery of DDT's pesticidal qualities in 1939 ushered in a new era for the chemical pesticides industry that encouraged rapid consolidation and high profitability for the firms at the top. As the industry shifted into the synthesis of pesticides from fossil fuel derivatives, what was once a small and fragmented industry became a highly concentrated one dominated by a small handful of very large firms. This rapid restructuring of the industry was remarkable given that the use of chemical methods of pest control was relatively new. The consequences were profound.

Throughout history, farmers have used a variety of biological, cultural, and mechanical practices methods to dissuade or kill insects, weeds, and plant fungi that threatened crops. There is a deep history, for example, of selecting seeds for pest-resistant varieties and intercropping to discourage insects and weeds from causing damage to other plants. The idea of applying specific substances to control pests also has a long history. In ancient Greece and Rome, for example, seeds were treated with plant and animal ingredients such as leek juice, powdered elephant tusk, and crushed cypress leaves to keep germinating plants safe from pests, while sulfur was used in various formulations to kill insects. Pyrethrum, a compound derived from chrysanthemum flowers that is toxic to insects, was used as an insecticide in ancient China and Persia. The application of salts and other minerals was another long-standing practice to control weeds.[1]

The widespread commercial trade in agricultural pesticides began in earnest in the nineteenth century. Initially these products were formulations of natural ingredients—primarily plants and minerals that were long used for this purpose—mixed in different combinations to be applied to plants or weeds. Technological changes brought about by the rise of organic chemistry in the early decades of the 1900s—first in Europe and then in North America—led to a major transformation of the industry that made it much more focused on research and development, intellectual property protection, and large-scale industrial production. This technological shift was accompanied by a governmental policy redirection from advocating natural control of pests to explicitly endorsing chemical approaches, with industry actively seeking to shape the rules. These changes encouraged a rapid concentration of the industry, such that by the end of World War II, the sector was dominated by relatively few large firms.

THE EARLY COMMERCIAL PESTICIDE INDUSTRY

Although mineral, plant, and animal ingredients were used for millennia to control pests, the commercial production of pesticides in agriculture—a general term for substances that control insects, weeds, fungi, and rodents—came only after the chemical revolution of the eighteenth century.[2] By the late 1700s, it was popular to use of pesticide formulations that combined several ingredients. For example, a wash mixture of tobacco, sulfur, and lime was used to kill insects and fungi.[3] Mixtures of this sort were expensive, however, and typically reserved for high-value horticultural crops. In Europe and North America, the growing need to control insect pests after the mid-1800s gave rise to a burgeoning commercial pesticide industry. In North America, the sector was initially small, but demand for pesticides grew as increased settlement across the midwestern portion of the continent began to close the frontier around this time, leading to more firms entering the industry.[4]

Intensive settler cultivation resulted in profound changes to landscapes in North America. What had been forests, grasslands, and areas of maize cultivation within the territory of Indigenous peoples were increasingly transformed into farms and homesteads throughout the 1800s. In the latter part of the century, settler agricultural patterns had become increasingly specialized for commercial markets, including markets in Europe. As human settlement densified on the North American continent, there were more contiguous lands under monoculture cultivation. That is, fields were planted with just one crop or type of crop—for example, corn in the Midwest, cotton in the South, wheat in the prairies, fruits and vegetables on the Atlantic coast, and fruit trees on the Pacific coast.[5] With new kinds of fertilizer products more frequently available by the late 1800s and early 1900s, as outlined in chapter 3, farmers also increasingly planted the same crops year after year in the same fields rather than in the rotation pattern that had previously been practiced in Europe as well as in the Americas.[6]

This transformation of the landscape into vast tracts of monoculture crops created a habitat that was ideal for insect and fungus infestations. Monocultures are simple ecological systems. Not only do they provide a vast landscape of pests' preferred foods, but they are also not very hospitable environments for those pests' natural predators.[7] Pests spread geographically by hitching rides on trains and ships in carloads of harvested crops that were increasingly being traded between North America and distant locations abroad. From at least the 1860s, European pests, such as the European corn borer, made their way to farm fields in North America, while the Colorado potato beetle established itself in Europe. As both monocultures and global trade in foodstuffs expanded in this era, pest infestations became a major global problem, causing massive crop damage.[8]

The common chemical products being sold commercially under proprietary names for pest control in the latter part of the nineteenth century were typically based, as they had been historically, on simple compounds and naturally occurring ingredients, and were sold as targeting particular types of pests. Mineral-based pesticides targeting insects included sulfur compounds, such as sulfur lime and copper sulfate. They also included arsenic compounds such as copper arsenate, calcium arsenate, and lead arsenate that went by more common names linked to their origins or color. Paris green, for example, was a copper arsenate compound, named for its vibrant, emerald-green color, as well as the fact that it was initially used in Paris to kill sewer rats.[9] It was developed in 1814 for use as a pigment in products like paint and wallpaper. Sold in powder form, Paris green was highly toxic and proved effective in killing insects, and it began to be used in the United States in the late 1860s against the Colorado potato beetle as well as to control pests in cotton fields.[10] London purple was a compound of calcium arsenate, a waste product of the aniline dye industry, which was commonly used to control boll weevils in cotton fields.[11] Petroleum-based substances like kerosene and petroleum distillate were also increasingly used for pest control, on their own or in combination with various chemical compounds. Salts, arsenic, sulfur compounds, and lime were also sold for weed control.[12] The growth in the use of mineral compounds at this time was in part a product of an expanding mining sector as well as advances in inorganic chemistry in the 1800s.[13]

Plant-based, botanical formulations for pest control were also common in the latter part of the nineteenth century, including pesticides with pyrethrum and nicotine as active ingredients.[14] Pyrethrum-based powders, for example, were increasingly marketed as insecticides after growing trade in the substance from Persia to Europe and the start of commercial production of dried chrysanthemum petals in the Caucasus region in the 1840s. The origins of the powder were largely unknown until the start of the nineteenth century, when an Armenian merchant discovered its origins and began to produce it commercially.[15] Europe was a key source of pyrethrum for international trade until World War I, after which it was supplanted by Japan and Kenya as the main producers. The United States began importing pyrethrum powder for use in pesticides as early as the 1860s.

The pesticides marketed in the nineteenth century were relatively easy to produce given that they were based on naturally occurring ingredients. They were not always sold as complete mixtures, and the individual components were often sold as powders that farmers mixed themselves with water or kerosene to suit their specific needs. The nascent pesticide industry in the latter part of the nineteenth century was thus highly fragmented, with many small producers and dealers operating within specific regions and countries. Firms tended to seek patents for their own formulations of ingredients, which enabled them to compete with others, though the formulas were often basic and were not always granted patents. For example, one firm was denied a patent for lead arsenate as a pesticide in the 1890s, and by the early 1900s, no fewer than eighteen companies were producing it.[16]

As was the case with seeds and fertilizers, sales of these early pesticides were often made by itinerant salespeople or by mail order, sometimes marketed as "magic" or "secret potions" to farmers who were desperate to try anything that might kill pests in their fields.[17] The sector was prone to frequent fraud. Salesmen often made highly exaggerated claims about the efficacy of their products but were long gone from the scene when farmers discovered that what they bought was ineffective or, worse, damaged their crops.[18]

NATURAL CONTROLS PUSHED ASIDE

At the same time that a commercial pesticide industry began to emerge in North America in the late 1800s, the field of economic entomology emerged, which was specifically focused on understanding insects and their relation to human activities, including the risks such pests pose for agriculture. Many of the early economic entomologists were naturalists and ecologists who were interested in studying broader ecosystems and typically were drawn to biological and cultural measures to control pests.[19] In the United States, for example, the Department of Agriculture (USDA) established the Division of Entomology by the 1870s, which gave advice to farmers through the agricultural experiment stations established in 1887 under the Hatch Act.

From 1879 to 1894, Charles Riley headed up the Division of Entomology. He strongly favored natural approaches to pest control, such as biological measures that used natural predators to kill pests and cultural practices designed to reduce insect habitat and other opportunities for pests to thrive. Riley was highly skeptical of the new chemical pesticides that were increasingly being marketed to farmers, and he made it his mission to test chemical products such as Paris green in order to ensure farmers were not being tricked into applying ineffective substances that could potentially harm plants and people. Riley's reports indicated that most of these tests of commercially marketed pesticides at the time failed to show significant pest reduction. For this reason, US government entomologists typically advised farmers to use biological and cultural controls as a first defense against pests and use chemical pesticides only as a last resort.[20]

When Riley stepped down from his role in 1894, the Division of Entomology was restructured and renamed the Bureau of Entomology, to reflect the expansion of entomological concerns at the USDA. Riley's assistant, Leland O. Howard, took his place and stayed in that role until 1927. Howard played an instrumental role in speeding up and cementing the shift toward chemical pest control in the United States in the early decades of the twentieth century by using his government office to advocate strongly for the use of commercial pesticides.[21] Although Howard initially took on his role by trying out natural methods of pest control, he became highly skeptical of these measures after several of his initiatives, such as his attempt to control the gypsy moth using natural predators, ended in failure. Stung by this experience, he increasingly viewed biological and cultural pest controls as being expensive and time-consuming. Instead, he was much more interested in finding chemical solutions to pest problems that could yield faster and more effective results, and he actively moved the bureau in that direction.

The chemical approach to pest control began to appeal to many farmers as well, who increasingly questioned the efficacy of natural approaches as their pest problems mounted. They were especially wary of cultural measures that required them to change their field practices, such as digging ditches or spacing their crops differently, which could increase their labor expenses and affect their output.[22] Many farmers at that time were also tenants on lands owned by others, and they were reluctant to make changes to a plot of farmland that they may not have access to the following year. To be successful, cultural measures also required all the farmers in the region affected by certain pests to follow those practices. Achieving full buy-in to cultural practices was far from easy in the absence of strict laws, which many states did not have the political support to pass.

Chemical pesticides were attractive to farmers because they could simply add them to their existing field practices, which was the easiest technological pathway for them given the growing pest problems they faced. Furthermore, according to some analysts, the use of chemical pesticides that farmers could apply to their own fields appealed to American farmers' individualist ethos.[23] With economic pressure to ensure that they did not lose a significant proportion of their harvest to pests, farmers warmed up to the idea of chemical pesticides so that they could take matters into their own hands. In short, it meant that they would not have to rely on their neighbors to "do the right thing" to control pests. They could control them on their own fields by applying chemicals themselves. Some states passed laws requiring farmers to spray their crops or incur the expense of having it done by the state to avoid the problem of unsprayed fields acting as a refuge for pests. These laws sought to protect farmers who did spray rather than those who did not.[24]

With rising demand for chemical pest control methods and a government arm in favor of that approach, many manufacturers of chemical pesticides entered the US market in the early 1900s. The problem of fraud and deception in the sector continued, however, and unsafe and ineffective pesticides were widely available as more sellers entered the market. As more firms joined the field, tensions grew between the larger, more established firms that portrayed themselves as more responsible businesses, and smaller ones, which the former blamed for most of the fraud.[25] The continuation of deceptive and fraudulent practices prompted the US government to pass the Federal Insecticide Act in 1910 to put strict rules and labeling standards into place to ensure that manufacturers gave accurate ingredient lists on their products. Some of the larger pesticide manufacturers actively sought to shape that legislation by funding a committee under the American Association of Economic Entomologists that ended up preparing a draft of the bill.[26] Although some of the pesticide manufacturers bristled at the increased government oversight in their industry that the bill legislated, others saw it as an advantage because they were concerned about the fierce competition in the sector brought on by what they saw as "less scrupulous competitors."[27]

Not surprisingly, the larger firms that sought to position themselves as being more reputable were able to easily meet the new regulations for pesticides. In fact, the larger firms supported more stringent regulations as a deliberate strategy to eliminate the smaller firms that they saw as damaging the reputation of the industry as a whole.[28] But the law itself, which focused on accuracy in labeling, did not require firms to prove that their pesticides were actually safe. The passage of the act was to mainly assure farmers that the products were of high quality. By 1910, the US pesticides industry was worth around $20 million, with Paris green and lead arsenate the most widely sold commercial products. Around 90 percent of that market was controlled by just a dozen or so firms that cooperated with one another to ensure that they marketed only "pure" pesticides.[29]

The shift to a greater reliance on chemical solutions to control pests was not without risks. The arsenic-based chemicals in wide use at the time were acutely toxic, including to humans and animals, and their efficacy was short lived. These features meant that farmers had to repeatedly apply chemical compounds to their fields, often by hand, increasing their risk of being poisoned. The use of these products also harmed beneficial insects, including bees, and often risked damage to crops and poisoning of soils. Concern about arsenic residues on fruits and vegetables was growing by the late nineteenth century.[30] Nevertheless, demand for pesticides continued to grow as monocultures increasingly dominated fields and pest infestations spread. As such, there were huge profits to be made in the pesticides industry.

World War I finally displaced what remained of natural measures of pest control and created space for a rapid expansion of the chemical pesticide industry. This shift occurred in part because many of the pests that became problematic, as noted earlier, had been inadvertently imported from Europe and had no natural predators in North America and vice versa. In addition, the war shut down the option of obtaining natural predators from other parts of the world to introduce as natural pest control. Perhaps more important, though, was the fact that the war also brought a growing sense of the need for expediency when dealing with pests during a time of conflict. Historian James McWilliams explains, "When the United States joined the Allies in 1917 they fought more than just the Axis powers. They also fought the insect pests that fought the allies. And if there ever was a specific geopolitical context that had complete disdain for gradualist, multifaceted, and ecologically sensitive approaches to pest control, war was it. After the war, cultural and biological approaches to insect control yielded as they never had before to chemical methods."[31]

Indeed, the war increased demand for quick solutions to pest problems and elevated the cause of pest control to one of national security, raising its profile in terms of government priorities. Funding for the US Bureau of Entomology under Howard's leadership, for example, expanded significantly in this context. When its budget grew, the bureau further extended the chemical mind-set as the first line of defense against pests, not just in agricultural fields to secure food supplies, but also to protect food warehouses, livestock, forests, and soldiers in trenches, all of which were of crucial importance for the war effort. The bureau made efforts to test a range of chemicals during the war for their pesticidal qualities, which saved significant research costs for the major chemical firms. Government testing also indicated to industry what kinds of chemicals the government was most likely to endorse. This government research effort ended up creating a close alliance between the chemical industry and the Bureau of Entomology during the war years.[32]

World War I stimulated increased demand for pesticides from farmers. Because fertilizer costs had increased during the war due to the disrupted supplies of nitrates from Chile and potash from Germany, as explained in chapter 3, farmers sought to use more insecticides to ensure that they did not experience crop losses on top of the decreased yields from using less fertilizer. There was also a shift toward chemical insecticides to deal with specific pests that mattered for the war effort. One example is the castor bean, the oil from which was used as a lubricant in airplane engines. The United States previously imported the beans from Mexico, but during the war, those beans were diverted to Europe. When farmers in the United States switched to growing castor beans to ensure domestic supply of the oil, they found the bean crops were ravaged by the southern armyworm. Demand for pesticides to address these pests grew and became a matter of national concern.[33] The idea of using chemical pesticides thus gained widespread public support as being important weapons in the "war against insects" within the broader wartime context and military metaphors against pests became common. Chemical pesticides, as environmental historian Thomas Dunlap notes, became associated with "victory."[34]

While demand for pest control substances increased in this period, some of the pesticides and their main ingredients were in short supply. The war cut off sources of some chemical pesticides based on natural substances, such as pyrethrums and rotenode, which the United States imported from Asia and South America and which were already quite expensive for farmers. Paris green also became scarce in 1917 and 1918. The war also interrupted imports of chemicals such as dyestuffs and other products derived from coal-tar derivatives, produced mainly by German firms like Bayer, Hoechst, and BASF and on which the United States relied. This shortage of chemicals in general prompted more US firms to get into the industry, with some seventeen firms entering the field in 1915.[35]

Chemical pesticides remained popular in the following decades. In the 1930s, under the Agricultural Adjustment Act brought in by Henry A. Wallace as agriculture secretary, the restrictions placed on the acreages farmers could cultivate encouraged them to try to increase yields on the fields they could plant. This meant using not just hybrid seeds, as outlined in the previous chapter, but also chemical fertilizers and pesticides.[36] As farmers increased their yields, the surpluses they generated pushed commodity prices downward, which further encouraged them to increase yields to maintain their incomes. Thus, farmers became locked into what analysts call a "pesticides treadmill," whereby they were effectively trapped in a cycle of chemical use from which it became increasingly difficult to exit.[37] The growing use of pesticides led to heightened concerns, however, over chemical residues on crops, particularly fruits, which were often liberally sprayed. These concerns led to increased regulations in the 1920s and 1930s that set safety thresholds for pesticide residues.

ORGANIC CHEMISTRY AND THE RISE OF SYNTHETIC PESTICIDES

Following the rise in status of chemical pesticides during World War I, more firms moved into the sector in the 1920s and 1930s. In Europe, German, Swiss, and British chemical firms moved toward the goal of synthesizing pesticides using modern chemistry methods rather than formulating them from naturally occurring ingredients. The European firms were among the first to venture into organic chemistry for this purpose, and indeed some German chemical firms had already begun to produce synthetic organic insecticides in the early 1900s.[38] This shift fit within the broader strategy of these firms to synthesize products using chemistry based on more readily available resources such as coal and its by-products rather than relying on foreign sources for natural raw materials. By taking such an approach, these countries aimed for chemical self-reliance. This strategy gave distinct advantages to larger firms, which had the capacity to engage in research and development of these new chemicals and could produce them on a large scale. These factors effectively created barriers to entry for smaller firms.

Taking up this approach were some of the large, established European chemical firms, such as the Swiss firm J. R. Geigy, originally founded in the 1750s, which moved into pesticide research in the 1930s. Other large firms moving into pesticide research at this time included the German conglomerate IG Farben and the British conglomerate Imperial Chemical Industries (both of which also produced fertilizers, as discussed in chapter 3). These European firms were leaders in the development of organic chemistry, including the synthesis of chemicals from coal tar—a by-product of steel manufacturing. Because some of these isolates were known to have pesticidal qualities, the shift into the sector seemed to be an obvious one, and these firms were looking to expand their product lines in the face of stiff competition in the dyestuffs sector that had previously been their mainstay of business. These firms began a more systematic search for pesticides in the early to mid-1930s, screening thousands of compounds for their insecticidal properties.[39]

North America also saw some of its larger and already established chemicals and pharmaceutical firms enter the pesticide industry in the 1920s and 1930s. As in Europe, the industry there similarly shifted from one focused on making products from natural ingredients to a more research-intensive effort to develop synthetic pesticides using modern chemistry. DuPont, for example, founded in 1802 as a gunpowder manufacturer, began to conduct research into agricultural chemicals, among other pursuits, in the 1930s. DuPont had acquired controlling shares in most of the other major US powder (explosives) companies in the first decade of the twentieth century and faced antitrust charges in 1907 due to its near monopoly on explosives. Found to be in violation of the Sherman Antitrust Act in 1912, the firm was required by the US government to break up, and it subsequently spun off two other firms—namely, the Hercules Powder Company and the Atlas Powder Company.[40] Nonetheless, the firm was widely viewed as having profited handsomely from war, earning it the derogatory moniker "merchant of death."

In the 1920s, DuPont sought to change its public image to one that was more scientific and consumer oriented. In this effort, the firm bought up a number of other chemical companies to diversify its business after World War I, and in 1928, the firm launched its fundamental research program around the same time that it also sought to produce synthetic nitrogen (as outlined in chapter 3).[41] The firm purchased the Grasselli Chemical Company in 1928, a US-based manufacturer of sulfur-based chemicals, including pesticides and fertilizers, that dated back to the mid-1800s.[42] These acquisitions made DuPont one of the largest chemical firms in North America at the time, and it was widely seen to be one of the world's major chemical firms alongside the newly merged massive European firms IG Farben and Imperial Chemical Industries (see chapter 3).

Monsanto, originally established in 1901 as a manufacturer of artificial sweeteners, expanded into the production of other chemicals, including those derived from coal tar derivatives by the 1920s and 1930s.[43] The firm began to produce sulfuric acid, a key pesticide ingredient, through the acquisition of a large acid-producing firm in 1918.[44] Union Carbide and Carbon Corporation was formed in 1917 as the product of the merger of several firms—Linde Air Products Company, National Carbon Company, Prest-O-Lite Company, and Union Carbide Company. The merged firm moved into the manufacture of a range of petrochemical products, including pesticides.[45] Rohm and Haas, originally a German chemical firm founded in 1904 that shifted its headquarters to the United States in 1909, also began to produce insecticides and fungicides in the 1920s.[46] Other established firms like the US-based paint company Sherwin-Williams also started to produce insecticides, as did a number of pharmaceutical firms, including Parke, Davis and Company and Sharpe and Dohme.[47]

The move by a number of large, established firms into the production of pesticides in the 1920s and 1930s was part of a broader shift among US chemical firms to emulate the German and Swiss companies that took a research-intensive approach to developing new chemical products.[48] The US firms were also eager to catch up with their European counterparts, which were ahead in research into possible new synthetic products developed through advances in organic chemistry. Firms like DuPont and Rohm and Haas fully committed to the strategy in the belief that synthetic chemicals based on organic chemistry would be more effective than those made from natural products, especially since there were growing reports at the time of pests becoming resistant to the botanical- and mineral-based products. Synthetic chemicals could also be produced at a lower cost on a large scale, promising huge profits if successful products could be developed. There were also hopes that pesticide products developed through organic chemistry could help solve problems like arsenic residues on fruits and vegetables from the mineral-based pesticides that were widely seen to be threats to public health by the early twentieth century.

To advance their research and development goals, the US pesticide firms began to develop closer relationships with university research labs, again mirroring the German and Swiss models that had close academic ties. This early connection between industry and university researchers established a model that agrochemical firms since that time have employed extensively—to fund university research in ways that advanced their own goals, not unlike the funding of a research lab by Funk Seeds several decades earlier (see chapter 4). Hercules Powder Company, for example, built relationships with US government entomologists at the state agricultural research stations and funded research at land-grant colleges that advanced its interests in developing insecticides.[49] In the 1920s, Monsanto's vice president in charge of manufacturing stressed the importance of this strategy: "In the organic chemical industry, the fellow who moves fastest gets the profits. The man who is second gets a much lesser prize, and the third and fourth fellows get left out in the cold."[50] It is thus not surprising that many of these same firms that engaged research programs at that time are still dominant players in the sector today.

DDT AND OTHER EARLY SYNTHETIC PESTICIDES

The shift in corporate strategy to develop pesticides synthesized from organic compounds led to a fundamental reshaping of the industry in both Europe and North America. The work these firms did in systematically scanning chemical compounds for those that might have pesticidal qualities began to show results by the late 1930s. These included the development of two main types of synthetic pesticides—organochlorines and organophosphates. The former had low acute toxicity but were persistent in the environment, while the latter were more acutely toxic but degraded more quickly in the environment.

Because a significant proportion of the business of the largest chemical firms in Europe was also in the development of dyestuffs for coloring fabric, their research had already been seeking substances that could make woolen cloth impervious to moths that damaged the fabric. Some of the compounds that IG Farben and J. R. Geigy were experimenting with along these lines were related to the discovery of the insecticidal qualities of the chemical compound DDT.

Paul Müller, a chemist at Geigy, was tasked with developing pesticides in the 1930s. In 1939, after synthesizing hundreds, if not thousands, of compounds, Müller and his team happened on the chemical structure of DDT—an organochlorine—and realized that it had insecticidal properties. The DDT molecule had actually been synthesized years earlier, in 1874, by Austrian graduate student Othmar Zeidler as part of his scientific experimentation, but its insecticidal qualities were not recognized until Müller's rediscovery of it in 1939.[51] Müller's scientific experiments showed that DDT effectively killed flies and other insects on contact, and he tested it in the field on the Colorado potato beetle and found it highly effective. In the wake of this discovery, which coincided with the start of World War II, Geigy moved quickly to patent the use of DDT as a pesticide in Switzerland, and then in the United States, Germany, and Great Britain. By 1942, Geigy began to market DDT under the name of Gesarol. Soon there were patent infringements during World War II, as Germany's IG Farben began to manufacture a product that contained DDT without having acquired a license to do so.[52]

Geigy shared samples of DDT with the US Bureau of Entomology in 1942, and the government tests showed that it was highly effective against lice and other pests. The United States moved quickly to ensure domestic production as it judged that DDT could greatly assist in the war effort because lice infestations were a major problem among the army troops. The prospect of a synthetic chemical for this purpose was highly attractive to the US military because its main source of pyrethrum to treat lice came primarily from Japan, the supply of which was cut off during the war. Geigy committed to produce the chemical in the United States, but its production capacity was below the amount demanded by the US Army.

The US government approached DuPont to enlist its assistance in making up the DDT shortfall. DuPont initially refused to produce the pesticide unless it was given a license from Geigy to continue to manufacture it even after the war ended, terms that Geigy eventually granted to the firm. Even with DuPont's contribution to manufacturing DDT in the United States, domestic production was still not sufficient for the US Army's demand, prompting the US War Production Board to secure Geigy's permission to allow additional US chemical firms to produce DDT. Several chemical firms were approached in this capacity to produce the chemical in the United States, including Monsanto, Hercules, and Merck. For these firms, the license to produce DDT was a huge boon, as they were able to profit not just from providing a chemical in demand during the war but one that could be refashioned for mass-marketed products in the postwar era. By the end of 1944, the firms producing DDT through government contracts were pumping out 2 million pounds of the chemical for military use.[53]

Throughout the remainder of the war, DDT was used to fight not just lice but also typhus and malaria, and the companies producing it earned major profits. DDT's success in fighting these problems gave it a generally positive reputation as a chemical that saved lives, which in turn boosted the reputations of the firms that produced it. After the war, with the decline in military demand for the chemical, DDT was released for civilian use and was marketed as a miracle pesticide for both agricultural and home use, building on its positive reputation during the war. Paul Müller went on to win a Nobel Prize in medicine in 1948 for his discovery of the insecticidal qualities of DDT, and sales of the chemical ballooned.

DDT was used liberally throughout the war because it was less acutely toxic to humans than chemicals that previously dominated the pesticide market. For example, it was applied directly soldiers' bodies to control lice without causing immediate serious illness or death. As a result, the chemical was widely assumed to be safe for use in a broad range of contexts. Market demand for synthetic pesticides increased sharply in the 1940s, and by 1945, fourteen firms were producing DDT in the United States, with more producing formulations that incorporated the chemical for sale as pesticides. Fewer than ten firms, however, manufactured the vast bulk of the DDT produced at that time.[54]

Other firms continued with their research and development of other types of synthetic pesticides throughout the 1930s and 1940s, and many new pesticides came on the market out of this research. At virtually the same time that DDT was discovered, Imperial Chemical Industries developed lindane, another widely used organochlorine pesticide. Other organochlorine pest control products developed in this period include chlordane, benzene hexachloride, aldrin, dieldrin, and heptachlor, among others.

In 1936, IG Farben researcher, working with what until then was a little-known class of chemicals known as organophosphates, discovered that these types of chemicals could be quite effective in killing insects. This discovery eventually led to the synthesis of additional potent pesticides, including parathion and malathion. While effective against pests, organophosphates were also highly toxic to humans, a major drawback for widespread agricultural use. Some of the organophosphate compounds developed at IG Farben were found to be lethal to humans and were subsequently used in chemical weapons such as nerve gas by the Nazi army. The firm continued to develop these chemicals as pesticides throughout the 1940s.[55]

Synthetic herbicides came onto the scene in the 1940s, and their use was promoted by the USDA. These early herbicides included 2,4-D and 2,4,5-T, produced by Monsanto and Dow Chemical. These chemicals were among the first selective herbicides that controlled broadleaf weeds in corn and wheat fields.[56]

Given a major boost by wartime demand, synthetic chemicals produced by a small number of very large research-oriented chemical firms soon became the dominant types of pesticides used in agricultural fields across North America and Europe, and eventually the rest of the world. Those few firms profited immensely from producing those pesticides for military use during World War II. By the 1940s, older chemicals based on naturally derived ingredients were no longer produced by the major players in the industry, and the USDA effectively abandoned nonchemical research for insect control.[57] The transformation of the pesticide industry was especially swift. It went from a small and fragmented group of firms focused on making formulations from naturally derived ingredients to one controlled by just a few very large-scale producers making synthetic chemicals derived through highly complex organic chemistry. Those firms at the top were able to grow large not just from sales of their new chemicals but also through mergers and acquisitions. According to environmental historian Bartow Elmore, Monsanto's expansion in the 1940s was largely the product of acquiring other firms.[58]

The production of synthetic organic pesticides required intensive research and a significant amount of capital to produce compared with the earlier pesticides based on naturally occurring ingredients. As a result, these firms increasingly sought to develop broad-spectrum chemicals that could be used on multiple types of pests in a variety of contexts, to ensure high levels of sales that could support their high research and development costs.[59] The companies also used aggressive sales tactics to generate demand for their products. The result was huge growth and high profit margins in the pesticide industry in the United States from 1939 to 1954, with the number of firms producing insecticides and fungicides ballooning from 83 to 275. From the late 1940s onward, however, five companies were by far the dominant players in the sector in the US market: DuPont, Union Carbide, Dow, Allied, and Monsanto.[60] In the United Kingdom, Imperial Chemical Industries became a major producer of pesticides after the war; Geigy was dominant in Switzerland; and BASF, Bayer, and Hoechst were the top producers in Germany after IG Farben was broken up by the Allies after World War II.[61]

Although the licenses for production of DDT were shared widely during the war, patent protection was vital to the dominant firms in the postwar era. This was especially the case for newer chemicals, as firms sought to recoup their high research and development costs. Monsanto and DuPont, for example, made huge investments in the expansion of their research efforts in the area of agricultural chemicals in the mid- to late 1940s.[62] As they ramped up their R&D activities, the large chemical firms became highly protective of their intellectual property, a key part of their business model, and they grew increasingly concerned about the costs imposed on them by what they saw as overly stringent safety and environmental regulations. These regulations took time for firms to meet, ultimately eating into the time period for their patents. According to former Imperial Chemical Industries executive John Braunholtz, "Patent protection is as vital to the agrochemical industry as it is in pharmaceuticals, and every move to diminish the scope or life of product, process or use patents is another blow to the validity of our research investment."[63]

Farmers became increasingly dependent on synthetic chemical pesticides such as DDT because they were relatively cheap and easy to incorporate into existing farm practices. In the United States, for example, DDT sales increased tenfold, from around $10 million in 1944 to around $110 million in 1951, with the bulk of this latter amount going to agricultural uses. The use of other pesticides also increased rapidly in the postwar era as new products were rolled out by the large firms that dominated the sector. Between 1945 and 1953, around twenty-five new synthetic pesticides were introduced onto the market. US production of pesticides grew from 100 million pounds in 1945 to around 300 million pounds in 1950 and doubled again in the period to 1960.[64] As the industry grew rapidly in this period, the chemical firms at the top of the sector grew in size and influence.

The growth in the production of synthetic pesticides after 1944 prompted efforts in the United States to amend its legislation because the 1910 Federal Insecticides Act applied only to substances that were by this point no longer widely in use. Moreover, there was little understanding at the time of the long-term impact of new synthetic pesticides. Regulators wanted to tighten controls by requiring manufacturers not only to label their products accurately, but also to register them (although this process did not require test results, just the label and summary of claims). Although initially skeptical of the idea of registering new products, the large chemical firms that were producing synthetic pesticides were willing to accept new legislation because, like their stance in the 1910 act, they believed it could serve to screen out smaller firms. At the same time, stricter rules would create a powerful barrier to entry for newer firms that might not have the capital to comply with new legislation as easily.[65] These firms portrayed their support for legislation as upholding high standards, but in practice, it enabled them to bat away potential competition from newcomers.

The large US firms had organized themselves politically through several pesticide industry trade associations, a key force in shaping the 1947 Federal Insecticide, Fungicide, and Rodenticide Act, which replaced the

1910 Federal Insecticides Act. The Agricultural Insecticide and Fungicide Association (the forerunner of what is today CropLife America) was formed in 1933 to represent fourteen firms in the industry. The National Association of Insecticide and Disinfectant Manufacturers (which is today the Household and Commercial Products Association), originally established in 1914 as the Insecticides Manufacturers Association, also played a role in shaping Federal Insecticide, Fungicide, and Rodenticide Act. Political scientist Christopher Bosso describes the passage of that legislation as the product of clientele politics, with a small group of powerful actors—in this case, the US Congress, USDA bureaucrats, and the large pesticide companies—calling the shots.[66]

THE SOCIAL AND ECOLOGICAL COSTS OF PESTICIDES

Enormous costs are associated with the growth of the pesticide industry. Although there were some early warnings regarding their safety, the broader impacts were not felt immediately, and thus action to address them was painfully slow. The health risks associated with early chemical pesticides were widely recognized when they were introduced, including their acute toxicity and short-lived action, which required repeated applications. They were also expensive for farmers, and sometimes, due to their reliance on naturally occurring substances, some of which were imported, they were not always readily available. The pesticide industry flourished nonetheless, as chemical control became the dominant approach to dealing with agricultural pests. When DDT and other synthetic pesticides came along in the 1940s, many saw them as a distinct improvement over earlier chemical formulations, and they were glad to put those earlier products aside in favor of new kinds of pesticides. These newer products were affordable and persistent, meaning that they could be sprayed less often.

But while there was great support for DDT and other synthetic pesticides when they were introduced and the market for them grew rapidly, there were early indications that DDT and other synthetic pesticides also carried serious risks. Although the US ban on DDT came only in 1972 following widespread public debate about its safety in the 1960s (discussed in more detail in chapter 6), the chemical raised concern on the part of some scientists almost from the time it was introduced to the market in the 1940s. For example, analyzing news items about DDT in the *New York Times* in the early postwar years, sociologists Valerie Gunter and Craig Harris found that approximately one in six articles on the topic raised safety concerns over 1944 to 1949, and by 1954, that ratio was approximately one in three.[67] These early concerns revolved around potential toxic effects of DDT on wildlife, pests that had become resistant to DDT, and potential cancer concerns.

Although DDT's acute toxicity was low, there was early evidence that it had effects on mammals and birds. Much of the early scientific work on DDT's safety focused on its impact on human bodies, although wartime testing of the chemical did include tests on animals, which showed liver and kidney damage in rats exposed to it.[68] Impact studies on wildlife found that smaller creatures, such as fish and some birds, were more at risk of mortality from exposure.[69] Some work also showed that humans exposed to large amounts of DDT suffered damage to the central nervous system. There was also awareness that DDT accumulated in the body and that it could be passed on to offspring in breast milk. Postwar tests reinforced these findings, although there were still many questions that remained unanswered about the impact of low levels of exposure over long periods of time. Some scientists working on DDT expressed fears about the cumulative effects of eating food sprayed with the pesticide and found the lack of extensive testing on chronic exposure deeply concerning. Indeed, by the early 1950s, DDT was found in the fat tissue of people who did not have occupational exposure to the substance.[70]

These concerns about the human safety of DDT were eventually debated publicly in US congressional hearings in 1950 and 1951 regarding whether legislation governing food additives and chemicals was sufficient. The regulations required firms to provide accurate labels but did not require firms to prove first that they were actually safe before they were put on the market. The chemical industry lobby, including the National Agricultural Chemical Association and the Manufacturing Chemists' Association, deeply opposed any new regulations. The hearings saw an array of evidence on both sides of the question, including Wayland J. Hayes Jr., a doctor frequently referenced by the pesticide industry who defended DDT as perfectly safe. The hearings did result in a decision to update legislation, including the requirement that firms register new pesticides and provide safety testing data before putting them on the commercial market.[71]

Beyond questions of safety, other costs were associated with pesticides. As in the case of seeds, there was a degree of "deskilling" that occurred with the widespread adoption of chemical pesticides, especially the synthetic varieties in the post-1945 era. As farmers came to increasingly rely on purchased synthetic chemicals to manage pests, deep knowledge of a wider range of pest control methods—including cultural practices and natural measures commonly used in the late nineteenth century—was lost. Knowledge about pest control was effectively transferred from farmers to chemical companies.[72] As farmers lost touch with the broader range of pest control strategies, they came to depend on the chemical companies for information on which products killed what pests. Indeed, it was not realistic to expect farmers to know in scientific detail what ingredients were in the bottles of chemical pesticides they purchased for use on their fields or the specifics of their potential broader impact, especially with so many new products coming on the market all at once. Farmers essentially obtained their primary information about pest control from private sector chemical companies, which had a vested interest in selling more products and thus were inclined to present their products as effective and safe.

Although DDT and other pesticides were cheaper than earlier formulations based on botanical and mineral substances, pest control became a larger expense overall because of the increased array of products to address specific pests. With lower cost per unit combined with diminished knowledge of the product's formulation and impact, many farmers began to overspray their fields as a kind of crop insurance. In other words, farmers went from spraying their crops only when there were pest outbreaks to spraying regularly to prevent such outbreaks. Chemical firms encouraged such practices by suggesting that farmers spray on a regular schedule, emphasizing that they did not need to make their own judgments about when to spray.[73]

With increased application of pesticides to crops, producers' livelihoods became dependent on the success of the pesticides. That is, this model of agriculture only "worked" if the pesticides did not fail. In the initial years, the pesticides did perform their assigned tasks, which played a big role in the abandonment of cultural practices. But the strong performance of synthetic pesticides did not last. Pest resistance to these pesticides emerged as a problem almost immediately. For example, while resistance was also a problem with earlier pesticides, it occurred rather quickly with DDT, perhaps because of the chemical's widespread use and persistence in the environment. By the late 1940s, studies showed that houseflies had already developed resistance to the chemical.[74]

As pests became resistant to pesticides, pest problems became increasingly harder to deal with because of the phenomenon of pest resurgence. In many cases, insecticides killed the target pest, but because they were nonselective and broad-spectrum chemicals, they also killed the pest's natural predators and other beneficial organisms, such as honeybees.[75] The result was that any surviving predators starved to death, while any surviving pests had ideal conditions for growth because they had no natural enemies.[76] In this way, the application of the pesticide had the effect of multiplying pest problems, which in turn required the application of additional types of pesticides to address. Pest resurgence, for example, happened in the apple industry in the United States in the 1950s with the excessive spraying of DDT.[77] Secondary pest outbreaks also became a problem with increased synthetic pesticide use, whereby insects that were not previously considered pests suddenly begin to cause crop damage. The cause, again, was the use of pesticides that killed insects indiscriminately, destroying natural enemies of insect pests.

When resistance, resurgence, and secondary pest outbreaks became problems, the typical response was often to spray yet more chemical pesticides. Sometimes more of the same chemical was applied in hopes of completing the job, but often a new combination of chemicals was used.[78] Policy analyst Angus MacIntyre likens this process to drug addiction: "Initial uses were followed by successively larger doses, then by troubled dependence, and eventually by some type of crisis."[79] The result of this increased use of pesticides was an incredible growth in the industry, which reaped huge financial rewards for the large, dominant chemical companies that had the capital to invest in research and development of new products.

While some of these costs were acknowledged early on, weak regulation, poor understanding of the impacts, and, on balance, more enthusiasm for chemical pest control methods, all contributed to a continued use of DDT and other synthetic pesticides as an integrated component of the emerging industrial agricultural system. A small number of firms came to dominate the sector as this reliance on synthetic pesticides increased. The message from those firms and others who defended the use of pesticides was that if used properly, they would be safe and effective. Because the effects were often distanced in that they were felt off the farm, and not immediately since bioaccumulation takes time to manifest and cause harm, it was hard to disprove those claims in the short term. And some of the problems we now associate with DDT and other synthetic pesticides, particularly bioaccumulation and its associated cancer risk, were novel concepts and out of the scope of the understanding of scientists at the time. The costs, when they did present themselves, were widely distributed and not borne by the firms that introduced the pesticides. In short, the dominant firms were able to externalize those costs as they reaped huge profits in a booming industry. The pesticide paradigm continued because farmers and the chemical industry had a shared interest in pesticides and were supported by the USDA, which also encouraged their use.[80] There was little incentive in this context to consider other options for pest control.

CONCLUSION

This chapter shows that the chemical pesticide industry came to be dominated by a small number of large firms by the 1940s, which benefited from a mix of market, technological, and regulatory advantages. While the industry was more fragmented in its early days, the move toward synthetic organic chemistry in the 1930s and 1940s marked a major shift for the industry and favored the development of large, dominant firms. The firms that rose to the top of the sector were typically already large, established chemical firms that had access to capital for the research and development necessary to develop new products. These firms also benefited from intellectual property protection in the form of patents and gained financially from licensing their protected chemical formulations to other firms. They were aided by government policy shifts that favored chemical pesticides over natural controls, as well as government testing that saved them R&D costs. These firms worked together to support more stringent legislation on pesticides through industry lobby associations, especially when doing so ensured that they were able to comply with this regulation while their smaller competitors were not. And as pesticide sales grew sharply, the largest firms benefited from economies of scale that made smaller competitors increasingly fall behind.

As a relatively small number of very large firms came to dominate the sector in this period, the wider costs of the pesticide industry were increasingly recognized, leading critics to call for more stringent regulations. At the same time, however, farmers became less skilled in controlling pests without chemicals, finding themselves on a pesticide treadmill, effectively locked into chemical use and reliant on the dominant firms to manage pests in their fields, all while chemical pesticide use climbed sharply and the dominant firms' profits soared.

II

CONSOLIDATION AND EXPANSION FROM THE MID-TWENTIETH CENTURY

6

LOCK-IN AND SHIP OUT

The decades following World War II saw further consolidation and entrenchment of both the industrial agricultural model and the firms that provided its basic components. As they had done in their initial rise to bigness, the agribusiness titans across all four of the input industries continued to benefit from a constellation of market, technology, and policy factors as their industries matured in the postwar decades. In this era, the interplay among these factors took on new dynamics. Growing technological integration of inputs into a more settled model of industrial agriculture and a more globalized economy, both supported by state policies in new ways, continued to reinforce concentrating tendencies in the sector.

As should be clear by this point, the new technologies that came to be the centerpieces of the input industries by the mid-twentieth century—farm machinery, chemical fertilizers, new seed varieties, and synthetic pesticides—became dominant farming methods in North America to the extent that it was difficult for farmers to eschew them altogether. In short, they had become locked-in technologies. Part of the reason they became so prevalent in farming practices is that the four inputs became progressively integrated with one another. That is, they were increasingly seen as a package rather than simply four distinct inputs from which farmers could pick and choose according to the specific needs of their farms. This lock-in of the industrial agricultural model ensured a continued market for the dominant firms across the four input industries that enabled them to maintain the oligopolistic market structures that had emerged in previous decades.

The lock-in of industrial agricultural inputs matters because it helps to explain why the industrial agricultural model was globalized, or shipped out, in the decades following World War II, despite its known costs, outlined in previous chapters. Although several of the large firms in the agricultural inputs sector had long engaged in international commerce, there was a concerted effort on the part of these firms to establish themselves as leading global firms in the postwar period. The modernization of the agricultural sector via the Green Revolution in countries such as Mexico, India, the Philippines, and Indonesia essentially created new markets in developing countries for industrial agricultural inputs. As they pursued a global strategy, dominant input firms positioned themselves to benefit from Green Revolution policies and programs by tapping into programs of assistance orchestrated by governments, philanthropies, and international institutions.

LOCK-IN OF THE INDUSTRIAL AGRICULTURAL MODEL

A small group of dominant firms is often typical in sectors where novel technologies emerge, in part because new economic dynamics are set in motion by technological breakthroughs. As previous chapters showed, such breakthroughs can create temporary asymmetries that give market advantages to first-mover firms, such as patent protection and other dynamics that typically follow new inventions and chance events. As technological paradigms move into a stage of maturity, lock-ins can further entrench the power of existing firms and contribute to corporate concentration.[1] These dynamics help to explain how the firms across four agricultural inputs were able to maintain their market dominance as industrial agricultural practices became increasingly locked in.

Lock-ins happen for several key reasons. One is what science and technology studies scholar W. Brian Arthur calls "increasing returns to adoption."[2] As individuals gain experience with a technology and become more adept at using it, they tend to benefit more, making it less likely that they will turn back to previous technologies. Additionally, wider communities that work with new technologies often gain from learning from each other, which can also encourage more widespread use. There are also network type effects, whereby additional products and services that are compatible with a technology emerge and become popular as use of that technology spreads, further entrenching a particular technological paradigm.[3] High demand for a particular technology enables scale economies of production, which also bring down the costs per unit, further ensuring that they remain in widespread use.[4] Additionally, technological interrelatedness, where several related technologies emerge to explicitly work with each other, also creates incentives to adopt a suite of technologies together.[5]

Science and technology scholars have also pointed out the ways in which institutional and behavioral factors can entrench certain technologies. Institutional decisions are often affected by the lobbying activities of dominant firms that seek to promote the use of certain technologies over others.[6] The result is often a network of policymakers, powerful firms, and institutional bureaucracies that reinforce both the political and economic dominance of the powerful actors. At the same time, a technological model can serve a person's individual needs in the short term, despite that individual's awareness of the wider societal considerations and long-term consequences of its broader use. Indeed, once technological and institutional forces lock in a certain set of technologies, making a decision not to follow along can actually undermine an individual's capacity to survive outside that technological paradigm.[7] In other words, lock-ins raise the costs of switching back to previous technologies or shifting to a different set of technologies.

Technological lock-ins can contribute to corporate concentration and power in several ways. Perhaps most directly, increasing returns to adoption can boost the profitability of firms producing the dominant technology as growing adoption expands the size of the market. As a technological paradigm matures, the pioneering firms tend to shift their innovation strategies to reinforce their position in the market rather than to disrupt the sector yet again.[8] As such, dominant firms gain power to act as gatekeepers by erecting various barriers to entry for others, keeping the sector concentrated and dominated by a small number of firms.

These broader insights on technological lock-ins are extremely useful for understanding the dynamics surrounding corporate concentration and power in the agricultural inputs sector outlined in previous chapters. The concept of lock-ins has been used as a framework to help explain the continued use of pesticides despite their known harms, the dominance of certain configurations of agricultural machinery, excessive fertilizer use, and the prioritization of industrial agriculture more generally over alternative paradigms such as agroecology.[9] A wider and longer-term perspective enables us to see that the lock-in of industrial agricultural inputs was a process that began as early as the mid-1800s and became increasingly entrenched. It also makes clear that the four industrial agricultural inputs were progressively designed by the leading firms to work together as a suite of technologies—that is, a technological paradigm of industrial agriculture—especially from the 1940s onward.

Network effects were unleashed as industrial agricultural inputs effectively became a package, whereby farmers who adopted one of them had to adopt them all. The shift from horse-drawn machinery to gasoline-powered tractors from the 1920s to the 1950s, for example, led to the development of a network of supporting technologies and infrastructures that farmers had to acquire. These included specific farm implements, designed to be attached to tractors—such as plows, fertilizer spreaders, and trailers—that were different from the implements used with horses.[10] A farmers who adopted a gasoline-powered tractor was highly unlikely to return to horse-drawn implements. Indeed, as tractors became more prevalent, the implements designed for use with horses became less available on the market, making it difficult for farmers to continue to use horse-drawn machinery. Economic historian Allan Bogue notes that farmers had to be prepared to make a "complete conversion" if they wanted to fully realize the benefits of tractor adoption, even though "the additional outlay beyond the cost of the tractor might be very large."[11]

As tractor adoption expanded, so did the use of other industrial inputs. As outlined in chapter 2, farmers who operated tractors were able to cultivate larger tracts of land, which typically meant that they also took up monocultural growing practices, because it became important to have uniform plants within large fields to make cultivation and harvesting by machine more efficient. Hybrids and other high-yielding varieties of seeds provided farmers with plant genetic uniformity in their fields that made it easier to harvest with other machinery too, such as mechanical corn pickers. With hybrid maize, for example, all the plants in a field had identical genetic makeup and thus matured at exactly the same time. These seeds were specifically bred by the large seed companies such that the ears of corn grew at the same height on each stalk and the plants had stiffer stalks, so they were easier to harvest by machine.[12] The ears also attached to the stalk much more firmly, which worked well with mechanical pickers but made them extremely difficult to harvest by hand. All of these factors made hybrid seed choices attractive to corn farmers who adopted tractors.

Once farmers adopted tractors and hybrid seeds, it became possible to plant rows of corn more closely together for easier harvesting. But this also meant using more fertilizers because the soil did not have enough nutrients on its own to support such an intensive monoculture. The surplus of nitrogen that was redirected from military uses to the fertilizer sector in the early postwar years helped to make this approach possible. Indeed, stiffer stalks on hybrid corn made them more responsive to the application of fertilizers.[13] From the 1950s to the 1980s, the number of maize seeds planted in fields in the United States doubled, and hybrid seed sales surged 60 percent. Over that same period, fertilizer application increased a whopping seventeen-fold.[14]

Large, monoculture fields with tightly packed crops that were heavily laden with fertilizers created optimal conditions for pests—insects, weeds, and fungi—to thrive. To address these problems, farmers became increasingly dependent on chemical pesticides. Their use of herbicides also grew because they helped to save on labor costs and keep weeds out of harvesting equipment.[15] Industrial agricultural inputs became not just a system that reinforced the use of each of the individual technological components in a static sense, but it also acted, as Jack Kloppenburg notes, as a kind of a "technological treadmill" that self-propelled the process forward.[16]

Many farmers were squeezed out of the farming business in the early postwar decades as agribusiness firms rose ascendant on the back of this technological determinism.[17] If farmers did not stay at the cutting edge of the technological developments that ensured higher production, they saw their incomes fall relative to others and often were forced to exit the sector and sell their farms to other producers who had the equipment and capital to expand their operations. In the United States, for example, the number of farms declined as the average size of farms rose in response to mechanization and other labor-saving technological changes in the sector. There were 6.8 million farms in 1935, but this number dwindled to 5.4 million in 1950 and to 2.7 million by 1969.[18] Average farm sizes meanwhile increased from 157 acres in 1930 to 440 acres by 1974.[19]

The lock-in of the industrial model was compounded by broader economic and political conditions that resulted in policies that favored the adoption of the entire package of inputs. As noted in chapter 4, the US Agricultural Adjustment Act in 1933 encouraged farmers to try to grow more on the land they were allowed to cultivate, which made the use of hybrid corn seeds along with the suite of other technologies all the more attractive to them. During World War II and in the early decades of the postwar era, governments around the world sought to increase production to ensure food supply in war-torn Europe as well as in the developing world. The use of food aid policies in the United States and Canada from the 1950s, and eventually in Europe in the 1960s, sought to dispose of surplus grain to prevent steep price declines as food production increased. But these policies only encouraged continued use of industrial inputs, as governments provided ready markets for farm output in this period. Food surpluses served powerful governments' political interests abroad, especially during the Cold War, where food assistance could serve as a tool for encouraging the cooperation of certain countries in the Global South.[20]

Although governments in grain-producing regions—the United States and Canada in the 1940s and 1950s and in Europe in the 1960s—were aware of some of the social and ecological problems associated with the industrial production model, they pushed ahead in encouraging its adoption in any case. Many policymakers viewed the use of these technologies and their associated costs largely as inevitable. For example, a major 1940 report of the US Department of Agriculture, *Technology on the Farm*, was clear in its understanding that technological change—in machinery, seeds, fertilizers, and pest control—was in progress and that it would result in harsh consequences for some. It saw the government's task not to stop technological inventions but to formulate policies in ways that reduce its negative impacts: "It is not that these scientific advances in themselves are to be blamed; the troubles, if any, arise from the inequality of adjustments and responses in agriculture and industry to such advances."[21] As such, it pushed for further technological advancement:

"Instead of preventing or slowing up technical progress, we need, rather, to speed up and give new direction to social and institutional changes in order to keep pace with technological change."[22]

This kind of view among government policymakers around the world—that industrial agricultural inputs are an inevitable step in the evolution of farming—contributed to an institutional bias that favored the entire package of industrial inputs. As industrial agriculture became more normalized in policy outcomes and in practice—effectively an institutional lock-in—the firms that were dominant in the sector benefited from the network effects that tethered the various input industries together, including through policies and institutions.

Because success in one of the inputs meant success in the others, these circumstances brought the firms across the four input sectors closer together through their shared interests. In some cases, tighter linkages among the firms led to investments between the sectors. Deere & Company and Monsanto, for example, each invested in fertilizer manufacturing facilities on these grounds in the 1950s.[23] Similarly, many of the firms in the chemicals sector, such as Imperial Chemical Industries and DuPont, produced both fertilizers and pesticides and were able to capitalize on synergies between these inputs. At the same time, the large agricultural input firms began to form industry associations to advance their collective interests in policy contexts, as with the formation of the Agricultural Insecticide and Fungicide Association in 1933, mentioned in chapter 5, and the Phosphate Exporting Association, mentioned in chapter 3. The 1950s saw the formation of more associations, including the Farm Equipment Manufacturers Association in the United States and its European equivalent, the Comité Européen des Groupements de Constructeurs du Machinisme Agricole (CEMA).

SHIP OUT: AGRIBUSINESS GOES GLOBAL

The industrial agricultural model went global in the decades following World War II, even as the lock-in of the four key input industries continued to solidify and the social and ecological costs became clearer. A number of the dominant firms had exported individual inputs, such as farm machinery and fertilizer, since the mid-nineteenth century. This early trade in farm inputs was mainly with countries in Europe, North America, Australia, Argentina, Russia, and South Africa—areas with vast tracts of arable land that could use machinery and implement large-scale staple crop production.

The globalization of the sector accelerated significantly from the 1950s through the 1970s, with the rise of foreign direct investment by the leading agricultural input firms. This explosion of investment transformed these firms into giant multinational corporations (MNCs) with extensive interests around the world. The main forms of foreign direct investment for the agricultural input companies included the establishment of worldwide marketing arrangements as well as joint ventures to build production facilities to crank out tractors, pesticides, fertilizers, and high-yielding seeds to serve local markets abroad. The agribusiness giants were encouraged to make these investments for a variety of reasons in their quest to reach new and potentially lucrative markets. Sometimes they sought to get around tariff barriers imposed by importing states. Other times they were obliged to meet government requirements for local content. And sometimes they simply sought to take advantage of lower production costs (including wages for labor and materials prices) and taxes in other countries.

This globalization of the firms in the agricultural inputs industry was part of the broader rise of global corporations following World War II. This expansion, according to political economist Robert Gilpin, was the product of political dynamics, especially the rise of the United States as a dominant world power in the postwar era. As the United States expanded its own political influence globally, so did its firms, aided by a revolution in communications and transportation. It was further supported by the post-1945 establishment of a new international economic order through the Bretton Woods institutions: the International Monetary Fund, the World Bank, and the General Agreement on Tariffs and Trade. These political and institutional dynamics on the global stage fueled a period of massive global economic growth in which MNCs actively sought to insert themselves. Investment by multinational firms, especially those with a home base in the United States or Europe, was greatest in countries where the United States and its Cold War allies established security interests, which made them seem safe places to invest. US firms were major players in outward foreign direct investment (FDI) in general in this period—with American FDI climbing from $7 billion in 1946 to over $100 billion in 1973.[24]

By the 1940s and 1950s, International Harvester and Massey (which merged with the British farm equipment firm Ferguson in 1953 and was renamed Massey-Ferguson) were heavily invested in the European market and had established their own factories in various European locations. Deere also expanded to invest in Latin America, establishing tractor assembly plants in Venezuela and Mexico in the 1950s, as the share of the firm's sales outside the United States grew rapidly following World War II. Deere's sales in Mexico, for example, rose from around 9 percent of its US sales in 1946 to nearly 18 percent by 1949. In this same period, no fewer than fourteen international firms were selling tractors in Mexico.[25]

The large commercial seed companies also invested abroad in this period, with Funk Brothers, for example, investing in the hybrid corn seed business in Italy in the early postwar period and eventually across Europe, South America, and Africa in the following decades.[26] The large agrochemical firms also went global, establishing subsidiaries and expanding their foreign sales to countries in Latin America, Asia, and Europe. European-based agrochemical and fertilizer firms also extended their foreign presence by investing in North America as well as in the developing world from the 1950s onward.[27] The US push for the adoption of an integrated package of industrial agricultural technologies across Asia and Latin America, which came to be known by the late 1960s as the Green Revolution, opened new opportunities for the agricultural input industries and the firms that dominated them.

CAPITALIZING ON THE GREEN REVOLUTION

Much has been written on the Green Revolution, and the intention here is to discuss how agribusiness sought to capitalize on this initiative. Its origins date back to 1940, when Henry A. Wallace, at the time the US vice president-elect, made a visit to Mexico to attend the inauguration of the newly elected Mexican president, Ávila Camacho. Wallace stayed in Mexico for over six weeks and toured the countryside to assess the agricultural situation, with a view to seeing how technological developments could improve the country's agricultural production and food security.

Although Wallace found a sophisticated agricultural sector, he also identified what he considered to be low yields as a problem hindering better nutrition in the country.[28] After Wallace returned to the United States, he met with Nelson Rockefeller and the president of the Rockefeller Foundation at the time, Raymond Fosdick. Wallace impressed on them that if the productivity of maize and beans could be improved in Mexico, benefits would follow, noting that it would help prevent the country from succumbing to a communist uprising.[29]

Mexican leadership was especially open to the idea of agricultural modernization, stressing its faith in science and technology for the sector. The Rockefeller Foundation launched its Mexican Agricultural Program (MAP) in 1943, employing a group of plant breeders and other agricultural advisers. The thrust of the initiative was to transfer technology and know-how to the country to improve crop yields, including high-yielding seeds, fertilizers, pesticides, and machinery—the entire package of inputs that underpinned the industrial agricultural paradigm that had become locked in in North America and was being increasingly adopted in Europe.[30]

New types of wheat seeds, for example, developed by US agronomist Norman Borlaug, who had worked for DuPont in the early 1940s, were a key focus of the Mexican initiative. The new wheat seeds were semi-dwarf, high-yielding, disease-resistant varieties (which have come to be known as high-yield varieties, HYVs). Because they were short and stocky, they did not lodge or fall over with the application of additional plant nutrients, making them highly responsive to fertilizer applications. The seeds came to be known as "miracle seeds" because, when combined with increased fertilizer use, they resulted in significantly higher yields. Pesticides were also explicitly integrated into the model, and by the end of the 1940s, the MAP was already experimenting with a range of synthetic pesticides.[31] Many machinery manufacturers had a keen interest in tapping into the Mexican market, especially as more land came under cultivation. The MAP succeeded in increasing production, and the Rockefeller Foundation later expanded its work to include similar projects in Colombia (1950), Chile (1952), and India (1955), for example. The US government also pursued this type of approach to rural development assistance in Asia, including in the Philippines and Indonesia.[32]

Much of the literature on the Green Revolution, especially that published since the 1990s, emphasizes the role of geopolitics, foundations, and international institutions as key forces behind efforts to encourage adoption of the package of inputs.[33] With the Cold War as the backdrop for this policy initiative, the US government sought to ensure that poor countries were able to produce enough of their own food to keep them from turning to communism. Philanthropic foundations and the World Bank played important roles in funding much of the research that developed high-yielding varieties of seeds stylized to conditions in developing countries. Much of this research took place in international agricultural research centers that were part of the World Bank–funded Consultative Group on International Agricultural Research (CGIAR), such as the International Maize and Wheat Improvement Centre (CIMMYT) in Mexico and the International Rice Research Institute (IRRI) in the Philippines.

The public sector, private foundations, and international organizations were important drivers behind the Green Revolution. Focusing exclusively on these actors, however, misses the important role of multinational firms from the start of the process. Many of the MNCs that dominated the agricultural inputs industries were key players, often working with governments, foundations, and international organizations in ways that advanced their business interests. Their involvement was driven by their strong desire to gain a global foothold in the marketplace for agricultural inputs, which the FAO projected to amount to some $185 billion in developing countries in the 1970s.[34]

Large multinational firms such as Bayer, Ciba-Geigy, Dow, American Cyanamid, ICI, Monsanto, Shell, and Union Carbide, for example, provided financial backing for several of the international agricultural research centers at the core of the Green Revolution.[35] Although the total corporate contribution to IRRI, for example, was small compared to other donors, the global input firms benefited enormously from public sector research into how the industrial model could be transferred to developing countries. Indeed, their involvement gave them expanded markets for their machinery, fertilizers, seeds, and pesticides, as well as access to seed germplasm. Political analyst Kevin Danaher noted that the corporations saw the policy effort of the Green Revolution as a "potential bonanza."[36]

The relative neglect of the role of MNCs in the more recent literature on the Green Revolution is puzzling given that during the 1970s, a number of analysts focused on the role of global corporations in the initiative, albeit from different perspectives. Lester Brown, for example, included an entire chapter on MNCs in his 1970 book, *Seeds of Change: The Green Revolution and Development in the 1970's*, which reads like an ode to the positive role those firms could play: "Once it becomes profitable to use modern technology, the demand for all kinds of farm inputs increases rapidly. And only agribusiness firms can supply these new inputs efficiently. This means that the multinational corporation has a vested interest in the agricultural revolution along with the poor countries themselves."[37] Brown and others warned that it would be difficult to envision how the needed agricultural investment for the Green Revolution could occur without large transnational input firms.

Other early analysts were much more skeptical about the role of MNCs in the Green Revolution. They saw their involvement as benefiting foreign firms more than small-scale farmers and believed it risked creating dependencies in developing countries. Critical scholars Hector Melo and Israel Yost, for example, saw the US promotion of the Green Revolution as encouraging a "massive takeover by US agribusiness" in the developing world.[38] Political scientist Kenneth Dahlberg similarly warned, "Given the reasonable probability that these multinationals will also seek integrated control over the whole green revolution package (seeds, fertilizers, pesticides, and equipment), there is a real fear on the part of many developing countries that they will be unable to control many of the basic decisions influencing the course of their own agricultural development."[39]

While there was both excitement and concern about the involvement of agribusiness multinationals in the Green Revolution in the early 1970s, capturing developing country markets was not easy for the global firms. The investment opportunities were not as lucrative as those firms initially expected.[40] Varying regulations and other barriers to investment in low-income countries frustrated firms because it made their efforts more complicated. They were also wary of transferring patented technologies into countries that might not protect their intellectual property.[41] As a result, they zeroed in on what they deemed to be the most lucrative markets and coordinated their efforts to make the investment environment in those countries more welcoming. The firms worked closely with governments, foundations, business associations, and intergovernmental bodies to ensure that they gained support and backing for their investments in what they deemed to be high-risk countries in the Global South. Through these efforts, they were able to get a foothold in medium- to- large countries, such as India, Indonesia, the Philippines, and Mexico, where they expected they would eventually play a major role in providing agricultural inputs.[42]

To achieve these goals, the agribusiness titans worked closely with their host and home country governments and benefited from tied aid regimes, whereby governments give bilateral aid to recipients tied to the purchase of goods from the donor country, such as tractors, pesticides, and fertilizers. Even if aid was not specifically tied to purchases from donor countries, development projects that provided "technical advice" often pushed the products of the firms based in donor countries.[43] These practices often imposed extra costs on recipient countries and effectively served as a subsidy for the firms, with costs of tied goods purchases, for example, averaging around 10 to 30 percent more than those purchased on free international markets. Fertilizers in particular were frequently overpriced by donors who sold them on concessionary terms to developing countries.[44] The United States also earmarked some funds from its PL480 food aid program, which was sold on concessional terms in local currencies, for assistance to multinational agribusiness firms that sought to make investments in those countries.[45] Multilateral assistance also funded infrastructure and industrial development, which further benefited the agribusiness firms by creating opportunities for joint ventures.[46]

AGRIBUSINESS WORKS TOGETHER IN GLOBAL GOVERNANCE FORUMS

Agribusiness multinationals actively worked together through the UN Food and Agriculture Organization (FAO), the World Bank, and other international development institutions to capitalize on projects associated with the Green Revolution. The Industry Cooperative Program (ICP), for example, was established at the FAO in 1965, spearheaded by a Herbert Felix, a Swedish industrialist in the food industry. It grew from an initial eighteen firms at its start to nearly ninety participating firms by the early 1970s. These firms included well-known agribusiness giants such as Ciba-Geigy, Ford, Hoechst, Massey-Ferguson, Deere, Mitsubishi, and Shell Chemicals.[47] Represented by top-level CEOs who were the formal members of the IPC, each firm paid $3,500 annually for membership. These payments supported the FAO, which in turn offered office space as well as access to the organization's data, which the firms found useful in determining which countries would likely yield the highest return on their investments. With the backing of the FAO, the ICP organized delegations to key countries in which agribusinesses sought to invest to gather information and press for favorable treatment.

Some analysts at the time, such as political scientist Louis Turner, saw the ICP as serving an important function in advancing agricultural modernization in developing countries.[48] Others were critical, seeing the ICP as nothing more than a lobbying group that undermined the official role and function of the FAO. Agrarian analyst Erich Jacoby noted with respect to the influence of the group at the 1974 World Food Conference, which was convened to deal with a global food crisis, "The close cooperation with transnational corporations necessarily divert[s] FAO's attention from one of the fundamental priorities of its Charter: the commitment to promote the welfare of the peasants. The strong position of the ICP became clearly apparent at the World Food Conference in Rome where its delegation of 69 members—by far the largest at the Conference—functioned as an institutionalised commercial lobby."[49]

Transnational agribusiness firms also worked through other organizations to press countries in the Global South to open their arms more fully to foreign investment and provide some sweetener to the deals to make it worth the while of the firms. The large firms participated in the Latin American Business Development Corporation, founded in 1970, which spearheaded foreign investment efforts in the region, including in the agrifood industry. Among this group's members were Deere & Co., Dow Chemical, and Monsanto.[50] The dominant firms in the sector also worked closely with the American Agribusiness Council (ABC), formed in 1967, which focused mainly on seeking out investment opportunities in Asia. The ABC was an offshoot of a corporate conference held jointly with the US Agency for International Development, entitled "The World Food

Problem: Private Investment and Government Cooperation."[51] Both the Rockefeller and Ford foundations funded the ABC in its early years, as they saw these firms as the only actors that could ensure the availability of agricultural machinery, fertilizer, and pesticides in low-income countries to make the "miracle seeds" deliver their promised yields.

These various cooperative arrangements that agribusiness forged with governments and intergovernmental organizations helped advance those firms' interests. Tractor manufacturers, for example, benefited from donor government aid programs that pushed Green Revolution technologies. Pakistan purchased some twenty-six thousand tractors from the big firms between 1962 and 1970, including from Massey-Ferguson, International Harvester, Ford, and Deere, at a cost of $55 million.[52] Massey-Ferguson relied on the Canadian International Development Agency to provide aid for purchasing its tractors in poor countries.[53] Massey-Ferguson was especially active in the ICP as well, and in 1964, even before the ICP's establishment, the firm worked closely with the FAO to set up a training program for farm machinery repair in low-income countries.[54]

The big fertilizer firms also were able to cash in on global markets during this period as demand for fertilizers in developing countries grew rapidly in the 1960s. Significant fertilizer sales in this period were tied to purchases from donor country firms.[55] In India, for example, around 40 percent of fertilizers used in the early decades of the Green Revolution were imported. The US government and the World Bank pressured the Indian and Pakistani governments to bring in MNCs as partners to build fertilizer plants in those countries.[56] The first ICP delegation in fact traveled to India to continue to press the cause, and Shell Chemicals came away from the trip with a license to build a fertilizer plant.[57]

Although the bulk of improved seed varieties were largely being developed in public international agricultural research institutes of the CGIAR, the private seed companies still were able to position themselves within global markets and capitalize on Green Revolution projects in this period. Pioneer Hi-Bred, for example, established a number of joint ventures throughout the 1960s, including in Australia, Argentina, and South Africa, as well as experiment stations in the Caribbean, as a way to gain new markets. DeKalb invested in India in close collaboration with the Rockefeller Foundation, the latter of which pressed for more private sector involvement in India's seed sector. The firm pursued a joint venture with an Indian seed firm and benefited from counterpart funds from the US PL480 food assistance.[58]

Most developing countries did not have the expertise to produce their own pesticides or to develop appropriate regulatory frameworks for their use. Instead, they relied on multinational agribusiness firms to provide the chemicals, training on how to use them, and assistance with regulatory legislation. Firms such as Ciba-Geigy worked with the FAO to help develop legislation on the safe use of pesticides in low-income countries, often seeking rules that would provide for easier importation of the chemicals and a more conducive investment environment.[59] Indeed, pesticide imports increased rapidly in countries receiving assistance for the Green Revolution, creating huge opportunities for those firms. From 1961 to 1965 alone, agrochemical imports doubled in Thailand and tripled in Pakistan.[60] In Mexico, for example, pesticide imports ballooned from 3,200 tonnes in 1949 to 33,000 tonnes by the mid-1950s, mainly imports from American and European firms, while total pesticide consumption (including both imports and domestic production) in Mexico reached 113,000 tonnes by 1960. This sharp increase in pesticide use in Mexico had firms like Shell Chemicals, DuPont, and Dow sidling up to the Rockefeller Foundation to try to get in on the action.[61]

The pesticides multinationals that participated in the FAO's ICP were also particularly active, forming a pesticides working group that sought to open up investment opportunities.[62] The major pesticides firms were concerned that many developing countries had worries about the safety of chemicals such as DDT, which were being sold to them at the same time that they were beginning to be more stringently regulated in industrialized countries. The working group went so far as to prepare over a dozen working papers on the topic as background documents to the 1972 UN Conference on the Human Environment.[63]

Although some countries in Asia and Latin America placed import restrictions on some pesticides, Bayer, which sought to invest in these regions, was able to secure export credit guarantees from the German government to protect its interests. The German government also provided support to Bayer, BASF, and Hoechst to establish a chemical factory in India in a joint venture with Hindustan Organic Chemicals in the 1950s under the label of development aid to India, which included protection against the risk of expropriation. Although this initiative did not last long, it gave Bayer and other firms an important presence in the Indian market, as it gave their brands name recognition.[64] Union Carbide also established a pesticide manufacturing plant in Bhopal, India, in 1969 as a joint venture with the Indian government.[65]

The interests of the input companies were made clear at a consultation with agribusiness firms in Toronto in preparation for the 1974 World Food Conference, which noted, "In order to fulfil its potential role and to become a more dynamic partner in the development process, industry relies on governments for a positive attitude towards multilateral and bilateral agreements and conventions, including the protection of intellectual property, and towards clearly stated rules regarding security of investment."[66] The industry consultation document went on to emphasize the importance of developing country governments upholding intellectual property rights over plant breeding, governments' role in providing infrastructure and raw materials at a low price for fertilizer production and for international financing of imports of pesticides into developing countries.[67]

CONSOLIDATING MARKET POSITION IN THE NEW GLOBAL AGE

With the lock-in and ship out of the industrial agricultural model in the postwar decades, the firms that provided the inputs saw an expansion of their profits and a continuation of their dominance in those markets. To be sure, there was some shifting in the degree of concentration and individual firms' market share both within countries and globally over this period. But by and large, the key firms that rose to dominance in the early twentieth century maintained their positions as key agricultural input firms into the 1970s while deepening their presence on the global stage.

Indeed, the concern about concentration in the fertilizer and farm machinery sectors that ignited antitrust activity against firms in these sectors in the early part of the twentieth century (discussed in chapters 2 and 3) continued into this period. Numerous studies were published in this era with titles like *The Fertilizer Industry: Study of an Imperfect Market*,[68] *The World Fertilizer Economy*,[69] and *Oligopoly in the Farm Machinery Industry*.[70] The government of Canada established the Royal Commission on Farm Machinery in the mid-1960s to study the structure of the market, and it issued a more than six-hundred-page report in 1971.[71]

There was less concern in the early part of this period about corporate concentration in the agricultural seeds and agrochemicals sector. By the 1970s, however, awareness was already growing about the power and influence of the dominant firms in these sectors. For example, a 1972 United Nations pamphlet on new agricultural technologies was blunt about the likely impact of large corporations making inroads into the seed sector in developing countries and linking their sales to other inputs: "In a situation of amalgamation of international companies, of the search of these huge and powerful companies for new lines of business, the relevant question to ask may not be 'Will seed sources be monopolized and inputs packaged in formulas?' but 'What is to stop large international agro-businesses from monopolizing and 'packaging' the inputs of HYV's cultivation?'"[72]

This focus of these various studies indicates the ongoing concern about the power and concentration of the firms at the top of these industries. Indeed, the numbers at the time justified this continued attention on the agribusiness titans. In the farm machinery sector in the United States in 1948, for example, four firms accounted for around 52 percent of the farm machinery sales overall, while in tractor sales specifically, the top four firms accounted for approximately 90 percent of the US market.[73] Several decades later, in 1966, the top four firms in the United States and Canada, taken together as a single market, held 56.5 percent of the farm machinery market and 75 percent of tractor sales.[74] In Canada, the percentage of tractor sales held by the top four firms in 1967 stood at 67 percent, and that ratio hovered around 70 percent for the previous decade. European countries also had high concentration ratios for tractor sales, although the specific firms at the top differed in each market. The percentage of the top four firms for tractor sales in 1964 was 87.5 percent in Britain, 84.2 percent in Sweden, 78.8 percent in Italy, 64.1 percent in France, and 52 percent in West Germany.[75] Most of the firms in the sector expanded their operations globally in this era and saw rising profits and growing market share. By 1970, Deere held 15 percent of the worldwide market, International Harvester 12 percent, Massey-Ferguson 10 percent, and Ford 7 percent, for a total of 44 percent of the global market held by these four giant North American firms.[76]

The fertilizer sector, which was more tied to regional and domestic markets, also maintained a high degree of dominance by a handful of firms, although there were some important changes in this period and specific developments in the different segments of N, P, and K production as well as mixed fertilizers. The "big six" US fertilizer firms that dominated the US market in 1914 were still the largest fertilizer firms in the United States in the 1950s.[77] These firms were typically chemical companies that produced other products as well, including pesticides. Concentration declined somewhat in the sector in the 1950s and 1960s. Part of the reason for this drop was the rise of the cooperative movement in the United States, which gained momentum during the Great Depression. By 1953, some sixty cooperatives operated over one hundred fertilizer plants in the United States, producing nitrogen, phosphate, and potash fertilizers. From 1950 to 1970, farmer purchases of fertilizers from cooperatives increased by a factor of four, and the market share of cooperatives in the fertilizer sector more than doubled, from 15 to 32 percent.[78] In this period, cooperatives accounted for around 20 percent of US nitrogen production capacity and 25 percent of phosphoric acid production, but only 3 percent of potash production.[79]

The rapid adoption of hybrid and other high-yield seed varieties in this period was a huge boon for the companies at the top of the sector. In the hybrid seed sector in the United States, just four firms dominated the market through the 1950s—Funk, Pioneer Hi-Bred, DeKalb, and Pfister—with these same companies accounting for at least 50 percent of seed sales. By the mid-1960s, several more firms joined the big four in dominating the US market, although Pioneer and DeKalb remained head and shoulders above the rest, together controlling around two-thirds of the US market in 1971.[80]

With respect to agrochemical pesticides, sales boomed after World War II, with DDT sales, as outlined in chapter 5, exploding for both farm and home use. The global market for crop protection chemicals grew from approximately $700 million in 1945 to around $2.5 billion in the early 1960s and reached $4.5 billion at the beginning of the 1970s.[81] As with fertilizers, agrochemicals were typically produced by integrated chemical companies, some of which were oil firms (since the chemicals were largely based on petroleum products). There were also important innovations in this sector with the development of new chemical herbicides, such as 2,4-D (developed by the American Chemical Paint Company) in the 1940s and glyphosate in the 1970s (developed by Monsanto), which quickly became widely used products on farms to tackle weeds (discussed in chapter 8). The German conglomerate chemical firm IG Farben was also broken up into separate firms in the 1950s, which included BASF, Bayer, and Hoechst. This breakup reduced global concentration, although the firms that came out of it were still exceptionally large and continued to play a dominant role in the global agrochemical market.

AT WHAT COST? CONSEQUENCES OF SHIPPING OUT THE MODEL

This chapter opened with an explanation of how technologies can get locked into common use even if they have harmful consequences. The lock-in of the industrial agricultural model benefited the firms, but it came at a huge cost in terms of its social and ecological effects. As the model was exported to the developing world under the banner of the Green Revolution, those same concerns were often multiplied when brought to new locations. The input technologies that were designed for use in North American and European contexts were in many cases additionally problematic when inserted into different unique contexts of developing countries that had totally different social, economic, and ecological conditions. A growing understanding of the risks associated with several of the technologies in all countries also gave new urgency to some of the problems they created in this era. There is a huge literature on the wider impacts of the Green Revolution, and only a brief summary is provided here as it relates to the technologies promoted by the large agribusiness firms.[82]

Among the concerns highlighted in the literature at the time were the uneven social and economic consequences of the adoption of industrial agricultural technologies in developing country contexts. Specifically, there was worry that larger commercial farmers with better soils would benefit from modern inputs more than poor farmers who had access only to smaller and more marginal lands. Some analysts warned that "the richer farmers will become richer," while the smaller and poorer farmers were likely to see a net reduction in their income.[83] There was also early evidence that the adoption of Green Revolution technologies in wealthier regions drove up land prices, making land unaffordable for smaller and poorer farmers in many countries. Related to inequities, the overall package of technologies was also widely critiqued for leading to rising indebtedness of farmers and for making them dependent on MNCs for their inputs, because the model meant that farmers who previously did not have to purchase seeds, fertilizers, pesticides, and machinery would now have to do so. In other words, farmers were being asked to suddenly lock themselves into the new system, which came with a reliance on large foreign firms.[84]

It is widely recognized that inequities were exacerbated by the adoption of mechanization as part of the Green Revolution package, which resulted in a displacement of people from farmlands, contributing to rural poverty and unemployment. Rural farmers and their families who were left landless and jobless were effectively encouraged to migrate to cities, although there were few employment opportunities for them there, as had been the case when the United States experienced similar rural displacement from farm mechanization in the 1930s and 1940s. The labor implications were complex: the Green Revolution in some ways increased demand for labor by enabling multiple growing seasons per year in some countries such as India and Indonesia, but mechanization also displaced labor. As labor was not particularly in short supply in these countries, the net effect in many cases was an increase in rural joblessness. This impact was especially hard for those who had lost access to their land because of the high debt levels they had to incur in order to borrow the funds they needed to purchase Green Revolution inputs.[85] In addition, there were critiques of the way in which the Green Revolution shifted income-earning opportunities to the input companies in industrialized countries that were responsible for labor displacement. As Jacoby lamented:

> The most fatal aspect of the operations of the transnational corporations is the transfer of a large part of the employment potential in Third World agriculture to the industries of the developed countries which produce fertilizers, chemicals, tractors and other goods needed for agricultural production. In other words, the workers of industrialised countries actually manufacture the very equipment which substantially reduces the employment possibilities of agricultural labour in underdeveloped countries. The focal point of Third World agriculture is gradually being transferred to the industrialised countries where the transnational corporations exercise the control of trade relations and finance sophisticated technical research whose application will only further disintegrate the rural community.[86]

Great concern was also expressed at the time about how widespread adoption of high-yield varieties was leading to a dramatic narrowing of the genetic base of food production. Because the package encouraged monocultures based on relatively few seed varieties, which replaced more diverse fields, the results were simplified ecosystems and biodiversity loss. Genetic narrowing was also problematic from a nutritional perspective. In India, for example, the adoption of Green Revolution wheat varieties led to a shift away from nutrient-rich pulses (legumes such as lentils, beans, and peas) and other traditional grains like millets. Moreover, while the wheat that was produced with HYVs weighed more and thus gave the appearance of higher yields, it had a higher water content and was less nutritious than traditional varieties.[87]

The narrowing of the genetic base of the food supply to just a few varieties of wheat, maize, or rice grown in monoculture fields also made food systems more vulnerable to pests and disease. The result was a massive increase in pesticide use in the Global South, even as industrialized countries were coming to a reckoning about the safety of agrochemicals for humans and the environment at that same time. As pesticides were being rolled out in developing country contexts, there was a severe lack of safety equipment, and the result was that pesticide poisonings occurred at a much higher rate in Global South contexts than in industrialized countries.[88] A particularly troubling effect of higher pesticide use was poisoning of waterways that killed fish in irrigation canals and rice paddies, important sources of dietary protein for many communities in Asia.[89]

Indeed, during the postwar decades, much more information became available about the risks and problems associated with pesticide use, including greater understanding of the capacity of certain persistent organic chemicals, such as DDT, to bioaccumulate in living organisms. Growing awareness of the capacity of DDT to accumulate in fatty tissues and to travel distances through a process of bioaccumulation and contamination of the food chain raised alarm bells. Moreover, organophosphate chemicals that were also developed in this era were acutely toxic and posed threats to humans and wildlife.[90]

In the United States, important hearings were held on the safety of DDT in the 1950s, resulting in new laws and regulations that required firms to provide detailed safety testing of all products before bringing them to market. Rachel Carson's 1962 publication of *Silent Spring* brought these issues to a wider audience and public debate over the safety of DDT that eventually led the United States to ban the chemical in 1972.[91] In the heat of the debate over the US ban, Norman Borlaug—by then widely viewed as the key agronomist that enabled the Green Revolution which earned him the Nobel Peace Prize in 1972—wrote: "*Silent Spring* was not typical of Rachel Carson's gentle, kind nature. It was a diabolic, vitriolic, bitter, one-sided attack on the use of pesticides, especially insecticides and weed killers."[92] Borlaug's condemnation clearly revealed how desperate the advocates of industrial agriculture were to protect DDT from regulatory constraints. But while it was banned for domestic use in the United States from 1972, US legislation did not ban the export of DDT to other countries for another decade. Thus, highly dangerous chemicals continued to be exported to the Global South, further spreading the problems associated with toxic pesticides.[93]

The danger was not just from the export of pesticides to the Global South, but also with the pesticide plants that the major chemical firms established within those countries. The 1984 Bhopal disaster at the Union Carbide India Limited plant is a tragic example of weak safety measures at the firm that was 50.9 percent owned by the US firm Union Carbide Corporation (UCC). A major gas leak at the plant resulted in what is widely seen to be the world's worst-ever industrial catastrophe. An estimated 3,800 people were instantly killed from exposure to the gas, and an additional 500,000 people were exposed, causing permanent disabilities and premature death for many thousands of people in the subsequent months and years. UCC closed the Bhopal plant but did not clean up the site, leaving a toxic legacy. Although the firm settled with the Indian government in 1989 for US$470 million in compensation to victims, the amount it paid was far less than would have been awarded to victims had the case been heard in the United States.[94] Moreover, as health analyst Edward Broughton notes, "At every turn, UCC has attempted to manipulate, obfuscate and withhold scientific data to the detriment of victims." While some firms, such as ICI, sought to improve safety standards in their Indian operations following the disaster, others, such as DuPont, incorporated a clause in its agreement with the Indian government that relieved it of all liability in case an accident occurred.[95]

CONCLUSION

As this chapter has shown, the interrelated dynamics of technological lock-in, globalization, and state support were defining features of the agricultural input sector in the postwar decades when industrial agriculture became established as a global norm. These processes were deeply entwined with one another. Lock-in dynamics among the four key industrial agricultural inputs meant that the industrial agriculture model promoted by the dominant firms was globalized via corporate foreign investment as well as the active coordinated involvement of those firms in states' promotion of the Green Revolution. Through these dynamics, the dominant corporations selling farm machinery, fertilizers, pesticides, and high-yielding seeds were able to maintain their dominant size and influence in the agricultural inputs sector overall. Meanwhile, the costs of the industrial agricultural model continued to be externalized by the firms and were extended to the Global South, leading to additional problems as it was rolled out in contexts that were very different from those in which it was originally developed.

The lock-in and ship-out dynamics entrenched the power of the dominant firms in the sector by expanding their markets as well as their avenues of influence over policy. In terms of markets, they benefited from network effects and from the way in which lock-in reinforced oligopolistic market structures. At the same time that these technologies were becoming more interconnected, the dominant firms also were able to extend their activities in ways that captured a wider range of international markets through their foreign direct investment. They also engaged directly with governments, foundations, and intergovernmental organizations to create and capture markets opened by the spread of the Green Revolution in the Global South. Throughout this period, these firms were able to maintain and extend their dominance over both domestic and international markets for agricultural inputs, which created barriers to entry for other firms that could not match the scale and scope of those operations.

7

MERGERS OF DISTRESS IN FARM MACHINERY AND FERTILIZERS

By the 1970s, with the industrial agricultural model fully locked in and going global, changes in the agricultural sector prompted significant consolidation in the inputs sector. This chapter focuses on the factors that led to a flurry of mergers and acquisitions in the machinery and fertilizer sectors from the 1970s to the early 2000s that fundamentally reshaped these industries. The profound changes in these industries during this period have received less attention in the literature than those that simultaneously occurred in the seeds and agrochemical sectors (which are discussed in chapter 8). Yet it is important to understand the reconfiguration of these industries in the latter part of the twentieth century that positioned the leading firms to deepen their dominance in those sectors.

The 1970s food crisis—and the agricultural boom and subsequent bust it generated—profoundly shaped the market context, leading to major consolidation in the farm machinery and fertilizer sectors in the last decades of the twentieth century in the wake of market distress in these industries. Technological change also mattered: new techniques for the synthesis of nitrogen fertilizers, for example, encouraged larger and more centralized production facilities. More sophisticated machinery to serve ever larger and more specialized farms also encouraged firms to seek greater economies of scale. Consolidation in these industries was additionally facilitated by government policies that affected farmers' planting decisions in this period, as well as a weakening of antitrust policies that coincided with the rise of neoliberalism in the 1980s.

Meanwhile, the broader social and ecological costs of concentration and the industrial agricultural model pushed by the firms at the top of the farm machinery and fertilizer industries became increasingly apparent. But with the industrial agricultural model largely locked in by this point, it was difficult to garner political will to address these concerns. The inclination of states to shift toward a more sustainable model of agriculture was thwarted by large firms in these sectors that continued to use the market, policy, and technology levers available to them to entrench the industrial model and resist calls for a different path toward more ecologically sustainable agriculture.

FOOD AND AGRICULTURE BOOM-AND-BUST CYCLE OF THE 1970s AND 1980s

The 1970s ushered in a prolonged era of global economic turmoil that was marked by rampant global inflation and commodity market volatility. These broader economic conditions were the backdrop to a major global food crisis that erupted in 1973 and lasted for several years, with profound implications for hunger and the organization of agricultural sectors worldwide. Rapidly rising food prices generated a massive agricultural boom followed by a major farm sector crisis that posed a serious threat to farmer livelihoods around the world. It was in this context that an intensified period of consolidation across the agricultural input industries took root and continued for several decades.

The 1970s global food crisis was the product of a confluence of multiple developments that resulted in significant turmoil on world food markets. One commonly cited contributing factor was widespread drought conditions in the early part of the decade, which affected large portions of the Soviet Union, Asia, South America, and North America. These dry conditions contributed to a drop in world food and agricultural output in 1972, the first such decline in twenty years. Lower agricultural production led to widespread fears about food availability and rising prices.[1]

World grain markets were further ruffled by the entry into the market of the Soviet Union as an importer in the early 1970s, in response to its own diminished agricultural production. The country purchased nearly 28 million tons of grain in 1972–1973, primarily from the United States. China had also reentered global grain markets in the 1960s following the 1959–1961 Great Chinese Famine, in which as many as 30 million people perished. China imported significant amounts of wheat in the early 1970s as the markets whipsawed.[2] With new major importers participating in world grain markets, global grain reserves dwindled. Food prices increased dramatically, exacerbating global inflation that had already taken hold. US commercial grain exports increased markedly in the following years, more than doubling to 42 million tonnes between 1970 and 1973. At the same time, US donations of food aid to poor countries declined sharply.[3]

Also contributing to agricultural market turmoil in this period was the quadrupling of oil prices in 1973, which resulted from a sharp reduction in supply from the Organization of Petroleum Exporting Countries. These countries restricted oil supplies to maintain the value of members' exports in a context of spiraling global inflation. The dramatic increase in oil prices had a major impact on the food and agriculture sector, given the tight interlinkage between petroleum and industrial agricultural production methods, pushing up the cost of farming and in turn raising food prices. The price of synthetic fertilizers, the production of which by this time was almost completely reliant on natural gas as its main energy source, rose sharply. These price spikes were especially sharp because fertilizer firms had scaled back production following a period of overcapacity in the 1960s, as discussed below. Farmers' expenses for agrochemicals also rose because these inputs were based on petroleum products. Higher prices for fuel, which more than tripled in the 1970s, also affected farmers' costs of operating farm machinery. But at the same time input prices were rising sharply, so were agricultural commodity prices, which enabled farmers to initially cover these rising input costs. Over the 1973–1975 period, prices for basic staple crops such as wheat, corn, and soy soared to levels that were on average over three times what they were in 1971.[4]

All of these factors contributed to a major boom in the agricultural sector in industrialized grain-producing countries in the first half of the 1970s. The United States especially benefited from these dynamics, as it was at the time the world's dominant grain exporter. US net farm income doubled over the 1970–1973 period, from $34 billion to $69 billion.[5] In this heady context, US farm policy encouraged producers to dramatically expand food production. Earl Butz, the US secretary of agriculture in both the Nixon and Ford administrations in the mid-1970s, called on farmers in 1973 to plant their farms "fencerow to fencerow" and reportedly called on them to "get big or get out."[6] To facilitate new farm investments, the US government offered subsidized farm loans and raised price and income supports for producers. Meanwhile, increased production was also promoted by European governments, with the European Community Common Agricultural Policy, in place since 1962, offering incentives to producers, including price supports.[7] The 1974 World Food Conference held at the FAO in Rome also encouraged developing countries to increase agricultural production to help bring down global food prices.

Although agricultural input prices were also rising quickly in the 1970s, many farmers took out loans to invest in their farms to increase production, often going into significant debt to do so. Galloping inflation meant that real interest rates (the formal interest rate adjusted for inflation) were extremely low and, in many cases, negative, in the mid-1970s. This favorable borrowing environment prompted many farmers to mortgage their farm properties to raise capital to purchase new farm equipment and expand the area of their farms.[8] Farm debt grew at levels not seen before in the United States, quadrupling during the 1970s. The number of acres under agricultural production in the United States soared from 293 million in 1972 to 356 million in 1980.[9] Many farmers assumed that they could easily repay their loans because commodity prices were high, raising their nominal income. But by the late 1970s, agricultural commodity prices began to decline as production continued to climb. As a result, farm incomes fell sharply.

Inflation peaked at double digits in the late 1970s, prompting the US Federal Reserve to step in and dramatically raise interest rates throughout the late 1970s and early 1980s. Inflation did fall in response to higher interest rates. However, the combination of continued high interest rates and low inflation meant a steep increase in the real rate of interest, which climbed to over 8 percent by 1981, a fivefold rise over the space of three years.[10] The consequences for the farm economy were devastating. By 1981, debt servicing costs had risen to 83 percent of farmers' net income.[11]

By the early 1980s, it was clear that the food crisis was morphing into a major farm crisis. As governments around the world followed the lead of the United States by instituting dramatic interest rate increases, farmers the world over found themselves saddled with high levels of debt that they were unable to repay because of falling commodity prices. Adding to farmers' woes, the US government imposed a temporary embargo on the sale of grain to Russia in response to the latter's 1979 invasion of Afghanistan, which meant lower demand for US grain on world markets. Corn prices fell by over 60 percent from 1980 to 1986 and soybean and wheat prices dropped by over 50 percent.[12]

The result of these various factors was a rapid decline in farm incomes, which affected farmers not just in North America but also in Europe and throughout most developing countries. Farmers who had borrowed to invest in expanding their operations were hit hard. In the United States, for example, farmers' net worth fell by as much as 50 percent in some parts of the country in the early 1980s. Land values fell precipitously, declining more than 40 percent between 1981 and 1987, undercutting the value of farmers' main asset that often served as collateral for their loans over the previous decade. Many farmers went bankrupt and were forced to sell their farms.[13] By the mid-1980s, the farm crisis was being characterized as the worst since the Great Depression.

This broader context is extremely important for understanding corporate restructuring in both the farm machinery and fertilizer sectors in the following decades. As farmers found themselves in increasingly perilous financial positions in the 1980s, they scaled back on purchases of farm inputs, including agricultural machinery, fertilizers, and pesticides. Tightening their belts put a strain on the input industries, especially farm machinery and fertilizer firms, leading to consolidation in the face of decreased market demand for their products.

FOUR HASTILY ARRANGED WEDDINGS AND A FEW FUNERALS IN THE FARM MACHINERY SECTOR

The 1980s and 1990s saw a dramatic acceleration of merger activity in the farm machinery sector, which was already by far the most concentrated of the farm input sectors. It is also the one on which farmers typically spend the most.[14] Earnings by the firms in the sector quickly fell from record levels during the 1970s farm boom to a deep trough by the early 1980s. Consolidation in the sector in the closing decades of the century was also the product of deeper shifts that had led to the consolidation of landholdings nearly a century earlier, which ironically meant that there were progressively fewer farmers to purchase farm machinery. The number of farms in the United States, for example, fell dramatically from the 1930s, when there were around 6 to 7 million farms, to just over 3 million in the mid-1960s.[15] As a result, even before the downturn in the 1980s, most of the main farm machinery firms found themselves experiencing weak performance overall in the 1950s and 1960s, prompting them to seek out foreign markets, as explained in chapter 6. Most of the farm equipment firms had already begun to reorganize and streamline their operations in this earlier period to reduce their swollen inventories and improve efficiencies.

This earlier restructuring in the farm machinery industry involved consolidation of production facilities and rationalization of retail outlets across the major firms at the top of the sector, including Deere & Co., Allis-Chalmers, and International Harvester. Several high-profile mergers took place in the 1950s and 1960s, including the merger of Massey with the British agricultural machinery firm Ferguson, which created Massey-Ferguson in 1953. White Motor Company purchased Minneapolis-Moline and Oliver in the early 1960s, which brought the auto firm into the farm machinery sector. The major conglomerate firm Kern County Land Company also purchased the majority of J. I. Case shares in 1964, after the firm had experienced financial losses in the early 1960s and was rescued by Morgan Stanley. Then, in 1967, conglomerate firm Tenneco acquired both firms and continued to produce J. I. Case–brand farm equipment. Other attempted mergers during these decades were thwarted by US antitrust authorities, including an effort by a major conglomerate, White Consolidated, to take over both White Motor and Allis Chalmers.[16]

As outlined in chapter 6, throughout the 1950s and 1960s, the sector continued to be dominated by a handful of farm machinery makers, with six dominant firms offering a full line of equipment: International Harvester, Deere, Massey-Ferguson, J. I. Case, Allis-Chalmers, and White Motor. Overall, the percentage of the North American market dominated by the top six firms remained somewhat stable at around 60 to 70 percent between 1948 and 1967. During that period, there was a shift in the market share of individual firms, most notably a decline in the market share of International Harvester and a rise in market share for Deere, which overtook International Harvester as the industry leader by the end of the 1960s.[17]

Rising commodity prices in the 1970s brought a major change in the prospects for these firms. Higher farm incomes in turn fueled demand for farm machinery, the sales of which climbed sharply in the late 1970s, reaching a record $12 billion in 1979 in the United States alone. But the bright prospects the farm machinery firms experienced in the 1970s quickly translated into deep crisis as the farm bust took hold in the 1980s. The sector suffered a serious sales slump that lasted for seven long years. By 1986, sales of farm machinery had plummeted to just over one-third of their level at the end of the 1970s.[18] The firms were caught with excessive inventory and few sales opportunities. Farmers made efforts to repair their machinery themselves or purchased used machinery from other farmers who were going bankrupt and selling their equipment. The farm machinery sector was operating at only 40 percent of its earlier capacity by the end of 1984, and many firms resorted to temporary closures of their factories to take pressure off inventory.[19]

Many of the firms that had dominated the market for farm machinery since the early twentieth century were teetering on the brink of bankruptcy by the mid-1980s. Firms across the industry began cutting the price of farm equipment extensively in order to clear their inventory and get ahead of their rivals. According to reporting at the time, retail prices of tractors that normally sold for $85,000 in the early 1980s were being sold for as little as $50,000. These dramatic discounts put a serious dent in corporate profits. By the early 1980s, it was widely rumored that a number of mergers were on the horizon, and bankers and investors were actively pushing for consolidation in the sector.[20] Donald D. Lennox, the chair and CEO of International Harvester, said colorfully at the time (and ironically in retrospect, given the fate of the company, as discussed below), "There's going to have to be some marriages, or there's going to have to be some deaths."[21]

International Harvester, Allis-Chalmers, and Massey-Ferguson were particularly hard hit by the farm crisis. Over 1978 to 1986, for example,

Massey-Ferguson dramatically scaled back expenditures and cut its workforce by more than 60 percent. The firm began to contract out the manufacture of its machines to other suppliers and shifted its focus to marketing.[22] Allis-Chalmers suffered huge losses in the early 1980s and filed for bankruptcy before being scooped up by the German firm Klockner-Humboldt Deutz for just over a third of its book value, to form Deutz-Allis.[23] Meanwhile, Ford Tractor purchased the conglomerate firm Sperry Corporation's ailing subsidiary, New Holland, a manufacturer of haying equipment, at a bargain price, forming Ford New Holland Inc.[24]

Over the course of the 1970s and 1980s, most of the North American firms increasingly organized their production similar to the automobile sector, with component parts such as engines—and sometimes entire machines—sourced globally to save on labor costs. By the 1980s, the major firms began to source especially from Europe, and increasingly from Japan from subsidiary firms they purchased abroad or from other producers. Deere, for example, established a subsidiary firm in Germany and also purchased some machines from Japanese firms, whereas Massey-Ferguson manufactured its products in Britain, France, and Italy and also purchased some machines from Japanese manufacturers. This global sourcing was especially the case for smaller tractors, under 80 horsepower, which were no longer made in North America as of the mid-1980s. One industry association representative said at the time, "I can remember the day when it would be sacrilege for Deere or Harvester to put their name or their paint on something they didn't produce."[25]

Although these were important shifts in the farm machinery industry, the most dramatic change came with the collapse of International Harvester, which was the lead firm in the sector since 1902. In 1977, the firm brought in a new chief executive officer, Archie McArdle, the first time it had selected a successor from outside the McCormick family. McArdle was not just from outside the family's inner circle; he was also from outside the farm sector, having formerly been a senior executive at Xerox. Analysts have noted that McArdle's lack of familiarity with the boom-bust business cycles in the farm sector, which do not always align evenly with broader economic cycles, led him to make fateful decisions about farm machinery production in the late 1970s and early 1980s.[26] International Harvester was particularly affected by overproduction and overcapacity by the early 1980s, with excessive inventories and rapidly accumulating debt. At one point in 1984, the firm had as many as fifty thousand large tractors sitting in storage, an inventory that normally would take ten to thirteen months to clear.[27] It was a classic case of growing too big and becoming inefficient as a result—the curse of bigness.

International Harvester seriously considered filing for bankruptcy after experiencing five consecutive annual losses, which forced it to cut costs wherever it could to avoid defaulting on its loans. Harvester's farm equipment arm was eventually purchased in 1985 by the conglomerate firm Tenneco, the parent firm of J. I. Case, which aimed to bring together the two firms, both of which were experiencing difficulties in the farm downturn.[28] Tenneco had already suspended tractor and combine production for six weeks in 1984 at a number of its US plants to cut costs and clear inventory after experiencing losses. To finance the purchase, it raised $300 million by issuing debt securities on financial markets.[29]

The US Department of Justice closely reviewed the proposal for Tenneco's purchase of International Harvester. Its concern was that the merger would bring together two of the main firms that had dominated the sector for so many years and would effectively eliminate one of J. I. Case's key competitors from the market. The merger was allowed to proceed, however, on the grounds that Tenneco was purchasing what was considered to be a failing firm, a circumstance in which antitrust authorities tend to be more lenient. Indeed, reporting at the time dubbed the antitrust review a "low-hurdle event."[30] The high hurdle event was ensuring that the firm was profitable. Tenneco eventually also purchased Harvester's European-based businesses. International Harvester continued its heavy truck business and subsequently changed its name to Navistar, but it was out of the farm machinery business for good.

Following the acquisition, Tenneco permanently closed the International Harvester farm equipment production lines and instead focused its production entirely on the J. I. Case brand. With this move, the International Harvester brand, which had become household name for farm machinery, was buried. The closure of the Harvester tractor plant at Rock Island, Illinois, alone cut around 40 percent of US tractor manufacturing capacity, removing competition for J. I. Case.[31] In order to clear the International Harvester machines out of its inventory, Tenneco pursued deep discounts across its machinery line, which in turn sparked distress in the remaining firms in the sector. The other firms had no choice but to respond with price cuts of their own just to stay afloat in an unwelcome price war, a virtual replay of the harvester wars that occurred in the late nineteenth century (see chapter 2).

Deere was the only firm that managed not to be cajoled into a merger or acquisition in the 1980s. Indeed, if it had, the deal likely would have been turned back by the US Department of Justice because the firm already had a nearly 40 percent share of the tractor market by that time. Deere, however, experienced a sharp drop in revenue in 1984 and faced a major strike in its workforce in 1986, the latter providing Tenneco with a lucky opportunity to clear out its remaining International Harvester inventory. Meanwhile, Tenneco dramatically scaled back the J. I. Case dealer network. Nonetheless, within months of the acquisition of International Harvester, Tenneco was threatened with forced restructuring by an activist investor, which the firm was able to hold off.[32]

Although the older firms in the sector were facing hardships throughout the 1980s, the Japanese firm Kubota saw its star rise in this period. Kubota has a long history, with its origins dating back to 1890, when it produced engines and steel products. In 1974, the firm formed a joint venture with Marubeni Corporation, a large Japanese *soga sosha* trading house, in France to produce small-sized tractors for the European and North American markets. The new venture challenged Ford and Massey-Ferguson, which had previously dominated in global sales of small- and medium-sized tractors.[33] By the mid-1980s, Kubota had already captured around 60 percent of the small tractor market in Canada and the United States.[34] The firm saw strong sales and opened a manufacturing facility in the United States in the late 1980s.[35]

In addition to the major restructuring in the farm machinery sector in the 1980s, a few additional megamergers occurred in the 1990s, largely completing the shift to the dominant firms that still reign today. In 1990, top executives at Deutz-Allis bought out the firm from parent company Klockner-Humboldt Deutz and renamed the firm Allis-Gleaner Corporation (now known as AGCO). The firm sought to specialize in financing and outsourced almost all of its manufacturing production, which it was able to do because many of the other firms in the industry had spare capacity. It also went on a buying spree and acquired, among other firms, White Tractor in 1991 and Massey-Ferguson in 1994. The automobile firm Fiat purchased the majority of New Holland's shares in 1991, and in 1999, New Holland merged with Tenneco's J. I. Case to form CNH Industrial. The deal with New Holland would have delivered CNH a huge segment of the market, which prompted the US Justice Department to challenge the merger. Both firms divested from certain parts of their businesses in response, after which the US government approved the deal.[36]

The restructuring and consolidation in the farm machinery sector in the 1980s and 1990s had huge implications in terms of the profile of the leading firms. Europe and Japan were much more present in the ownership and production of farm machinery following the mergers mentioned above. In the United States, for example, sales from Europe and Japan accounted for around 50 percent of total farm machinery market in the late 1970s, but by the late 1980s, 85 percent of American sales of farm machinery were made abroad.[37] It was a remarkable shift from a century earlier, when most of the firms making farm machinery were based in North America. A depiction of these changes is shown in figure 7.1.

A MERGER FRENZY IN THE FERTILIZER SECTOR CLOSES OUT THE CENTURY

The fertilizer sector has historically been highly concentrated at the domestic level and controlled at the international level by cartels, as outlined in chapter 3. But even with this kind of market structure, many firms were still operating in the sector in the 1960s and 1970s, largely because of the relative separation of firms specializing in nitrogen, phosphorus, and potassium and the unique dynamics of domestic markets. The fertilizer sector has always been subject to volatility because it is reliant on and integrated with markets for its key nutrient inputs and for energy, an important ingredient of synthetic nitrogen production. All of these inputs are globally traded commodities, and thus their prices reflect broader trends in the global political economy as well as agricultural conditions and prices, which influence supply and demand, and hence the final prices of fertilizers.

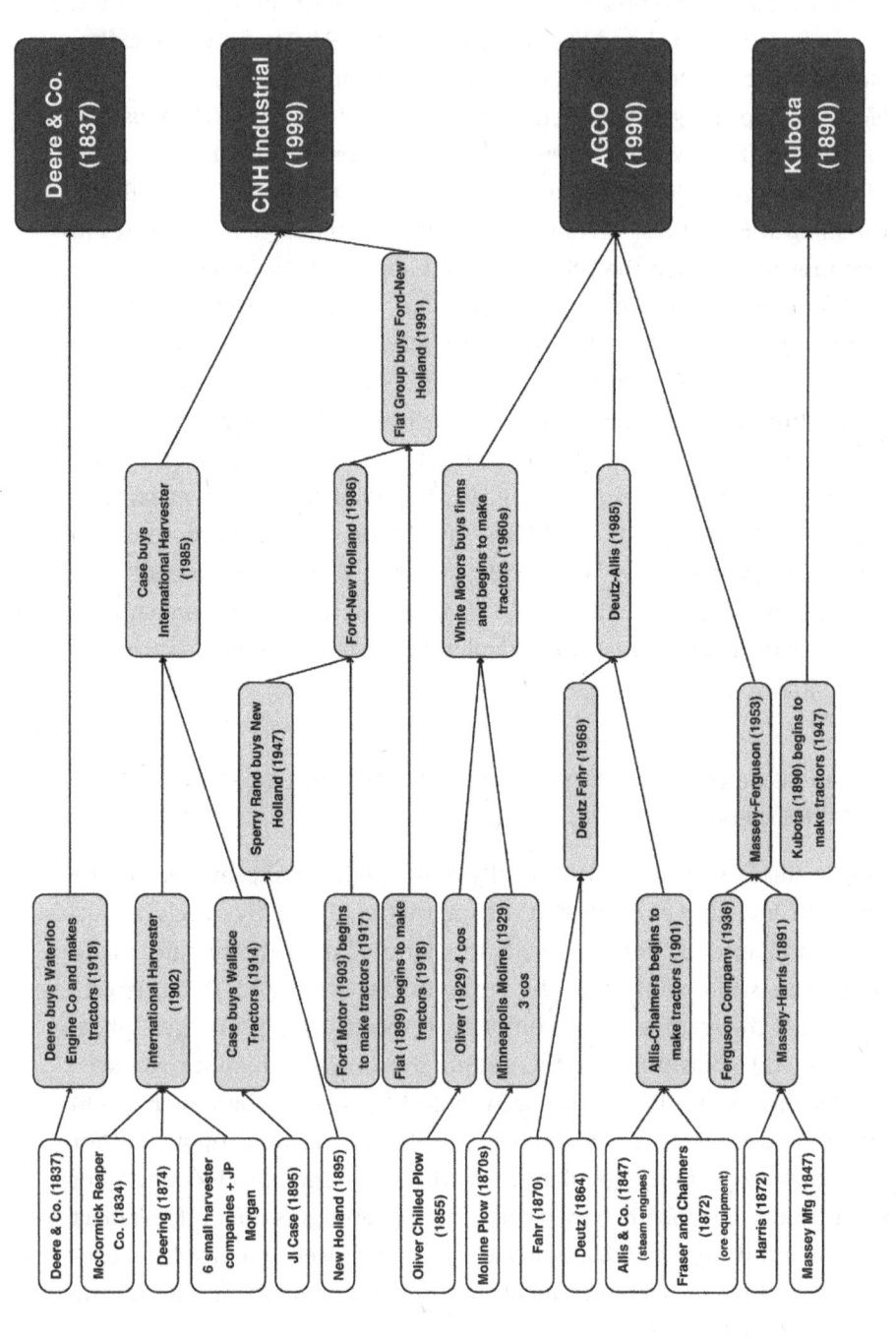

7.1 Major mergers and acquisitions in the farm machinery sector since the 1830s. Sources: Business press; corporate websites; sources cited in this book.

The fertilizer industry is also particularly vulnerable to overproduction. There has long been a risk of overmining of phosphorus and potash especially, especially once industrial equipment made it possible to mine on a massive scale. With respect to synthetic nitrogen production, changing production techniques altered the scale of production needed to achieve efficiencies. Whereas in the late 1950s firms had to produce 100–500 tonnes of ammonia per day to be profitable, by the mid-1960s, they had to produce a minimum of 1,000 tonnes per day to achieve profits. As a result, there were large increases in the productive capacity of fertilizer firms throughout the 1960s, which outpaced demand and resulted in lower prices.[38] The price of anhydrous ammonia, for example, fell to just $75/tonne in 1970, half its price in 1969.[39] Sagging profits from sliding prices led several producers to leave the market, including some oil companies that had moved into the sector in prior decades, whereas others reduced their capacity by shuttering old plants and choosing not to build new ones.

Weak profits in this era also encouraged increased cartel activity among the fertilizer firms that sought to fix prices at home as well as with foreign producer to boost profits. As noted in chapter 3, such cartels were exempt from US antitrust laws under the 1918 Webb-Pomerene act, so long as they did not result in domestic market distortions. Member firms of the Concentrated Phosphate Export Association (which succeeded the earlier Phosphate Export Association) were successfully sued by the US Department of Justice for domestic price fixing in the 1960s. After losing the case, the association disbanded but reappeared in 1971 as the Phosphate Chemical Export Association, also known as PhosChem.[40]

The sector was jolted out of the doldrums in the early 1970s, as higher grain prices prompted farmers to expand their acreage, in turn increasing demand for fertilizer. This spike in demand occurred just a few years after some firms had left the sector, leading to an especially sharp increase in fertilizer prices. Many of the firms that scaled back production in the previous decade were reluctant to make significant new investments to expand their capacity, given the experience of overproduction and slumping prices that followed when they implemented that strategy in the 1960s. Moreover, any new investments in production plants would take two to four years to become fully operational. As a result, fertilizer shortages deepened not just in the United States but also globally, as many countries, including in the developing world, had weak production capacity.

The situation was exacerbated by the increased export of US fertilizers, which captured higher prices on global markets due to domestic price controls imposed by the Nixon administration in an effort to tame inflation as food prices spiked in the early 1970s. When the United States abandoned fertilizer price controls in late 1973 amid growing concerns about shortages, the domestic price shot up sharply, prompting farmers to accuse the industry of purposely engineering a shortage to drive up profits.[41] In this context, some farmers experimented with lowering the amount of fertilizer they used on their crops in an attempt to reduce their costs.

Declining demand led to weak profits for fertilizer firms in the 1980s after the boom years of the 1970s. Not only were farmers trying to cut back on fertilizers, but US government policy encouraged cuts to crop production in the face of falling grain prices. The agricultural sector slump lasted more than five years in both Europe and North America, prompting many fertilizer companies to file for bankruptcy, drastically cut back their operations, or sell off their assets. This serious downturn in the sector eventually fueled a new frenzy of mergers and consolidation from the mid- to late 1980s, a process that lasted over a decade and completely restructured the sector.[42] Firms sought to consolidate to reduce their fixed costs and improve their efficiency. But surplus capacity was stubbornly persistent and profit levels remained low throughout the 1980s.

Beyond the broader market dynamics within the farming sector, several other factors contributed to the trend toward greater consolidation in the fertilizer industry that began in the 1980s. First, there was a push for greater integration of complementary products and technologies within the sector. Most firms up until the 1970s were specialized in the production of one of the three nutrients of nitrogen, phosphorus, or potash. The reason for this separation was the geographical connection to physical mining operations for both potash and phosphorus, which were under the control of specific domestic firms working in the region where the minerals were present. Similarly, synthetic nitrogen fertilizers required a source of cheap energy, meaning that plant facilities were also specific to certain geographical regions.

By the late 1970s and early 1980s, many of the firms in the sector sought to gain an advantage in the marketplace by bringing together the production of two or three of these elements in one firm. Some large firms specializing in one or another of the key fertilizer ingredients looked to merge with or acquire other firms specializing in the other nutrients. This kind of consolidation can be considered horizontal, in that it brought related products at the same stage in supply chains together under one firm. For example, IMC Global, one of the largest US phosphate fertilizer producers (known earlier as the International Minerals and Chemicals Corporation), was at risk of going bankrupt in the early 1990s until it diversified by acquiring a potash firm. Cominco Fertilizer was spun off from its parent mining firm and changed its name to Agrium in 1995, when it purchased an American phosphate company to complement its existing specialization in potash and nitrogen production. Similarly, the Potash Corporation of Saskatchewan acquired a nitrogen-based fertilizer firm in the 1990s.[43]

Having access to all three key fertilizer ingredients gave these firms the possibility of vertical expansion into fertilizer mixing and preparation as well as retail, functions that previously had been undertaken by intermediary fertilizer mixing firms that purchased ingredients from the mining and nitrogen-producing industries. Further mergers occurred that solidified vertical integration whereby the large firms bought up smaller firms at different points along the supply chain. Agrium, for example, purchased retail operations in the mid-1990s and focused on marketing directly to farmers. Terra Industries, a US firm that began with nitrogen production in the mid-1960s, made a number of acquisitions, including in the United States and Canada, and in 1997, it purchased Imperial Chemical Industries' fertilizer operations and moved into fertilizer retail.[44]

Many nitrogen-producing facilities that were upgraded in the 1960s had become inefficient by the 1980s and required further modernization. Technological changes in the production of synthetic nitrogen continued, and by 1980, the minimum amount of ammonia production needed to maintain profitability had increased to 1,500 to 2,000 tonnes per day.[45] The large plant size required for profitability acted as a major barrier to entry that crowded out smaller firms. Some firms, such as Koch Industries, a conglomerate firm and one of the largest private US companies, acquired nitrogen fertilizer assets in the late 1980s, which enabled it to enter the industry. These developments within the nitrogen market were important for the fertilizer industry overall because nitrogen is typically more important in terms of both volume and value compared to the other minerals.

Broader market forces are also important for understanding consolidation in the fertilizer sector in this period. The rise of neoliberal economic policies in the 1980s accelerated the process of economic globalization and encouraged the entry of some new producers that had access to the necessary resources for fertilizer production. For example, with the fall of the Soviet Union in the early 1990s, there was suddenly abundant natural gas, potash and phosphate at rock-bottom prices that could be sourced from Eastern Europe, which challenged the dominant global fertilizer firms to adjust. Many European fertilizer firms took advantage of the ability to purchase inexpensive natural gas from Russia, as well as potash and phosphates from Russia and other Eastern European countries, bringing these inputs into global fertilizer supply chains. At the same time, relying on Russian inputs brought its own geopolitical risks, as there were concerns that the Kremlin could cut off the spigot at any time.[46]

These market, technological, and political dynamics encouraged firms in the sector to expand and conglomerate in order to take advantage of new global markets for energy and minerals. Consolidation was also encouraged by rising demand for fertilizer imports from countries such as India and China, as new markets could help to absorb the excess supply of fertilizers that were still present in the sector in the 1980s and early 1990s.[47] These dynamics encouraged many new global fertilizer deals. For example, Norsk Hydro bought a Canadian fertilizer company in 1996, giving the firm access to the North American market.[48] BASF sold its fertilizer unit, which specialized in nitrogen, to its former subsidiary K+S, another German firm specializing in potash, in the 1990s. This conglomerate subsequently merged with the Potash Corporation of Saskatchewan, giving the latter access to the European market.[49] Also in this period, IMC

Global, a major phosphate fertilizer producer, bought up potash interests, further consolidating the market and bringing together multiple nutrients into one multinational firm. In 2004, IMC Global merged with grain trading firm Cargill's crop nutrition division to form a new fertilizer giant, Mosaic. Cargill maintained a 64 percent ownership of Mosaic until 2011, when Cargill divested its share of the firm.[50]

As this rapid and extensive consolidation unfolded, there was also a growing trend toward the privatization of state-run and cooperative fertilizer companies. As noted in chapter 3, many of the early fertilizer companies had deep ties to states through either state-run or associated firms or state-controlled cartels, particularly because nitrogen was an important ingredient for explosive weapons. With the rise of neoliberal policies in the 1980s, which emphasized the retreat of states from economic policymaking and the privatization of state-run industries, the fertilizer sector saw some important changes. The Potash Corporation of Saskatchewan (PCS), for example, was established by the Canadian provincial government of Saskatchewan as a Crown corporation in 1975. With the sector overall facing depressed profits and with PCS suffering heavy losses in the 1980s, the provincial government of Saskatchewan moved to privatize the firm in 1989.[51] Once it was privatized, PCS went on a massive buying spree, snapping up other fertilizer companies to improve its competitive position relative to other firms that were also engaging in consolidation, buying firms that specialized in nitrogen and phosphorus. By 1996, PCS was the third largest producer of potash in the world.[52]

The cooperative firm Central Farmers Fertilizer Company, which later came to be known as CF Industries, had long operated as a mechanism to pool purchasing power among buyers. Its original aim was to ensure a steady supply of farm inputs for its members at low prices, such as nitrogen and phosphate fertilizers purchased from the Tennessee Valley Authority.[53] Following the slump in the fertilizer industry in the 1980s and the volatile market experienced in the 1990s, there was a push from within Central Farmers Fertilizer Company to either divest the company or merge with a stronger firm. Following initial discussions with both Terra Industries and Agrium regarding a buyout that did not ultimately materialize, the firm adopted a new business model that prioritized profit over its original cooperative aims. Central Farmers became listed as a publicly traded company in 2005, effectively becoming a private firm, CF Industries, which went on to become one of the largest fertilizer companies in the world.

In 2004, Norsk Hydro, a private firm in which the Norwegian government had long had significant share ownership, spun off its fertilizer unit as Yara, a publicly traded company. Although Norsk Hydro's origins were in fertilizer production dating back to the early 1900s, the firm's unique hydropowered process for nitrogen synthesis had become obsolete by the 1920s. The firm moved into energy and aluminum production alongside its fertilizer business but decided to split off its agricultural arm by the early 2000s. At that point, Yara was one of the largest fertilizer companies in the world. Although it became a private firm, the Norwegian government owned just over a third of its shares. The spinoff enabled Yara to make acquisitions without having to compete for capital with other arms of Norsk Hydro. Once it was solely focused on fertilizer, Yara went on an expansion binge and acquired or pursued joint ventures with a number of fertilizer firms around the world, largely in Africa, Asia, and Latin America.[54]

Overall, the reconfiguration of the fertilizer industry over this relatively short period was dramatic. As European fertilizer executive Frans Visser remarked to the press in 1990, "In 1985 there were 70 companies while now there are 30, of which six command more than 75 percent of capacity."[55] Figure 7.2 depicts the major changes in the fertilizer sector (including through the post-2015 period, which is discussed in depth in chapter 9).

CONSEQUENCES OF FARM MACHINERY AND FERTILIZER CONSOLIDATION

The consolidation that took place in the farm machinery and fertilizer sectors in the 1980s and 1990s gave the firms that remained at the top increased influence over the food system, which manifested in different ways. A small number of firms ended up with large market shares in the fertilizer and machinery sectors, giving them not only more market power but also greater influence over the technological trajectory of the sector, including the wider social and ecological consequences of those

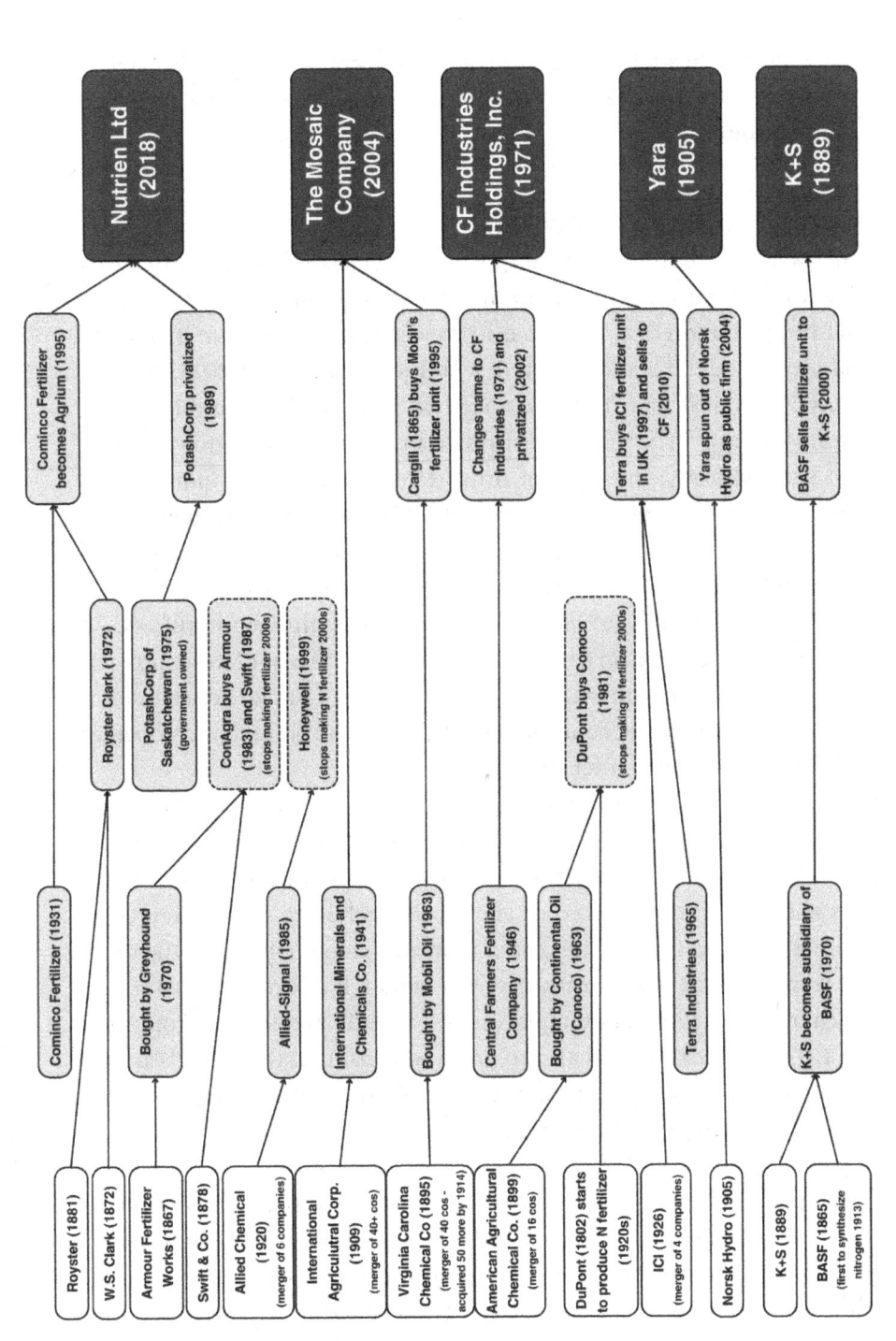

7.2 Major mergers and acquisitions in the fertilizer since the 1880s. *Sources:* Business press; corporate websites; sources cited in this book.

technologies. In addition, the firms at the top of the sector gained greater influence over government policies, including in ways that benefited their bottom lines.

LACK OF MARKET COMPETITION

Increased concentration enhanced the market power of the firms that rose to the top in this period. In the US farm equipment sector, the market concentration of the top four firms went from 53 percent in 1980 to 58 percent in 2002, and rose further still to 61 percent in 2012.[56] By the early 2000s, just four firms controlled 80 percent of tractor sales in the United States.[57] The dominant firms also commanded a growing market share globally: the top four firms were estimated to command over 50 percent of the global market by 2009.[58] Fertilizers also saw heightened concentration by the close of the twentieth century as the number of firms fell and those that remained became more vertically integrated. In 1996, 48 percent of the US market for synthetic nitrogen fertilizers, 73 percent of the phosphate fertilizer market, and 89 percent of the potash fertilizer market were controlled by just four firms.[59] Similar concentration was occurring in other countries as well, while the dominant companies increasingly operated internationally.

This high level of concentration in the farm machinery and fertilizer sectors raised numerous concerns about potential abuses of market power in several countries as it unfolded. In the United States, for example, farmers were increasingly concerned about being beholden to just a few companies for these inputs. The cost of farm equipment relative to the value of crops changed dramatically over this period. If a farmer wanted to pay for a tractor in corn, for example, the cost would have doubled from 1969 to 1974, despite the fact that corn prices were rising at the time.[60] Farmers also resented their reliance on just a handful of fertilizer companies that they accused of deliberately restricting supply to drive up prices.[61]

Beyond farmers' widespread suspicions of market abuse, firms in both the farm machinery and fertilizer sectors were investigated by antitrust authorities from the 1970s to the 1990s. For example, in 1976, nine major potash corporations, including IMC and the Potash Company of America, were indicted in the United States for violating antitrust laws. The indictments were connected to a scheme that allegedly began in 1969, which aimed to limit production in order to stabilize prices of potash. The firms were also accused of attempting to convince government officials in Saskatchewan to join the conspiracy. The companies were eventually acquitted, however, after a mistrial was declared when the jury was not able to reach a verdict.[62] In 1984, Deere was fined $1.4 million by the European Commission for violating the European community's antitrust rules. It was accused of actively seeking to prevent farm equipment dealers in countries where the machinery was less expensive from selling it on to residents of other countries in Europe where the equipment was more expensive.[63]

As concern heightened, Dan Glickman, the US secretary of agriculture, formed the Advisory Committee on Agricultural Concentration in 1996. In its first report, which focused on concentration in the meat and livestock industries, the committee set out concerns regarding concentration in the agricultural sector more broadly:

Farm producers find themselves facing processors or manufacturers in very concentrated markets, who have incentives to expand because of scale economies in consumer products. This situation offers incentives for collusive price behavior at worst, and for diminished information flows at best. Where information concerning prices is not easily available or accessible, uncertainty and anxiety often translate into hostility and distrust. . . . As we move to competing in a global marketplace, we frequently find monopolistic behavior to be subtle and not easily verified. Advantages of large firms now seem more important in international competition, while regard for small, domestic firms seems to have declined. In addition, the apparent effectiveness of public agencies also may have declined. In light of these factors, the historical pattern of antitrust enforcement has come to be regarded as a less powerful force in detecting and modifying anticompetitive behavior.[64]

Although the issue of tackling corporate concentration in agriculture garnered support across the political spectrum, few substantive legislative changes occurred. This was despite some active efforts to bring about legislative reform. For example, several bills introduced in the US Senate in the late 1990s and early 2000s sought to place a moratorium on large agribusiness mergers in the country. Several other bills were introduced around this time to ensure fair competition for farmers. Glickman remained concerned about farmers losing power in relation to the large agricultural companies. Although several hearings were held on the theme in the US Senate over the next few years, little change in terms of policy or practice resulted.[65]

These efforts floundered because they occurred in a context where US antitrust legislation was being weakened in the wake of an economic policy shift toward neoliberalism in the 1970s and 1980s. The ideas espoused at the time by the Chicago school approach to economics, which called for less robust oversight of markets in the name of generating market efficiencies, were increasingly adopted in policy contexts, including in the interpretation and application of competition policy in the United States. As a result, antitrust policy became effectively "economized," though this attempt to distance it from politics was anything but apolitical.

This shift in antitrust policy followed the publication of Robert Bork's influential 1978 book, *The Antitrust Paradox*, which explicitly aimed to reshape the political interpretation of the law in ways that fit the neoliberal agenda.[66] Bork argued that the purpose of competition policy should be to maximize consumer welfare and increase economic efficiency, not to rein in corporate power. Antitrust legal analyst Tim Wu calls Bork's ideas "a radically narrow reading of the Sherman Act" because it dismissed the broader concerns about market structure and corporate power that was embodied in the original law.[67] Historians Naomi Oreskes and Erik Conway put it bluntly: "Ignoring the actual history of antitrust legislation, Bork elided concerns about inequality, private power, and the defense of democracy."[68]

Bork's arguments had enormous sway in the broader political context of neoliberalism, which led to a reinterpretation of antitrust laws away from regulating the structure of markets and toward maximizing consumer welfare.[69] The result of this shift was that proposed mergers and growing market control in key sectors were reviewed not with an eye to whether they stifled competition or increased market power. Rather, merger reviews increasingly focused on whether they affected consumer prices or led to market inefficiencies that might harm consumers—which became known as the "consumer welfare standard." In short, consideration of the impact of market structures on competition was no longer the primary driver of antitrust policy. If firms could convince regulators that larger firms meant lower prices, even if there was little follow-up to ascertain whether that was actually the case, proposed mergers were likely to be approved.

DEEPENING TECHNOLOGICAL LOCK-INS
In addition to gaining more power to shape the market, the firms at the top of the machinery and fertilizer sectors played a role in deepening the lock-in of industrial agriculture through the sale and promotion of their products. With just a handful of firms dominating both markets, those companies played a huge role in determining what farm machinery was available to farmers, and the firms actively worked to increase demand for fertilizers. Throughout this period, even while these firms were promoting the use of ever-higher-tech equipment and increased use of fertilizers, there was growing awareness of the wider social and ecological costs of the adoption of these inputs. But with farmers already locked in to these technologies and firms continuing to promote them, these wider problems only became more entrenched.

As outlined earlier, farmland consolidation was a major concern in North America from the 1940s to the 1960s, when there was a dramatic decline in the number of farms and an equally dramatic rise in the average size of farms. This process of consolidation continued in the last decades of the twentieth century. As farm machinery became more available, bigger, and more sophisticated, it allowed farmers to manage ever-larger acreages. While in the early 1980s most cropland in the United States was made up of farms under 600 acres, by 2013 most cropland was made up of farms at least 1,100 acres in size, with many farms being as much as ten times that size.[70] Similar trends of increasing farm sizes combined with a decline in the overall number of farms occurred in other parts of the world as well, including across most industrialized countries.[71]

The availability of farm machinery also encouraged farmers to specialize their operations to make the management of larger farms simpler, and more stylized equipment designed for very specific tasks abounded. Between 1970 and 2005, for example, the number of acres a farmer could manage using the tractors and planters available at the time increased from 40 to 420, as machinery became larger and more sophisticated. A USDA report on farm size notes that "a farmer could harvest more than

12 times as much in a day in 2010 as in 1970."[72] As machinery became more powerful, it also became more sophisticated and included more bells and whistles. In the late 1970s, for example, some tractor manufacturers began to add luxuries such as closed cabs with air-conditioning and heaters, sound systems, and even television sets, as farmers were spending more hours in their tractors because they had to harvest ever more land. One farmer explained the need for these extras to the *New York Times*: "To make a living today you need to farm at least 500 acres—it used to be 60. Now, I can plow at least 60 a day. I can plant 100 acres of beans a day. But I spend between 12 and 15 hours a day in the tractor. It gets boring after a bit."[73]

When the farm crisis hit in the 1980s, many farmers were unable to service their debts and ended up leaving farming altogether. They often sold their farms to those who remained, leading to a further consolidation of farmland holdings. These trends reinforced earlier patterns of Black farmers being disenfranchised from farms they had once owned or rented. New farmers, including young people and recent immigrants, were also often excluded due to the high costs of getting into farming.[74] In 1969, the number of Black farmers in the United States stood at 87,000 (down from 925,000 in 1920), constituting only 3.2 percent of farm operators. This number fell further in the following decades, such that by 1997, there were just over 18,000 Black farmers in the United States—only 1 percent of the farm operators in the country.[75] The common image in children's storybooks of a white male farmer on a tractor may be reflective of the general farmland and tractor ownership in North America, but it obfuscates the history of dispossession and exclusion that came with farmland consolidation and the rise of farm machinery as part of the industrial agricultural model, a process that has continued for well over a century.

The central role of machinery in industrial agriculture also raised important concerns during this era, including concerns that farmers were being increasingly tethered to broader economic trends, such as the price of energy on global markets. The growing use of fossil fuels to power ever-larger machinery also contributes to greenhouse gases that cause climate change. And as machinery became larger and heavier, it also became associated with soil compaction and fertility loss.[76]

The dominant firms played a large role in promoting greater use of fertilizer, stressing to farmers that it is indispensable for their operations. Indeed, world consumption of fertilizer shot up sharply after 1945 and continued to accelerate from the 1960s onward (see figure 7.3). But the growing use of synthetic nitrogen fertilizers in particular has been widely associated with numerous environmental problems. The uptake of synthetic nitrogen in farm fields is notoriously low; for example, it is below 50 percent in numerous European Union (EU) countries, whereas the global food system as a whole (i.e., taking dietary composition into account) has a nitrogen efficiency of just 15 percent.[77] What this means in practice is that fertilizers run off the fields where it is applied and into watercourses, depositing high levels of nitrate and phosphorus pollution in water sources and causing eutrophication, problems that have been recognized since at least the 1950s but which have accelerated as fertilizer use climbed sharply. Nitrogen runoff also raises emissions of nitrous oxide, a powerful greenhouse gas and contributor to acid rain. Additionally, synthetic fertilizer production uses an extremely high amount of natural gas, which also adds to its overall climate impacts. In total, the

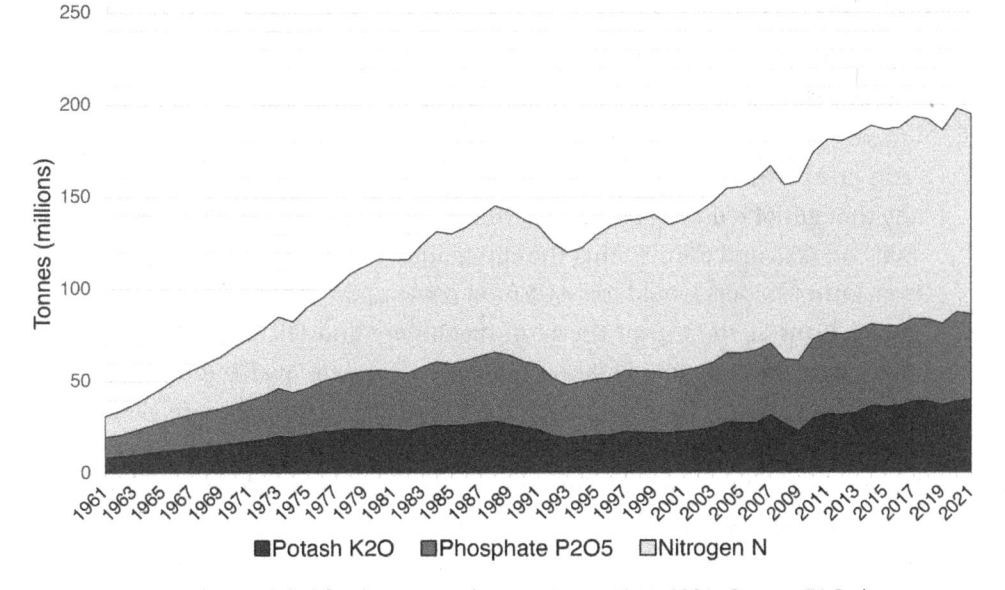

7.3 Cumulative global fertilizer use, select nutrients, 1961–2021. *Source*: FAO data.

chemical fertilizer industry accounts for around 2.4 percent of global greenhouse gas emissions.[78]

SHAPING POLICY IN SUPPORT OF INDUSTRIAL AGRICULTURE

Despite greater awareness of the problems associated with ever-greater use of farm machinery and synthetic fertilizers, these industries maintained active lobby operations to try to influence policy and governance in ways that support the industrial agricultural model—and with it, demand for their products. For example, a prominent industry lobby group for the fertilizer sector based in the United States, the Fertilizer Institute (FI), took up several causes in the 1980s and 1990s to advance its interests while criticizing efforts to address the farm crisis and support sustainable agriculture. It lobbied extensively against US farm programs that encouraged farmers to scale back on the acreages they planted when farm surpluses were mounting and prices were falling, because any reduction in planting would mean less demand for fertilizer.[79]

In the early 1990s, the FI launched a campaign to push back against "low-input sustainable agriculture" (at the time called LISA for short) that drew interest from farmers as a means to save on fertilizer and other input costs. When the US government allocated funds to the USDA for research into LISA, the FI openly attacked it, claiming that the USDA was supporting an effort based on no scientific evidence. Along with the chemical industry, it launched a campaign to discredit the approach throughout the farm press.[80] In an attempt to scare policymakers and farmers away from any thought of reducing chemical fertilizer use, the FI also funded a major study on LISA and claimed that the elimination of fertilizers and pesticides from farm practices would drive US food prices up by some 45 percent.[81]

The firms at the top of the farm machinery and fertilizer industries lobby government policymakers regularly. Data are available only on the lobby activities of these firms in the United States from the late 1990s, in Canada since 2008, and in the EU since 2015, when transparency legislation began to require it. But even a quick glance at the reports from the United States indicates that these firms spent hundreds of thousands of dollars each (and collectively millions of dollars) in the late 1990s and early 2000s. Firms met with policymakers to discuss a range of topics, from emissions standards for engines, to environmental regulations, to farm policies that could affect the acreages planted.[82] We know that farm policies have generally favored large farms as well as industrial agriculture. How much of this policy is the result of lobbying is hard to determine, but what we do know is that large agricultural firms actively sought to shape the policies that mattered for their bottom lines.[83]

CONCLUSION

The restructuring of both the farm machinery and fertilizer sectors in the 1980s and 1990s marked a profound change in these industries. As in earlier eras, market, technology, and policy factors played a large role in the consolidation of the farm machinery and fertilizer industries. A major contributing factor to the mergers in both sectors in this period was the farm boom and bust of the 1970s and 1980s, which first drove up demand and then gave way to dramatically lower demand for farm machinery and fertilizer. In this sense, most of the deals in this era were "mergers of distress," which resulted in significant restructuring of the two industries.

Firms in both sectors pursued consolidation strategies that aimed to make them more resilient in the face of volatility in the farm economy. In the fertilizer sector, that meant both horizontal and vertical integration. In the farm machinery sector, it meant more global sourcing and mergers with larger conglomerate firms that had businesses in other sectors as well. This consolidation was made more complex by technological changes in both sectors, including changing production methods for fertilizers as well as more complex machinery needs for ever larger and more specialized farms. Further, the policy context also shifted, with a weakening of antitrust policies that accompanied the rise of neoliberalism in this era.

As these industries underwent major restructuring, the firms at the top maintained their capacity to shape markets, technological trajectories, and the broader policy context in ways that served their interests, such as undermining market competition, deepening technological lock-ins, and lobbying policymakers. Yet even while these firms pushed their vision of the further extension of industrial agriculture—and indeed fertilizer use ballooned, and land consolidation continued—awareness of the associated costs continued to grow.

8
MERGERS OF OPPORTUNITY IN SEEDS AND PESTICIDES

From the 1970s, a series of mergers and acquisitions resulted in the amalgamation of the agrochemical and seed industries into just a handful of giant firms that specialized in both products. These transformations meant that the inputs sector that had been dominated by four sets of concentrated firms was transformed into a sector dominated by just three sets of even larger and more concentrated firms, with one set of firms now producing two of the main inputs—seeds and pesticides. Consolidation of these industries took place in two main phases in the latter decades of the twentieth century, the first beginning in the 1970s with several large chemical, pharmaceutical, petroleum, and other industrial firms buying up seed companies alongside consolidation among existing seed firms. Another round of consolidation began in the late 1980s and lasted into the first decade of the 2000s and cemented the pesticide and seed sectors more fully together. Both of these intensive periods of consolidation contributed to larger firms dominating in the inputs sector.

The mergers that brought together firms producing seeds and pesticides were the product of several factors. The market context was important, as growing public concerns about the health and ecological impact of agrochemical pesticides—which include insecticides, herbicides, and fungicides—led to lower demand and flagging profits for agrochemical firms. Weaker profits of the firms were also in part due to stronger regulations that increased the cost of developing new agrochemical products. These dynamics intersected with the advent of agricultural biotechnology, which opened the possibilities of designing seeds and pesticides to work together in a more integral way with genetically modified seed-herbicide technological packages. The pursuit of agricultural biotechnology generated new rivalries between the giant firms for expanded market share for both seeds and agrochemicals. But at the same time, the fact that so few firms dominated the sector by the early 2000s encouraged those firms to sometimes act together in ways that reinforced their power in the marketplace and extended the lock-ins of industrial agriculture. The pursuit of new agricultural biotechnologies also led to expanded herbicide use, which came with costs in terms of health and the environment.

LARGE CONGLOMERATES SET THEIR EYES ON SEEDS

As early as the mid- to late 1960s, large firms with ties to the agrochemical industry began to acquire seed companies. This early wave of consolidation in the sector brought the seed and pesticide industries closer together as petroleum, pharmaceutical, and chemical companies moved into seed breeding and sales. There were around ten major seed companies that dominated the market in the United States at this time, in addition to others that had global presence. As outlined in chapter 4, however, the main companies that engaged in field crop seed research and development and dominated the hybrid seed market were Pioneer Hi-Bred, Funk Brothers, DeKalb, and Pfister. Both the larger and smaller firms in the seed sector at that time were typically independent, family-run companies, and the smaller firms were often reproducing seed varieties for the larger ones.[1] Many of both the small and large seed firms were brought into the fold of large chemical, oil, and pharmaceutical firms that produced agrochemicals.

In one of the earlier acquisitions, Upjohn, a conglomerated pharmaceutical and chemical firm, purchased several US-based seed companies in the 1960s. These included the 1968 acquisition of Asgrow, a seed firm that had recently begun to sell herbicides. By the 1970s, larger firms were buying up seed companies in ever-larger numbers, concluding sixty-one such deals, with twenty-seven mergers and acquisitions alone occurring between 1978 and 1980.[2] For example, the chemical firm Ciba-Geigy purchased Funk Brothers Seed Company in 1974 and then expanded its investment into seed genetics research. Sandoz purchased several seed firms in the mid-1970s, and Royal Dutch Shell purchased Nickerson Seeds, a UK-based seed company, at around the same time.[3]

Meanwhile, there was also consolidation within the seed industry itself. Several of the larger US-based seed companies, namely Pioneer Hi-Bred and DeKalb, remained independent firms but grew larger as they acquired other seed companies. These two firms maintained a commanding market share throughout the 1970s and 1980s. In 1975, a relatively new cooperative seed company, Limagrain, which was established in France in 1965, bought out the much older Vilmorin & Cie.[4]

This first wave of seed industry consolidation further accelerated in the 1980s, with over ninety mergers and acquisitions occurring throughout that decade.[5] For example, ICI acquired six seed companies in the mid-1980s and subsequently stepped up its research into pesticides, also purchasing Stauffer chemicals, a US pesticide firm, in 1987. Monsanto also acquired several seed companies in the 1980s, while French chemical and pharmaceutical firm Rhône-Poulenc acquired five seed firms that same decade. Sandoz continued its purchasing spree of seed interests and eventually acquired eight companies, also in the 1980s.[6]

These are just some of the examples of mergers and acquisitions that took place involving the seed industry in these decades. It is nearly impossible to provide a full breakdown of every merger and acquisition that took place at this time because many of the firms were private, family-owned businesses, so the information is not widely available. By the end of the 1980s, a significant proportion of the seed industry had been acquired by a small number of large firms whose main business was focused on other industrial products, but with interests in agrochemicals. Figure 8.1 shows the fate of the four dominant hybrid seed companies during this period.

REGULATORY HURDLES AND GROWING COSTS

Several dynamics encouraged the flurry of seed company acquisitions over the course of the 1970s and 1980s. The chemical industry more

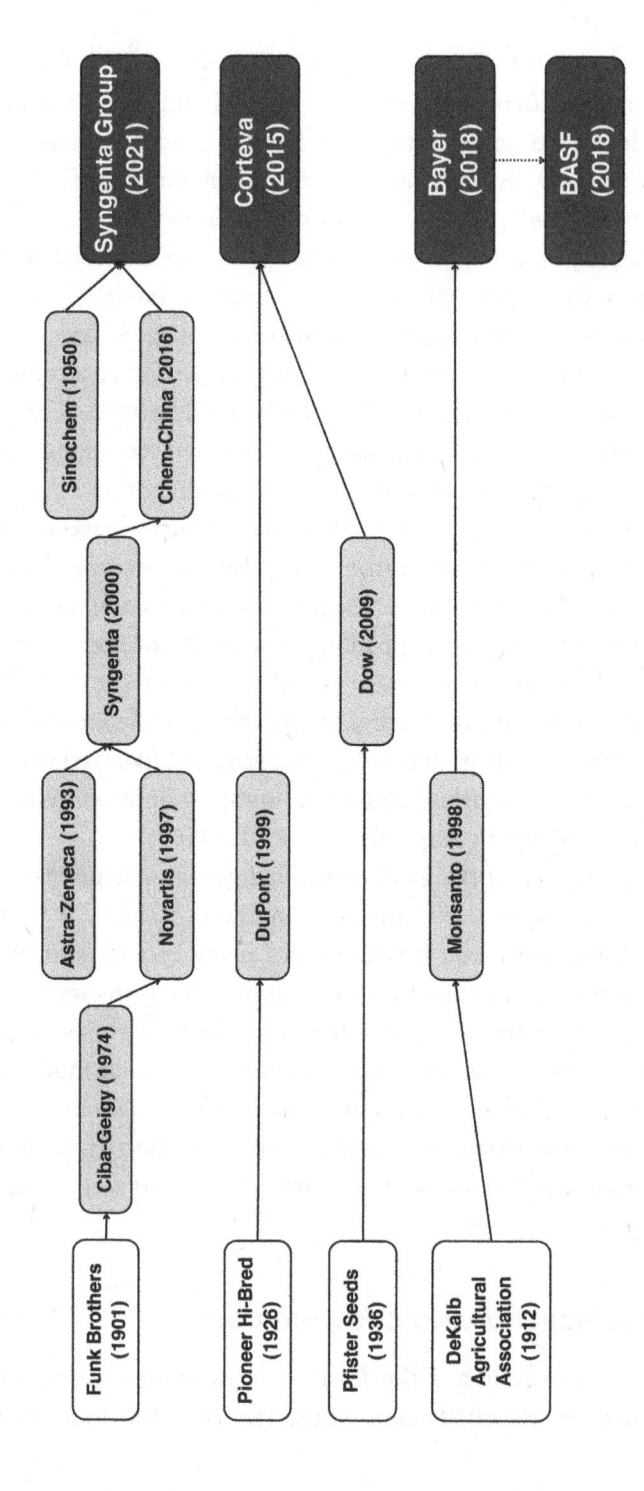

8.1 Fate of the four dominant hybrid seed companies after the 1970s. Sources: Business press; corporate websites; sources cited in this book.

broadly was facing weakened profits in the 1960s and early 1970s, in part due to increased environmental regulations linked to growing health concerns from exposure to agricultural chemicals. The publication of Rachel Carson's *Silent Spring* in 1962 generated huge public awareness of the problems with these chemicals, as outlined in chapter 6. While much of the attention at the time focused on the insecticide DDT, Carson's work provided a strong critique of all agrochemicals, including herbicides.[7] As the issue of toxicity of agrochemicals entered the public consciousness, it prompted stricter regulations. Demand for agricultural chemicals also began to decline in the late 1960s, especially after they were increasingly linked with health problems, including cancer.[8]

By the early 1970s, it had become clear that the days of chemical companies introducing new pesticides onto the market without worrying about their broader potential impact were over. Some of the older agrochemical products—including organochlorine pesticides like DDT, aldrin, and dieldrin—were in the process of being banned in the United States and in other countries. In some cases, agrochemicals were taken off the market before the firms that developed them had a chance to recoup their R&D investment.[9] Some of the banned chemicals, such as DDT, were still produced for export to developing countries, however, where those chemicals were not yet banned.

The growing stringency of regulations governing chemical registration in the United States and in other industrial countries meant higher costs for research and development of new agrochemicals, as well as increased time frames for the introduction of those new products. By the early to mid-1970s, agrochemical firms began to complain about these costs. Dow Chemical, for example, went so far as to categorize regulations as what it considered to be "appropriate," "questionable," and "excessive." The firm then calculated the cost of what it considered to be questionable and excessive regulation, which it figured was around $83 million in 1976, a 38 percent increase over the previous year. The cost of developing new pesticide products increased from around $1 million in 1950 to $5 million in 1970 to $20 million by 1977.[10] Industry was also concerned about the time it took to bring an agricultural chemical to market in the United States, which increased from around 2.75 years in the 1950s to around 4.6 years in the early 1960s, and then to 7 years in the 1965–1975 period.[11]

The reason behind the growing costs and time frames was that regulators required an increasing number of tests to be completed on each chemical before it could be approved for release onto the market.

Rising costs for the introduction of new products put a serious dent in the profits of chemical companies. These firms had come to rely on buoyant sales of pesticides in the 1950s and 1960s. The market for herbicides had grown rapidly since they were widely introduced in the 1950s as farmers adopted them into their regular practices. By the early 1970s, farmers applied these weed-killing chemicals on upwards of 90 percent of their fields for some crops, such as corn. As a result, agrochemical companies sold far more herbicides than they did insecticides and fungicides.[12] The firms were thus eager to ensure that they could maintain high net revenues from the sales of herbicides and were disappointed at the rising costs to register new chemicals.

The farm crisis that began in the late 1970s and early 1980s also affected the profitability of the agrochemical sector, especially when new policies were put in place in the United States and Europe to encourage farmers to reduce their production to avoid the kinds of excessive surpluses that pushed down commodity prices in the 1930s. As farmers scaled back production, their demand for inputs naturally declined.

Within this broader context, the chemical industry more generally was experiencing a downturn in innovation that followed thirty years of rapid growth in the sector during which firms were screening thousands of compounds to develop new chemicals. By the 1960s, the useful properties of most chemical compounds had already been discovered and the number of novel innovations began to drop. For example, between the 1930s and 1980s, there were sixty-three major innovations in the chemical sector—forty of which occurred in the 1930s and 1940s. In the 1950s and 1960s, there were only twenty new major innovations, and by the 1970s and 1980s, only three new innovations emerged from the sector.[13] In this context, an ever-growing number of compounds needed to be screened in order to obtain a single successful commercial pesticide. In 1956, for example, a firm would typically have to screen around eighteen hundred compounds to find a chemical that could be marketed successfully as a pesticide. By 1967, over five thousand compounds needed to be screened, and by 1977, around twelve thousand compounds had to be screened to find a single successful pesticide.[14] At the same time, patents on some key agrochemicals also began to expire in the 1960s and 1970s, leading in many cases to a drop in prices and increased competition from new generic producers.[15]

THE ALLURE OF SEEDS

In this first round of seed acquisitions, agrochemical firms increasingly looked to connect with other parts of the agricultural input sector that could generate more buoyant profits, and seeds were promising in that regard.[16] There were also opportunities to extend complementarities between seeds and pesticides. The acquiring firms, for example, were interested in obtaining the sales and distribution networks of the seed companies, including smaller independent firms that mainly reproduced publicly developed seeds or varieties of the dominant seed firms rather than conducting their own research and development, which they thought could be useful outlets to also market their agrochemicals. Many of the acquisitions at this time were European chemical firms—ICI, Sandoz, Ciba-Geigy, Rhône-Poulenc— buying US-based seed companies to make inroads into North American markets. These acquisitions encouraged some US agrochemical firms, such as Monsanto, to join in the frenzy of seed company acquisitions to keep up with their European counterparts.

There were also other reasons that the chemical industry considered seed companies an interesting investment at this time. The hybrid seed industry was, similar to the agrochemical sector, a research-intensive industry that benefited from patent-like intellectual property protection of its products. As such, chemical, pharmaceutical, and oil companies found it easy to understand the profit model of these products, which required heavy outlays of capital for research and development.[17] Not only did hybrid seed have in-built intellectual property protection because it could not be reliably replanted and the parent lines were not identifiable from the seed itself (see chapter 4), but also from the 1960s and 1970s, there was increased intellectual property protection for plant varieties from policies at both the international level and in the United States. The 1961 adoption of the International Convention for the Protection of New Plant Varieties (UPOV) in Europe—which came into force in 1968—provided a system for protecting intellectual property rights for plant breeders that was similar to patent protection for a period of no less than fifteen years. The adoption of this agreement was intended to stimulate private investment in new plant varieties by establishing property rights for breeders at the national level.[18]

Similarly, the passage of the 1970 Plant Variety Protection Act (PVPA) in the United States strengthened intellectual property rights for plant breeders for sexually propagated plant varieties. The PVPA provided patent-like protection to both hybrid and nonhybrid varieties of sexually reproducing plants, which previously did not benefit from this type of intellectual property protection.[19] The PVPA grants the owner of a protected plant variety exclusive rights to sell, reproduce, import, and export that variety for a period of eighteen years, although with some exceptions. These exceptions include permission for farmers to save and sell seed that they themselves produced and they also allow researchers to use protected plant varieties as part of their research and development of new seeds.[20]

UPOV and the PVPA effectively created barriers to entry to the production of new seed varieties and spurred increased investment in research. The strengthening of intellectual property protections is widely seen to have played a large role in sparking the early wave of acquisitions of seed companies by petrochemical and pharmaceutical corporations.[21] Large firms were able to spend extraordinary amounts to advance research and acquire intellectual property rights that enabled them to introduce new products that more traditional seed companies, many of which were still largely reproducing publicly bred seed varieties, were simply unable to match. According to legal analyst Robert Leibenluft, consolidation during this period drove an incredible concentration of intellectual property protection among a handful of firms:

As of March 1979, five companies and their subsidiaries held 30% of all the plant patents that had been granted since 1970. On the individual crop level, concentration was significantly higher: as of December 1979 three corporations held 80% of the patents on beans, four corporations held 45% of the patents on cotton, four corporations held 60% of the lettuce patents, four corporations held 48% of the soybean patents, and four corporations held 36% of the wheat patents.[22]

This overwhelming market dominance—which food system analysts Carey Fowler and Pat Mooney characterize as "monopoly control"[23]—granted to the firms by the PVPA was extremely important to the success of the large multinational firms in the sector.

The seed industry was also hugely profitable in this period, and the chemical companies with sagging profits saw diversification into seeds as one way to boost their financial performance. Analysis at the time put profit margins in the seed sector in the 1970s at around 20 percent, among the highest of US industries at the time. A decade later, seed industry profit margins in the sector were estimated to be as high as 45 percent.[24] Part of the reason for this strong performance was the 1970s food crisis, which led to dramatically higher food prices and thus growing demand for seeds. These dynamics were accompanied by the oil price shocks in 1973–1974, which gave firms in the petroleum sector enormous profits that they could use to diversify their operations, including into the seed industry.

The agrochemical companies were acutely aware of criticisms against them in the 1960s and 1970s, and seeds, importantly, had a much "cleaner" reputation. Diversification into the sector provided the large chemical, petroleum, and pharmaceutical firms an opportunity to burnish their reputations and reposition themselves in a positive light. The chemical industry also reasoned that with declining demand for pesticides and herbicides due to health and environmental concerns, there would be a greater need for new plant varieties that were resistant to pests to meet rising food demand.[25] Monsanto, for example, strategically used its investment in seeds as a way to draw attention away from its reputation as a chemical company with a storied past, especially with respect to its production of Agent Orange, PCBs, and other toxic chemicals.[26] While seeds were attractive for these reasons, they also provided an opportunity for the firms to sell more agrochemicals, because seeds could be used as a delivery mechanism in the form of pesticide-coated seeds that were assumed at the time to be safer in terms of both health and environmental risks.

For a range of technological, regulatory, and market reasons, the chemical, petroleum, and pharmaceutical industries each found themselves investing in the seed industry. These rationales reinforced one another in ways that completely transformed the agricultural inputs sector by the late 1970s.

A SECOND WAVE OF CONSOLIDATION

A second wave of mergers and acquisitions involving seed and agrochemical companies began in the latter part of the 1980s and continued into the 1990s and early 2000s. This new round of consolidation took off just as some of the earlier investors in the in the seed industry, especially the petroleum companies, moved out of the sector. And the companies primarily focused on seeds, which had remained independent and still standing throughout the 1970s and were eventually swallowed into larger chemical and pharmaceutical firms, such that by the early 2000s, just six large firms dominated the market, often referred to as the "big six": Bayer, Monsanto, DuPont, Dow, Syngenta, and BASF. Following is a review of some of the higher-profile mergers that took place in this era, as well as a discussion of the reasons behind these market shifts.

Ciba-Geigy (which by this point owned Funk Brothers) and Sandoz, two large Swiss pharmaceutical firms with specialization in both biotechnology and agricultural chemicals, merged to form Novartis in 1996. In 1999, DuPont, primarily a chemical company, acquired Pioneer Hi-Bred, the largest seed company at the time. As these large mergers unfolded, Monsanto, which had purchased a variety of seed and biotechnology firms throughout the 1990s, engaged in serious discussions with other firms—including Novartis, DuPont, and Pfizer—about a potential sale of all or parts of its business, as it was under pressure due to its falling stock price. Although a deal did not materialize at the time, Monsanto did attempt to purchase US cottonseed firm Delta and Pineland in 1998, but dropped the idea when the US Department of Justice threatened to sue to stop the deal on antitrust grounds.[27]

The consolidation continued. In 2000, the agrochemical divisions of AstraZeneca (itself a product of a merger between Astra, a Swedish pharmaceutical firm and the agrochemical division of ICI that was spun off in 1993 and renamed Zeneca) merged with the Swiss pharmaceutical firm Novartis which subsequently spun off its own agricultural chemical arm to form Syngenta, based in Switzerland. Also in 2000, Monsanto merged with pharmaceutical firm Pharmacia & Upjohn, from which its agricultural input business was spun off in 2002 as a separate firm that kept the name Monsanto. Monsanto did eventually acquire Delta and Pineland in 2007 but was required to divest from its US-branded cottonseed business.[28] Dow undertook a joint venture with American pharmaceutical firm Eli Lilly in 1989 to pursue agricultural biotechnology, with the former buying out the latter in 1998 and rebranding itself as Dow Agrosciences. The firm then acquired Mycogen and various other seed, chemical, and biotech firms, including Rohm and Haas Agricultural Chemicals and Cargill's seed interests In 2002, Bayer acquired Aventis, the latter of which was itself the product of a 1999 merger between chemical firms AgrEvo and Rhône-Poulenc.[29]

This frenzy of merger and acquisition activity resulted in a second massive realignment within the sector, such that by the late 1990s and early 2000s, it looked completely different than it did at the close of the 1970s. This long period of consolidation saw six to ten major agrochemical companies rise to become the dominant players in a growing international agricultural biotechnology seed industry. At this same time, five of the top seven firms producing herbicides were also major agricultural biotechnology seed companies (Syngenta, Monsanto, DuPont, Dow, and Aventis). By 2006, just five companies conducted 74 percent of research and development into agricultural chemicals.[30]

As was the case with the earlier wave of consolidation in this sector, it is difficult to track all the mergers and acquisitions that took place over this period, in large part because of the dizzying pace of corporate tie-ups. These acquisitions in some ways carried on the trends that had begun in the 1970s, which linked chemical firms to seed firms. But they were also the result of new dynamics, including the advent of agricultural biotechnology, which created new opportunities to profit from the linkage between seeds and agrochemicals.

THE PROMISE OF AGRICULTURAL BIOTECHNOLOGY

Agricultural biotechnology gave large agrochemical and pharmaceutical firms further reasons to continue purchasing seed companies. These firms were increasingly interested in acquiring biotechnology start-up companies that specialized in research and development around this new technology. Such a strategy allowed them to be first movers in agricultural biotechnology, while the acquisition of seed companies gave them access to novel germplasm with which to develop new products. The large chemical firms were uniquely placed, as the agricultural biotechnology start-up firms lacked access to plant germplasm, while the seed companies lacked access to agricultural biotechnology know-how, and both often lacked the capital required for such deals. There were some exceptions, however. The start-up firms Agrigenetics, Calgene, Biotechnica International, and Mycogen undertook acquisition of seed companies beginning in the 1970s and 1980s.[31] By the 1990s, however, the large chemical and pharmaceutical companies were the dominant players acquiring both the agricultural biotech start-ups and the seed firms. Moreover, they had the agrochemicals that would be essential for ensured profitability for those firms from the new agricultural biotechnologies.[32]

It was in this context that some of the early investors in seed companies, particularly the oil firms, began to divest their seed subsidiaries, even as firms from other sectors were piling in. For example, Royal Dutch Shell, which at one point in the 1970s had become one of the world's largest seed and agrochemical producers, sold off its seed acquisitions, including its prized UK-based Nickerson seeds, by the early 1990s. Other investors from the earlier era, including Occidental Petroleum, British Petroleum, and Upjohn, also bowed out of the seed business.[33] The multinational corporations that stayed in the sector and expanded their operations, particularly in the United States, were those with significant investment in agricultural biotechnology. A handful of corporations took the lead in pursuing strategic mergers and acquisitions in order to integrate agricultural biotechnology into their seed breeding activities.[34]

Monsanto is a clear example of a major chemical firm that went on a whirlwind buying spree of both seed and biotechnology firms in order to establish itself as a leader in agricultural biotechnology. Monsanto increasingly moved into agrochemicals as a chemical company, as outlined in chapter 5. In 1974, it began to market Roundup, a nonselective glyphosate-based herbicide that came on the market just as farmers increased applications of weed-killing chemicals on their farms.[35] Sales of Roundup were a financial boon for the firm. As noted, the firm acquired both seed and biotechnology firms in the 1980s and 1990s, bringing it more squarely into the agricultural biotechnology space. In 1998, Monsanto also purchased the seed giant DeKalb. By the early 2000s, Monsanto had become the dominant player in the development of genetically modified (GM) seeds and moved into areas such as food ingredients and pharmaceuticals under a broader life sciences model.

Key to Monsanto's success was research and development into the genetic modification of seeds to make them resistant to applications of its flagship herbicide, Roundup. There were early promises from corporate quarters that agricultural biotechnology could deliver crops that were resistant to drought and pests, thus requiring less chemical use. But in practice most of the research focused on engineering plants to make them tolerant to the application of herbicides. This strategy was taken up almost immediately. By 2003, 82 percent of all commercialized GM crops were engineered for herbicide tolerance, with Monsanto as the dominant GM seed firm, thus making Roundup a dominant herbicide.[36] The firm promoted this strategy as an environmentally positive one, as glyphosate was widely viewed to be less toxic than many of the older herbicides.

Given that herbicides had become the most widely used agrochemicals in farmers' fields, at least in North America, the development of crops with herbicide-tolerant traits was significant. Farmers could now spray glyphosate on fields sown with genetically engineered seeds to kill the weeds but leave the crops intact. This innovation meant that glyphosate, which, previously used as a nonselective herbicide because it killed everything with which it came into contact, could be sprayed in fields not just prior to planting or after harvest to manage weeds on either side of the growing season, but also throughout the growing season without damaging the crops. It thus saved labor that previously had been devoted to weed control during the growing season.

Agricultural input firms worked on developing a range of herbicide-tolerant crops, such as soy and canola, throughout the late 1980s and early 1990s. They also engineered crops such as maize and cotton to be pest resistant by genetically altering them to contain the natural bacteria *Bacillus thuringiensis* (Bt), which was toxic to certain insects. The corporations that moved into this technology were able to integrate their research into seeds and agrochemicals under one research program centered on agricultural biotechnology. Genetically engineered seeds were approved for commercial planting in North America in 1996, and approvals followed in many other countries, including in South America, where production of soy was accelerating.[37]

FINANCIAL AND INTELLECTUAL PROPERTY INCENTIVES

The ability to bring these technologies together was a key incentive for consolidation in the sector. But it was also in part a response to the broader regulatory and market conditions. As noted, from the late 1960s and early 1970s, the agrochemical industry came under increasing pressure due to the introduction of new regulatory requirements regarding the health and safety of pesticides. These regulations made it increasingly costly for these firms to develop new agrochemicals, which required more testing prior to approval for commercial use. The amount of time required to develop new agrochemicals also climbed as regulatory requirements increased. By the mid-1990s, it took over eight years to bring a new pesticide to market. This increased time was necessary for research and development as well as registration of the chemical, which typically began once a patent was secured on a new active ingredient. In this sense, the time to market after the patent was granted effectively reduced the capacity of firms to capitalize on IP protection, which is typically twenty years. The growing time and cost to develop new agrochemicals, depicted in figure 8.2, weakened profitability in the sector throughout the 1980s and into the 1990s.

By contrast, the development and commercial introduction of a new genetically modified crop using techniques of agricultural biotechnology cost firms only around $10 million in the mid-1990s—just a fraction of the cost of developing a new chemical herbicide. It also took a lot less time—around six years in the mid-1990s—to develop a new GM crop, which was also an improvement on the average ten-year time period it took to develop a new crop or variety with traditional crop breeding.[38] Together, these differentials in terms of costs and time between traditional crop breeding and the introduction of new agrochemicals, and the new approach of genetically modifying seeds to work with existing chemicals, played a big role in encouraging the large agricultural input companies to focus on the latter through newly consolidated corporate structures over the course of the 1980s and 1990s.[39] These firms required access

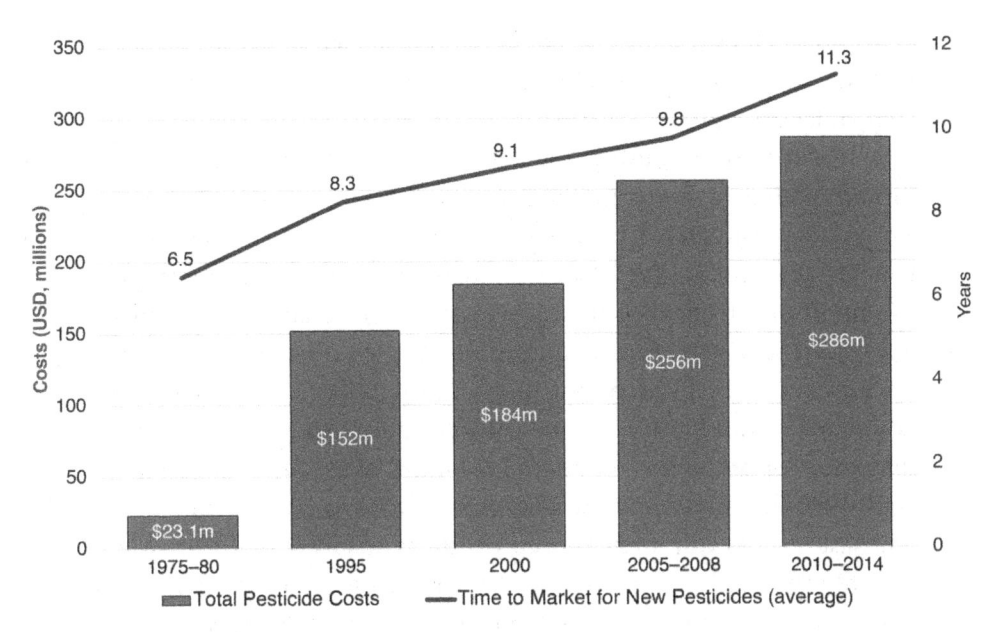

8.2 Rising costs and time to develop and bring a new pesticide to market, 1975–2014. *Sources*: Phillips McDougall (2016); Clapp (2021).

to agricultural biotechnology know-how, superior germplasm, as well as large amounts of capital for research and development to breed seeds to work in conjunction with existing chemicals. For this reason, agrochemical firms were highly incentivized to acquire both agricultural biotechnology start-ups as well as seed companies in order to expand their research and development capacities and gain market share.[40]

The early to mid-1980s also saw important legal decisions in the United States that led to a strengthening of intellectual property rights for genetically engineered seeds that encouraged consolidation in the sector. The PVPA was strengthened in 1980 to extend its coverage, enabling the United States to join UPOV 1983. Also in 1980, a US Supreme Court decision, *Diamond v. Chakrabarty*, extended patent rights to genetically engineered microorganisms. This landmark legal decision to allow patents on genetically modified organisms sparked a wave of research in agricultural biotechnology for commercial purposes. Intellectual property rights for genetically modified seed varieties were extended with a 1985 court decision that granted patent protection for seeds and plants derived from agricultural biotechnology. These developments led to a significant rise in R&D spending on agricultural biotechnology by agricultural input companies throughout the 1980s.[41]

The leading firm in using this strategy, Monsanto, was eager to move forward with genetically modified seeds as soon as possible. The patent for its glyphosate-based herbicide, Roundup, was due to expire in the United States in the year 2000. The firm's ability to shift its technological innovation focus to genetically modified crops and away from the development of new agrochemicals allowed it to profit not just from selling new seeds under patent protection but also to continue to sell Roundup.[42] Indeed, the herbicide part of the package was crucial, given that Roundup accounted for around one-third of the firm's profits in the early 1990s.[43] To ensure these dual market returns, Monsanto required purchasers of its GM seeds to sign contracts ensuring that they would use only the firm's Roundup herbicide with those seeds, effectively selling them as a bundle.[44] The requirement that farmers sign such contracts marked a huge shift in the way the companies interacted with their customers. It also enabled Monsanto to control 80 percent of the market for glyphosate-based herbicides even as late as six years past the expiration of the Roundup patent.[45]

While intellectual property protection enabled the firms to develop large shares of the market for their genetically modified seeds and agrochemicals once they were firmly dominant players by the mid-2000s, they began to engage in more cooperative relationships through the cross-licensing of seed traits. These agreements enabled firms to license the use of specific genetic traits that may be patented by other firms in order to bundle different traits in new ways and market them as new products. Firms typically pay a licensing fee to use traits from other firms, but they can have big payoffs if the resulting seed with multiple traits finds a market.

All of the big six firms had signed cross-licensing agreements with the others in the 2005–2010 period, and the resulting varieties accounted for around 50 percent of the seeds sold on the market.[46] Agreements between Monsanto and Dow Agrosciences, for example, led to the development of SmartStax corn seeds, which included eight different transgenic traits. In this way, cross-licensing had the same effect as patents and worked to benefit both firms.[47] These kinds of arrangements also benefited firms as the patents on their traits expired. As several key traits came due for expiry, the firms engaged in cross-licensing expiring traits with newer ones while removing older products from the market, thus locking in sales of newer products with stronger intellectual property protection.

CONSEQUENCES OF THE SEEDS AND PESTICIDES MASH-UP

The major reconfiguration of the seed and pesticide sectors into one set of firms that now focused on marketing packages of genetically modified seeds stylized to work with specific agrochemicals had huge consequences for markets and for the technological trajectory of industrial agriculture. It also expanded the capacity of the resulting firms to influence the policy context.

HEIGHTENED MARKET INFLUENCE

Corporate concentration in the sector by the early 2000s was quite stark. Whereas in 1994 the top four firms in the seeds and agrochemicals sectors commanded 21 percent and 29 percent of the global market for those inputs, by 2000 it was 33 percent and 41 percent, respectively.[48] What these global figures fail to convey is the market concentration in specific seed and pesticide markets at the national level, which was often much, much higher. For example, the top four hybrid seed companies in 1979—Pioneer Hi-Bred, DeKalb, Funk Brothers (owned by Ciba-Geigy), and Trojan (owned by Pfizer)—controlled 57 percent of the US hybrid corn seed market, which made up nearly all of the corn seed market in the United States by that point.[49] By the late 1990s, the top four corn seed firms in the US market held 67 to 69 percent of the market, while the top four soybean seed firms held 49 percent of the market, and the top four cotton seed firms held 87 percent of the market.[50]

Concentration was also high and rising in specific pesticide markets around this time. According to a 1980 study conducted for the US Environmental Protection Agency (EPA), the top four firms in the corn herbicides market in the late 1970s had around 90 percent of sales, while the top four firms in the soybean herbicides controlled over 75 percent of the market in that same period. These figures underemphasize the degree of concentration because within the category of corn herbicides, the markets are segmented into complementary products. Just two firms, Ciba-Geigy and Shell Chemicals, accounted for over 76 percent of the broadleaf corn herbicide market while the other two firms, Monsanto and Stauffer, accounted for over 92 percent of the grass control corn herbicides at that time. By 2002, the top four firms in the US domestic pesticides sector held over 64 percent of the overall market.[51]

Cross-licensing arrangements between the dominant seed and agrochemical firms are also widely viewed to be potentially anticompetitive because such arrangements can deepen dominant firms' market power.[52] Concentration ratios and other measures of corporate concentration do not typically include consideration of R&D and cross-licensing agreements. Information on cross-licensing agreements is not always publicly disclosed, however, making assessments even more challenging. Sociologist Philip Howard has outlined some of the agreements that can be discerned by examining products on the market that contain stacked traits owned by multiple firms. He argues that these cross-licensing agreements present strong barriers to entry for small firms in a highly concentrated industry.[53] Multiple and overlapping patent claims, known as "patent thickets," in the agricultural biotechnology sector also tend to present barriers to entry for new firms because it is costly for them to navigate the patent landscape.[54]

High degrees of concentration in any sector tend to raise concerns about anticompetitive practices, including price manipulation. Monsanto and other leading firms in the sector were widely suspected and frequently accused of engaging in anticompetitive practices once they had gained dominant market share in the 1990s and early 2000s. A group of farmers brought forward a class action lawsuit against Monsanto and several other firms—including Bayer, Pioneer (DuPont), Novartis, and AstraZeneca (as noted above, the latter two subsequently merged to form Syngenta)—for price fixing in 1999. The farmers alleged that these firms violated antitrust provisions by charging high fees for corn and soy seeds based on patent license agreements with Monsanto. The farmers lost the case, however, because the judge denied the class action on the grounds that seed pricing had regional specificities and complexities and that it seemed impossible to prove that a large group of farmers was negatively affected.

It was later revealed that the judge in the case had previously represented Monsanto in another case but did not disclose this relationship and did not recuse himself from the case.[55]

Several other antitrust controversies took place in this period, including revelations in 2004 that Monsanto and Pioneer engaged in high-level talks that included discussions on pricing for genetically modified seeds, which would be considered illegal if the firms intended to fix prices. Reporting at the time indicated that Monsanto had encouraged Pioneer to charge higher prices for genetically modified seeds that incorporated traits from Monsanto, which Pioneer had licensed at a low price several years earlier. Monsanto was keen to ensure that Pioneer would not undercut its profitability by charging less for those traits. Executives from Novartis and Mycogen told the press at the time that they had been pressured as well to coordinate their retail pricing strategies with Monsanto but rejected those suggestions because of concerns about potential illegality and anticompetitive effects.[56]

These revelations occurred around the time that the US Department of Justice was investigating Monsanto for potential anticompetitive practices, including price fixing, around the sale of its glyphosate-based herbicide Roundup. In this instance, Monsanto was investigated for allegedly preventing other companies from developing genetically modified traits that worked with glyphosate or glyphosate-similar herbicides—even after Monsanto's patent on glyphosate expired in 2000. Monsanto pursued this outcome by requiring distributors to make it difficult for competitors to sell other glyphosate-based herbicides.[57] Monsanto also actively pursued incentive programs with dealers, particularly in the United States, that encouraged them to carry Roundup brand and not generic glyphosate products. If the dealers did not follow the practices that Monsanto mandated, they risked being dropped as suppliers.[58] The DOJ pursued a complaint about these practices in 2007 as a potential violation of US antitrust laws. Soon after, Monsanto backed off from these practices, and the case was eventually dropped.

Given the weakening of antitrust policy implementation in the United States in these decades, as outlined in chapter 7, it is not surprising that it was difficult to secure court wins against corporations that were amassing enormous market power from highly concentrated agricultural input markets. The discourse at the time, as was evident from numerous publications from the US Department of Agriculture, was that highly concentrated markets need not always be considered problematic because they could in fact increase efficiency and lower prices.[59] Yet at the same time, the US Government Accountability Office outlined in a report that by the late 1990s, seeds derived from agricultural biotechnology were more expensive than conventionally bred seeds, linking this trend to high and rising technology licensing fees for GM seeds.[60] In 2007, technology fees made up around 30 to 75 percent of the cost of GM seeds in the United States and the European Union countries.[61]

Data from the USDA show that from 1975 to 2015, the price of corn and soy seed per acre as a percentage of the amount of revenue farmers received for those crops per acre nearly tripled for both crops. By comparison, prices for wheat seeds did not increase at the same pace as corn and soy over this same period. The lower price of wheat seeds is likely due to the fact that wheat is not a genetically modified crop and thus does not have technology fees associated with it. There is relatively little private sector R&D in wheat seeds because it is a self-pollinating crop, with much of the US wheat seed varieties provided by the public sector, although this is changing with growing private sector interests in hybrid and genetically modified wheat development.

Although there are many factors that affect farm input prices, several recent studies examining this period found that in addition to technology fees, seed prices have increased at least in part due to market power. Barriers to entry in the sector due to high costs for research and development meant that the fewer players in the market for genetically engineered seeds and connected herbicides were able to enjoy a degree of price premium that they otherwise would not have had. These peer-reviewed studies found that market concentration is one factor among several that contributed to higher seed prices for genetically modified seeds.[62]

A NEW TECHNOLOGICAL LANDSCAPE

The development of integrated seed-chemical packages led to a reconfiguration of the technological landscape by further locking in seeds and chemicals in ways that eroded the rights of farmers. Farmer organizations and civil society groups have highlighted the impact of integrated seed and chemical technology on farmer autonomy, as the new technologies made it challenging for farmers to adopt alternatives once they were already in the industrial agricultural model. For example, by the early 2000s, it had become increasingly difficult for farmers in North America to access non-genetically modified seeds for crops in which GM seeds have become dominant—in particular corn, soy, cotton, and canola. This trend was exacerbated by some of the market-shaping strategies of firms already discussed, including their incentivization of dealers to prioritize sales of GM seed and chemical packages.[63] The dominant firms also forced farmers to sign contracts that prohibited them from saving seeds for replanting the following year.[64] Monsanto, for example, filed lawsuits against hundreds of farmers for saving seeds with proprietary traits—whether it was done intentionally or not—for which the firm won millions of dollars in settlements from farmers.[65] At one point, Monsanto set up a hotline so that farmers could report their neighbors for saving and replanting its GM seed.[66]

Technological lock-in of genetically modified seeds after 1996 led to a massive increase in the planting of those seeds for maize, soybeans, and cotton. By 2007, 98 percent of the global acreage planted with GM crops was already sown with seeds supplied by the dominant companies.[67] By 2014, 85 percent of genetically modified crops were engineered to be resistant to the application of chemical herbicides (as either a single or stacked trait), the most common being glyphosate, the active ingredient in Monsanto's Roundup (see figure 8.3).[68] Other companies have engineered seeds that are resistant to other herbicides, such as Bayer's Liberty brand. While ostensibly responding to environmental concerns regarding pesticides, herbicide-resistant crops further locked in glyphosate use, which was advertised as safer and less ecologically damaging, but which we have come to learn is associated with numerous problems.

The cultivation of glyphosate resistant crops, such as Roundup Ready soybeans, drove up the use of glyphosate herbicides sharply and on a global scale. In the 1970s and 1980s, before the advent of genetically modified seeds, Roundup was just one of several nonselective herbicides on the market. But once seeds were modified to be resistant to it, its use soared. According to chemical industry analyst Charles Benbrook, from

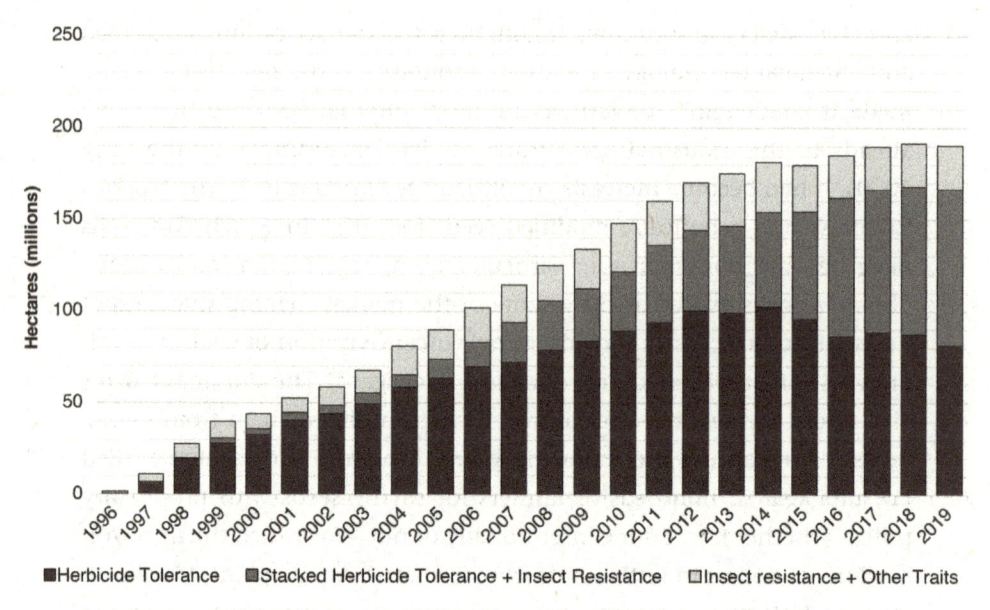

8.3 Global area of biotech crops 1996–2019, by Trait. *Source*: ISAAA data, https://isaaa.org/.

1996 to 2014, global agricultural glyphosate use increased nearly fifteenfold (see figure 8.4).[69]

Glyphosate use has increased not just in the Global North, but also across a diverse range of countries in the Global South, although the data for use in the latter are often inaccurate and wildly underestimated. According to new estimates by Annie Shattuck and colleagues, while global pesticide use grew some 20 percent by volume globally, it increased by over 150 percent in low-income countries over that same period.[70] Brazil and Argentina, for example, which have experienced a major expansion in the cultivation of GM soybean acreages, have seen especially dramatic increases. Growing herbicide use has prompted protests, including among groups of mothers in Argentina concerned about the impact of spraying on the health of their children and grandchildren.[71]

Although initially the herbicide glyphosate was promoted as a relatively benign pesticide, concerns about its safety began to grow by the early 2000s. But with the chemical being locked in and with generic versions increasingly available after the patent for it expired, its use continued to

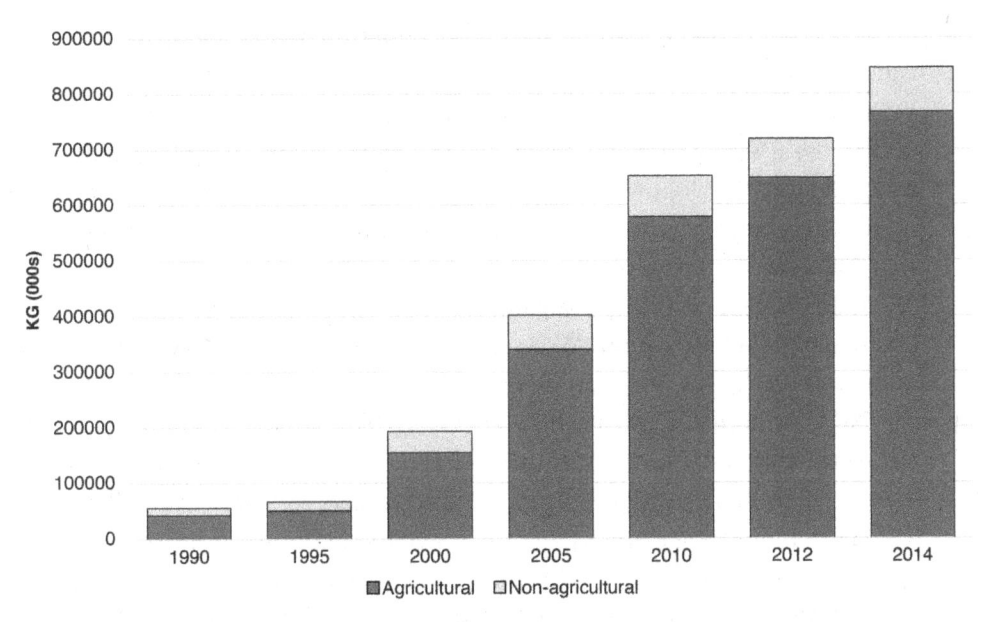

8.4 Global glyphosate use, 1990–2014. *Source:* Benbrook 2016.

climb. Generic glyphosate—the raw ingredients for which were increasingly being supplied by chemical firms in China—sold for a much lower price than Roundup, encouraging its further use.[72] The increased application of pesticides presents numerous environmental and health risks, although there is debate over the extent to which the chemical is implicated in these problems. Many weeds have developed resistance to glyphosate and it has been associated with certain kinds of lymphoma cancers, risks to pollinators such as butterflies, and water pollution.[73]

Industrial agriculture based on high-tech seed and chemical packages has also been associated with a narrowing of crop genetic resources. The large agribusiness companies have tended to focus on seed-chemical technical packages for a handful of key crops: corn, soy, canola, and cotton. These crops are typically grown in large-scale monocultures that pose a threat to agricultural biodiversity. Glyphosate and other agrochemicals sprayed on herbicide-tolerant varieties can damage plant genetic diversity in and around fields, which can pose a threat to wildlife, including key pollinators such as bees and butterflies that rely on those plants for their survival.[74]

Seed and chemical mergers have also raised questions about implications of consolidation for agricultural innovation. As the agricultural biotechnology agenda grew more prominent in the late 1990s and early 2000s, there was a growing trend toward privatization of agricultural research and development, which meant that seed research became increasingly profit focused. Although there was a boost in innovation that followed the mergers of the 1970s to 1990s in the agricultural biotechnology space as firms amalgamated their R&D operations to bring about new GM seed technologies, innovation weakened as the sector became more highly concentrated by the late 1990s and early 2000s.[75] As USDA economist Keith Fuglie and colleagues note, concentration in the sector and high capital costs can also stifle innovation in other ways, because high R&D costs present significant barriers to entry for smaller and more innovative firms. The result is a reduction in the number and types of innovations, thus leaving farmers with less choice.[76]

With the acceleration in mergers in the sector, agrochemical R&D became concentrated in fewer firms. Between 1972 and 1989, for example, the number of pesticide firms with US R&D operations dropped from thirty-three down to just nineteen.[77] Throughout this period, the large seed and chemical firms did not commercialize any new herbicides, as their innovation agenda focused almost exclusively on developing genetically modified seeds, which as the analysis here indicates, was simply a less expensive profit strategy for them. In the 1960s and 1970s, new active ingredients for herbicides were typically introduced every year or two in a bid to create new markets as patents expired on previous chemicals. However, as corporate consolidation trends intensified after the late 1980s and early 1990s, R&D into new active ingredients for herbicides dwindled.[78] Research and development spending in the pesticides sector fell in real terms from 1994 to 2010.[79] The number of registered patents for herbicides declined from around 180 in 1995 to just 50 in 2002.[80] Only around 20 modes of action for weed control were used in agriculture by the early 2010s, all of which had been discovered many years ago when many more firms were in the business.[81] Monsanto, for example, ceased to conduct R&D into crop protection chemicals altogether after the expiration of its glyphosate patent in 2000.[82]

As R&D became more privatized, the dominant corporations became one of the main sources of information for farmers on genetic modification and the use of GM seeds with herbicides. The growing role of firms as sources of information for farmers has become an issue not only in the Global North but also in the Global South, where corporations were among the few actors with resources to take up this role. This trend is seen by analysts as contributing to the problem of "agricultural deskilling" with respect to both seeds and pesticides as outlined in chapters 4 and 5, only now on a global scale. Anthropologist Glenn Stone, for example, explains the deskilling tendencies of genetically modified seeds in Warangal District in India, "The technology introduces new sources of inconsistency and unrecognizability and accelerates technological change."[83] Others have pointed to the ways in which growing reliance on genetically modified seeds in particular have contributed to ecological deskilling among farmers, characterized by a loss of ecological knowledge and practices as well as weakened agency among farmers.[84]

INTENSIFIED POLICY INFLUENCE

The reconfiguration of the agricultural seed and chemical industries into a concentrated set of agricultural biotechnology firms gave those firms at the top increased power to influence policy and governance. They employed familiar strategies in their attempt to achieve their regulatory aims, but this time, they met with more resistance than they had in the past. Agricultural biotechnology was controversial from the start, and as such, critics have closely watched the tactics of the firms. This scrutiny, however, did not deter these firms from trying to influence policy and regulation in ways that strengthened their own bottom line. Indeed, these firms actively worked to influence the policy context for agricultural biotechnology and agrochemicals, especially herbicides, in ways that shaped their ability to amass even more market power.[85]

The firms in this period were especially active in direct lobbying of government regulators over several issues that they saw as crucial for their business model to succeed. Once intellectual property protection was secured in the United States in the 1980s, for example, the corporate actors investing in agricultural biotechnology pursued an extensive lobby strategy to ensure that these rules would be globalized to enable them to expand their markets internationally. The 1994 Trade Related Intellectual Property Rights (TRIPs) agreement of the World Trade Organization (WTO) was an important avenue through which these firms sought to achieve this goal.[86] The TRIPs agreement harmonized intellectual property protection across countries and required member countries to adopt some form of intellectual property rights for plants and other life forms.

The dominant firms also lobbied hard regarding rules for approval and labeling of foods derived from agricultural biotechnology. The big players in the sector spent some $547 million lobbying in the United States between 1999 and 2009, with the annual amount doubling in that time period from $35 million to $71 million.[87] They also spent enormous amounts funding politicians and employed hundreds of lobbyists, many of whom were former politicians who cycled through the revolving door between industry and government.[88] Monsanto, for example, played a large role in shaping policies that affected agribusiness in the United States. Before she became chair of the US Federal Trade Commission, Lina Khan wrote in 2013:

Few firms have as methodically mastered the revolving door between Washington and industry as Monsanto—whose former employees and lobbyists frequently enjoy top posts at agencies like the Food and Drug Administration and on legislative committees—or groomed deep ties with both Republican and Democrat administrations. The company spent close to $6 million on lobbying in 2012, more than any other agribusiness organization, and three times the sum dished out by the second-highest paying firm, Archer Daniels Midland.[89]

Indeed, in the 2010s, Monsanto had successfully lobbied in the United States against the labeling of GM foods and for the approval of Roundup Ready alfalfa and sugar beets.[90]

In addition to directly lobbying governments, the firms also participated in industry associations that embarked on campaigns to influence policies. Most of the top firms in the sector worked through trade associations like CropLife International to lobby on behalf of the agrochemical firms. The top firms also worked through the Biotechnology Industry Organization, which was founded in 1993 as a merger of the Industrial Biotechnology Association and the Association of Biotechnology Companies. The firms also engaged in national and regional associations that advocated their interests, such as CropLife America, EuropaBio and the Global Industry Coalition. These industry associations have actively lobbied on behalf of their members in a range of contexts, including international negotiations on the trade in genetically modified organisms. They also have lobbied at the national level, including with respect to biotechnology and pesticides use in countries in the Global South, such as Costa Rica and Brazil.[91]

In addition to direct lobbying, the top firms have also engaged actively in this period in attempts to shape public discourse about agricultural biotechnology and associated agrochemicals. Monsanto, for example, sought to position itself as a global leader in sustainability in the 1990s through its promotion of agricultural biotechnology. Robert Shapiro, then CEO of Monsanto, put forward his vision that linked the need to grow enough food to feed an expanding world population with the need to adopt agricultural biotechnology to limit the environmental impact of increasing food production.[92] In a 1995 speech, Shapiro invoked a neo-Malthusian tone: "We're clearly going to need, if we're going to have any hope at all, a different model of development; and for this we're going to need brand-new technologies."[93]

The dominant firms also worked very much behind the scenes in ways we would likely not learn about were it not for recent court cases that led to the release of corporate documents that Monsanto handed over in the discovery process. These documents, which are discussed in chapter 12, indicate that the firm actively sought to influence scientific studies on glyphosate safety and agricultural biotechnology dating back to the 1990s. For example, the firm funded academic research, engaged in ghostwriting of scholarly papers, and prepared presentations for academics.[94] In many cases, the firms' fingerprints in these activities were well hidden—by not signing the names of the employees and by the listed authors not disclosing their ties to the firm—to give the appearance that the findings and messages were coming from independent scientific voices.

CONCLUSION

From the 1970s to the early 2000s, two waves of mergers occurred that resulted in the conjoining of the agricultural seeds and pesticides industries into a single set of dominant firms. While the specifics of these two waves of consolidation were somewhat different, they shared some elements in common. They were both in part a response to growing ecological and health concerns about pesticide use that changed the broader socioeconomic context in which the firms operated. The regulatory environment became more stringent, requiring increased testing and documentation for firms seeking to register new pesticides. These new requirements in turn affected the market context, driving up the costs of introducing new products, while broader environmental concerns dampened demand for their older, more toxic products.

These socioeconomic and regulatory factors intersected with new technological possibilities, including the development of agricultural biotechnology. The latter opened new technological opportunities to address key societal and regulatory concerns about agrochemical safety through the modification of seeds designed to work with what were considered at the time to be much safer chemicals, especially certain herbicides that were already registered. These regulatory, market, and technology dynamics were key factors in driving a second round of consolidation in the seed sector, particularly for agrochemical firms that saw agricultural biotechnology as a way to recover their profitability and remain viable. As such, these were largely mergers of opportunity.

The firms that resulted from this reconfiguration of the sector used their new, more consolidated status to influence markets and shape the technological landscape in ways that increased sales of their products while further locking farmers into the use of industrial inputs—herbicides and new genetically engineered seeds—that were now themselves tethered together as a package. They also sought to shape regulations in ways that cleared the path for them to further develop their products along these same lines. The increased use of these technologies sparked enormous public controversy around their safety in terms of both human exposure and the environment, especially with respect to the massive increase in herbicide use.

III

TWENTY-FIRST-CENTURY MEGAMERGERS AND THEIR CONSEQUENCES

9
DRIVERS OF RECENT AGRIBUSINESS MEGAMERGERS

By the early 2000s, the agricultural inputs industry looked dramatically different than it did a century earlier. It was also about to see another radical transformation. Beginning in 2015, a frenzied period of mergers and acquisitions took place that resulted in further corporate concentration with relatively few agribusiness titans at the helm. The consolidation of what were already giant firms also led to increased overlap in the products and services offered by the different sets of firms across the main input industries. This chapter explains the forces driving consolidation in the twenty-first century and their significance for reshaping the agricultural inputs sector. The subsequent three chapters examine the various consequences of this period of consolidation—namely, how concentration has enhanced the market, technological, and political power of these firms and generated further social and ecological costs.

The trend toward greater concentration in the sector after 2015 was driven by a new configuration of market, technology, and policy dynamics that generated both mergers of distress and mergers of opportunity. First, market shifts, including a new boom-and-bust cycle in the farm economy, put pressure on the large firms to take part in massive merger deals to secure their market share, especially once agricultural commodity prices began to soften after 2013. Heightened financialization in this period also increased investors' leverage over firms to press for increasing returns, including through consolidation. Second, the rise of precision agriculture—or digital farming—alongside new mechanisms for plant genetic engineering, such as genome editing and other forms of synthetic biology, created pressures on firms to be first in line to capitalize on these new technologies. The shift into digital technologies on the part of all the firms in the sector signals they are not only hoping to stay ahead of the curve of technological change, but also that they are seeking to use those technologies to smooth out the effects of the boom-and-bust cycles that have defined them for centuries. A third major factor was weak antitrust regulation that did little to stop the mergers and acquisitions that led to ever-larger firms able to capture greater market shares. Although the forces leading to weakened antitrust legislation began in the 1980s, the looser approach to evaluating mergers and acquisitions had become entrenched by the early 2000s.

CONSOLIDATION INTENSIFIES

As the previous two chapters made clear, the major reconfiguration of the agricultural inputs industry that unfolded in the decades leading up to the early 2000s resulted in three sets of global firms dominating markets for the four main agricultural inputs. But it was not long before the next dramatic round of mergers and acquisitions took place that further consolidated the sector. Monsanto's purchase of several start-up firms was a precursor to this transformation. Having survived a difficult period in the 1990s during which it almost sold off its businesses, as outlined in chapter 8, Monsanto sought to make inroads into the digital farming space with its 2012 acquisition of Precision Planting, a firm that developed high-speed planting equipment linked to software applications. The following year, Monsanto also purchased Climate Corp, a software firm that developed digital farming applications that was started in 2006 by two former Google employees. With these acquisitions, the firm sought to build its own digital farming software platform.[1]

Buying up these digital firms was not Monsanto's only important act. As early as 2014, it seriously considered making a major acquisition, setting its sights on a megamerger with the Swiss agrochemical firm

Syngenta. Monsanto made several attempts to acquire the firm, including making an offer of $46 billion in 2015. Had this merger taken place, it would have brought together one of the largest seed companies in the world with one of the largest agrochemical companies in the world, furthering the linkage between the seed and chemical industries. The move would have enabled Monsanto to relocate its headquarters to Europe, with the benefit of lightening its tax burden.[2] Syngenta, however, was not interested in the merger, which prompted Monsanto's CEO at the time, Hugh Grant, to insist the firm was better off going solo. However, analysts remarked that Monsanto was itself vulnerable to a takeover, given that the value of its shares fell sharply in 2015 due to its entanglement in legal disputes and increasingly vocal questions over the safety of its glyphosate-based flagship herbicide Roundup.[3] That same year, Monsanto put Precision Planting up for sale.

Although Monsanto's earlier overture to Syngenta did not result in a merger deal, it signaled changing circumstances in the sector, and a spate of other megamergers among agricultural firms swiftly followed. Toward the end of 2015, two of the largest and oldest chemical firms in the United States, Dow and DuPont, both of them key producers of pesticides, announced their intent to merge to form new company worth $130 billion. In this case, both firms had a similar product mix of agrochemicals and seeds. They claimed that the merger made sense because it would enable the elimination of duplicative research and development spending.[4] Following the merger, the new entity subsequently split into three firms, with one of them, Corteva Agriscience, focused exclusively on agricultural chemicals and seeds. This move effectively created a gigantic new firm squarely focused on agricultural inputs.

Hot on the heels of the Dow and DuPont merger announcement, ChemChina, one of China's largest state-owned firms, announced in early 2016 that it had struck a deal to purchase Syngenta for $43 billion. Until this point, ChemChina had focused its efforts squarely on the domestic Chinese agrochemical market, including supplying both fertilizers and pesticides. The firm was interested in gaining access to Syngenta's agricultural biotechnology assets, although Syngenta was also a major player in agrochemicals. In 2021, after several years of discussions, ChemChina was then absorbed into an even larger state-owned Chinese chemical firm, Sinochem. Syngenta Group was then formed as a spinoff that includes the seed and chemical divisions of the merged firms.

With these major shifts in the agricultural chemical and seed sectors, it became evident to the remaining firms that they would also need to restructure or risk being marginalized. By mid-2016, Bayer announced that it had put in a bid to acquire Monsanto. Given its weakened position, Monsanto was open to the idea but was ultimately disappointed in the price that was offered and turned down the deal. BASF and Monsanto briefly engaged in talks about a potential merger after Monsanto rejected Bayer's initial offer, but a deal did not come to pass.[5] Bayer did not give up, however, and by the last quarter of 2016, Monsanto finally accepted a purchase price of $66 billion, and the deal was closed in 2018. With this acquisition, Bayer moved more squarely into the market for genetically modified seeds, having previously focused mainly on agrochemicals. Bayer also was eager to acquire Monsanto's Climate Corporation to facilitate its move into digital farming (discussed below).[6]

The German agrochemical firm BASF was left out of the merger dance at this time. Despite not moving into seed production like many of the other large agrochemical firms in earlier decades, BASF continued to be a dominant player in pesticide markets. Although it was not engaged in a major merger or acquisition deal after 2015, BASF underwent big changes nonetheless as it purchased assets that the merging firms were required to sell to gain regulatory approval. BASF's head of crop protection critiqued the Bayer-Monsanto merger at the time: "Size on its own . . . isn't a recipe for success. . . . Farmers want the freedom to choose, they want choice and alternatives. . . . They don't just want to be dependent on 3 to 4 [suppliers] on a global scale."[7] Despite this skepticism, BASF went on to acquire significant parts of Bayer's seed and agrochemical businesses, including its genetically modified LibertyLink seeds and its Liberty brand glufosinate-based herbicide, which were in direct competition with Monsanto's Roundup ready seeds and Roundup herbicide.[8] Figure 9.1 depicts the main mergers and acquisitions in the pesticides industry since the late nineteenth and early twentieth centuries, including this most recent period.

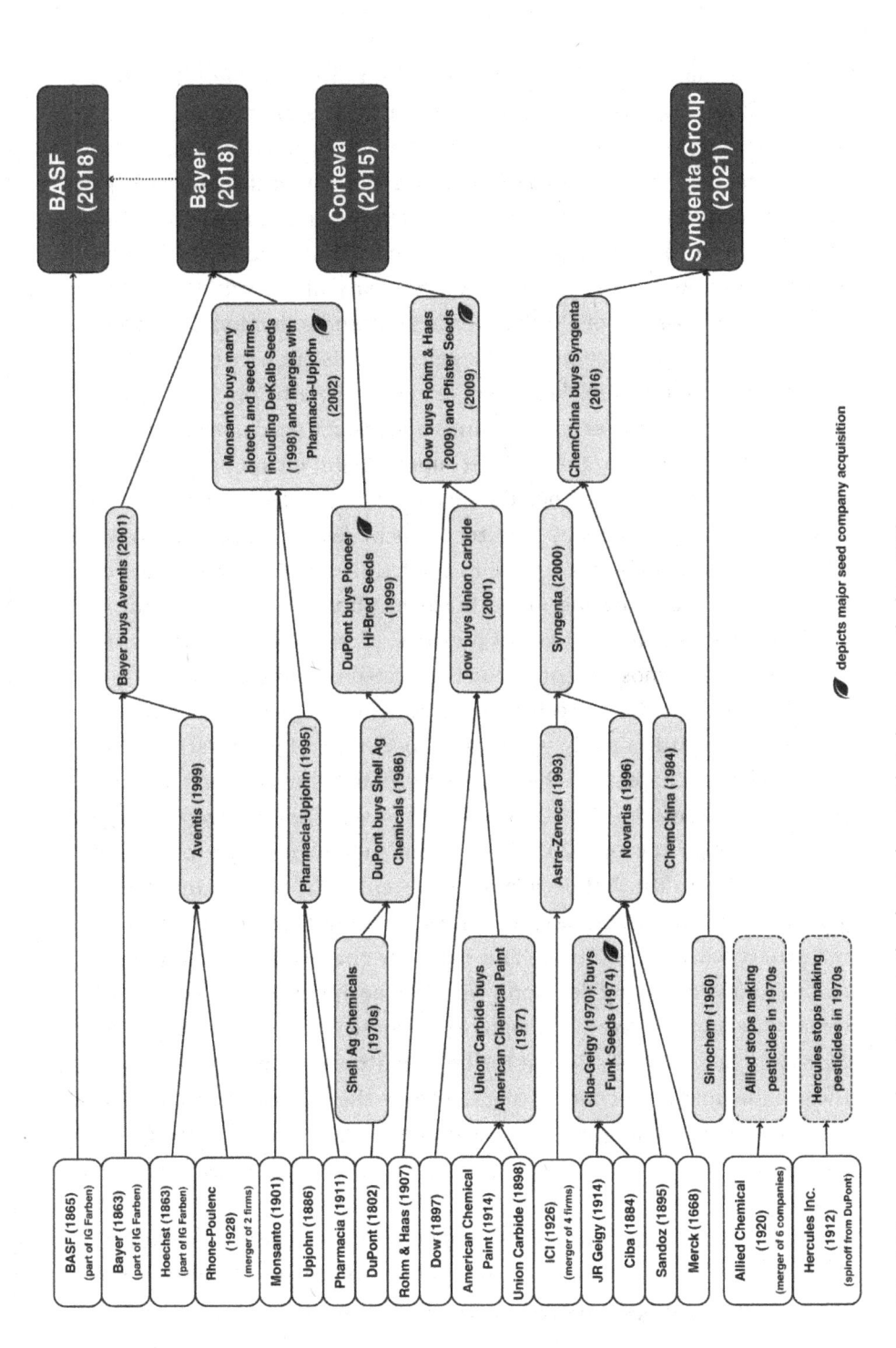

9.1 Major mergers and acquisitions in the chemical pesticide industry since the late 1800s.

Major restructuring also took place in the $150 billion fertilizer market after 2015. By that point, the top four firms—Agrium, Yara, Mosaic, and PotashCorp—already accounted for around one-quarter of the global fertilizer market.[9] In 2016, two of the world's largest fertilizer firms, both based in Canada, the PotashCorp and Agrium, announced that they would merge into a new firm under the name Nutrien, worth $30 billion. This move created the largest fertilizer company in the world, accounting for over 60 percent of North America's potash production, 25 percent of its phosphate production, and 22 percent of its ammonia production for fertilizer manufacture.[10] Prior to the merger, PotashCorp had steadily acquired stakes in smaller fertilizer firms outside of Canada, while Agrium diversified up and down the fertilizer supply chain, including into retail, as outlined in chapter 7. Once the merger was complete, Nutrien made a number of acquisitions of fertilizer firms in Australia and the United States. Other deals also took place in the fertilizer sector after 2015. For example, Yara acquired the major Brazilian phosphate firm Galvani in 2018, increasing that firm's global presence. (Consolidation in the fertilizer sector in this most recent period is depicted in figure 7.2.)

The farm machinery sector also saw some consolidation in this period, although it already was quite concentrated by the early 2000s, as outlined in chapter 7. The dominant global firms—Deere & Company, CNH Industries, AGCO, and Kubota—were not engaged in large megamergers in the post-2015 period, but they increasingly purchased software firms in the first decades of the twenty-first century in a bid to gain digital platforms. These platforms would allow them to develop farm machinery with both software and hardware that would enable the use of data to guide farming decisions, with the machinery equipped for data interconnectivity. Deere also sought to purchase Precision Planting when Monsanto put it up for sale, but the US Department of Justice challenged the deal because of its concern that they were the only two firms offering precision planting equipment. As such, the merger would effectively create a monopoly on the technology. Instead, ACGO purchased Precision Planting in 2017.

What explains this massive reconfiguration of the sector, marked by megamergers that shook up the major players and resulted in the remaining firms positioning themselves in new ways? As with the reconfigurations that happened in earlier periods, the mergers that occurred in the early decades of the twenty-first century were the product of shifting market, technology, and policy factors.

PRESSURES OF THE BOOM-BUST FARM CYCLE

Similar to the wave of mergers that occurred in the 1980s and 1990s across all of the agricultural input industries, an agricultural boom-bust cycle played a major role in driving the megamergers that occurred after 2015. Gradually rising agricultural commodity prices over the course of the early 2000s quickly gave way to a full-blown food crisis by 2008, which brought sharply higher crop prices punctuated by extreme food price volatility that lasted through 2012. Spiking commodity prices were triggered in large part by a major financial crisis that began in 2008, as well as soaring oil prices that pushed up the cost of farming. The crisis in the agricultural sector was also a product of policy shifts that encouraged the increased use of biofuels in Europe and North America in the years just prior to the crisis, which increased demand for agricultural commodities.[11] On top of these pressures, China increasingly began to source a portion of its soy and cereal grains from global markets in the early 2000s, which followed decades of policies aimed at food self-sufficiency in that country.[12] These factors combined to push up agricultural commodity prices.

As the prices of staple crops such as wheat, rice, corn, and soy doubled in the first half of 2008, financial speculators, seeking lucrative investments amid a global financial crisis, piled into these markets to profit from rising crop prices. Speculative investments in agricultural commodities futures and other derivatives pushed food prices to new heights.[13] Food price volatility was exacerbated and extended by drought that occurred in multiple grain-growing regions over the 2010–2012 period that affected global supply and further incentivized speculators. An extended period of higher and more volatile food prices contributed to rising world hunger while at the same time benefiting many farmers who were producing staple grains for export in industrialized countries. Rising farm incomes, for example, enabled producers to invest in their farming operations to increase production. The financial crisis also led many governments to lower interest rates, which meant that credit was widely available for farmers to make purchases of land and agricultural machinery. High and volatile food prices remained throughout the 2008 to 2012 period as drought conditions in the United States and other countries kept commodity prices at elevated levels.

Like most other farm booms, this heady period of high commodity prices was followed by a bust, which began to take hold in 2013. The increased investment in crop production eventually led to oversupply, which in turn reduced pressure on prices. The decline in agricultural commodity prices was swift and sharp. By 2018, for example, US net farm income was only half of what it was five years earlier.[14] Economic growth fell in this period across emerging economies reliant on agriculture. These included Argentina and Brazil, which by 2014 had become some of the largest markets for agrochemicals because their production of soy, largely destined for Chinese markets, soared.[15] During the commodity boom, these countries were a key source of market growth across all of the agricultural input firms. As the boom ended, these markets contracted.

As farm incomes around the world fell with the drop in commodity prices, farmer demand softened for farm machinery, genetically modified seeds, agrochemicals, and fertilizers as farmers looked to reduce costs.[16] These trends were especially prominent in emerging economies, which directly affected the financial performance of the big firms. Although this farm crisis was not as dramatic or long-lasting as the farm crisis in the 1980s, the drop in income among the major input companies substantially reduced their profits. Dominant firms viewed consolidation as a promising strategy to counter falling profits because it offered opportunities to cut costs and rationalize production by combining businesses and eliminating duplication.[17]

In the fertilizer sector, these broader economic pressures played a central role in the mergers. For example, reporting in the *Financial Times* at the time of the Agrium–PotashCorp merger noted that the two firms "are struggling with industry overcapacity, although some producers hope a series of mine closures and suspensions over recent years will stabilise the industry."[18] Adding to the fragility in the fertilizer sector during the downturn was the 2013 collapse of both PhosChem, a fertilizer export cartel whose members included PotashCorp and Mosaic, and the Belarusian Potash Company cartel. In the wake of the collapse of these cartels, global fertilizer prices declined further, and PotashCorp began to lay off workers to keep down its costs.[19]

FINANCIALIZATION AND ACTIVIST INVESTORS

The heightened power of financial investors, which had been growing especially since the 1980s, appears to have further pushed firms toward consolidation. Although financial factors have long been important in explaining consolidation in the sector, these pressures have become more pronounced in recent decades. Financialization—the growing importance of financial motives, actors, and trends in shaping activity in the global economy—played an important role in reconfiguring the agrifood sector in ways that made it more responsive to investor pressures.[20] Many analysts see financialization as a key factor in the rising importance of shareholder value (i.e., return on equity) relative to other goals (such as job creation and long-term building of the firm) as a benchmark of the performance of firms in the global economy.[21] When firms do not deliver the short-term profits that financial investors expect, even when outside economic conditions are the primary cause, they become vulnerable to shareholder pressure to make changes in their corporate structure to boost returns. These financial dynamics have interacted in ways that help to explain the scope and timing of the recent merger activity among the major agricultural input firms.

Looking at the financial performance of the dominant agricultural input firms, it is clear that each experienced lackluster profits and share values as commodity markets softened after 2013 compared to the overall economic growth and the performance of stock market indices. For example, Syngenta's net income fell 17 percent in 2015 due to declining profits in Latin America as demand for its products in that region shrank.[22] In 2015, DuPont saw its lowest returns in nearly a decade as farmer demand dropped in the face of weak grain prices, particularly in Brazil, where the company had heavy exposure.[23] Monsanto similarly had weak financial performance in 2015 and 2016, also linked to lower commodity prices, which dampened demand for its flagship herbicide Roundup. Bayer too underperformed relative to the overall stock market in this same period. In addition, Agrium and PotashCorp saw falling equity prices in this period, with share values dropping below the S&P 500 benchmark.[24]

It was in this broader context that shareholder pressure came bearing down on the Big Ag input firms to improve their returns, including pushes to restructure as a means to save costs and shore up profits. Shareholder activism—when one or several investors purchase a large number of shares in a firm that they consider undervalued and then exert pressure on the firm's management to increase its returns—has been on the rise in recent decades as the global economy has become more financialized, and the agricultural sector has been no exception. Activist investors, even though they typically own just a few percentage points of the total shares in a firm, can pressure management to make major changes. According to business analysts Bill George and Jay Lorsch, "With increasing frequency they get deeply involved in governance—demanding board seats, replacing CEOs, and advocating specific business strategies."[25] The strategies of activist investors can include pressure to restructure, including undertaking mergers and acquisitions.[26]

In the Dow and DuPont cases, several activist investors were instrumental in pushing the two firms to make structural changes that ultimately led to the merger. Activist investor Nelson Peltz's Trian hedge fund purchased just under 3 percent of DuPont's shares in 2013 and subsequently began to push for a restructuring of the firm to counter its weak financial performance. Daniel Loeb's Third Point activist hedge fund revealed that it held just over 2 percent of Dow's shares in 2014. These amounts may seem small, but they were enough for these investors to make vocal demands for change at the firms. Both investors felt the firms were not performing at their full potential and made their assessments clear to leadership at the firms.[27] The Dow–DuPont merger came just a few months after resignation of DuPont CEO Ellen Kullman, who had fought off a proxy challenge from Peltz in 2014 and 2015 in which he pushed for a breakup of the firm. According to reporting at the time, Peltz played a central role in hashing out the details of the deal, even inviting Dow's CEO to his mansion in Palm Beach to work out specifics, with the aim of finding cost savings.[28] Kullman was not thrilled with the outcome. Of this kind of deal, she lamented, "Break up, recombine. Breakup, recombine . . . That doesn't create any value except for bankers and lawyers."[29]

Activist investor pressure was also a factor in several other agribusiness mergers in this period. When Monsanto was courting Syngenta in 2015, it sought to engage with Syngenta shareholders directly to play up the benefits of its proposed takeover. The hedge fund Paulson and Co. was rumored to have built up a large stake in Syngenta shares in an attempt to push the firm to accept the deal, although it ultimately fell through.[30] Syngenta's refusal of the deal sent the firm's shares into free fall, dropping 20 percent within days, which resulted in the resignation of Syngenta's CEO at the time. To placate shareholders, Syngenta undertook a $2 billion share buyback in September 2015 and signaled that the sector would look quite different in six months, likely foreshadowing acceptance of its purchase by ChemChina only a few months later.[31] Similarly, the Agrium–Potash Corporation merger was preceded by activist pressure from the hedge fund Jana Partners just a few years before the creation of the combined firm Nutrien. In this case, Agrium had been able to fend off the proxy challenges from Jana Partners, but a few years later, in 2015, another activist investor, ValueAct, revealed a nearly 6 percent stake in the firm.[32] Although the new activist investor did not publicly apply pressure to the firm to restructure, it was not long before Agrium and Potash Corporation joined forces to form Nutrien in 2016.

Shareholders in large firms are not always in favor of mergers. Their views largely depend on whether they think merging with another firm will add value to their shares. Many of Bayer's shareholders, for example, were initially unhappy with the firm's bid for Monsanto and were instead intent on keeping the company's focus on pharmaceuticals rather than building up its agricultural inputs business. They were wary of expanding the firm's agrochemicals portfolio and were skeptical of Monsanto's poor environmental reputation, which many saw as potentially damaging for shareholder value. Some analysts, though, argued that the merger would increase Bayer's returns from 7 to 8 percent per year to 11 to 12 percent per year. In the end, Bayer's shareholders approved the takeover.[33]

Adding to these financial dynamics was a context of very low interest rates, which made corporate borrowing highly attractive. After seven years of historically low interest rates globally, corporate borrowing was both cheap and easy, which was convenient for financing giant mergers. The *Financial Times* reported in 2015 that many firms were also "sitting on large piles of cash," which encouraged them to make deals.[34] Investment banks actively sought to encourage the financing of merger deals as a way to increase their own profits. As a result of these conditions, firms took on debt in order to pay dividends to shareholders and to buy back shares in an effort to raise capital. Several of the agribusiness megamergers from this period were funded along these lines: ChemChina's purchase of Syngenta was mostly financed by loans, leaving the firm with a debt level at the time of 9.5 times its annual earnings, and Bayer's net debt quadrupled when it purchased Monsanto. Both ChemChina and Bayer borrowed from a suite of banks and lending institutions to finance the deals.[35]

COMMON OWNERSHIP INFLUENCES CORPORATE INCENTIVES

Heightened financialization in the agrifood sector has also influenced consolidation in ways beyond just encouraging activist investors. The institutionalization of savings through pension funds and other types of institutional investment instruments has been a growing trend in recent decades. A large share of institutional investors' funds is now managed by professional asset managers, who are typically rewarded based on their investment performance. As a result, asset management firms have strong incentives to push the firms in which they invest for higher returns. Pension funds and other large institutional investors, such as university endowment funds, are typically referred to as "passive investors" because they buy into firms through indexes that track shares of groups of companies as a block, and these investments are typically held for long periods of time. Institutional investors collectively hold around 70 to 80 percent of US publicly traded firms, and often the same asset management firms hold shares across a number of firms in the same industry. The top asset management firms collectively own at least 10 to 20 percent of most American companies, including those in the same sectors.[36]

In addition to managing the money of passive investors, financial investment firms that sell index products to institutional investors often engage directly with the firms in which they invest, particularly if they are concerned about a firm's performance. But even if they do not directly apply explicit pressure to increase returns, most firms understand the concerns of these asset managers and are likely to act accordingly.[37] In

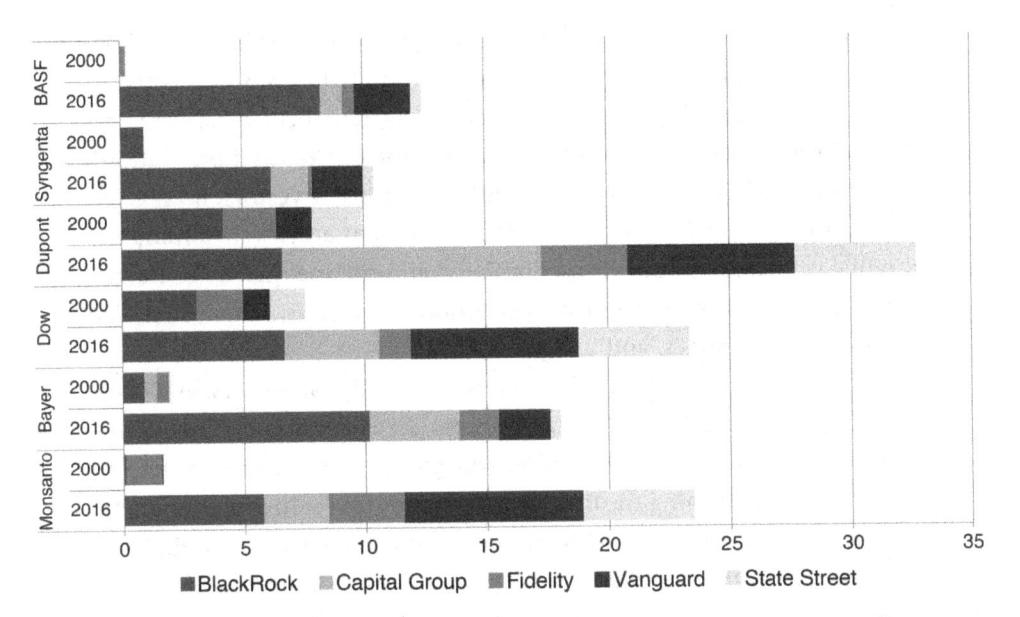

DRIVERS OF RECENT AGRIBUSINESS MEGAMERGERS 233

9.2 Ownership of seed and chemical firms by large asset management firms. *Source*: Thomson Reuters Eikon Database (percentage of shares as of December 31, 2016). Adapted from Torshizi and Clapp (2021).

other words, large asset management corporations' holdings in firms across entire sectors of the global economy—referred to as common ownership—exert constant pressure on firms to generate more profits and increase shareholder value. Mergers are a common response to these pressures because they offer a simple and immediate strategy to boost returns, even though those returns are not rooted in a solid base of corporate growth. Interestingly, it is not just individual firm performance that matters in this context, but industry performance across an entire sector, including competitors.[38] Thus, when all the firms in a sector do well, so do the investors, because they have a stake in all or most of those firms.

This kind of common ownership is strikingly evident in the agricultural inputs industry. For example, around the time of the mergers that were announced in 2015 and 2016, BlackRock, Capital Group, Fidelity, the Vanguard Group, State Street Global Advisors, and Norges Bank Investment Management each owned significant shares in all of largest seed and chemical companies.[39] The scope of common ownership in the sector, and its change between 2000 and 2016, is shown in figure 9.2.

Asset management ownership was also high in the fertilizer and farm machinery sectors around the time that consolidation was occurring. In 2016, the top five institutional owners of Agrium held nearly 20 percent of the firm's shares, whereas 16 percent of Potash Corporation's shares were held by firm's the top five institutional investors. Both Capital Group and Royal Bank of Canada's investment arms were among the top five investors in both firms. Similarly, around one-quarter of Deere's shares were held by its top five institutional investors, which included BlackRock, State Street, and Vanguard.[40]

In these cases, a small number of large institutional owners, especially asset management firms that own shares across multiple firms in the sector, can pressure firms to pursue strategies to keep short-term returns high, including pushing the firms in which they invest to engage in mergers and acquisitions. Like with the pressure from activist shareholders, pressure from the large asset management firms that are their common owners—whether explicit or implicit—no doubt weighed on corporate decisions to pursue the megamergers in the agricultural input industries in the post-2015 period.

PRODUCT COMPLEMENTARITY AND TECHNOLOGICAL INTEGRATION

Although the wider economic context played a large role in encouraging the spate of mergers in the agricultural inputs sector that took place after 2015, it was not the only factor at play. The mergers also reinforced product complementarity and technological integration among the dominant firms.[41] This strategy was clear with the Dow and DuPont merger, for example. At the time, DuPont was the second-largest seed company in the world, with around 21 percent of global seed sales. Originally a chemical company, DuPont diversified with its purchase of Pioneer Hi-Bred in 1999, and although it continued to sell agrochemicals, by 2015 it had only around 6 percent of the global pesticide market. By contrast, Dow Corporation had more expertise in pesticides, where it held around 10 percent of global sales, whereas it had only around 4 percent of the global market in seeds.[42] In this sense, bringing these two firms together under one roof resulted in a firm that had a more even balance of seed and agrochemical expertise, especially when Corteva Agriscience was spun off to focus solely on agricultural inputs.

Similarly, the matchup of Bayer and Monsanto brought together the former's dominance in the agrochemical market, which included around 18 percent of global sales of pesticides at the time of the merger, with the latter's dominance in seeds, for which it commanded approximately 26 percent of the global market.[43] However, these market shares shifted after the mergers, as regulators in a number of jurisdictions, including the United States and the European Union, required Bayer to sell major portions of its seed and agrochemical assets, as noted above. BASF, which purchased assets from Bayer, thus moved into the seed market for the first time to complement its agrochemical product line.

Both ChemChina and Syngenta primarily focused on agrochemicals, but the former's purchase of the latter nonetheless led to a more balanced product mix between seeds and agrochemicals for ChemChina. The Chinese government has long had its own research program in genetically modified crops, and the country released a policy paper in early 2016 calling for a cautious rollout of GM crop technology in the food sector.[44] Syngenta, which owned around seven thousand seed varieties, effectively gave China access to plant genetic material for the country's GM crop research.[45] The opening of the Chinese market to GM crops is appealing for agrochemical and seed companies more generally, especially because demand for GM crops and associated chemicals peaked in North America and weakened in other key markets during the commodity market downturn, including in Latin America.

The PotashCorp and Agrium merger that created the new firm Nutrien also continued the trend of bringing complementary arms of the fertilizer business together, as outlined in chapter 7. Agrium was already a supplier of all three main fertilizer nutrients—N, P, and K—and it also had a strong retail subsidiary, which gave it some protection from the fluctuations of the bulk commodity nutrient trade.[46] The merger with PotashCorp bolstered the combined firms' potash interests, as both firms had significant mining capacity in western Canada.

Although product complementarity was clearly evident in these prominent megamergers, there were some differences from the merger waves that took place in earlier decades, especially in the case of seeds and agrochemicals.

The earlier mergers that brought together seeds and agrochemicals directly followed a strengthening of intellectual property protections in the 1970s and 1980s for plant genetic material. Stronger IP protections rewarded larger research and development operations that could generate innovations to tie seeds and herbicides more closely together through agricultural biotechnology. This time around, however, there were no major changes to IP rules that preceded the push for new mergers, although the firms remained committed to continuing the genetic modification of seeds to work with specific agrochemicals. Some analysts have suggested that patents are no longer spurring innovation now that the market shares of the top firms are so big. In other words, patents and market concentration can serve as substitutes for one another, as both give firms a degree of market power that allows them to set prices above their marginal costs.[47]

Moreover, as mentioned in chapter 8, patents on the first set of GM seeds were beginning to expire in the early 2000s, and competition from generic producers of herbicides was growing. These forces played a role in spurring firms to coordinate with cross-licensing agreements to develop new seed varieties that were not just using novel patented traits but also combining existing traits in new ways. For example, the dominant firms increasingly developed products that featured "stacked traits"—that is, combining multiple separate traits developed by different firms into a single seed that were nearly impossible for other firms to replicate. Monsanto had cross-licensing arrangements with all of the other players, including Bayer, which eventually bought the firm. Dow and DuPont also had cross-licensing arrangements for seed traits prior to their merger that formed Corteva Agriscience.[48]

NEW FORMS OF GENETIC ENGINEERING

The big firms across all of the agricultural inputs sector have invested heavily in acquiring the know-how to employ new technologies through their acquisition of start-up companies, as access to cutting-edge technology can help them to maintain their dominance. One of those technologies is the broad category of new techniques for the genetic manipulation of organisms, which are being used to develop new kinds of seeds, agrochemicals, and fertilizers. For example, seed and agrochemical firms have begun to invest in the acquisition of and rights to use genome editing technologies, which promise lower costs and faster means by which to alter the genetic makeup of seed varieties. These technologies also typically face less regulatory oversight than genetic modification techniques using agricultural biotechnology.[49] The development of CRISPR and other data-driven gene editing technologies ushered in entirely new ways to modify the DNA of plants.[50]

The dominant firms in the seed industry are particularly interested in these novel genome editing technologies because they are much more precise than more traditional methods of genetic engineering in plants. Earlier techniques simply inserted genetic material from other organisms into plants in a somewhat random fashion, which required extensive testing to determine which plants expressed the desired traits. Gene editing focuses instead on rearranging the DNA of an existing plant rather than adding foreign genetic material to it. Although there is a great deal of research using these techniques to enhance the qualities of crops (e.g., to make them more resistant to drought and floods), there is also ongoing research to edit crops to make them resistant to herbicides, which is especially interesting to the dominant seed and chemical companies, as outlined in more detail in chapter 11.

Most of the initial advances in gene editing—and the associated patents—are linked to university-based research labs. The big firms were quick to develop linkages with university research groups to acquire licenses to use CRISPR and other gene editing technologies. Similar to patterns that emerged in the seed and chemical industries in the 1980s and 1990s, firms also began purchasing gene editing start-up companies so that they could rapidly establish research programs for gene-edited crops.[51] They then pursued patent protection for crop varieties that involved a complex mix of genetic edits to combat herbicide-resistant weeds and to make crops resistant to herbicides.[52] For example, Syngenta, Bayer, and Corteva Agriscience have all made investments in plant breeding programs that make use of gene editing. As of 2022, Corteva Agriscience amassed the largest number of CRISPR patents in the agricultural arena.[53] Syngenta has also begun to use gene editing techniques for plant breeding drawing insights from China's government-sponsored CRISPR research, with a focus on the Chinese market.[54]

Firms in the seed, agrochemical, and fertilizer industries have also started investing in other kinds of synthetic biology, including what the industry calls "biologicals," to develop new agrochemicals and fertilizers.[55] Biological products use large-scale biological data sets and genome editing techniques to modify microbes, extracts from plants, organic matter, and beneficial insects to develop new methods of pest control and fertilization of agricultural crops. Similar to agricultural biotechnology and genome editing, the renewed focus on developing biological products using highly sophisticated data-driven technologies has spurred a boom in investments in and acquisitions of firms working in this space, including by the dominant agricultural input firms. Corteva, Bayer, Syngenta, and BASF have all made significant investments in synthetic biology start-ups, as summarized in figure 9.3.

THE RISE OF DIGITAL AGRICULTURE

Companies across all of the input sectors have also made significant investments in digital technologies, which has led to further integration of the agricultural input industries. Investments by the large farm machinery firms in both hardware and software firms have enabled them to pursue automation of their equipment and deepen their interface with new digital farm management technologies that connect to all of the agricultural inputs. Deere's attempt to acquire Precision Planting in 2016 was just one example of the movement of equipment firms in this direction. Over the past decade, the equipment firms have made extensive acquisitions of digital start-ups, including Deere's purchase of various artificial intelligence (AI) and automation start-ups in recent years (see figure 9.3). With the procurement of these firms, Deere has moved closer to its aim of developing autonomous farm equipment that can use cameras and AI for navigation and to identify weeds in the field that can then be sprayed automatically. This kind of technology can be highly lucrative for inputs firms, as software can earn up to 85 percent in gross profits, compared to profits of just 25 percent on machinery. Deere noted that it expects 10 percent of its annual revenue to come from software sales in the coming decade.[56]

Other machinery firms are investing in similar ventures. In 2021, CNH acquired stakes in several digital software and precision agricultural equipment firms. CNH also invested in electric vehicle, clean energy, and autonomous vehicle firms, as well as a start-up developing technology to identify and kill weeds with electricity rather than chemicals.[57] AGCO not only bought Precision Planting when Deere was unable to do so in 2017 due to US Department of Justice concerns, but in 2022, it also acquired an automation firm for digital agricultural machinery, as well as other software and electronics firms.[58] Meanwhile, Kubota acquired a Canadian-based firm specializing in automation technology, in addition to establishing partnerships on digital platforms, including platforms dedicated to carbon accounting.[59]

It is not just machinery firms that have made inroads into digital technologies. Many of the top firms in the seeds and chemicals industries, as well as in the fertilizer sector, have also invested in digital agriculture technology platforms, often through acquisitions of start-ups and other firms. Firms across all of the agricultural input industries appear to be vying for dominance in what might be considered a new agricultural input essential to the industrial agricultural model: data and associated cloud-based digital farm management tools. These digital technology platforms represent a combination of sophisticated software programs that can analyze satellite and other data to determine climate and soil conditions in individual fields. These software programs provide farmers with specific advice regarding the inputs they should be using and in what amounts across different parts of their acreage. When combined with machinery hardware, AI-assisted sprayers can apply fertilizers and pesticides with precision.[60] The firm that ends up with the dominant digital platform will be able to benefit from platform power and network effects (discussed in chapters 6 and 11), as customers will be driven to the most useful digital farming services.

The rise of these types of digital technologies was part of the motivation for the Bayer-Monsanto merger. As noted earlier, Bayer was eager to access Monsanto's Climate Corp platform. The announcement for the merger between the two companies emphasized these digital technologies alongside its seed traits and chemical products, which it referred to as

9.3 Some recent digital and biological acquisitions of the major agricultural input firms. *Source:* corporate webpages and news sources.

"integrated solutions," such that the newly merged firm can be a "one-stop shop" for farmers.[61] Firms in the seed and chemical sectors, as well as in the fertilizer sector, subsequently made a series of acquisitions of smaller firms and start-ups to enable them to get a foothold in the digital farming business. For example, Bayer, in addition to marketing Climate FieldView, acquired ForGround in 2022, a digital platform specifically geared to measuring soil quality and tracking carbon sequestration. BASF, Syngenta, Corteva, Nutrien, and Yara have all invested in digital software platforms in the past decade.

These information technology platforms can replace the need for patents on plant genetic material if enough farmers sign on to use them. Farmers who use these platforms are often asked to send data from their fields via satellite back to the firm, which combines those data with data provided by other farmers to generate input prescriptions it can sell to farmers, as will be discussed in more depth in chapter 11. Some of these platforms are linked to specific equipment companies, as is the case with the interface between Climate FieldView and John Deere tractors. Launches of digital platforms face far fewer regulatory hurdles compared to the introduction of new pesticides and seeds, making them much easier to bring to market.[62] In this way, firms can use less expensive pathways of technological innovation to lock in sales of their own brands of seeds and chemicals that are designed work with specific software.

THE CULMINATION OF THE UNWINDING OF ANTITRUST

US antitrust policy is grounded in several laws and acts put in place over a century ago. These laws explicitly sought to rein in the political power of corporate giants by regulating the structure of markets. Specifically, they aimed to prevent a small number of very large firms from dictating the terms of any particular market. They tried to do that in a number of ways, including by removing conditions that would allow dominant firms to collude to raise prices, engage in predatory pricing, or to erect other market barriers that could drive competitors out of business. These laws were exercised robustly in the earlier part of the twentieth century and were a key force behind the trust busting that broke up several large monopolies in the United States, such as Standard Oil, which controlled not only the oil market but also the infrastructure on which it was traded.[63]

From the late 1970s, the political interpretation and application of competition law—in the United States as well as in other countries—shifted in important ways that effectively loosened controls on consolidating firms. This shift, outlined in chapter 7, coincided with the rise of neoliberal economic policies that sought to reduce government intervention and oversight of the market. In this period, merger reviews increasingly centered on their impact on efficiencies and consumer prices, rather than the ways in which proposed mergers might affect market structures and competition, which was the original focus of antitrust law.

Analysts have associated this policy direction with a rise in mergers and acquisitions in the decades that followed. Interpreted through this more outcome-focused lens, mergers that likely would have been prevented under previous legal applications—because they would either allow dominant firms to amass significant market share (e.g., through horizontal mergers that result in fewer players controlling the bulk of the market), or to dominate multiple stages along supply chains in ways that would stifle competition and lock in customers (as would be the case with vertical mergers)—were deemed permissible if they led to lower consumer prices or an increase in market efficiencies.[64] This more economistic and effects-based approach to evaluating mergers was reflected in the various overhauls of the US merger guidelines since the 1980s.

Unsurprisingly, in the subsequent decades, there were fewer regulatory challenges to corporate consolidation, especially vertical mergers.[65] The shift in the US interpretation of competition policy toward consumer welfare has since extended internationally and reshaped competition policy around the world. For example, the best-practices guidelines of the International Competition Network, established in 2001, heavily reflect the US merger guidelines.[66] The EU's approach to antitrust also saw some convergence with that of the United States on certain elements, including a more economistic approach to evaluation by the 1990s.[67]

By the time the big mergers in the agricultural inputs sector began around 2015, this weaker approach to antitrust had become fully entrenched. The mergers and acquisitions in this most recent era have thus benefited from shifts in the interpretation and enforcement of antitrust rules, not just in the United States but also globally. Although the US and Canadian governments and the EU did require the firms to make certain changes before the mergers could continue, regulators did not sue to block the mergers outright, and they were ultimately permitted to proceed.

CONCLUSION

The post-2015 megamergers were part mergers of distress and part mergers of opportunity. The broader economic context, including the weak performance of the farm sector following the 2008–2012 agricultural boom, played an important role in shaping firms' decisions to pursue mergers with and acquisition of their rivals. Shareholder pressures within new financial ownership structures, combined with low interest rates, created conditions in which firms saw clear financial benefits in consolidation both within and across input sectors. Based on these factors, there was an element of distress driving the mergers.

At the same time, technological imperatives regarding product development and competition for market share at the firm level also played a role in the smaller acquisitions that were taking place in this period. These included factors such as access to plant genetic material for further development of agricultural biotechnology, including the seed and herbicide combinations outlined in the previous chapter, as well as access to know-how for new seed modification techniques, such as genome editing. There was also growing corporate interest in developing and capitalizing on new digital platforms for farm management software and services, which could provide stylized advice to farmers on which inputs to use and in what combinations for specific portions of their fields. As such, consolidation in this period was also fueled by new technological opportunities. Of course, both the economic and technological factors interacted with each other in complex ways.

10

THE POWER TO SHAPE MARKETS

The reconfiguration of the agricultural inputs industry after 2015 generated immediate apprehension from many quarters, including farmer organizations, civil society groups, environmental nongovernmental organizations, government policymakers, and academics. Their worry was not just about the market dominance of a handful of large agribusiness firms following the megamergers outlined in the previous chapter, although that is certainly a big concern. They were also troubled by the firms' promotion of a technological model associated with wider social and ecological costs, as well their growing political power to shape policy and legislation.

These concerns echo long-standing critiques of corporate concentration and control in the sector, as outlined in previous chapters. But the impacts about which critics expressed concern are in many ways of a new order in this current period because of the extreme levels of concentration, as well as the increasing overlap and dominance of ever-larger firms in the sector. Growing hostility toward corporate power in national and international economies, especially with the rise of the Big Tech firms in recent decades, has also fueled heightened scrutiny of corporate dominance in the agricultural sector. Competition authorities in the EU and in the United States, for example, stepped up their oversight of the Big

Tech firms in the late 2010s over what were widely deemed to be anticompetitive practices among those firms. The public critique of corporate economic dominance was of such magnitude in the United States that in 2021, President Biden issued an executive order to address concentration in the US economy, including in the agrifood sector. In response, the USDA invited comments in an effort to gather information about the impacts of concentration in the US food system to guide potential future legislation to rein in corporate power in the sector.[1] From the early 2020s, Canada has also stepped up its efforts regarding competition policy and has made agriculture a particular focus of its activities.[2]

The main issues that critics raised in the wake of the recent agribusiness mergers are outlined in this and the following two chapters. This chapter focuses on market power and its consequences in food systems. Chapters 11 and 12 examine the technology power and the political power of the agricultural input firms, respectively. Although the repercussions of market, technology, and political power of the dominant firms in an era of heightened concentration are discussed in separate chapters, in practice, these different types of corporate power overlap and intersect with one other in ways that reinforce the influence of the top firms in the sector.

CONCENTRATION AND MARKET POWER

The recent megamergers have prompted worry that the dominant firms have gained even more power to shape markets. *Market power* refers to the capacity of firms to influence supply and/or demand elements of a market in ways that enable them to raise prices well above their costs to generate excess profits (i.e., profits that exceed a normal return on capital). Highly concentrated markets are usually a sign that the dominant firms have some degree of market power. The power of the top firms to shape the contours of the market typically increases as the percentage of the market held by the top four firms rises. For example, if the top four firms control 70 percent of a market, they are likely to have more market power than a situation where the top four firms control 30 percent of the market. It typically works like this: if one of a small number of dominant firms raises prices well above their production costs, then the other top firms usually follow suit because there is less competition from smaller firms to pressure the top firms to keep their prices lower. Price increases of this type can occur via coordination, explicit or implicit, among the dominant firms.[3]

Dominant firms often compound their market power by taking actions to hinder competition. For example, beyond simply buying up rivals, dominant firms often try to dissuade other firms from entering the market by creating barriers to entry, which ultimately results in fewer firms vying for market share.[4] Firms with technologies that have high R&D costs and intellectual property protection typically benefit from market power because the barriers to entry in those industries are already high, thus keeping those markets concentrated. Firms can also actively work to keep out competitors by other means, such as demanding that customers sign usage agreements that make it hard for those customers to switch brands. Dominant firms can manipulate markets to enhance their influence in other ways too—such as by incentivizing retailers to bundle or prioritize sales of certain products or by only selling to retailers that follow such practices—which ultimately shapes both supply and demand conditions in the market. These kinds of practices make it difficult for other firms to compete in those markets.

Competition authorities are typically on high alert regarding the potential for market power to distort markets when an already concentrated sector pursues further consolidation. Economists typically consider a 40 percent market share among the top four firms to be the threshold beyond which market distortions are likely to occur due to market power.[5] If a merger is likely to result in a 60 percent or higher market share among the top four firms, regulators typically apply additional scrutiny. As agricultural economist James Macdonald noted in the wake of the latest mergers in the agricultural inputs sector, "Mergers today are likely to attract antitrust concern if they lead to a reduction of four sellers to three, three to two, or two to one. They may attract antitrust action in some less concentrated markets (six sellers to five, or five to four), if other factors, such as high barriers to entry or high costs to buyers switching among sellers, support market power among the sellers."[6]

In the immediate aftermath of the post-2015 megamergers outlined in chapter 9, several organizations issued reports on the extent of concentration that resulted across the agricultural inputs sector.[7] According to estimates in these reports, concentration ratios of the top four firms (CR4) remained high and have increased somewhat in their intensity after the mergers were completed. From 2018 to 2020, the top four seed and agrochemical firms—Bayer, Syngenta Group, Corteva, and BASF—controlled between 60 and 70 percent of the global pesticides market and between 50 and 60 percent of the $45 billion global seed market.[8] The concentration figures for these sectors are higher than they had been in earlier decades. According to USDA analysis, the global CR4 in crop seeds and biotechnology was approximately 20 percent in 1994, 30 percent in 2000, and around 50 percent in 2009. For pesticides, the global CR4 was approximately 30 percent, 40 percent, and 50 percent in those same years.[9]

In the fertilizer sector, although global firms increasingly dominate the market, most of the available data on concentration are at the national level. For example, in 2019 in the United States, four companies—CF Industries, Nutrien, Koch, and Yara-USA—supplied 75 percent of nitrogen-based fertilizers, and just two companies—Nutrien and Mosaic—supplied 100 percent of North America's potash fertilizer. One firm, Mosaic, was estimated to supply nearly 90 percent of the US market for phosphorus-based fertilizers.[10] In the farm machinery sector, the top four firms—Deere, Kubota, CNH Industrial, and AGCO—captured around 45 percent of the global market, and the top six held nearly 50 percent of the global market.[11] In the United States and Canadian national markets, Deere accounts for around 60 percent of sales of heavy-duty tractors.[12]

Concentration ratios differ depending on markets for specific kinds of inputs, such as particular seed varieties or certain chemicals. When those more specific markets are considered, concentration levels are often much higher because some markets are only served by a few firms. For example, genetically modified (GM) seeds comprise around half of the global seed market, and even before the recent mergers, virtually all of the market for GM traits was dominated by the top six firms.[13] In countries that plant significant acreages of GM crops, the concentration in the seed sector is starkly evident. In the United States, for example, where genetically modified seeds account for most of the corn and soybeans planted, concentration in those markets is especially high. In the 2018–2020 period, the top four seed companies controlled 84.4 percent of the

US corn seed market and 78.1 percent of the US soybean seed market. The top two firms alone—Bayer and Corteva Agriscience—controlled 72 percent of the US corn seed market and 66 percent of the US soybean seed market.[14]

This kind of concentration is not surprising when one considers that the top three firms—Bayer, Corteva, and Syngenta—own 95 percent of the patents in the United States for GM corn, 78 percent of the patents for GM soybeans, and 93 percent of the patents for GM canola issued over the 1976–2021 period.[15] Concentration is similarly high in the seed sector across many other national markets, including the United Kingdom, Turkey, Italy, Thailand, Denmark, South Africa, and Brazil, where the top four firms controlled over 80 percent of the market for corn seed in 2016. For soybeans, over 80 percent of the market that same year was controlled by the top four firms in Argentina, Brazil, Paraguay, South Africa, and Uruguay.[16] Although the precise level of concentration is difficult to determine in some cases, concentration in the sector remains very high—more than double the 40 percent threshold that economists warn is likely to result in market distortions. Concentration levels are also typically much higher for GM crops than for non-GM crops, such as wheat and barley.[17]

Some analysts have raised concerns that the dominant firms within a sector may command more market power than even these measures signal because of their common shareholder ownership structure—outlined in chapter 9—which is not reflected in concentration ratios. Common ownership is a pattern for many of the firms in the agrifood system, whereby a significant proportion of shares in each of the companies is owned by the same large asset management firms. As shareholders, the gigantic asset management firms such as BlackRock, State Street, and Vanguard are in a position to pressure the CEOs of these firms to deliver higher returns, which can lead to elevated prices across all firms in which they own shares.[18] Critics have argued that this is an important aspect of market concentration that competition authorities should consider, especially in the agrifood sector where these dynamics are prevalent.[19].

Although the CR4 and other measures of market concentration can point analysts to where market power may reside in the economy, it is not always a perfect measure of the exercise of that power. Not only is concentration tricky to measure, but the capacity it potentially confers to firms to raise prices well above their production costs does not necessarily mean firms are doing so in practice. To determine whether dominant firms are flexing their market power, economists also look at other metrics, such as price markups—that is, the amount that firms charge for their products above their marginal costs—as well as corporate profit ratios. These other measures provide a good indication of whether the firms that dominate in concentrated sectors are in fact exerting their market power in ways that are excessive or socially harmful.

Recent research has determined that markups and profits are indeed rising as markets are becoming more concentrated. For example, economists Jan Eeckhout and Jan De Loecker have shown that globally, the average markup firms charge has increased significantly. Prices were around 1.1 times higher than marginal costs in 1980 and rose to nearly 1.6 times higher than marginal costs in 2019—with rates in North America (1.76) and Europe (1.64) having increased more than in other parts of the world.[20] The increase in markups was especially sharp in the 1980s and 1990s, and again after 2010—periods when there were rampant merger and acquisition waves in many economies, including in the agricultural inputs sectors, as outlined in chapters 7 to 9. Similarly, new research shows that corporate profits as a share of sales increased between the 1980s and mid-2010s, from around 1 to 2 percent of sales in 1980 to around 7 to 8 percent of sales in 2016. By 2021, corporate markups and profits in the United States had increased to their highest recorded level since the 1950s. And although these averages are revealing about the rise in the exercise of market power, recent economic research also shows that markups were higher among the largest and most dominant firms, especially those in high-tech and manufacturing sectors.[21] In other words, the dominant firms in concentrated markets are typically the ones that have access to market power, and they are exercising it actively to their advantage.

Beyond price markups and profits, evidence that firms are actively working to create barriers to entry to stifle competition is also an indicator of the exercise of market power, even if such practices are difficult to measure precisely. Like in the wider economy, the top firms in agricultural inputs sector in the post-mergers context have increased prices beyond their costs, have increased their profit margins, and have sought to create barriers to entry for other firms.

SEED MARKETS

The seed sector is one of the most highly concentrated input industries, especially when considering genetically modified seeds in specific markets.[22] The data on concentration ratios noted above are just one aspect of this concentration. Beyond the market for seeds themselves, the ownership of intellectual property (IP) for seed traits is also concentrated in the hands of just a few firms. For example, the USDA analyzed ownership of IP and found that in 1990, the top four companies held 41 percent of intellectual property protection for corn in the United States, with just one firm, Pioneer, owning 38 percent. By 2010, the IP ownership of the top four firms had risen to a whopping 93 percent. As of 2022, the top four firms owned an incredible 95 percent of the IP for corn, 97 percent for canola, 84 percent for soybean, and 74 percent for cotton. These very high levels of IP concentration far exceed that of wheat—a non-GM crop for which much of the breeding takes place in public sector institutions—which has an IP concentration among the top four firms of 51 percent.[23]

In Canada, when Bayer initiated its purchase of Monsanto, alarm bells rang for both farmers and regulators because 95 percent of canola seeds sold in Canada contained either the Bayer-owned LibertyLink trait (55 percent) or the Monsanto-owned Roundup Ready trait (40 percent). Without some sort of intervention, the tie-up between the two firms would surely result in what would effectively be a monopolistic market. The Canadian Competition Bureau identified this concentration as a threat to competition and made its approval of the merger conditional on Bayer divesting its canola seeds and traits business.[24] BASF was the purchaser of Bayer's Canadian canola seed assets.

There is a great deal of concern that corporate concentration in the seed sector—for sold seed and in IP for genetically modified traits—gives the dominant firms the power to establish prices above levels that would prevail in a more competitive market. Indeed, the USDA reported that prices for genetically engineered seeds increased by 700 percent between 1990 and 2013, while prices for other field crops increased by 218 percent.[25] Ascertaining whether these price increases are the product of concentration or other factors, such as technology licensing fees, is tricky because most of the required data are not publicly available. Rather, the data are often kept behind paywalls by private sector data companies. For example, it can cost upwards of six figures to attain the twenty years of seed price data necessary to show trends over time.

Technology licensing fees, which make up a large proportion of genetically modified seed prices, were easy to track in the United States until recently because they appeared on a separate line in the seed contracts that farmers signed with firms. These fees have since been rolled into seed prices, however, making it hard to separate their effect.[26] At the time that the megamergers in the seeds and chemicals sector were unfolding, studies predicted that prices would likely increase around 2 to 6 percent due to the resulting concentration. The predicted effect of the Bayer-Monsanto merger on cotton seed prices was much more pronounced, with an anticipated 17.4 to 19.2 percent increase.[27] However, given the turmoil on global agricultural markets caused by the COVID-19 pandemic and the Russian invasion of Ukraine that contributed to overall inflation, it has been especially difficult to parse out the various concentration effects on seed prices in recent years.

Despite these data constraints, some analysts have acquired enough data to show that market concentration has influenced seed pricing. As noted in chapter 8, several studies based on time-series data for key crop seed markets in the United States found that market concentration is at least one significant factor contributing to higher seed prices.[28] The OECD recently analyzed proprietary cross-country seed price data for the year 2016 and also found a linkage between concentration and seed prices in cases of very elevated levels of market concentration—which prevails in many local and national markets for certain specific crop seeds.[29]

The seed companies insist that their products enable farmers to achieve greater overall agricultural productivity, which should offset any price increases. However, the vast majority of the agricultural biotechnology traits marketed by top firms are not designed to increase yield. Rather, as outlined in chapter 8, nearly all of the traits marketed by seed firms are for herbicide tolerance or insect resistance—or, increasingly, firms market stacked traits that combine these various traits. Of course, protecting seeds from weeds and insects can result in greater output per field, but the evidence is scant that GM seeds outperform conventional seeds to the extent that it covers the additional cost. USDA data show that the prices of farm inputs, led by seeds, have increased more rapidly in recent decades than the prices farmers have received for their crops. As the American Antitrust Institute notes, "Seed price increases have outpaced yield increases over time—the very problem that biotechnology is purportedly designed to solve."[30] Given the complexities of the issue, most critics agree that more data transparency and further studies are urgently needed.

Beyond pricing impacts, concentrated seed firms can dissuade new entrants into the market. Critics have pointed to practices among firms in the agricultural biotechnology sector with respect to intellectual property ownership, such as licensing and cross-licensing of seed traits and varieties in ways that make it difficult for new firms to enter the marketplace. As inputs to a 2022 USDA consultation on concentration in the seed sector revealed, large firms are able to dictate unfavorable terms to smaller-scale seed dealers, who have little choice but to comply because they have no alternative sources for specific traits.[31] The large biotech seed companies were also criticized in submissions to that same consultation for their efforts to prevent other firms from producing generic versions of their products when their patents expired. One comment filed in the consultation noted that BASF allowed the license for its LibertyLink seed trait to lapse several years before the patent was due to expire, thereby ensuring that the trait was removed from the public domain. The firm also prohibited dealers from selling any seeds containing that trait for several years in order to prevent other firms from producing a generic version once the patent expired in 2023.[32]

Other concerns have been raised about the market power associated with access to licenses for CRISPR techniques for commercial seed breeding. CRISPR is widely touted by its advocates as a democratizing technology because it is less expensive and more accessible than agricultural biotechnology. Hundreds of the basic patents held by the inventors of CRISPR via university consortia and their spinoff firms have open access policies for noncommercial research. But at the same time, the university patent holders have granted exclusive rights to those patents to surrogate firms—namely, spinoff companies connected to the university research teams, which can grant licenses to those wishing to access the technology.[33] Although these surrogate firms offer access to the technology to noncommercial researchers free of charge, they have granted exclusive licenses to private firms for commercial research. The granting of exclusive rights to surrogate firms that then choose to which firms they will sublicense can hinder competition, as those firms that are not able to obtain a sublicense cannot compete in the market for that trait.[34]

One example is Caribou Biosciences, the spinoff company of the University of California, Berkeley, team that developed some of the key CRISPR gene editing technology. The firm granted an exclusive license to DuPont in 2015 (just before it merged with Dow to form Corteva) for the commercial development of row crops using CRISPR technology, as well as nonexclusive rights in other agricultural applications.[35] In 2018, the firm also gained both exclusive and nonexclusive rights in the agricultural area from other patent holders, as well as sublicensing rights. Corteva Agriscience has since amassed over sixty patents for crops developed using CRISPR, and as of 2022, the firm held more CRISPR patents for agriculture than any other firm.[36] Corteva, according to a report written for the European Greens, "is the main gatekeeper for CRISPR patents in the agricultural arena and has gained unprecedented market power due to its ability to grant access to this patent pool."[37] Although Corteva has said that it will make the technology accessible to researchers, those licenses are granted only for noncommercial research, whereas commercial licenses are far too expensive for smaller firms to access.

INPUT SUPPLIERS CROWD OUT NEW RETAILERS

The large seed, agrochemical, and fertilizer firms were targets of several class action lawsuits in 2021 in the United States and Canada for their refusal to sell their products through online retail businesses, such as Farmers Business Network (FBN) and AgVend.[38] In the 2010s, these retail operations set up shop to sell agricultural inputs through online platforms that enabled farmers to compare input prices across different retailers for the first time. This was a significant development because the large firms typically sold inputs such as seeds and agrochemicals only through licensed local dealers that did not offer online sales, making it hard to compare prices.[39] A lawsuit filed by a group of farmers in Idaho, for example, claimed, "The crop inputs market is structured, from top to bottom, to maximize opacity and deny farmers access to the objective pricing data and product information they need to make informed decisions about the crop inputs they buy."[40] Among the defendants in these cases were the seed and agrochemical giants Bayer, Corteva, BASF, Syngenta, and the fertilizer firm Nutrien, all accused of conspiring to boycott these online sellers because they refused to license them as dealers.

The large input firms were especially concerned about the entry of Farmers Business Network into the market. In 2017, these firms discussed FBN's arrival in the inputs retail sector at the annual meeting of CropLife America, a major lobby group to which these firms belong, and which the plaintiffs in the court case saw as a vehicle for collusion.[41] In an attempt to gain access to products from the large firms, FBN purchased the Canadian physical retailer Yorkton Distributors, which had supply agreements with the major firms. Shortly after FBN's entry into the market, however, the large firms cancelled their contracts with Yorkton. Whereas FBN began to develop its own inputs in response to being shut out of the market, AgVend simply shut down its online sales platform.

The Canadian Competition Bureau investigated this case, but in 2022 announced that it would not pursue the case further. The bureau noted that although the suppliers indeed communicated with each other on this issue, it did not see this communication as resulting in a formal agreement or arrangement that crossed the threshold of evidence for acting with anticompetitive intent. According to the Canadian Competition Bureau's formal statement, "The evidence suggests that certain market participants engaged in communications with the goal of influencing manufacturers or wholesalers with respect to FBN. Although the evidence surrounding these communications fails to establish an agreement or arrangement between competitors, these communications are nonetheless concerning to the Bureau."[42] In other words, without evidence of a formal agreement, collusion was hard to prove. However, when there are so few firms in an industry, a formal agreement is hardly necessary for firms to collude.

The large input firms have also been targeted by regulators for undertaking market-distorting practices with their licensed dealers in pesticides sales. In 2022, the US Federal Trade Commission (FTC) along with ten state attorneys general filed a lawsuit against Corteva and Syngenta Group for offering rebates through loyalty programs to compensate dealers who agreed to limit the quantity of generic products for off-patent pesticides that they sold in their stores.[43] The suit claims that these programs have cost farmers hundreds of millions of dollars annually in additional expenses for their purchases of pesticides, because these practices hinder sales of cheaper, generic products while allowing firms to charge higher prices for their brand-name products. The distributors also benefit from these schemes, as the loyalty payments they receive are higher than the margins that they would earn through the sale of generic products. The makers of generic products are harmed by not being able to compete fairly in the market.[44] The US FTC Chair, Lina Khan, remarked on the case: "The FTC is suing to stop Syngenta and Corteva from maintaining their monopolies through harmful tactics that have jacked up pesticide prices for farmers.... By paying off distributors to block generic producers from the market, these giants have deprived farmers of cheaper and more innovative options."[45] Corteva and Syngenta Group maintained that these are longstanding practices that are compliant with antitrust rules. These types of arrangements do indeed harken back to the early twentieth century, when US Steel paid rebates to International Harvester—and at that time, the latter was sued by federal regulators over the practice (see chapter 2).

Critics have also raised the alarm about fertilizer giants expanding into retailing, which could give them even more control over prices. When Nutrien was formed following the merger of Agrium and Potash Corp, as discussed in chapter 9, it became one of the largest fertilizer companies in the world, and the merger moved the firm more fully into the retail side of the business. Although the 1990s mergers in the sector, outlined in chapter 7, began the process of vertical integration—from mining and nitrogen production to the processing of mixed fertilizers to the retail sector, all managed together in giant global firms—the formation of Nutrien in 2016 solidified that trend. These new retail outlets are now selling much more than just fertilizer; they are also retailing seeds and pesticides. This is an important development, especially as the lines between these industries has begun to blur, as discussed more fully in chapter 11. The growing vertical integration of these firms creates barriers to newcomers lacking the capital to compete at multiple points along supply chains. It also enables the vertically integrated firms to manage retail prices by adjusting supply levels along key points in the supply chains that they control.

DOMINATING THE MARKET FOR FARM MACHINERY REPAIRS

In recent years, there have been growing complaints about the market dominance of the big farm machinery firms, especially their tight control over the market for repairs. As farm machinery—such as tractors and harvesters—has become more sophisticated, including, for example, embedded controls driven by copyright-protected software, the dominant firms have taken measures to constrain access to information on the systems necessary for repairs. They have been accused of keeping repair guidance from farmers and third-party repair shops, as well as using software that fails to function when machines are repaired with nonproprietary spare parts.[46] When farmers purchase such equipment, they are now routinely asked to sign contracts known as end-user license agreements (EULAs) that set out rules on what the purchaser can do and cannot do with their equipment in order to respect the copyright of the software that controls the machinery. For example, in the EULA that it forces farmers to sign, Deere, which controls over 50 percent of the US tractor market and a significant market share in other countries, prohibits almost all types of repairs and modifications of its equipment that are not carried out by authorized Deere dealerships and repair shops.[47]

This sort of end-user agreement that constrains farmers' use of technologies is similar to the contracts that agricultural biotechnology firms have required farmers to sign since the 1990s, as outlined in chapter 8. Farmers have been required to sign such agreements regarding use of their farm machinery for at least the past decade.[48] The terms in these agreements severely limit farmers' options for the repair of newer tractors, a growing problem as they begin to replace older equipment. Older tractor models were easier for farmers to repair themselves, because they were basic engine-based machines that were not controlled by software and electronics. Indeed, as discussed in chapter 7, many farmers during the 1980s farm crisis resorted to repairing their own machinery rather than buying new.

The small number of farm machinery firms that dominate global markets now hold considerable power over the farm equipment repair market. There are increasing concerns not only about the ability of these firms to charge higher prices for repairs, but also that they are effectively creating barriers to entry that prevent small-scale repair shops from entering the market, as well as preventing farmers from making cheaper do-it-yourself repairs. As Rob Larew, president of the US National Farmers' Union, stated in testimony to a US House of Representatives hearing in 2023, "Family farmers are put at a great disadvantage if they are forced to choose between the ability to independently fix their own tractor or to reap the benefits of the technological advancements of modern equipment."[49]

Farmers are concerned about their inability to repair their own equipment because timing is critical for their profitability. If a tractor breaks down during harvest, timely repairs can mean the difference between getting crops out of the field—and to the market—and losing them to poor weather. Farmers have been frustrated by lengthy waiting times for licensed dealers and repair shop representatives to assess and repair farm machinery. In the past, farmers could perform those fixes themselves and be back at work within hours, but now it can take many hours to several days to get their machinery serviced. The constraints resulting from this highly controlled approach to repairs by the large farm equipment firms have spurred many farmers to join the growing right-to-repair movement to defend their right to repair their own machinery.

The fact that farmers cannot repair their own machinery also contributes to a deepening trend of deskilling in the farm sector, whereby farmers are increasingly unable to engage directly in decisions about their own work because information about the inputs they use is kept from them.[50] As deskilling accelerates, farmers find themselves increasingly locked into certain technology pathways from which it is hard to break free because of high switching costs between a small number of tractor manufacturers and high switching costs between industrial and alternative modes of farming.[51] In this way, deskilling erodes farmers' agency by limiting their choices and making them dependent on a handful of large firms.

A number of farmers in the United States have sued Deere & Co. in recent years, accusing the firm of breaching antitrust laws with respect to the constraints it places on equipment repair. These farmers argued that

Deere is violating the Sherman Antitrust Act because it is monopolizing the market for service and repair of Deere equipment.[52] Several of these lawsuits have been consolidated into class action cases that, as of 2024, are still before the courts. Deere has defended itself by contending that it does not have monopoly power because farmers can choose to purchase any brand of farm equipment they wish and that farmers understand the policies restricting repairs when they buy their machinery because they are asked to sign a EULA. The US Department of Justice issued a statement in support of farmers' right to repair in early 2023 in relation to one of the lawsuits, which refuted Deere's position on the issue. The DOJ statement pointed to a past case involving accusations of monopolization of repair markets involving the camera company Kodak in the 1990s. That earlier case set a precedent that after-market repairs should be considered distinct from the initial purchasing market.[53]

Political pressure has grown in many countries and subnational jurisdictions to pass legislation to enshrine the right to repair, including for agricultural machinery, and farmer groups have been active in this movement. The large agricultural equipment firms have pushed back in many instances, as discussed more fully in chapter 12.

ACCUSATIONS OF CORPORATE PROFITEERING

The prices of farm inputs rose sharply after 2020 as general inflation increased due to supply chain disruptions and labor shortages caused by the COVID-19 pandemic. In addition, prices for fertilizer, seeds, agrochemicals, tractors, and other farm equipment spiked in the wake of Russia's invasion of Ukraine. For example, fertilizer prices rose to record levels in the first part of 2022, increasing to roughly four times their price in 2020.[54] Farm groups expressed concern that the world's agribusiness titans were taking advantage of the market turmoil caused by these crises by raising prices they charged to farmers far beyond their own increased costs for materials. Farmers were suspicious that firms were charging more for agricultural inputs simply because farmers were earning more in a period of higher agricultural commodity prices.

If the input firms were only raising prices because their own costs increased, then there would be an expectation that they would not be making undue profits. But farmer groups point to the fact that the input firms' profits have soared to new heights, leading to complaints of corporate profiteering. As US Agriculture Secretary Tom Vilsack noted, "As I talk to farmers, ranchers and agriculture and food companies about the recent market challenges, I hear significant concerns about whether large companies along the supply chain are taking advantage of the situation by increasing profits—not just responding to supply and demand or passing along the costs."[55] In the post-megamergers context, it is important to examine whether firms indeed used the recent external market disruptions to exercise their market power.

Profiteering complaints have been especially loud regarding the fertilizer industry. The firms that dominate the fertilizer sector are in a unique position to influence price trends because that sector is tightly connected to commodity markets for NPK nutrients, the production or extraction of which are largely under the control of a relatively small number of firms. As noted in earlier chapters, the fertilizer sector has long operated under cartel arrangements that allowed fertilizer firms to coordinate their activities and manage supply in ways that enabled them to charge prices that significantly exceeded their marginal costs of production.[56] For example, fertilizer prices doubled during the food price crisis in 2008, just prior to the post-2015 merger period. A major study published by the American Antitrust Institute examined empirical data on pricing and market structures in the sector during this period and found that "global fertilizer producers have likely acted in a coordinated fashion to raise prices, to the detriment of competitors and consumers."[57] Cartels are also rampant in African fertilizer markets, where the top firms have been involved in collusive arrangements in a number of African countries.[58] In short, fertilizer firms have long coordinated to cut production, boost prices, and enhance their profits.

Although several of the international fertilizer cartels have collapsed since 2013, the dominant firms still have the capacity to manage supply in ways that can affect prices. The few larger players that resulted from massive mergers in the sector can control production even without a formal agreement simply because there are very few of them and opportunities for even tacit collusion are high. The firms in this sector can still close production facilities when there is overcapacity. In the context of the

COVID-19 pandemic and the war in Ukraine, with farm groups raising concerns that agribusiness firms were making windfall profits, the USDA warned, "These companies' possession of scarce resources, often in other countries, and control over critical production, transportation, and distribution channels raises heightened risks relating to concentration and competition."[59]

The top nine fertilizer firms saw their profits triple from 2018 to 2022, from an average of $14 billion to $49 billion. At the same time, their operating profit margins nearly doubled, from approximately 20 percent to 36 percent. This dramatic rise in profits indicates that they were exercising their market power to expand their profits, even as their costs of production increased due to higher energy prices in the wake of post-COVID inflationary pressures and the Russian invasion of Ukraine.[60] The dramatic upward trajectory of the net incomes and the net profit margins of the top four global fertilizer firms are shown in figures 10.1 and 10.2.

With fertilizer prices rising so sharply over the course of 2021 and 2022, a large number of US farm groups encouraged the federal government to investigate the market power of the firms, in particular their capacity to fix prices.[61] The farm groups were already concerned that fertilizer prices were rising sharply throughout 2021, well before Russia invaded Ukraine. With fertilizer prices typically comprising over a third of farmers' operating costs, the impact of higher prices is felt especially hard.[62] Echoing farmer arguments about fertilizer firms in the 1970s, the groups called the increased fertilizer prices simply a profit grab by the firms, especially as the rising prices of fertilizers closely tracked rising agricultural commodity prices. According to the coalition of organizations that complained about the matter, "Recent record-breaking fertilizer prices coincided suspiciously with an increase in income farmers were earning from commodity crops."[63]

The large fertilizer firms pointed to higher natural gas prices in late 2021 and in 2022 after Russia invaded Ukraine, which sent prices of fuel and fertilizer soaring. But farmer groups countered that the firms were making record profits despite higher prices for fertilizer nutrients N, P, and K. For example, the groups pointed out that even before the start of the war, Nutrien's gross profits rose by more than six fold, much more than the cost increases it experienced.[64] Indeed, the firm's gross profit

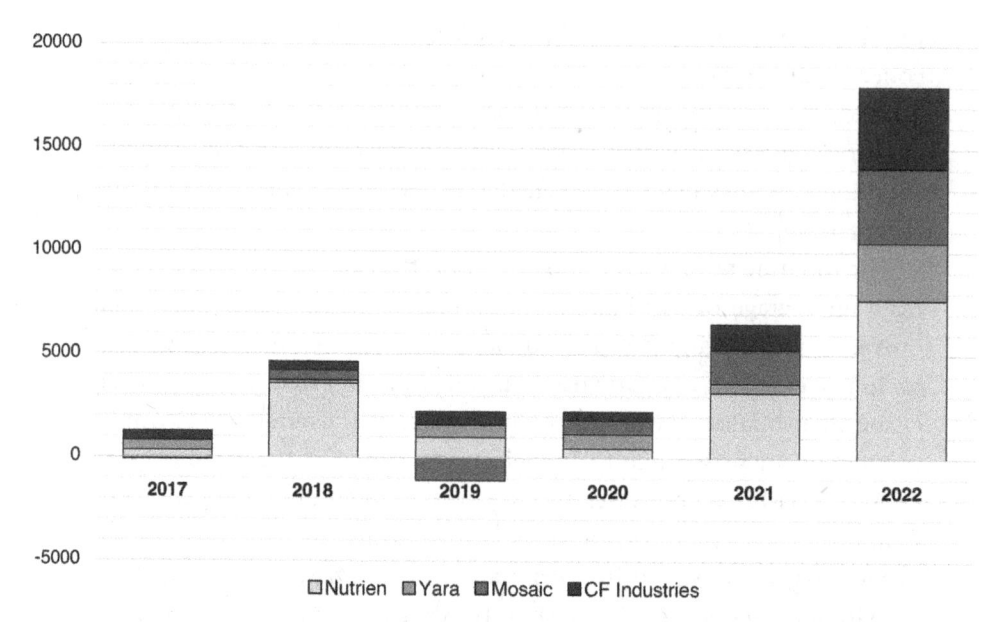

[Bar chart showing net income of Nutrien, Yara, Mosaic, and CF Industries from 2017 to 2022, with values rising dramatically in 2021 and 2022.]

10.1 Net income of major fertilizer firms, 2017–2022. *Source*: S&P database.

margin was 80 percent higher in 2021 than it was in 2020, and in 2022 it was 64 percent higher than in 2021. Gross margins fell in 2023 as crop prices softened, even as sales volume increased.[65] Similarly, reporting at the time indicated that in the first nine months of 2022, there were also massive profit increases at Mosaic and CF Industries compared to that same period the previous year.[66]

As profits were booming for the big fertilizer companies, they reported to shareholders that natural gas prices had only a limited impact on their production capacity. Prior to the fertilizer price increases, Yara's 2020 earnings report noted that the firm curtailed production of ammonia, the basic ingredient for nitrogen fertilizer.[67] For Farm Action, this indicated that the firms were simply using the Russian invasion of Ukraine as a "shield for fertilizer firms to hide behind, as their attempts at pandemic profiteering were beginning to attract attention prior to the invasion of Ukraine."[68] Nutrien admitted as much in its 2021 annual report, referring to record profits across its nitrogen, potash and phosphorus operations that far exceeded its increased costs for materials. With respect to its phosphorus operations, for example, the report noted that "higher

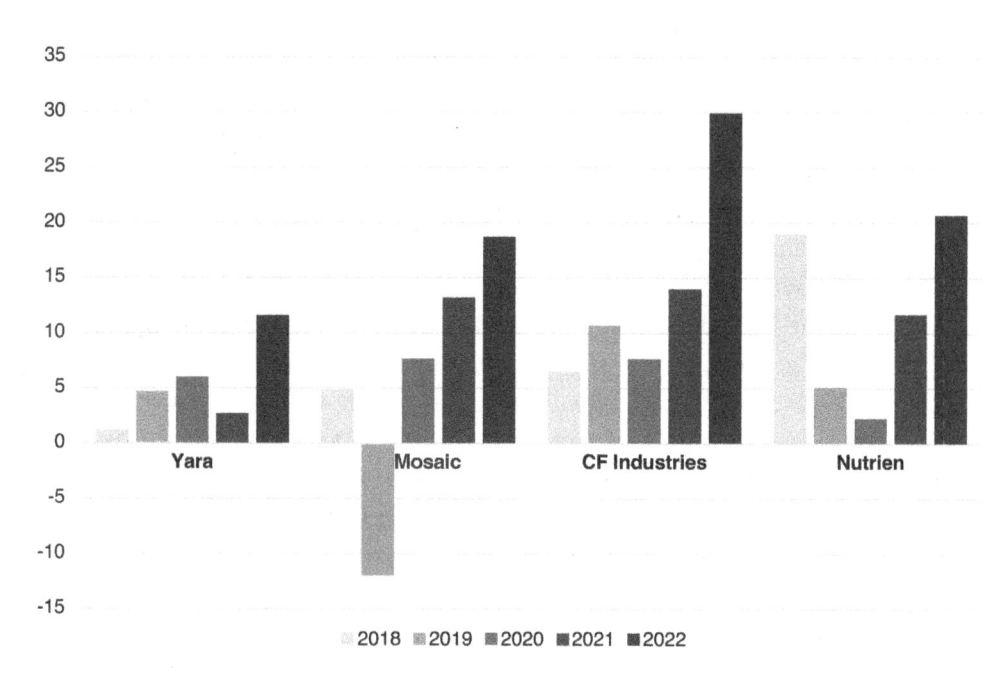

10.2 Net profit margin for the major fertilizer firms, 2020–2022. *Source*: S&P database.

selling prices more than offset higher raw material costs and lower sales volume."[69]

A similar situation occurred in the seed and agrochemical markets. For example, in its earnings statement for 2022, Bayer noted that its revenues from herbicide sales were up in the Americas as well as Europe, the Middle East, and Africa, "in particular thanks to higher prices" due to tight glyphosate supply. Regarding seeds, Bayer's report noted that "price increases in all regions more than offset a decrease in acreages in North America and lower license revenues."[70] Although the firm said supply chain problems and inflation were behind the higher prices, its operating profit margin in its crops science division ticked upward to an "industry-leading" 27.3 percent.[71] Again, farmers were concerned that seed and agrochemical firms were actively pricing inputs in response to rising prices for commodities—basically increasing prices to what the market could bear rather than based on their own cost increases. Syngenta Group's operating profit in 2022 surged by 34 percent over the previous year, with a huge jump in herbicide sales volumes and increases in local prices for those products.[72] Corteva also saw significant profits in this period and noted in its 2022 financial statement that "pricing and volume gains and productivity actions more than offset higher input costs, including raw material costs, and the unfavorable impact of currency."[73]

Farm machinery profits were also up between 2020 and 2023. Deere & Co., for example, was able to counteract its rising costs of materials and labor (including the cost of a major strike in late 2021 that shut down factories in the United States for five weeks). The firm's net income tripled from 2020 to 2023. It saw especially high profits—upward of 26 percent in 2023—in its precision agriculture business due to a higher volume of sales as well as improved "price realization."[74] Deere was able to pass higher costs onto customers easily because of the buoyant farm commodity prices that drove up demand for farm equipment and data services. According to the USDA, farmers once again borrowed heavily to buy farm assets such as machinery in the United States in this period, although borrowing slowed as interest rates rose after 2022.[75]

THE WIDER COSTS OF MARKET POWER

The market power that unfolded in the wake of increased concentration in the agricultural inputs industry—in the form of higher prices, barriers to entry for new firms, and constrained choices for farmers—has wide-ranging impacts. Price increases, for example, play out through the farm sector and beyond in important ways. When firms can charge higher prices due to their market power—be it due to implicit coordination because of excessive concentration or engagement in explicitly collusive price-fixing arrangements—the cost of farming goes up.

Farmer livelihoods are directly affected by the market power of the input companies. When prices of fertilizer rise suddenly and sharply, for example, it cuts into farmers' own profitability, especially when fertilizer prices rise more than crop prices. In the period just prior to the recent mergers (1990–2015), the cost of farm inputs, especially seeds, rose more quickly than the prices farmers received for their crops.[76] Although it is hard to calculate exactly what the cumulative costs of these price increase were, antitrust analysts C. Robert Taylor and Diana Moss estimate that "damages from supra-competitive pricing of fertilizer likely amount to tens of billions of dollars annually, the direct effects of which are felt by farmers and ranchers."[77] Farmers in developing countries have been especially hard hit by rising fertilizer prices since 2020, which rose by as much as three times world prices in the first six months of 2023 in East and Central African countries. Small-scale farmers in sub-Saharan Africa in particular have had difficulty accessing imported fertilizer because of the higher costs and high debt levels in those countries that limit the ability of national actors to borrow funds to purchase fertilizer imports.[78]

The impacts of higher farm input prices also extend to consumers of food the world over, as increased farming costs are translated into higher food prices. Civil society critics have argued that the recent megamergers will likely have an adverse effect on those who are already in poverty by making food less affordable. For example, a 1 percent increase in the price of fertilizer translates into a 0.45 percent increase in the price of food commodities.[79] The unaffordability of fertilizer in the developing world has led to reduced use and lower production, which further constrains food availability and in turn puts upward pressure on food prices.[80] The cost of a healthy diet has increased in all regions of the world since 2019, and in 2020, 3.1 billion people could not afford a healthy diet—an increase of 112 million compared to 2019.[81] The sharp increase in food price inflation in 2021 and 2022 only exacerbated this trend. Although many factors have contributed to food price inflation, at least part of this increase is attributable to the rising cost of farm inputs.

The broader impacts of enhanced market power also go beyond the pricing effects that ripple through the economy. Increased market power in the agricultural inputs sector affects entrepreneurial opportunities as well as farmer autonomy and choice. The examples outlined here regarding the right to repair machinery, patent control on seed technologies, and fertilizer companies manipulating supply highlight these wider impacts. By using their market power to block the right of farmers and third-party repair shops to repair farm machinery, the large equipment manufacturers undermine farmers' agency while closing off livelihood opportunities for independent small-scale repair firms.[82] By using their market power to control who can and cannot access seed technologies, the large seed and agrochemical firms are closing off both livelihood opportunities for smaller firms as well as limiting farmer choices regarding what seed traits they can plant in their fields.[83] And by using their market power to control production to influence supply and prices, fertilizer firms make it that much more difficult for smaller-scale fertilizer firms to enter the market.[84] These impacts impose huge costs by reducing individual agency within food production systems and limiting opportunities for diversity that are necessary for more resilient food systems.

The exercise of market power by the dominant input firms also exacerbates inequality more broadly in society. There is growing recognition that as the top firms in the economy have exercised their market power, inequality has increased.[85] One dynamic that has raised concern among economists is that as the top firms have increased their markups and turbocharged their profits, the share of the national income that is allocated to workers declined from roughly 65 percent in the 1970s to around 59 percent in 2017. As Jan Eekhout explains, the drop in the labor share of national income is not simply due to a reallocation of profits from workers to owners of firms with market power, but also a product of economic inefficiencies from overly concentrated firms that are a drag on the economy in ways that reduce wages.[86] These kinds of broader inequalities that arise from the exercise of market power, including among the agricultural input firms, privilege corporate executives and financial investors over all others in society.

CONCLUSION

Concerns about the market power of the large agricultural input firms have grown since the post-2015 megamergers in the sector. Although competition authorities sought to reduce potential market power among the firms by requiring them to divest key assets when they merged, the capacity of these firms to shape markets in ways that diminish competition has remained. In the post-merger context, the market shares among the top four firms in the agricultural input industries have remained at high levels and in many cases have increased, especially when considering more geographically or product-specific markets.

At the same time, there have been increasing complaints about the dominant firms in the sector working to erect barriers for other firms trying to enter the sector, which not only weakens competition but also has negative impacts on farmer agency and choice. The massive uptick in profits of the dominant agricultural inputs firms in the 2020–2023 period raises new questions about the market power of these firms in the context of market turmoil caused by the COVID-19 pandemic followed by the Russian invasion of Ukraine. The key concern is that the dominant firms used the uncertain situation to raise their prices by more than their own costs increased, which the firms themselves confirmed in their own financial statements. In exercising these various aspects of their market power, the firms have imposed enormous costs on food systems by making both food and farming more expensive and less accessible.

11

THE POWER TO SHAPE TECHNOLOGY

As the agricultural inputs industries have become more concentrated through the latest round of mergers, the dominant firms have deepened their power to shape the leading agricultural innovations that define the sector. The firms have argued to competition authorities that the mergers were necessary to ensure continued high levels of innovation in the sector. For example, when Bayer and Monsanto announced their merger, they emphasized that the combination would "create an innovation engine for the next generation of farming."[1] Critics, however, have raised concerns about the extent to which those firms have gained the power to shape technology and innovation pathways in ways that serve corporate interests first, which are not always congruent with the interests of society more broadly. The recent megamergers in the agricultural inputs sector have cemented the influence of the dominant firms over the direction of the main trends in technological innovation in the sector.

The key areas of innovation in which these firms are investing include digital farming, which is being taken up by farm machinery, seeds and chemicals, and fertilizer firms, and genome editing, in which firms in the seeds and chemicals and fertilizer industries are investing. Firms across the inputs sector are also establishing carbon-offset programs that they are integrating with their digital farming platforms. Through their investments in these technologies, firms that previously were not in direct competition with one another are increasingly vying for the same markets. This trend represents an important shift in the sector—one that may signal future consolidation across inputs, similar to the consolidation of the seed and agrochemicals industries in the latter part of the twentieth century. At the same time, broader concerns have also emerged about the latest technological features of industrial agriculture that the corporations are marketing, especially regarding digital farming and genome editing. These concerns include the continued dominance of herbicide-centric agricultural practices, as well as the potential implications for farmer autonomy and expertise, equitable access to technology, data privacy, and ecological impacts.

GROWING PRIVATE SECTOR SHARE OF AGRICULTURAL R&D

The influence of the top firms over the direction of technological innovation in the agricultural inputs sector grew as the industries became more concentrated after the 1980s and 1990s. In subsequent decades, private sector agricultural research and development (R&D) began to outpace public sector R&D, leading to increased corporate influence over innovation in the sector. This trend has been especially prominent in the United States, which historically had been a leader in public agricultural R&D spending. For example, by 2012, just prior to the latest wave of consolidation, private sector agricultural input R&D spending alone surpassed all US public agricultural R&D spending. Total US private sector agricultural R&D increased nearly threefold from 1990 to 2014, reaching nearly $14 billion.[2]

This trend toward greater private sector R&D expenditure is reflective of major shifts in the agricultural research landscape that have occurred globally. As the share of public agricultural R&D spending in the United States fell, it rose in middle-income countries. Indeed, agricultural R&D expenditure in these countries now outpaces agricultural R&D spending in high-income countries.[3] In China, for example, public and private sector agricultural R&D spending now surpasses that of the United States on both fronts. Private sector R&D in the agricultural sector in China has also been rising relative to public sector spending, and in both China and the United States, the private sector accounts for around two-thirds of all agricultural R&D.[4] The latest round of consolidation in the agricultural inputs industry took place in the context of these broader shifts in R&D in the sector.

Not surprisingly, the bulk of private sector spending on agricultural innovation focuses on areas where the top firms have business interests, such as seed traits and agricultural biotechnology, agricultural chemicals, and farm machinery. In the United States, for example, over 40 percent of all private sector agricultural R&D by 2014 was dedicated to the development of seed traits and the genetic improvement of crops.[5] Other important areas where research and development are essential for the agricultural sector, such as environmental conservation, safety, and community development, have been largely left to the public sector. Private sector R&D in agriculture is also typically more narrowly targeted than public sector R&D. For example, seed companies tend to focus research efforts and spending on crops with high returns, such as soy, maize, and cotton, whereas public sector research typically covers a broader range of crops.[6]

THE INFLUENCE OF HYPER-CONCENTRATION ON INNOVATION

Despite the claims of the large agricultural input firms that the post-2015 mergers were necessary to spur game-changing innovations, critics have pointed to the ways in which market concentration affects the rate and types of innovations pursued by the large agricultural input firms. They argue that the dominant firms focus their R&D spending on the technologies that make them the most money, regardless of the broader social and ecological costs of those innovations—costs that these firms are largely able to externalize.[7]

The current era of concentrated market power has given new relevance to a long-standing debate over whether having large firms in concentrated sectors is a prerequisite for investment in innovative R&D. Nearly a century ago, Austrian political economist Joseph Schumpeter argued that large firms with market power tend to be the main source of innovation.[8] He argued that capitalism developed through "creative destruction," whereby economic structures change when new, superior technologies replace old ones, which then become obsolete. Schumpeter posited that large firms were the main actors capable of innovating because their market power granted them sufficient rates of profit to invest in R&D or related activities. He reasoned that large firms, because they do not have to borrow funds for research and development, are a more "stable platform" for such innovation.[9] He further argued that large and concentrated firms had incentives to innovate because doing so would secure their position as leaders in the marketplace. As such, Schumpeter saw concentrated sectors dominated by large firms as a requirement for transformative technological innovations. In fact, he saw these firms as essential to human progress:

> As soon as we go into details and inquire into the individual items in which progress was most conspicuous, the trail leads not to the doors of those firms that work under conditions of comparatively free competition but precisely to the doors of the large concerns—which, as in the case of agricultural machinery, also account for much of the progress in the competitive sector—and a shocking suspicion dawns upon us that big business may have had more to do with creating that standard of life than with keeping it down.[10]

American economist Kenneth Arrow took issue with Schumpeter's analysis, instead arguing that investment in innovation requires competition.[11] Arrow argued that monopolists who dominate markets could continue to enjoy profits even without innovation. Moreover, if large and dominant firms invest in innovation, it might not lead to additional sales for those firms, because the development of new products might simply displace sales of existing products—what is often referred to as the "replacement effect."[12] By contrast, Arrow argued that competitors have a lot to gain by innovating, because they could capture the business that their larger rivals held.

These contrasting views sparked enormous debate on the question of market power and innovation, with many empirical studies producing contradictory results, as much depends on the specific factors and forces within different sectors. A middle-ground position argues that although large firms may spend more on innovation, they do so only up to a point, and that precise threshold differs across industries. After that point, R&D spending declines because of a lack of competition. In other words, there is an inverted U-shaped relationship between corporate concentration and spending on innovation.[13] Schumpeter may have been correct that innovation increases up to a certain level of firm concentration, but then the relationship changes and becomes negative, which was Arrow's concern.

Some analysts have found that the inverted U-shaped relationship with respect to innovation seems to hold in parts of the agricultural inputs industry. A 2011 study by the USDA found that research intensity—that is, firm spending on R&D as a percentage of sales—remained somewhat steady in the crop protection chemicals and farm machinery industries even as concentration in those sectors rose in the 1990s and early 2000s, as discussed in chapter 8. But in agricultural biotechnology, the inverted U relationship is clear. Although research intensity initially picked up after the mergers in the 1990s in the sector—from a rate of 11 percent to 15 percent—by 2009 it had dropped to just 10.5 percent. This decline occurred as the four-firm concentration ratio rose from 21 percent to 54 percent over that same period.[14] In short, increased concentration in the agricultural biotechnology sector was not associated with a permanent increase in R&D intensity.

In the context of the most recent mergers, similar questions have arisen about the impact of consolidation on innovation. For example, Corteva's head of business platforms, Rajan Gajaria, emphasized only positive innovation effects, stressing that "consolidation in this case is giving customers more choices."[15] Similarly, Hugh Grant, CEO at the time of Bayer's takeover of Monsanto, noted to investors in a conference call that the firm's acquisition by Bayer was driven by the need for technological innovation:

This transaction wasn't born in a boardroom. It started in the field where we had our farmers call for greater innovation and more sustainable solutions. We've considered multiple strategic options and ultimately we believe that this combination best positions us to deliver a wide set of solutions to meet growers [sic] needs on a truly global scale regardless of their size. And [in] this new era of agriculture, farmers need greater, more sustainable solutions and technologies and they need them now faster than ever before.[16]

The agrochemical and seed giants are advertising what they see as benefits arising from more integrated farming solutions, combining seed traits, crop protection, and digital farming platforms. But at the same time, several of the newly consolidated firms clearly stated that they planned to make cutbacks to R&D budgets rather than increasing them. Soon after the Dow–DuPont merger was announced, both firms shed thousands of jobs—seventeen hundred at DuPont and over two thousand at Dow.[17] When Bayer purchased Monsanto, the firm widely advertised that its proposed deal would result in significant "synergies," referring to cost savings because of their ability to eliminate duplicative research and development expenditures. In early 2019, Bayer announced plans to eliminate twelve thousand jobs—10 percent of its workforce—in a cost-cutting move.[18] These cutbacks occurred in the immediate aftermath of the mergers, raising important questions about their commitment to overall investment in innovation. As the *Financial Times* asked in 2016, when Bayer announced its planned acquisition of Monsanto, "How many mergers between two very large companies have resulted in the creation of an innovative hybrid product line? That so few leap to mind is sobering."[19]

Indeed, there is concern that large firms in concentrated sectors have little incentive to invest in breakthrough innovations because doing so would cannibalize sales of their existing products—the same concern Arrow expressed decades earlier. In other words, why innovate new and better seeds and chemicals when you could continue to sell the existing ones? This sentiment rings true especially for firms with the dominant products on the market. Introducing new innovations is costly and could potentially lead to lower rather than higher returns on the R&D investment. This concern came up when the US Department of Justice rejected Deere's proposal to acquire Precision Planting from Monsanto in 2016. The DOJ was worried that innovation around precision planting technologies would decline if just one firm had such a large share of the market.[20] Precision Planting developed its planting technique in a way that enabled farmers to retrofit their existing planting equipment, no matter the brand, whereas Deere typically bundled planter technologies with its own equipment brand.[21] A merger of these firms would likely have dramatically reduced competition and stifled the incentive to innovate.

TURNING DEFENSIVE

A related concern is that dominant firms in concentrated industries focus only narrowly on "defensive" R&D expenditures—that is, spending on innovations that extend sales of existing products rather than developing breakthrough technologies. The firms that dominate in the seed and agrochemical sector, for example, devoted huge amounts of their R&D investments into efforts to extend their profits from genetically modified seeds that let them continue to sell chemicals that were coming off patent.[22] As explained in chapter 8, when patents for herbicide-resistant seeds neared their expiration dates, the firms that owned those patents began to develop seeds with stacked traits, which effectively extended their intellectual property protection over those traits. This strategy conveniently enabled them to continue to sell the herbicides for which those seeds were engineered to be resistant.

Defensive R&D was also evident when the dominant firms responded to the growing problem of herbicide-resistant weeds, which weakened the effectiveness of their herbicides.[23] In this instance, the firms capitalized on the problem and introduced genetically engineered seeds that were resistant to multiple kinds of herbicides, including glyphosate, as well as older and more toxic chemicals, such as 2,4-D and dicamba. In this way, their R&D efforts enabled the firms to extend the sales of multiple types of existing herbicides rather than developing newer and safer ones or, indeed, moving away from the model of herbicide-resistant seeds altogether. With seeds now resistant to multiple types of herbicides, farmers have more options for weed management. But the increased spraying of dicamba, which is prone to drifting and affecting adjacent fields, introduced further concerns about exposure to toxic chemicals. In addition, some analysts are worried that weeds will also develop resistance to dicamba, repeating the same cycle as occurred with glyphosate.[24] These strategies implemented by the dominant firms led to a massive increase in herbicide applications associated with the use of genetically modified seeds.[25]

A coalition of farmer and civil society groups expressed frustration about these practices that further entrench the use of toxic herbicides in a letter to US regulators opposing the merger of Dow and DuPont: "The seed companies have fostered a dependence on seed and chemical cropping systems with declining effectiveness—and the industry's response has been to develop newer and more expensive traits."[26] In other words, the firms chose not to invest in newer and safer modes of weed control that moved away from stylized seed-chemical packages. Instead, they doubled down and extended the patent life of their earlier products by mixing existing herbicide-resistant traits in new combinations that constituted only a marginal change to the technology.

Herbicide scientists have expressed concern that there have been no new active herbicide ingredients brought to the market in over thirty years.[27] This dearth of new R&D into herbicides is in large part due to the high costs of herbicide development discussed in chapter 8. For example, weed scientist Stephen Duke suggests that corporate consolidation has not only reduced the number of scientists working on these problems but has also lowered diversity in research groups, which has weakened innovation.[28] Indeed, as noted earlier, following the announcements of the most recent megamergers, the firms involved stated that they were planning to make cutbacks to R&D budgets. Just prior to their merger, both Dow and DuPont referred to these cuts, which resulted in the loss of thousands of jobs, as the "global optimization of R&D" in their agriculture divisions.[29]

This defensive mode for R&D became a significant trend just prior to the most recent mergers, with an industry report noting in 2013, "On a global basis, the number of agrochemicals in development is falling, primarily due to fewer companies being involved, a greater focus by these companies on the seeds and traits area and a greater share of R&D investment being spent on defending products as they come off patent, including seed treatment and formulation technologies."[30]

The result of this defensive approach to herbicide R&D was a further lock-in of the herbicide-genetically modified seed technological package. This kind of narrow approach to innovation has been compounded by the large firms' decisions to discontinue certain seed and chemical products in order to drive purchases of more profitable products. The large companies, for example, have decreased the availability of nongenetically modified and earlier versions of genetically modified seeds from the marketplace to promote sales of their latest, still patented GM varieties.[31] The example of BASF taking LibertyLink seed traits off the market, outlined in chapter 10, is representative of this type of practice. The removal of LibertyLink seed traits from the public domain prior to the expiry of the patent serves as a barrier to entry for generic firms, and it also limits farmer choice. As activist Pat Mooney explained to the *Financial Times*, farmers continue to buy GM seeds for only two reasons: "One is that farmers have little choice ... Speaking as a Canadian, it is almost impossible to buy conventional canola in Canada. The other reason is that for the last 20 years the companies have put their plant breeding talent into the GM portfolio and neglected conventional crops."[32]

Firms have also been criticized for further bundling products together in ways that limit farmer and consumer choice and drive sales of certain products. In addition to combining seeds and chemicals into a single package, which has occurred since the 1990s through genetically modified crops, firms are now increasingly bundling the sales of these inputs through their digital software platforms. This practice deprives farmers of the option to mix and match products. These concerns have been expressed by a range of voices, not just by the staunchest critics of these firms. As a group of analysts who work at the USDA noted, "With only a few companies accounting for most R&D spending in these industries worldwide, critical decisions about the kinds of technologies to develop (e.g., GM or non-GM varieties), for what crops, and for what production environments may rest with a relatively small number of corporate boards."[33]

THE RISE OF DIGITAL FARMING

At the same time that corporate concentration can dampen innovation or encourage defensive R&D, the process of consolidation can give merging firms access to new kinds of technologies that were developed by more innovative start-up firms. The desire on the part of the big firms to connect their business models to digital farming played a role in the post-2015 mergers and acquisitions outlined in chapter 9. Dominant firms pursued this strategy not just because it opened up new technological opportunities, but also because digital farming could be employed to extend sales of existing products. As with previous agricultural innovations, including tractors and agricultural biotechnology, digital farming originated largely outside the leading firms in the sector.

Early precision or digital farming innovations were primarily initiated in the early 1990s by start-up firms. Although Deere was one of the first farm machinery firms to use sensors on its tractors in the late 1990s, the technology was not connected with cloud-based data servers or analytics software at that time, so these early technologies mainly collected information for use on the farm.[34] The more modern software platforms for farm data analytics since the 2010s were largely developed by digital technology start-up firms, which were subsequently acquired by the large input companies.

Another difference today is that firms across all segments of the inputs industry—seeds and agrochemicals, farm machinery, and fertilizers—are developing digital farming software products and services (see table 11.1). In many ways, data analytics and information services can now be considered a fifth key input into farming, particularly for some crops in certain parts of the world. This is increasingly the case for commodity crops in North America and Europe, and that is the way the leading firms would like it to be. Indeed, Deere calls on farmers to "fuel your farm with data."[35] In 2024, Deere established a strategic partnership with Big Tech mogul Elon Musk's SpaceX company to link its machines to the latter's Starlink satellite network, with the goal of reaching rural farmers facing internet connectivity challenges.[36] Through these kinds of efforts, various input firms are vying to become the dominant digital software service for farmers. To be the top firms in this sector would give them platform power—the power to control online data and the software infrastructure that connects different services and products.[37]

It is not just the software that matters in the development of digital farming, but also the hardware, which is where the farm machinery firms have an edge over the other input industries. For example, in 2022 Deere announced it was close to releasing autonomous AI guided tractors into its digital product portfolio. Not only do automated tractors save labor because they do not require an operator to be on site, but they are also fully integrated into the firm's digital farming software platform, which serves as an incentive for farmers to rely on the firm for both software and hardware. Relying on neural network algorithms that underlie AI, these machines take in information from cameras and sensors to guide their path through fields and determine its functions. The firm advertises that the farmer needs only to passively monitor the machine remotely from their mobile device. When the vehicle was announced, Deere's chief technology officer Jahmy Hindman noted the significance of this development: "I think it's every bit as big as the transition from horse to

Table 11.1 Major Agricultural Input Firms' Business Activities, 2023

Company/technology	Seeds	Pesticides	Fertilizer	Farm machinery	Digital agriculture	Carbon credits
Bayer	X[a]	X[a]			X	X
Corteva	X[a]	X[a]	X[a]		X	X
BASF	X	X[a]	X		X	X
Syngenta	X	X[a]	X		X	
Nutrien	X	X	X[a]		X	X
Yara			X		X	X
CF Industries			X			X
Mosaic			X		X	
Deere & Co.				X	X	X
CNH Industrial	X			X	X	
AGCO				X	X	X
Kubota				X	X	

[a] Denotes genome-edited products.
Sources: Corporate websites as of 2023.

tractor. . . . We've now figured out how to decouple the labor from the machine." Initially, the AI tractors will focus mainly on plowing, but the plan is to make them capable of a range of functions from planting to harvesting. As of mid-2024, Deere was still training and beta testing these machines, but anticipates an imminent release.[38]

Interestingly, such developments were even anticipated by some almost a century earlier. Cyrus H. McCormick's grandson was eerily prescient when he pondered in *Century of the Reaper* in 1931 what farming would be like in 2031:

Of course, there will be improvements in the instruments of power farming. Oil or alcohol may reduce the tractor's fuel bill, more refined tractor attachments may succeed in applying power more directly or more usefully to farm work, scientific farming methods will play an increasingly important part. In the future, octogenarians will doubtless say, as the old guard says to-day, "We worked a lot harder in those early days." To be sure—they used muscle where we are using mind; but perhaps some future man will be able to demonstrate that 1931 did not realize, as another century may do, how best to summon abstract forces to his aid.[39]

Indeed, it did take nearly a century to integrate the abstract forces of artificial intelligence and big data into farm machinery and software platforms, which marks a major transformation in the sector.

The firms that end up controlling the dominant digital platforms and associated machinery can exert market power because they can act as gatekeepers that let some firms into the market while creating barriers to entry for other firms. For example, the owners of dominant platforms have the power to decide with which other platforms and equipment brands to make their data interoperable. Those that control the dominant platforms also gain direct benefits from network effects linked to the data that they have acquired through their operation, with which they can train their algorithms. In other words, the dominant firms will have the privileged ability to sell products and services associated with their platform. Firms that dominate platforms also have leverage to establish themselves in related markets, and they can use the information they have collected from their clients to further deepen their market position by targeting their products to specific users.

The big firms often present digital agriculture as addressing many of the problems that have long been associated with industrial farming. These include environmental and health hazards associated with pesticides, the impact of heavy use of fertilizers, soil degradation, carbon emissions, energy use, and biodiversity loss.[40] For example, digital technologies that rely on big data and artificial intelligence analytics can help farmers manage chemical use more precisely on their farms. Precision spraying equipment can enable farmers to reduce chemical spraying to the minimum amount required. Cameras on the end of sprayers can detect weeds and direct machinery to spray only the amounts of herbicides needed in those specific locations. Cameras can also assess the color and quality of plants to determine whether certain parts of the field require fertilizer and, if so, in what amount.[41] Farm management software can also be integrated with carbon credit programs to encourage practices that reduce agricultural emissions.

Although these new digital technologies may offer ways to improve current industrial farming practices and reduce agriculture's ecological footprint, critics are voicing concerns about the way these technologies are being rolled out—largely as an extension of the industrial agriculture paradigm. Studies have found that precision technologies can deepen technological lock-ins while at the same time extending the power of the dominant firms.[42] The fast-growing literature on digital agricultural technologies has identified a number of concerns, several of which echo and deepen the critiques of earlier technological changes along the path to modern industrial agriculture, whereas others are new.[43]

One of the main ecological critiques of digital agriculture is that although it may make some marginal improvements in the efficiency of resource use on farms, it is still tethered to the industrial agricultural model. The digital model remains reliant on the application of synthetic fertilizers, uses fossil fuel energy to power the machinery, and is set to create a mountain of e-waste when equipment becomes obsolete. Moreover, the use of AI computing capacity to analyze the data, and the servers on which that data is stored and analyzed, require massive amounts of energy. AI technology also consumes significant quantities of water for hardware production as well as the cooling of servers. Data centers that house gigantic servers for digital data storage and processing are also putting pressure on land use, including agricultural land. In addition, there are serious social and environmental consequences associated with the mining of critical minerals to power digital technologies. The increased demand for digital and AI products and services, including in the agricultural sector, only intensifies these pressures.[44]

The data analytics software behind digital farming platforms has also been associated with an additional deskilling of farmers, as it further detaches food producers from decisions that used to be part of the art of farming. Drawing on their access to big data on farm fields and weather conditions, the data analytics services that the large input firms offer provide prescriptions to farmers about what crops to plant in which fields, how much fertilizer to apply, and so on. As rural sociologist Michael Carolan notes, although digital agriculture can increase some skills, such as the use of new technologies, it often comes at the expense of "analogue knowledge" about how to "read fields and animals" and creates dependencies on digital platforms.[45] This kind of reliance reinforces lock-ins, especially as farmers lose the capacity to make independent decisions and repairs to their machinery.[46] Yet this dependence is precisely what the input firms are striving for because it extends their influence over the direction of the technological system.

Indeed, firms such as Bayer have been open about their aims with digital farming tools. Liam Condon, then head of Bayer CropScience, stressed in 2019 after the firm bought Monsanto and acquired the largest digital agriculture platform, Climate FieldView, "We are still largely living in an input world where we sell bags of seeds and jugs of pesticides, and give agronomic advice. But with digitalisation we can move towards a model where we get paid for the outcome that the farmer gets. . . . We take risk away from the farmer and our partnership will become much closer. That is where we see a huge advantage."[47]

Condon was clear that the firm planned to sell detailed advice to farmers and in return take a cut—around a third—of the farmer's "additional revenues." Such an approach would use the digital technology to lock farmers into providing the firms with a steady revenue stream that would insulate the firms from the boom-and-bust cycles that have long affected their viability. This vision that Bayer outlined is similar to the early hybrid seed companies' offers to farmers in the 1920s and 1930s to try hybrids for free on the condition that they share the additional crops with the seed companies, as discussed in chapter 4. But with digital agriculture, all the decisions are made by the software algorithms based on big data, and the farmer is merely the implementer of the plan, much like a contract farmer who is provided all of the inputs and must deliver the crops at harvesttime. This business model was presented as a future vision that to date is not yet a reality. But if this model is ever implemented, it is unclear how any "additional revenues" would be calculated and what would happen if a farmer's crops failed to deliver them.

The collection and corporate ownership of large amounts of data about specific plots of farmland also raises questions about what firms are doing with these data to advance their own interests.[48] These concerns are ultimately related to the large firms' acquisition of platform power. For example, farmers have expressed worries about sharing data with the large input firms because it is not always clear who exactly owns the data and whether those data are interoperable with other digital services, especially if the firms act as gatekeepers to create barriers for other firms to operate on their platforms.[49]

Data collection and access to digital farming platforms are mainly regulated by user agreements created by the platform developers, which farmers are required to sign. But these agreements are difficult to navigate, leaving farmers concerned about others accessing data about their farms without their permission or knowledge.[50] In other words, firms collecting the data have privileged access to granular information about farmers' lands and their neighbors' lands, which gives them leverage over farmers as a group in terms of both the data services and the products that those firms seek to sell to them. The collection of large amounts of data regarding specific plots of land can also facilitate the "assetization" of land to make it legible and accessible to financial investors. This trend could accelerate pressures toward land consolidation via farmland investment funds, which agglomerate landholdings and then rent them back to farmer-operators.[51]

In short, the ability of the large input firms to collect and control data gives them multiple advantages and opportunities to profit. An executive from Deere predicted that by 2030, around 10 percent of the firm's annual revenue would come from software fees alone, and an industry analysis report estimated that average profit margins on farming software was approximately 85 percent, compared to 25 percent for farm machinery.[52] The digital subscriptions these firms sell also bolster the sales of their own-brand products and equipment. Deere refers to this as a "technology stack," which leverages the firm's "digital capabilities, automation, autonomy, and alternative power technologies"[53] Pursuing a similar integration of technologies, Bayer noted that its product sales to corn farmers that had signed up to its digital platform Climate FieldView had already increased by around 5 percent in 2022.[54] This power of data is inextricably linked with broader market power concerns.

Although many of the critiques of digital farming have thus far been based on experiences in the Global North, digital farming apps are quickly spreading to countries in the Global South, including digital systems linked to the big firms. For example, Bayer markets its Climate FieldView software in Latin America and South Africa. Other digital software programs for farming in less industrialized countries are emerging from start-up firms and are focused on serving small-scale producers, such as Hello Tractor and WeFarm in sub-Saharan Africa, among others. However, the larger data platforms to which these apps are connected are linked to Big Tech firms such as Amazon, Microsoft, and Alibaba.[55] Hello Tractor, for example, has Deere and IBM listed as "technology and distribution" partners. In addition, Yara and IBM have partnered to develop a global digital farming platform that is targeted at Asia, Brazil, and Europe, with intentions of moving into Africa as well.[56] There is a significant chance that even local start-ups in the Global South will become the targets of takeovers by the large agricultural input firms as the latter seek dominance in the digital agriculture space.

GENOME EDITING

As firms across the sector are seeking platform dominance in the digital space, both the fertilizer firms and the seed and agrochemical giants are also shaping technology pathways by investing in synthetic biology technologies such as CRISPR and other genome manipulation techniques. As noted in chapter 9, these new technologies are being employed to develop novel products such as gene-edited seeds, nitrogen-fixing microbes, and bio-pesticides and bio-herbicides. Firms like Corteva were quick to acquire licenses to use those technologies and have developed crops that they have subsequently patented.[57]

Companies pursing synthetic biology techniques for agriculture argue that these technologies usher in more environmentally friendly approaches to crop production. Gene editing can be used, for example, to alter the genetic structure of plants in ways that confer new traits, such as flood and drought resistance and increased yield. Furthermore, biological fertilizers based on gene-edited microbes that fix nitrogen to the roots of crops can reduce reliance on synthetic nitrogen and decrease fertilizer runoff. And the development of biological sprays to address the problems of weeds and insect pests can facilitate the adoption of less toxic products and reduce farmers' reliance on hazardous petroleum-based synthetic herbicides and pesticides.[58]

The theory sounds good. But critics have pointed out that in practice, the bulk of gene editing innovation by the big firms is still within the industrial agricultural model.[59] Although some researchers are experimenting with gene editing to make plants more resilient to stresses and to deliver higher yields,[60] a large proportion of gene editing research and development in the large agribusiness firms is defensive, at least in the case of genome-edited seeds and some bio-herbicides. In particular, gene editing strategies for seeds are still primarily wedded to the concept of matching seeds with specific herbicides, an approach that has seen waning effectiveness due to the growing problem of herbicide-resistant weeds and the dangers of chemical exposure.[61]

The large seed and chemical firms are working on ways to use gene editing techniques to engineer faster fixes that make seeds resistant to new combinations of chemicals, much the same as they were already doing with other agricultural biotechnologies. Critics have warned that this research direction by the big firms is likely to result in more rather than less herbicide use.[62] The firms have also responded to the emergence of herbicide-resistant weeds by researching ways to use gene editing to disable those weeds' resistance to glyphosate, so that the weeds would effectively regain their vulnerability to glyphosate spraying.[63] Monsanto, for example, invested in research along these lines as early as 2012.[64] If such a technology is successful, it would enable Bayer—which has since purchased Monsanto—to continue to sell its glyphosate-based herbicide Roundup. In short, the big firms' research into gene editing to overcome glyphosate-resistant weeds represents a classic defensive R&D strategy.

On the surface, it may appear that modern biological products harken back to the basic biological approaches to pest control and fertilization of the late nineteenth and early twentieth centuries, discussed in chapter 5, which were eventually supplanted by industrial processes that drew on organic chemistry and the synthesis of nitrogen-rich ammonia. Indeed, the large industrial players portray their latest products in that way, arguing that they are safer than synthetic chemicals and therefore should not be regulated. However, these new biological products are based on very different techniques that involve the use of fossil energy to run powerful AI computer models to identify ways to more quickly move genetic material not just within but also between plants and organisms in ways that cannot always occur in nature. For this reason, some critics warn that these technologies introduce new kinds of risks.[65] But it is too early to know for sure yet the possible ecosystem impacts of widespread use of gene-edited crops and microbes. As philosopher Christian Illies warned of gene-edited organisms, "The deliberate or accidental release of these organisms into the environment introduces potential ecological hazards of a hitherto unknown magnitude."[66]

CARBON FARMING DEEPENS CORPORATE TECHNOLOGY LOCK-INS

Many of the main companies across the agricultural inputs sectors—including Bayer, Corteva, Nutrien, Deere & Co, Yara, and BASF—have established or signed integration agreements with carbon credit initiatives in what is often referred to as "carbon farming." These programs have served as yet another technological vehicle for the firms in the sector to entrench and exercise their power, albeit with questionable environmental benefits. These carbon credit programs typically focus on sequestering soil carbon by paying farmers to undertake certain farming techniques, such as no-till and cover-cropping practices. Such carbon credit programs have proved to be a politically popular way to address climate change in general and agriculture's climate footprint more specifically, with the aim of making agricultural soils a carbon sink rather than a carbon bomb. All of the major firms are associated with at least one carbon credit initiative, and once they pay farmers to sequester carbon, the firms can use those credits to trade on carbon exchanges or to offset their own carbon emissions. For example, Indigo Agriculture, which integrates its data systems with Deere's digital farming software and also partners with Corteva, has gone on to sell carbon credits from soil sequestration to large firms including Barclays, JP Morgan Chase, and IBM.[67]

The agricultural input firms use these programs to advertise their environmental credentials as part of their corporate social responsibility activities, as many firms have pledged "net zero" carbon goals.[68] Often the pressure on these firms to make corporate social responsibility pledges come from their shareholders, including large asset management firms. Corteva Agriscience executive Ben Gordon noted to the press, "When you look at BlackRock and other investment companies, they're essentially saying they will not support a company unless it has a climate plan."[69] Although these carbon sequestration programs are relatively new since the late 2010s and early 2020s, there are already millions of acres committed to these efforts, including across the United States, Canada, Brazil, Europe, and India.[70]

As carbon credit programs have increased in popularity since the early 2020s, critics have pointed out numerous problems with them, including the difficulty of actually measuring and verifying soil carbon sequestration. Soil carbon levels tend to change over time, and it can take decades, and even centuries, to see meaningful increases in soil carbon resulting from surface-level practices. The Canadian National Farmers Union has critiqued these initiatives as "essentially unworkable." [71] It argued that in addition to the long time frames needed to sequester carbon, this method of carbon storage is not permanent because any disturbance to the soil, such as tilling, will just re-release all of the carbon into the atmosphere. Manitoba farmer Gunter Jochum—who is also president of the Western Canadian Wheat Growers Association—noted to reporters about carbon credit programs, "I smell complete bullshit—it's a terrible idea."[72] Environmental groups have complained that the resultant carbon credits are traded on voluntary exchanges with no cap on emissions, so there is no guarantee that carbon emissions are being reduced. Moreover, the dominant firms are able to control their own carbon offset markets while also trading carbon credits in other platforms on their own account, raising questions about conflicts of interest.[73]

The issue is not just that it is difficult to verify soil carbon sequestration. The fact that most of the large agricultural input companies are actively operating in this space indicates that associating with carbon credit initiatives is good for their bottom line, which critics note strengthens their power. The large firms have used their carbon credit initiatives as a way to lure farmers into signing on to their digital farming platforms. This approach gives these firms more opportunities not only to gather data from farmers but also to advance their ambition to become a dominant digital platform and gain advantages from the network effects that come with that dominance. For example, Bayer's carbon credit program requires farmers to have membership in its own digital subscription service, Climate FieldView, and offers farmers who sign onto it a one-year free subscription to its software service.[74] Corteva Agriscience offers its own Granular software app to farmers for free, but as with Bayer's program, farmers must use the app to link with the firm's carbon credit program.[75] By requiring farmers to use their digital farming platforms in order to access their carbon credit programs, these firms are placing themselves in a position to receive more data from farmers, which bolsters their digital farming software services and their technology. It also creates opportunities for product bundling, whereby firms can offer packages of products to carbon credit subscribers, which further adds to their market power.[76] Nutrien, for example, has been explicit about its plans to use its carbon credit initiative to sell high-margin products to farmers, including microbe-based pesticides and slow-release fertilizers.[77]

The deep connection between carbon credit programs and the large firms' digital software platforms also amplifies the concerns about lock-in and data privacy. To participate in the firms' carbon credit initiatives, farmers must submit not just current data but also five years of historical data before they can qualify for carbon credits. Gaining access to such data is a huge boon for the firms in terms of strengthening the accuracy of the farming advice that their digital programs offer. It also benefits the firms that moved first into the space by serving as a barrier to entry for new firms. Additionally, farmers are asked to sign multiyear carbon sequestration contracts—in some cases up to twenty years—which locks them into working with a specific firm's digital platform, as well as the agricultural practices that the program requires. This lock-in makes it difficult for farmers to shift to other systems while guaranteeing the firms' long-term access to farm data. Indeed, in practice, digital farming systems are a linchpin of the carbon credit programs.[78]

Finally, although the carbon credit programs are ostensibly designed to improve farm sustainability, they also ironically deepen many of the environmental problems associated with the industrial farming model put forward by the large agricultural input firms. By offering carbon farming options to their customer base, the dominant players put themselves in a privileged position to be able to define what counts as climate-friendly agriculture.[79] The practices mandated in the carbon market programs are narrowly focused requirements, which draw attention away from broader, systemic changes in food systems, such as the transition to agroecology, that are necessary to address urgent social and environmental challenges.

Instead, these carbon market approaches can be easily incorporated into the existing industrial agriculture paradigm based on large-scale, monocultural farms that rely on agrochemicals. For example, no-till farming requirements rely heavily on the use of herbicides, such as glyphosate.[80] As food system antitrust expert Claire Kelloway points out, Bayer sells glyphosate-based herbicides while also promoting no-till practices through its own carbon credits initiative, which constitutes a massive conflict of interest.[81]

WIDER COSTS OF AGRIBUSINESS TECHNOLOGY POWER

The ability of the large and dominant firms to shape technological outcomes in the agricultural sector also has wider, less direct costs that go beyond the specific concerns outlined above. A prominent concern is linked to the long-standing association between the industrial farming model promoted by the dominant firms and farmland consolidation. Critics see the rise of digital farming and associated carbon credit initiatives as exacerbating this trend. Digital tools make it possible for farmers to manage even larger tracts of land, much like the advent of mechanical harvesting machinery and tractors did over a century ago. At the same time, only the very large, mechanized farms with acreages in the hundreds or thousands are likely to be able to recover the costs of switching to digital practices and attain benefits from carbon credits. Recent studies point to farmers expressing a desire to expand their farm sizes to make digital farming worth the investment.[82] To ensure that they continue to profit even as farm sizes grow, Bayer and other big firms are now charging farmers per acre fees for the use of digital services. These charges are applied in addition to an annual fee for a subscription to the service, as well as the costs to purchase connectivity equipment, plus seed and chemical sales recommended by the prescriptions.[83]

These trends have enormous implications for equity.[84] More expensive technology that favors ever larger farms is likely to continue to create barriers for individuals and groups who are underrepresented in farming, such as Black, Indigenous, female, and new farmers in North America and Europe. As Friends of the Earth stressed, "Access to land is already the primary barrier to entry for farmers of color and other under-represented producers, such as new and beginning farmers. Integrated platforms that promote tremendous bundling of inputs will exacerbate existing economy of scale issues to a point where land is even more inaccessible, and we see more consolidation."[85] Marginalized groups in other parts of the world are also likely to face displacement from further land consolidation as digital technologies spread to those regions, as happened with the adoption of mechanization in India and other countries during the Green Revolution, discussed in chapter 6. Furthermore, if the availability of carbon credit programs leads to higher farmland prices, this will strain the ability of marginalized populations to enter farming even further.[86]

The power of the dominant input firms to shape technological developments in the sector also contributes to wider costs associated with the industrial agricultural model. By perpetuating the reliance on seed-herbicide combinations, the firms encourage the growing use of pesticides and herbicides, which have significant health and environmental consequences. For example, as noted in chapter 8, studies have shown that exposure to glyphosate is associated with non-Hodgkin's lymphoma, a type of cancer, although this connection remains highly debated.[87] In addition, a growing number of studies have shown that traces of glyphosate are present in many commonly consumed food items, and it has also been detected in supplies of drinking water.[88] The Canadian Food Inspection Agency, for example, tested over three thousand food products and found that nearly 30 percent contained glyphosate residues. Four percent of the grains tested had glyphosate residue levels that exceeded the maximum recommended limit.[89] The chemical has been found in the urine of a very high proportion of humans and animals—for example, glyphosate was found in over 99 percent of samples in France and over 80 percent of samples in the United States—sparking enormous controversy over whether the levels found in food and water sources are safe.[90] Other studies have found that glyphosate-based herbicides pose a threat to biodiversity due to their toxicity to aquatic organisms and soil microflora.[91] Glyphosate runoff from farm fields into waterways has also been found to contribute to high phosphorus loads in aquatic ecosystems, which can damage and destabilize those environments.[92] These effects are likely to continue as the global glyphosate market continues to grow, which reached a value of approximately $10 billion in 2022, up from $5 billion in 2017.[93]

Allowing the large and dominant agribusiness firms to shape the direction of technological development in the sector also deepens the industrial agricultural paradigm in ways that undermine efforts to shift toward more sustainable production systems. The long trajectory of technological change in the sector, as outlined in this and earlier chapters, is a story of deepening technological lock-ins driven by the corporate quest for profit, which favors certain innovations over others. Defensive innovation strategies that entrench synthetic chemical use, genetic engineering, and now digital agriculture are all outgrowths of this long history, building on it in ways that further lock the current trajectory into place. The result is a path dependence that makes it ever harder—for farmers, firms, and governments—to transition to a completely different agricultural production paradigm, such as agroecology, that does not rely on industrial inputs.[94]

CONCLUSION

The latest round of consolidation has strengthened the power of the agribusiness titans to shape technology and innovation landscapes in ways that have profound societal and ecological implications. One of the key factors in the recent megamergers is the desire of the dominant firms to gain a foothold in new technological developments, which largely emerged outside the sector but from which they see opportunities to extend their profits. The dominant firms have positioned themselves in emerging markets for new technologies such as digital agriculture software and hardware, genome editing techniques, and carbon credit initiatives through the acquisition of and partnerships with a range of start-up firms. This acquisition and partnership strategy enabled the large firms to quickly rise to be dominant players in these new markets. As such, they have been able to shape the direction of these technologies in ways that advance their own bottom lines. Although the firms present these new technological directions as improving the sustainability of farming by increasing resource efficiencies, the way these firms are shaping these technologies through defensive strategies also deepens the lock-in of industrial agriculture rather than providing transformative technologies that enable farmers to pivot away from it.

These new technologies have raised broader social and ecological concerns. For critics, they prompt urgent questions about data ownership and privacy, and they have the potential to deskill farmers in new ways that further distance those who work the land from decision making about how that work should proceed. These new services are also exclusionary: they are expensive and geared toward farmers with large acreages, further disadvantaging marginalized groups and deepening inequalities. Moreover, although the technological strategies the firms are pursuing help to position them as environmental leaders, enabling resource use efficiencies and carbon sequestration, such strategies still fall squarely within an industrial agricultural paradigm and are associated with continued herbicide dependence.

12
THE POWER TO SHAPE POLICY AND GOVERNANCE

The most recent round of mergers increased the ability of the agribusiness titan firms to exert political power. Although consolidation resulted in fewer lobby voices overall, those that remain are much louder and well-funded, giving them more concentrated airtime with policymakers and the public. The large agricultural input firms make use of multiple types of strategies—some more visible and some less so—to shape regulatory environments that work in their favor. These include not just direct lobbying, but also other strategies that put pressure on regulators. The strategies they pursue often overlap with and reinforce one another, as is clear from a closer look at the examples that follow. Corporate tactics to influence policy are part of a broader playbook employed by corporate actors all across food systems in their attempts to influence policies.[1]

Although large agribusiness firms often shroud the strategies they employ from public view, investigative journalists and civil society have uncovered many instances of such campaigns, which show a clear pattern of efforts to exert influence over political processes. Some countries have mandatory lobby registries, which also provide useful information. As these firms have gotten larger and markets have become more concentrated following the most recent mergers, they have sought to increase their political influence over governance processes. Their success in shaping many policy contexts in ways that serve their agendas highlights the extent to which their exercise of political power undermines democratic participation in food governance contexts where corporate interests are prioritized over public interests.

CORPORATE POWER AND INFLUENCE OVER POLICY

As outlined in chapter 1, agricultural input firms make use of different strategies to shape regulatory environments that work in their favor, which confers different kinds of political power on them. Examples of these strategies have appeared in previous chapters, and I provide a brief reminder here.

Direct lobbying of policymakers—that is, meeting with or writing to elected officials and civil servants responsible for developing and implementing regulatory frameworks with the intent of swaying their actions—is the most direct form of corporate political influence. Firms can also exert direct influence on policy through what is often referred to as a revolving door of sector executives who cycle between corporate and government regulatory positions.[2] Although industry actors may hold specialized knowledge that can be useful in regulatory contexts, the practice of individuals alternating roles between industry and government raises important concerns about conflicts of interest, especially when there are no or only minimal periods of cooling off between roles. Engagement in public-private partnerships (PPPs) with governments or international organizations is another avenue of direct influence.[3] These partnerships have become increasingly popular with governments since the 1990s and early 2000s as a means to share costs with industry on specific initiatives, especially as states have scaled back their role in governing the economy in an age of neoliberalism. However, such initiatives also give industry a direct means to shape the rules that govern them.[4]

Corporate actors also have less direct means of influence over policy processes. Because of the economic significance of these industry actors— for example, in terms of providing employment, taxes, and political donations—governments often prioritize the interests of the dominant firms even when those firms are not making direct requests that they do so. In this way, large firms can shape regulatory agendas even without having to lobby governments. They can also indirectly shape the policy context by engaging in corporate social responsibility or voluntary codes of conduct that are not mandated by governments, which in turn can influence government to ease up on regulatory requirements.[5]

Large, dominant firms can also influence policy indirectly by taking an active role in public and scientific debates about issues that matter to their business models. In this way, they shape broader discourses that can sway public opinion in their favor and prompt regulators to approve rules that serve corporate interests. Large firms often engage in public debates on social media and in advertising campaigns to get their views across to a wide audience. They also often sponsor scientific studies to bolster their positions on key issues as well as to lend legitimacy to their perspectives.[6] There is, in practice, considerable overlap between these types of political influence and the ways in which large firms use certain strategies, as illustrated in the examples that follow across the agricultural inputs industry in the period following the most recent mergers in the sector.

INFLUENCE CAMPAIGNS OF THE AGRIBUSINESS TITANS

Agribusiness lobbying in general has increased markedly in the United States since the early 2000s. The amounts that firms have spent on lobbying in the sector have doubled from around $80 million per year in 2000 to over $165 million in 2022.[7] Not surprisingly, the largest agricultural input firms have been among the biggest lobbying spenders in the agrifood sector. Among the top ten in lobby spending on agricultural services and products in 2022, for example, were Corteva Agriscience at over $3 million, Nutrien at $2.3 million (the top two spots), and Deere and CNH Industrial at $1.7 million and $1.5 million, respectively. Industry lobby groups to which these firms belong also spent millions, such as the pesticide lobby group CropLife, which clocked in at $1.8 million and the Fertilizer Institute, which spent $1.36 million. The big firms have also spent massive sums on lobbying in the EU, with Bayer spending nearly $7.6 million in 2022. Other firms were also big spenders in the EU, with BASF allocating over $3 million and Yara over $2.5 million toward lobbying in 2022, and Syngenta spending nearly $1.5 million in 2021.[8]

Spending on lobbying in the United States and the EU must be disclosed as required by legislation in these jurisdictions. But not all countries have such strict requirements. In Canada, for example, lobbyists' communications with government officials must be disclosed, but firms are not required to report the annual monetary amounts that they spend on their efforts. Still, we can glean some information in the Canadian case. In 2022, for example, Bayer CropScience communicated with government policymakers ten times, Corteva Agriscience eighteen times, the pesticide industry lobby group CropLife thirty-four times, and the fertilizer giant Nutrien, which is based in Canada, communicated with government officials over eighty times that same year—the equivalent of once every four to five days.[9] This kind of meeting frequency between industry lobby groups and government officials reveals that the firms that make up the membership of these industry associations keep a constant watch on policy developments and seek to ensure that their interests take priority.

The case of the lobbying over gene editing legislation in Canada illustrates how these groups seek to influence government regulatory processes. Over the course of 2019 to 2023, several industry lobby groups including CropLife Canada (with Bayer, BASF, Syngenta, and Corteva as members) worked with Canadian federal regulators behind closed doors to develop regulatory guidance on gene edited foods and seeds. Industry and government regulators met regularly under the code name "Tiger Team," including outside of government offices, to work on a joint strategy. During this time, CropLife Canada shared numerous reports and other resources with the government officials, outlining industry's view that gene editing is safe and thus foods and seeds based on this technology should have only minimal regulatory oversight. Investigative reporting for Radio Canada based on access to information requests showed that the initial document outlining the draft regulation was created by a director of CropLife Canada.[10] The broad contours of the regulatory framework were already in place when the government held public consultations on it in 2021, which was scheduled during planting season when farmers were not able to participate. Despite critique from farmers and civil society groups about the process as well as the proposed regulations, the new rules reflected industry's interests. They did not require firms to notify the government before new gene edited products are introduced and exempted many gene edited foods and seeds from safety assessments. Instead, industry was merely invited to voluntarily disclose new products at their own discretion.[11]

The lobbying disclosure requirements and access to information legislation in place in the United States, the EU, and Canada are more unusual than usual. For most countries around the world, especially those in the Global South, lobby spending and corporate influence remain largely in the shadows due to the lack of transparency and reporting requirements. In some cases, though, we have a glimpse of the pressure campaigns by the large agribusiness input firms in developing countries. For example, the large European agrochemical firms, including Bayer and BASF, lobbied hard in the EU to push for the EU-Mercosur trade agreement that is projected to increase EU exports of agrochemicals to South America.[12] The European chemical firms also worked with Brazilian agribusiness associations, including CropLife Brasil, to weaken environmental protection measures in that country, which is one of the largest pesticide consumers in the world. They have pushed to have more agrochemicals approved for use in Brazil, including those that are banned in the EU, directly lobbied the Brazilian congress, and worked to build a major public relations campaign in favor of the deal.[13]

There are also many known cases of the revolving door between agribusiness firms and governments, including pesticide manufacturers placing employees in regulatory positions. Indeed, a significant proportion of the lobbyists hired by these firms in the United States are former government employees, who worked as regulators, congressional staff, or politicians.[14] In 2023, for example, over 90 percent of Bayer's lobbyists had previously worked in government.[15] One case that attracted attention in the United States involved a Syngenta pesticide lobbyist who moved directly into a top position advising the head of the US Environmental Protection Agency on agricultural issues in 2017. The case drew fire because during the short six-month tenure of the adviser, the EPA made the decision to drastically reduce a fine that Syngenta was to pay for the violation of a pesticide regulation.[16] In another case, the CEO of Syngenta's South America operations was named as a chief presidential adviser in Argentina, which swiftly drew criticism from environmental groups in the country.[17]

THE BATTLE OVER GLYPHOSATE

Given the significance of the herbicide glyphosate to the industrial agricultural model since the advent of agricultural biotechnology in the 1990s, the agricultural input firms—first Monsanto and then Bayer after the latter purchased the former—have gone to great lengths to ensure the continued registration of the herbicide. These firms went into high gear when questions were raised in the 2010s about the safety of glyphosate, the key ingredient in Monsanto's flagship herbicide Roundup. The International Agency for Research on Cancer (IARC), an agency of the World Health Organization (WHO), was among those raising concerns. Monsanto was aware that the IARC was preparing a review of the safety of glyphosate, and in response the firm designated twenty staff members to work on a strategy to "neutralize [the] impact" of the report, should it be negative. This strategy included pushing out a critique of the IARC and "engag[ing] industry associations" in "outrage."[18]

The IARC's report on glyphosate, released in 2015, was based on a review of the available academic studies on the safety of the chemical. Notably, the report classified glyphosate as "probably carcinogenic."[19] The IARC's conclusion showed that, on balance, there were elevated rates of non-Hodgkin's lymphoma among people with exposure to glyphosate compared to those who were unexposed. The IARC's report was issued at the same time that the EU began its own review of glyphosate as part of its regulatory process to renew registration of the herbicide for commercial use. Other countries, including Canada and the United States, were also set to reevaluate glyphosate's registration, in 2017 and 2019, respectively. Reviews of this type to re-register chemicals are typically undertaken by governments every ten to fifteen years.

Given their strong commercial interest in the re-registration process for the chemical, it is not surprising that the large agricultural input companies responded aggressively to the IARC's report on the toxicity of glyphosate. Monsanto allocated $17 million for a public relations campaign to defend the use of the chemical.[20] It insisted that glyphosate was safe and complained that the IARC reviewed only a select subset of studies on the toxicity of the herbicide, mainly those that were not based on industry-sponsored research.[21] Monsanto labeled the IARC's work as "junk science" and accused the agency of "cherry-picking" data to support an "agenda driven bias."[22] The firm went so far as to demand that the IARC retract its report. The IARC nevertheless strenuously defended its study, although the agricultural input firms continued to criticize it.[23]

Monsanto's influence campaign went far beyond the public vilification of the IARC's report. Internal corporate documents were made public in 2017 when Monsanto was sued by a groundskeeper in the United States who was diagnosed with cancer after being exposed to glyphosate. Those documents, known as the Monsanto Papers, revealed that the firm had also directly contacted the scientists who participated in the IARC's review panel with a view to intimidating them. The firm went so far as to demand that those scientists hand over the documents involved in their decision. Monsanto also hired third-party firms to post glyphosate and Monsanto-positive messages on social media at "arms-length" to shape public opinion about the safety of glyphosate.[24]

That was not all. Court papers revealed that Monsanto strategized to write its own studies and to contract outside scientists to stand in as the authors to those studies. To orchestrate this scheme, Monsanto hired a Canadian consulting firm to recruit scientists to participate in writing no fewer than five academic articles involving fifteen scientists who gave favorable assessments of glyphosate. These papers were published in 2016 in the journal *Critical Reviews in Toxicology*. The firm not only arranged and paid for those scientists to "author" the papers, but also took an active role in reviewing and editing the papers that the other scientists signed as authors, without the latter declaring their connections to the firm.[25] Critics called out the firm for "ghost-writing" the papers to give them the conclusions it wanted to convey.[26] In one case, a Monsanto employee wrote to the consulting firm to say, "OK, I have gone through the entire document and indicated what I think should stay, what can go, and in a couple of spots I did a little editing."[27] Then, referencing these same studies, Monsanto pressured government regulatory agencies to re-register glyphosate to ensure its continued use.[28]

After Bayer completed its purchase of Monsanto in 2018, the firm continued to try to influence the regulatory environment. One of its first measures was to publish a fifteen-page document that simply listed quotes from "leaders" that emphasize "glyphosate's vital role in modern agriculture."[29] The regulatory decisions on glyphosate in the EU, Canada, and the United States, all eventually supported the position of the agricultural input companies that the chemical was safe, and it was approved for use in all three jurisdictions. In the EU, the approval was initially limited to a period of five years while further evaluation took place.[30] In each of these regulatory decisions, the evaluation contained a review of the available studies on the safety of glyphosate, but unlike the IARC review, they did consider the industry-sponsored studies in their assessment, including the studies paid by, written for, and reviewed by Monsanto.[31] In Canada, for example, the review leading to the decision to reregister glyphosate included all five of the papers written for Monsanto.[32] A report for the European Parliament later revealed that the EU decision was based on an assessment report that had plagiarized sections on health risks from industry reports.[33]

When the EU's initial approval expired in 2022, the approval of glyphosate was extended by another year while safety assessments were ongoing. Then, in 2023, the EU approved glyphosate for an additional ten years, with new restrictions on maximum application rates. This decision was made despite split views within the European Commission. Environmental and citizen groups, as well as some EU lawmakers, immediately moved to challenge the decision on the grounds that the safety assessments relied too heavily on industry-funded studies.[34]

Even as the EU, the United States, and Canada approved glyphosate for reregistration for agricultural use, a number of other countries and jurisdictions began to put restrictions in place on the use of glyphosate, largely in response to the IARC report's findings.[35] In 2016, six countries of the Gulf Cooperation council—Saudi Arabia, Kuwait, the United Arab Emirates, Qatar, Bahrain, and Oman—were among the first countries to put national bans in place on the use of glyphosate for any purpose. St. Vincent and the Grenadines banned the import of glyphosate in 2018, and Vietnam banned its use in early 2019. Thailand also announced plans to ban the chemical in 2019, while Luxembourg announced plans for a ban by the end of 2020, and Germany announced it would ban the chemical by 2023. In 2020, Mexico announced that it would phase out glyphosate use in the country, as well as imports of genetically modified corn, by 2024.

While the announcement of multiple bans on glyphosate across a number of countries shows the extent to which the ground is shifting regarding policy on the chemical, there has also been swift backlash against these policy moves by actors with strong interests in the pesticides industry. Several of the earlier announced bans have already been reversed under pressure from the US government working with the large industry players. In Thailand, for example, the government dropped its plans for the glyphosate ban just a few days before it was due to come into effect. According to documents obtained under a freedom of information request by the US environmental group Center for Biological Diversity, Bayer sought the help of the US government to put pressure directly on Thailand's prime minister to drop the ban. When the news story broke, Bayer emphasized that its close coordination with the US government to pressure Thai authorities was simply routine and nothing out of the ordinary.[36]

In Mexico, the pesticides lobby used similar pressure tactics in coordination with the US government to try to convince Mexico to drop its planned phaseout of the herbicide. Emails from the Office of the US Trade Representative, again obtained through a freedom of information request by the Center for Biological Diversity, showed that US government representatives were pressured by Bayer and CropLife America to emphasize to Mexico that the phaseouts were not compliant with the US-Mexico-Canada Free Trade Agreement.[37] In late 2022, Corteva also pressed the US government to initiate a dispute settlement process on the matter in an effort to intimidate the Mexican government.[38] In early 2023, the United States demanded that Mexico show the science behind its decision, suggesting that the move was not grounded in sound science. The Mexican government did lay out its concerns and kept its the plan to phase out glyphosate. But less than one week before Mexico's ban was due to come into effect in 2024, and under continued heavy pressure from industry and the US government, the Mexican government announced it would delay the ban until a suitable alternative became available.[39]

In 2020, Bayer, just a few years after its acquisition of Monsanto, agreed to pay $10.9 billion to settle over ninety-five thousand legal claims against the firm for continuing to sell glyphosate without proper warning labels. It made this decision to settle after losing several major cases in which it was forced to pay millions of dollars to plaintiffs who accused the firm of not being forthright with respect to the risks associated with the chemical. Although it paid the plaintiffs in the class-action settlement, the firm did not admit liability or any wrongdoing.[40] A year later, the firm set aside a further $4.5 billion to cover any additional claims. By 2024, some fifty thousand lawsuits over Roundup remained unresolved, and the firm had lost some of those cases on the grounds that warning labels on the product failed to meet state-level requirements. In an attempt to reduce their liability, Bayer has taken to lobbying US state-level governments to pass laws that curtail the ability of states to enact safety regulations on pesticides that are more stringent than those set by the US EPA.[41] The big firms in the pesticides industry have continued to follow similar playbooks to influence policymaking with respect to the safety of other pesticides, such as Syngenta's recent strategy to defend the pesticide paraquat.[42]

THE EU FARM-TO-FORK STRATEGY UNDER PRESSURE

Beyond fighting tooth and nail to preserve their markets for glyphosate, the large agricultural input firms have also engaged in a broader attack on policies and regulations aimed at mitigating the environmental impact of industrial farming. Concerned that such policies could dampen demand for agrochemicals and fertilizers in particular, which have been targeted by policymakers due to their toxic effects and contribution to climate change, the dominant firms have engaged with other lobby groups to quash such initiatives.

A prominent example is the sustained attack on the EU's Farm to Fork (F2F) strategy by advocates of industrial farming, including the large agricultural input firms.[43] The F2F initiative aims to encourage a radical shift toward a more environmentally sound model of agriculture. The strategy pays particular attention to agrochemicals, which account for over 10 percent of the EU's greenhouse gas emissions, with ambitious targets for their reduction. Specifically, the F2F calls for the use of pesticides to be halved by 2030 and a 20 percent reduction in the application of chemical fertilizers within that same time frame. Additionally, the F2F aims to achieve the objective of having at least one-quarter of EU's farmland designated as organic by 2030. Industry actors claim that the F2F strategy will backfire, resulting in lower crop yields and higher food prices, thus harming both farmers and consumers. The industry influence campaign incorporated several tactics and has been undertaken with the leadership of CropLife, a lobbying group for agribusiness firms, to which all of the big agrochemical giants belong. The corporate lobby has actively worked alongside Copa Cogeca, a European farmer's association.

An early critique of the F2F emanating from industry was that in their view, the strategy was not based on sound scientific evidence, including studies that projected the impact of the regulations. Industry groups made repeated calls for impact assessments to be undertaken and then, as in the case of glyphosate, arranged for studies to be written that reached conclusions that were more to their liking. Various industry groups sponsored impact studies—five in total are known—with the aim of persuading governments to weaken the legislation. For example, one of the studies sponsored by CropLife was written by a group of researchers based at Wageningen University in the Netherlands. The preface of that study notes the close involvement of CropLife in its execution: "We thank the representatives of CropLife Europe and CropLife International and other stakeholders who have guided the project and commented on the output of this study." It also thanked a CropLife representative for "the open and involved manner in which he supervised this project."[44]

The Wageningen study drew conclusions that fit with the narrative of CropLife and its big agribusiness members: that farming without chemicals would be disastrous. The study projected that the F2F targets would on average lead to a 10 to 20 percent decline in crop production and that some crops would see up to a 30 percent drop in production.[45] Corporate Europe Observatory, an NGO that works to raise awareness of corporate influence in European policymaking, obtained a leaked copy of CropLife's social media strategy that planned to promote the Wageningen study "to build 'surround sound' and pressure."[46] The organization critiqued the study for neglecting to mention the costs of not implementing the F2F targets, including damage to the environment and public health, as well as its failure to mention the benefits of chemical reduction measures for soil, biodiversity, and the climate.

In addition to using impact assessments as a scare tactic to build pressure against the F2F measures, industry players also actively argued that it was more important to reduce the impact of pesticides than to regulate their volume. At the same time, the firms positioned their own technologies as the way to address any problems associated with agrochemical use. In a paid content piece in *Politico*, for example, Bayer argued that "when regulating pesticides, we should focus on *impact* reduction, not *volume* reduction."[47] The firm also called for the EU to loosen restrictions on gene-edited crops—since the EU regulates gene editing under the same rules as genetically modified organisms, which is much stricter than US regulations. Bayer also advocated for digital farming technologies as the best way to ensure efficient use of pesticides and fertilizers. CropLife pursued similar strategies, in conjunction with Bayer, BASF, and Syngenta, calling on EU policymakers to focus on promoting digital technologies as a way to ensure "sustainable" pesticide use. It also called for industry-drafted guidelines rather than stringent regulations.[48]

After the Russian invasion of Ukraine in February 2022, industry players capitalized on the situation to further publicly attack the European strategy to cut agrochemical use. In May 2022, as food prices spiked, Syngenta's CEO, Erik Fyrwald, aggressively condemned organic farming, claiming that it resulted in up to 50 percent lower yields. He complained that "the indirect consequence is that people are starving in Africa because we are eating more and more organic products."[49] He went on to say his views were independent of Syngenta's business objectives. It was clear, however, that in the face of global food market turmoil, he brought out the well-worn neo-Malthusian narrative to push Europe to increase its food production by reducing regulations on pesticides. Although he was harshly critiqued for expressing this view, industry actors were given extensive roles in a European Commission "expert group" on food security as the war raged on. Industry representatives made up 80 percent of the group's participants (members and observers), including representatives from Bayer, Syngenta, Corteva, Yara, and CropLife, and significantly outnumbered NGOs.[50]

FERTILIZER INDUSTRY ON A MULTIPRONGED OFFENSIVE

Fertilizer industry firms have long been active in lobbying governments to enact legislation that supports rather than hinders their business, and that pattern has continued as corporate concentration has become more pronounced following the most recent mergers. Across many countries, these actors have gone to great lengths to influence policy.

Even as industry resisted the EU's F2F target to reduce fertilizer use by 20 percent by 2030, other governments have similarly sought to reduce reliance on synthetic fertilizers in order to address climate change and import reliance. In Canada, for example, the federal government included a fertilizer emissions reduction target in its climate plan in late 2020.[51] The main Canadian fertilizer lobby, Fertilizer Canada (an offshoot of the US industry lobby group, the Fertilizer Institute), went into high gear to ensure that the Canadian plan to meet that target did not mirror the European approach, which was to reduce the amount of fertilizer used. The top fertilizer companies and Fertilizer Canada relentlessly pressed Canadian civil servants working on the strategy to adopt industry's voluntary approach rather than pursue hard reduction targets for fertilizer applications. Furthermore, it sought to ensure that the approach to reduction focused on emissions per bushel of crops rather than overall emissions.[52]

Industry's voluntary approach was to promote what it calls the 4R method, a focus on the "right source" of nutrients at the "right rate" of application, applied at the "right time," and in the "right place."[53] This voluntary approach is advocated by the Nutrient Stewardship, an industry initiative established by the Fertilizer Institute. Partners with the initiative include Fertilizer Canada, the International Fertilizer Association, and the International Plant Nutrition Institute, along with major agribusiness firms Nutrien, Bayer, BASF, Corteva, Deere, Mosaic, Syngenta, and Yara. The 4R approach, these industry advocates argue, will enable more efficient fertilizer use that can reduce emissions intensity per unit of crops. Critics have pointed out that this approach, which is similar to the argument of the Canadian oil industry that it makes more sense to reduce greenhouse emission intensity per unit of energy rather than overall emissions, does not in any way guarantee that overall emissions will decline. Indeed, under the 4R approach, emissions can climb if farmers expand the areas they cultivate, even if the intensity per unit of production declines.

To push the 4R narrative, the fertilizer industry was in constant contact with the Canadian government officials working on shaping the fertilizer emissions policy following the government's emissions reduction target. Over the course of 2022 alone, Fertilizer Canada contacted the regulatory authorities over one hundred times, while Nutrien contacted the Canadian government over eighty times. Some of these communications occurred on the same day, indicating the constant pressure that these entities put on the Canadian government.[54]

The fertilizer industry's contact with government regulators intensified around the time that Fertilizer Canada was preparing a report projecting the impact of fertilizer reduction targets. It warned of crop production declines and C$48 billion in lost income for farmers over the following eight years if the federal government imposed the fertilizer reduction target.[55] Industry's projections assumed that the Canadian policy would mirror the EU's approach and call for a reduction in overall fertilizer use. The report was released shortly after the 2021 Canadian federal election and the intent was to send a message to the incoming agriculture minister that taking the approach of the EU would meet strong resistance.[56] The Canadian government responded by assuring the industry that it would follow its suggestion to support the 4R program, and the pressure campaign eased up. This episode is similar to the Fertilizer Institute's efforts in the United States in the 1980s to oppose fertilizer reduction plans (discussed in chapter 8) and the studies funded by CropLife regarding the EU Farm to Fork Strategy more recently.

The fertilizer lobby also engaged in a fierce persuasion campaign in the US context, with the Fertilizer Institute spending some $1.36 million on lobby activities in 2022 alone (and over $19 million between 2012 and 2022).[57] In this case, the effort was not about watering down legislation on emissions. Rather, it was about weakening the competition. The largest US fertilizer company, Mosaic, attempted to influence trade policy as it related to fertilizer imports. The firm launched a major lobbying effort aimed at influencing the Trump administration only a few months into its term in early 2017. The firm campaigned heavily to convince the government to impose tariffs on phosphate fertilizer imports from Russia and Morocco based on the claim that those governments were providing unfair subsidies to their domestic fertilizer industries.[58]

With a past fundraiser for Donald Trump's 2016 presidential election campaign as their main lobbyist, Mosaic was able to arrange high-level meetings with trade officials in the White House to make its case, as was revealed by a freedom of information request by the nonprofit watchdog, American Oversight. Mosaic petitioned for countervailing duties, and the Trump administration eventually recommended the imposition of tariffs in 2020. The tariffs on Moroccan phosphate were set at 20 percent for five years, with tariffs on Russian fertilizers ranging from 9 to 47 percent.[59] Mosaic openly praised the move, declaring in a press release, "Today's decision upholds our belief that fair trade is a cornerstone of a healthy U.S. economy, and that American farmers will benefit from having a more competitive American fertilizer industry."[60] But the effect in practice was that the duties gave Mosaic control over 90 percent of the US phosphate fertilizer market.[61]

Meanwhile, CF Industries also filed a petition to the US International Trade Commission (ITC) and Department of Commerce arguing that Russia and Trinidad and Tobago—both of which have ample natural gas supplies—provided unfair subsidies to urea ammonium nitrate (UAN) production, a vital input for the production of nitrogen fertilizers. It asked the government to impose tariffs on UAN imports.[62] A US Department of Commerce investigation made a preliminary determination that UAN was being dumped by these countries, and proposed duties as high as 113 percent on producers from Trinidad and Tobago and 130 percent on Russian producers.[63]

US farmer groups were upset by these developments because they had the effect of pushing up fertilizer prices. Average fertilizer costs as a proportion of overall farmer costs in the United States have increased sharply from around one-third in the 1990s to nearly half by 2022.[64] Jon Doggett, head of the National Corn Growers Association (NCGA), complained that "While other corporations and firms are attracting public scrutiny for how their practices impact Americans, fertilizer executives are making out like bandits at the expense of the people who feed and fuel America. Let's just refer to them as the Fertilizer Oligopoly."[65] As fertilizer prices soared after the Russian invasion of Ukraine over the course of 2022, as outlined in chapter 10, a number of US politicians and farmer groups complained. In response, the ITC revoked the plans for the duties against UAN imports from Russia and Trinidad and Tobago. The NCGA and four other farm groups launched a lawsuit to have the duties repealed. In late

2023, the US lowered duties on Moroccan phosphate fertilizers but raised them on phosphate fertilizers from Russia.[66]

The fertilizer industry also has a formidable influence over policy in other countries. Yara, for example, lobbies actively at the international level, as it pushes for greater fertilizer use in countries in the Global South.[67] The firm also seeks to influence policy and governance in multiple ways in these contexts. It has played a role in shaping agricultural value chain governance via the establishment of knowledge and information networks in national contexts, including in some African countries. In Tanzania, for example, the firm played a key role in supporting the establishment of the Southern Agricultural Growth Corridor of Tanzania, a public-private partnership that served as a platform for the firm to influence governmental agricultural policy.[68]

MACHINERY MANUFACTURERS' EFFORTS TO BLOCK RIGHT-TO-REPAIR LEGISLATION

As outlined in chapter 10, the inability of farmers to repair their own machinery as it becomes increasingly embedded with complex software has prompted farmer groups to join with others in a broader right-to-repair (R2R) movement. One of the chief aims of this movement is to advocate for legislation to enshrine into law the right to repair one's own equipment. The farm machinery giants have actively lobbied policymakers across a number of jurisdictions against adopting any sort of formal legislation that enshrines the right to repair machinery.

In North America, the large farm equipment manufacturers have lobbied against R2R legislation, individually as well as under the umbrella of the farm equipment manufacturing associations to which they belong. Deere & Co, which holds 53 percent of the US tractor market, has been especially vocal in opposing any legislation that would enshrine the right for farmers to repair their own farm equipment.[69] These firms are wary of sharing their proprietary software with third-party dealers and with farmers on the grounds that doing so and allowing modifications could compromise safety and performance, not to mention that the software constitutes "trade secrets" that they do not have to disclose. For these firms, unauthorized repairs constitute a breach of copyright.[70] They have argued that farmers do not technically own their equipment outright, but rather that they have an "implied license" to use it instead. This approach is similar to the arguments made by the agricultural biotechnology firms that farmers do not own the traits contained in the seeds that they purchased, as discussed in chapter 8. The farm equipment firms also expressed concern that farmers might try to hack the equipment's operating software to evade emissions requirements mandated by the government.[71]

Despite their initial efforts to head off legal protection for R2R, legislation has been introduced in some forty US states since 2014 to protect the right to repair equipment, with twenty pieces of state-level legislation introduced in 2023 alone.[72] Deere and other large agricultural equipment firms mounted strong opposition to these specific efforts. In Montana and Nebraska, for example, the Association of Equipment Manufacturers and the Equipment Dealers Association—which have top farm machinery companies Deere, CNH Industrial, AGCO, and Kubota among their members—mounted an internet information campaign claiming that the manufacturers supported farmers' right to repair, but that legislation to protect R2R would encourage modifications to farm machinery that would make it unsafe and unsustainable.[73] A representative from CNH Industrial, for example, testified in a 2017 hearing on R2R legislation in Nebraska, stating that the firm "strongly believe[s] that industry is best suited to solve this issue without legislative intervention and we have a history in our industry of solving consumer issues through our own cooperative efforts."[74] The legislation in that case did not pass. Similar efforts have been employed by the farm machinery firms across the United States as more and more states have proposed R2R legislation.

The US R2R movement got a boost in 2021 when President Biden issued an executive order promoting competition in the national economy, which explicitly mentioned the agricultural sector and called on the US Federal Trade Commission to enact regulations to prohibit manufacturers from barring repairs by individuals and independent repair shops.[75] Several bills were introduced to the US Congress in 2022 and 2023 that would enshrine the right for farmers to repair their equipment but none of these bills has yet been bought to a vote.[76]

In this context of increased pressure for R2R legislation, major firms in the farm machinery industry signed a memorandum of understanding (MOU) with the American Farm Bureau Foundation (AFBF) in early 2023 on the right to repair. Deere signed the first MOU with the AFBF, which stated that its purpose is to ensure "timely availability, on Fair and Reasonable terms, of Tools, Specialty Tools, Software and Documentation originating from Manufacturer, and Data from the operation of Agricultural Equipment originating from Manufacturer."[77] It also stresses the importance of protecting the firm's intellectual property from illegal infringement or modification, as well as ensuring that safety and environmental requirements are not compromised. Shortly after the Deere MOU was signed, CNH Industrial and AGCO signed similar MOUs with the AFBF. Many analysts see these MOUs as efforts to weaken legislative efforts on the issue, and critics remain skeptical.[78]

Although the American Farm Bureau states on its website that the agreement with Deere "ensures farmers' and ranchers' right to repair their own farm equipment," the MOU itself is explicit in stating that the AFBF "agrees to encourage state Farm Bureau organizations to recognize the commitments made in this MOU and refrain from introducing, promoting, or supporting federal or state 'Right to Repair' legislation that imposes obligations beyond the commitments in this MOU."[79] The MOUs are not binding, and the parties can exit them with fifteen days' notice.

Despite these efforts to squelch legislation, Colorado passed the first R2R law in the United States in April 2023. The legislation is widely seen as a major win for the R2R movement, although it included provisions that prevent farmers and repair shops from making modifications to functions related to safety or emissions, in line with the industry's key concerns. Nonetheless, Deere's response to the legislation was that it was "unnecessary and will carry unintended consequences."[80]

Legislative efforts on R2R are moving apace in other countries as well as farmers around the world buy tractors in highly concentrated markets and face similar issues. In some of those jurisdictions, legislation is more advanced than it is in the United States, while in others, it is less so. In the EU, for example, Framework Regulation 167/2013 calls for nondiscriminatory access to agricultural and forestry vehicle repair information, recognizing that this information is necessary to improve the functioning of markets.[81] An initiative to introduce a more general R2R regulation was launched in 2022 as part of the EU's efforts toward a more sustainable economy, as repairs rather than replacement of products can reduce waste.[82] In India, a committee was established in 2022 to develop R2R legislation, explicitly including farm equipment alongside other electronics, vehicles, and consumer goods.[83] Legislation was also introduced in Canada in 2022 to amend the copyright act to allow access to information for the purpose of repair, although the farm machinery industry came out strongly against the effort.[84] Nonetheless, the bill passed in the Canadian House of Commons in 2023 and as of 2024 is before the Senate.

CORPORATE INFLUENCE AT THE FAO

The large transnational agricultural input firms also work actively to influence governance beyond national-level policy and regulations, including at the global level. They do this using a range of strategies, including through engagement in public-private partnerships (PPPs) that open pathways to influence policies promoted by international institutions. Even before the most recent consolidation in the input sector, for example, many firms, including Bayer, Syngenta, Yara, and Monsanto, participated in the New Alliance for Food Security and Nutrition, launched in 2012, which promoted Western aid to Africa in return for policy changes friendly to business. The initiative received a torrent of critique within just a few years and was discretely dismantled by 2019.[85] There are many other examples of these types of initiatives that the agricultural input industries are engaged with, and there is only room to examine some of the more recent ones here.

A prominent example of an industry partnership involving the input industries is the partnership of CropLife International (CLI) with the Food and Agriculture Organization (FAO) of the United Nations. Social movements, civil society, and environmental groups have denounced this partnership as undue influence of the corporate sector in the work of a UN agency. FAO and CLI signed a letter of intent in October 2020 with the aim of working together to "find new ways to transform agri-food systems and promote rural development through on the ground investment and innovation."[86] Specifically, the letter of intent calls for collaboration on the sound management of pesticides to minimize their risk for "sustainable crop production intensification and better protection of human health and the environment," as well as "data and information sharing regarding pest and pesticide management."[87] Although FAO's relationship with CLI dates back to 2010, when the two organizations worked on the removal of obsolete and highly hazardous pesticides, the signing of the letter of intent marked the first time that the FAO director general spoke in front of the board of CropLife International, which includes representatives from the major agrochemical firms—BASF, Bayer, Corteva, and Syngenta.

The FAO press release on the partnership noted the international organization's interest in "improving pesticide management" as well as digitalization offered by the private sector.[88] CropLife International's chair of the board at the time, Liam Condon, who was at the time also head of Bayer CropScience, declared the partnership "the start of a new and exciting journey for both organizations."[89] The focus on pesticides management, as well as data and information sharing, closely mirrors the pesticides working group of the Industry Cooperative Program at the FAO some forty years earlier, for which the FAO was widely critiqued for having too cozy a relationship with industry (see chapter 6). Indeed, the partnership between CropLife International and FAO may be one way that industry is seeking to influence regulatory decisions in FAO member countries regarding pesticides.

Critics have expressed deep concern about the FAO CropLife partnership, especially because the body represents agribusiness firms that are deeply involved in the production and sale of pesticides, including those that are highly hazardous. The nongovernmental organization Pesticide Action Network (PAN) launched a global campaign against what it called a "toxic alliance" between FAO and CropLife. Several open letters and reports about the partnership were issued from groups including the Alliance for Food Sovereignty in Africa, Pesticides Action Network, FIAN International, Institute for Agriculture and Trade Policy, and Third World Network, among others.[90] These communications accuse the FAO of backing away from its own stated priority of reducing pesticide use and point to the FAO's own statements that note the importance of progressively banning highly hazardous pesticides. The potential for harm from these pesticides, the groups note, is especially high in Africa, Latin America, and Asia, which the large agrochemical firms target as new markets for their products but where legislation is weak. The groups also argue that this approach undermines work toward more ecological agricultural systems, such as agroecology, that do not rely on chemical pesticides.[91] By the end of 2021, the campaign had collected nearly 200,000 signatures from 107 countries to protest the partnership.[92]

FAO leadership responded to civil society and academic concerns, stating that the organization must engage in strategic partnerships with the private sector in order to best advance "innovative approaches to support sustainable agriculture." It also stated that "FAO can only influence the way the private sector supports sustainable development through engagement and partnering around common goals."[93] But the organization faces formidable pressure from industry. According to former FAO employee Allan Hruska, "FAO and CropLife have tangled with each other over pesticide use for decades. While the two parties have sometimes been able to work together, the relationship has been tense, as the industry constantly pushes its agenda of promoting pesticide sales and use, especially in developing countries."[94] Civil society groups continued to apply a pressure campaign against this partnership, and in October 2023 the FAO quietly ended its partnership with CropLife International.[95]

The FAO's partnership with CropLife is not the only relationship it has with Big Ag input companies. In 2023, the FAO's partnership portal listed a partnership with Syngenta Group, one of the top global seed and agrochemical companies, although this partnership was no longer listed on FAO's website as of 2024. The FAO also boasted partnerships in recent years with other big agribusiness industry associations such as the International Fertilizer Association, the European Agricultural Machinery Association (CEMA), and the International Fertilizer Development Center (IFDC). The IFDC is an international organization with heavy corporate funding that seeks to promote increased fertilizer use in the Global South. A number of the big input firms are members of the IFDC, for example, including Yara, Mosaic, CF Industries, Nutrien, and BASF. Given the extensive industry involvement in the IFDC, it is not surprising that the partnership focuses on minimizing the impact of fertilizers by increasing the efficiency of fertilizer use rather than its reduction.[96] The

FAO partnership with the CEMA seeks to promote farm mechanization in developing countries via the Agrievolution Alliance, which promotes itself as "the global voice for agriculture equipment manufacturers."[97] CEMA's members are national equipment manufacturing associations, including all the large farm machinery firms: Deere, AGCO, CNH Industrial, and Kubota.

AGRIBUSINESS FLEXES ITS INFLUENCE AT THE UN FOOD SYSTEMS SUMMIT

Agricultural input firms have also played a role in other multistakeholder initiatives and took a prominent role in the 2021 UN Food Systems Summit (UNFSS). Civil society groups have argued that summit was a direct result of a strategic partnership that was signed between the UN and the World Economic Forum (WEF) in 2019. This partnership was established in a context of declining UN resources, which prompted it to forge closer linkages with transnational corporations under a "multistakeholder" governance model.[98] The WEF describes itself as an "International Organization for Public-Private Cooperation."[99] Most of the big agricultural input firms are closely associated with it and have links on the WEF website to their own profiles and content, which serves as a platform for them to shape narratives around their contributions to addressing food security and environmental issues associated with industrial agriculture.

The UNFSS took on the public-private cooperation approach and some have described it as effectively being a giant multistakeholder initiative.[100] The close links between industry and the UNFSS leadership made many civil society groups deeply uncomfortable. The Civil Society and Indigenous Peoples' Mechanism (CISPM) of the UN Committee on World Food Security (CFS) voiced its concerns and made its own participation in the summit conditional on the inclusion of deliberations on the impact of corporate power in food systems.[101] The summit leadership did not respond to this request, prompting the CSIPM to boycott the summit, although other civil society organizations did choose to participate. But outside of those groups calling most loudly for attention to the role of the corporate sector in the deliberations, there was little focus in the UNFSS deliberations on the influence of corporations on food systems.

The summit's leadership promised that corporations would not have major roles in leading the work of the summit or defining its outcomes.[102] Critics argued that transnational food and agriculture corporations were nonetheless offered a priority seat at the table and given ample opportunity to shape the agenda.[103] The private sector engagement guidelines of the summit called for business to engage primarily through industry associations, so that no individual corporations would have an outsized role.[104] But the guidelines did not prevent representatives of individual firms from taking place in dialogues and other public events associated with the summit. Many representatives from the world's major agrifood firms were invited to speak at these events, including individuals from many of the world's largest agricultural input firms. Bayer CropScience, for example, was represented at the UNFSS Science Days event, promoting the firm's genetically modified seeds, crop protection, and digital agricultural technologies and services.[105] CEOs from Yara and Syngenta presented in videos featured at the summit. The high-level involvement of these firms and their industry associations in this event gave them a unique opportunity not only to advertise themselves as champions of sustainable food systems, but also to shape the direction of the deliberations as well as the broader discourses emerging from the summit.

Even with all the critique of the UN collaboration with the WEF around the UNFSS, not to mention the pushback against the FAO partnerships with CropLife, Syngenta, and other input industry associations, the FAO moved ahead in 2022 to establish a separate collaboration with the WEF. The FAO director general, who also happens to co-chair the WEF board of stewards for Agrifood Systems, signed the letter of intent, which the FAO noted will feature collaboration on "common areas of interest, in particular data and digitalization to support inclusive, efficient, sustainable and healthy agrifood systems as well as the increased investment required to catalyze improvements."[106]

WIDER COSTS OF CORPORATE POLITICAL POWER IN FOOD SYSTEMS

Corporate influence over policy and governance processes and outcomes has enormous implications. Social movements, civil society, and environmental groups have raised major concerns about the ways in which political influence campaigns of the large agribusiness firms are affecting food systems. For these critics, processes by which these firms have been able to influence policy contexts via the revolving door, lobby campaigns, partnerships, and multistakeholder initiatives indicate problems with representation in governance contexts. They are examples of blatant corporate overreach into governance spaces that should be more open and transparent and serve public rather than private interests. And because corporate actors have more resources than ordinary citizens, social movements, and civil society groups, they are well placed to get more airtime and have a larger impact in these processes.[107]

The growing frequency and visibility of corporate attempts to influence the policy process have effectively normalized the presence of dominant agribusiness firms in food and agriculture policy contexts. The rise in multistakeholder forums such as the UNFSS is a particular concern, because these processes tend to prioritize "stakeholders" such as powerful firms over "rights holders" such as citizens, including food producers.[108] Although civil society groups are often invited to participate in multistakeholder initiatives alongside corporate actors, the power differentials between these actors are replicated in ways that effectively give corporate actors more sway over policy and governance outcomes. Meanwhile, the interests of corporate stakeholders are shaped by their shareholders, who put financial returns above all else. Civil society actors are wary of participating in these contexts because they are at risk of being used to legitimize what is in their view an unbalanced process that is biased toward corporate and financial interests.

Corporate-biased policy processes also affect the quality and effectiveness of governance outcomes. When corporations have a strong role in shaping these outcomes, regulatory decisions and rules tend to be weak and ultimately serve the interests of the dominant firms that shaped them. Corporate actors are unlikely to call for stringent regulations unless it serves their interests, such as creating barriers to other firms, as was the case with the chemical firms in the early 1900s that shaped US policies on pesticide labeling. Rules shaped by commercial interests are also less likely to make it easy to hold corporate actors legally and financially accountable when ecological and social harms are caused by their actions.

In these ways, corporate political power works to undermine democratic participation in food systems, which in turn can undermine food security and livelihoods. When corporate actors dominate processes and water down policy outcomes, the effect is to weaken the agency of others not only to relate to food systems on their own terms but also to have a voice in how food systems are shaped and governed. The most marginalized food systems participants—including women, Indigenous and racialized communities, small-scale food producers, food systems workers, and young people—are often the ones whose agency is most undermined by corporate dominance in food policy and governance processes.[109]

CONCLUSION

The giants of the agricultural inputs industry have gone to great lengths and employed a vast array of strategies in the past decade, and especially since the start of the most recent round of consolidation began in 2015, to exercise political influence over the policy context. This playbook of strategies—lobbying, revolving doors, sponsorship of scientific studies, public information campaigns, and more—has enabled large firms to flex their political power in ways that encourage policymakers to serve the interests of corporate actors over those of society and the environment more broadly. Through these strategies, the firms in the agricultural inputs sector have actively portrayed pesticide and fertilizer use as essential and safe and have argued that they should not be regulated. The farm machinery firms have also actively fought against right to repair legislation, going so far as to encourage other groups to refrain from supporting the laws that enshrine the right. And the firms in the sector as a whole have taken an active role in shaping food and agriculture governance at a global level via partnerships with the FAO and participation in the UN Food Systems Summit process.

Through these various types of influence campaigns, the agribusiness titans have had more opportunity to shape food and agriculture policy and governance than other nongovernmental actors. Critics have raised important concerns about the ways in which corporate political power works against democratic participation in food systems governance and how it can undermine the quality and effectiveness of policy outcomes.

IV
CONCLUSION

13
THE UNCERTAIN PATH AHEAD

My aim in writing this book was to explore the origins of corporate bigness and power in the agricultural inputs industries to give context to today's growing consolidation and control by just a few very large farm machinery, fertilizer, seeds, and pesticides firms. The analysis shows that the roots of corporate dominance in the agricultural inputs sector go back further than we often realize, to the beginnings of the widespread commercial trade of those inputs that began as early as the mid-1800s. Many firms were selling machinery, fertilizer, seeds, and pesticides in the early days of each of these industries. However, by the early to mid-1900s, a relatively small number of firms had grown to be dominant sellers of these inputs and their concentration has persisted. This book advances several arguments about the rise of the dominant input firms—the agribusiness titans—that have come to dominate and shape the sector.

The first argument is that the leading firms gained their dominant position through a mix of market, technology, and policy factors. In some cases, economies of scale played a role, but this factor is often overemphasized as a leading driver of bigness. The dominant firms grew big largely through mergers and acquisitions, often pressed for by investors and made possible by their privileged access to investor finance and the primacy of shareholders within industrial capitalist markets. They were also able to finance consolidation from the profits they accrued through intellectual property protection and at times from coordinated activities with other large firms that often served as barriers to competition. Technology dynamics also mattered, such as first-mover advantages for firms that were placed to benefit from new innovations and production methods. Technological lock-ins and network effects also secured markets for the major firms and created barriers to entry for newcomers. Policy factors supported the rise of the agribusiness titans, such as state protections on intellectual property that afforded firms temporary monopolies from which they could benefit. A host of other state policies also influenced outcomes, such as direct and indirect subsidies for certain industries, regulatory regimes that shaped incentives, state-sponsored research and development activities that benefited the private sector, and weak and uneven competition policies. These market, technology, and policy dynamics overlapped and reinforced one another over the past century and more as the firms that dominate the agricultural inputs industry grew to be enormous players.

The second argument is that as these firms began to get big, even from very early on, they were able to wield several kinds of power that enabled them to influence the very forces that benefited them in their path to bigness. The processes of growing to be big and using their power to stay big often overlapped in messy ways. The dominant firms leveraged their market power to ensure that they profited handsomely while keeping other firms out of their markets. They used their technology power to shape innovation pathways in the sector in ways that maximized their own profits even when there were better alternatives that were more accessible to farmers, and as a result narrowed choices available to farmers by ensuring that their innovations further locked in the industrial model of agriculture. They employed political power through a variety of strategies from lobbying to revolving doors to sponsoring research studies and shaping discourse in a bid to effect policy changes that benefited their bottom lines. These various forms of power intersect and reinforce one another, and the firms pursued multiple strategies to shape the same market, policy, and technology contexts in ways that favored their interests and their expansion. In short, the dominant firms made industrial agriculture what it is today: a production system that drives enormous profits for just a few firms, concentrates and distorts markets, rewards only profit-oriented innovations, and exerts influence over policy and regulations in ways that support the interests of dominant firms.

The third argument I advance in this book is that corporate concentration and power in the sector have resulted in wide-ranging costs, including adverse social and ecological effects associated with the model of industrial agriculture promoted by the dominant firms. High levels of concentration in the sector have contributed to elevated prices and a dampening of innovation, which ultimately constrains choices for farmers and consumers. It also undermines democratic participation in food system governance as policy processes are captured by corporate interests. The corporate-led industrial agricultural model has contributed to wider social, ecological and health impacts that we are still coming to grips with today. By encouraging farm consolidation and higher prices, this model contributed to highly unequal access to resources that left marginalized populations with the least access to land and inputs. It led to difficult labor conditions for those working in the input sector. And industrial farming has contributed to enormous ecological problems, such as soil degradation, a narrowing of agricultural biodiversity, pollution from the overuse of pesticides, herbicides, and fertilizers, and a huge increase in greenhouse gas emissions, all of which also have significant human health consequences. As I show in this book, examples of these kinds of impacts span over a century or more, including in less industrialized countries, especially after the globalization of the major firms and the export of the industrial agricultural model via the Green Revolution. While it is important to recognize that different countries have experienced differing levels of adoption of industrial agricultural inputs and their contexts are unique, the costs of the industrial model of agriculture are widespread. These costs were expressed by critics from very early on with the roll-out of each new technology, although the ardent promotion of their highly uneven benefits by the leading firms has often overshadowed those critiques.

In this final chapter, I reflect further on the policy challenges of addressing the problem of corporate power and its costs in the sector. As I have outlined in this book, corporate dominance as it has unfolded in this sector has generated dynamics that contribute to a variety of social and ecological problems in important ways. As we move to address these problems in the current era, the corporate-led industrial agricultural system—which thrives on bigness, uniformity, and techno-fixes—claims to have solutions. We have heard these promises for well over a century, yet the solutions frequently pose new and complex challenges. For many, the dynamics that perpetuate corporate concentration in this system are standing in the way of the kind of diversity that many analysts say we need to achieve a fundamental transformation to more social and ecologically sustainable food systems. I next outline some of the kinds of policy shifts that could begin to address the situation, recognizing that corporate concentration is widely prevalent in other sectors of the economy and as such the problems in the agricultural sector are deeply interlinked with broader processes. Because this is already a long book, there is only space to point briefly to priority areas for policy shifts. An in-depth analysis of the potential and progress regarding these policy directions would take another book to explore. In outlining these potential policy directions, I also briefly point to some of the movements pushing for them and discuss their prospects for success.

A TURNING POINT?

The future trajectory of corporate dominance in the agricultural inputs sector is not yet clear. One scenario is that we could head further down the path of ever greater concentration in the sector, continuing the trend that I have outlined in this book. There could be continued waves of megamergers, combining not just the largest firms within each input industry into ever larger and more dominant firms, but also bringing different input industries together—such as fertilizer firms merging with seed and chemical firms and farm machinery firms—as they all vie for power in the digital agriculture industry that serves as a platform for all the agricultural inputs. This type of scenario—what the International Panel of Experts on Sustainable Food Systems (IPES-Food) and ETC Group call "agribusiness-as-usual"—would likely see the increasingly giant firms, backed by powerful financial interests, continue to focus on the development of digital agriculture and synthetic biology, amplifying the problems associated with these technologies.[1]

Such an outcome is unfortunately likely without a major groundswell pushing for public policy changes to reverse course. The history of the rise to corporate bigness in the inputs industries makes clear that simply assuming the dominant firms will voluntarily address the problems associated with concentration is unlikely to get very far. The firms at the top of the sector have used the power available to them to shape food systems in ways that serve their own needs first rather than the needs of society more broadly. While the firms may pledge to take voluntary measures seriously through corporate social responsibility programs or by engaging in partnerships, research over the past decades across various sectors has shown the flaws in this approach due to the power of the large firms to influence how these measures roll out on the ground.[2] For example, firms may make some marginal improvements to sustainability but are unlikely to advocate a complete transformation away from industrial agriculture. While such measures may appear to be better than nothing, they may also hinder the transformation to more just and sustainable agricultural systems because they reinforce the existing industrial agriculture paradigm.

It is also unrealistic to assume financial investors will suddenly shift their interests in large enough numbers to pressure firms via ratings on their environmental, social, and governance (ESG) performance, at least not in the current context. Analysts have warned that even the massive rise in sustainability investing will not save the planet.[3] Moreover, efforts to effect change by means of shareholder pressure have been hampered by a lack of reliable data as well as dropping interest among investors, especially in the United States, with the rise of polarized politics that attacks the very idea of ESG investing.[4]

A hyper-concentration scenario does not have to be the ultimate outcome. Indeed, as competition policy expert Matt Stoller makes clear, "Nothing about monopolization is inevitable."[5] Strong public policy has an important role to play in addressing the problems with ever more concentrated and powerful firms controlling the agricultural inputs sector. The key to addressing the concentration of power in the food system is to foster more diversity in terms of market structures, inputs into political processes, and agricultural production systems. Such an outcome will require action on multiple fronts and at different scales to foster that diversity, especially given the different types of power available to the dominant firms. Efforts on all these fronts will require governments at multiple scales to play a strong role in order to enact meaningful policy measures that tackle the main kinds of power available to firms. Some movements are actively pushing for policy changes in these directions.

What are the prospects for addressing the problems associated with long-standing corporate concentration and power in the food system along the lines outlined above? As already noted, robust societal support would strengthen the likelihood that policymakers would adopt reforms that move in the directions identified. Although there were critics who raised alarms about the problems with corporate concentration more broadly as well as the industrial model of agriculture marketed by the leading firms for at least the past century, these voices have had an uneven impact on policy change. There have been moments, such as the late 1800s and early 1900s, when broad public concern regarding corporate concentration resulted in strengthened competition policies. And there have been moments, such as in the 1960s, when critiques of the widespread use of pesticides brought tighter regulations, as was the case with growing awareness of the harms of DDT. But there have been other times—especially in the recent neoliberal era—when it seems that the critics of corporate bigness and industrial agriculture have been unable to convince governments to bring about fundamental policy reforms, despite their best efforts in calling for major change.

The current moment is one where there is growing public attention to the issue of corporate power in food systems, which may signal a turning point. Calls for change are coming from a number of different quarters—from farmer unions and competition experts to global social movements and food consumers of all stripes. All are calling for more sustainable and just food systems, which could provide an opening to address the ways in which corporate dominance and power have contributed to problems within those systems.

Calls for policy reform have grown louder after 2020. The COVID-19 pandemic and the war in Ukraine were huge shocks that upended food systems, highlighting the fragility of the corporate-led industrial agricultural model.[6] These shocks sparked rampant food price inflation that fueled growing public concern about corporate reach into food systems and their governance. In Canada, rapidly rising grocery bills prompted the Canadian Competition Bureau to undertake a major study of the grocery retail sector, which found that the sector is highly concentrated and lacking sufficient competition.[7] In the United States, the Biden administration issued an executive order to restore competition in the US economy, which prominently mentions the need to address concentration in the food system. And across countries in Europe and many others, similar questions are being raised about the connection between concentrated sectors in food systems and problems like food price inflation.[8]

This widespread concern about the corporate role in agriculture and food systems adds to an already growing recognition of a need to fundamentally transform food systems to make them more ecologically and socially sustainable. Across the political spectrum, industrial food systems are widely understood to be contributing to inequities and environmental problems. The epic failure to meet United Nations Sustainable Development Goals (SDGs), including SDG 2—to end hunger and adopt more sustainable food systems—further reinforces the rationale for transformation. Actors at all scales, from individuals to states to international organizations and private firms, are reconsidering how food systems are organized, from production to consumption.

As the analysis in this book shows, corporate concentration and power in food systems have wide-ranging costs. They affect the dynamics of markets, technology, and politics in ways that have enormous impacts on social, ecological, and health outcomes. For this reason, for any food systems transformation agenda to be successful, it must address corporate power. I next outline three areas where policy change, both outside and within the food system sector, could help address the challenge of corporate dominance in the agricultural inputs sector.

MORE ROBUST COMPETITION POLICIES

Most industrialized countries have had competition policies in place since at least the early to mid-twentieth century. Those policies, as outlined in earlier chapters, were weakened in the decades following the late 1970s as neoliberalism began to dominate the global economy. Competition policies in many developing countries, where they exist, are relatively recent, and in many cases are weak. For example, nearly half of sub-Saharan African countries lack competition policies, while policies in many other countries on the continent are relatively new and vastly underresourced.[9]

Given the surging market power of the dominant firms, it is important to support more diverse market structures. This means stronger, more comprehensive, and more consistently applied competition policies that foster market diversity. The fixation of competition policies on consumer welfare impacts over the past fifty years—in particular the effect of mergers on consumer prices—has resulted in skewed market structures that have enabled the big firms to get bigger and gain even more market power. Although combining firms may have argued that as a single larger firm they could achieve efficiencies and lower prices, their subsequent increase in market power enables them to later raise prices and gain excess profits without fear of being undercut by competition. The evaluation of merger deals should take the implications for market structures more fully into account, considering the impact of consolidation on opportunities for small- and medium-scale businesses in order to ensure sufficient competition in the marketplace to keep prices at normal competitive levels.

Reform advocates have also argued that competition authorities should also not be shy about breaking up the existing giant firms that dominate entire sectors, as sometimes this is the only effective remedy to the colossal market power of dominant firms.[10] Such a strategy has been employed in the past and should be kept open as an option in the agricultural inputs sector, where the market power of the largest firms has had wide ranging consequences. Unless there are more openings for a range of small- and medium-scale enterprises to thrive in the farm economy, there is the risk that opportunities for a more diverse base of entrepreneurship will be closed off.

The attention to market structures is especially important in the agricultural sector because those markets affect farmers' livelihoods far beyond just influencing prices. Although farmers purchase inputs, they are not simply consumers, but also small businesses that operate as suppliers to other firms in the agricultural economy. When farmers face potential harms from vertical and horizontal integration of the firms on which they rely for inputs and for the sale of their crops, they can get the raw end of price manipulation on both fronts—higher input prices and being paid lower prices from other firms that buy their goods. In other words, they face a "price-cost squeeze" whereby they face extremes of market power from both supplying firms and buying firms.[11] When there is simultaneous vertical and horizontal integration—as occurred with seed and chemical firm mergers, in the fertilizer sector, and now across all of the inputs as a result of digital farming—it squeezes farmers even more. These dynamics also create enormous barriers to entry for other firms that offer more diverse options and that might enable farmers to break out of the lock-ins to the industrial inputs for which they are captive to the big players. It is important that competition policies take these unique circumstances of farmers into account.

Financialization and rising patterns of common ownership also need to be taken more fully into account in competition regulation. As noted in earlier chapters, growing share ownership by common financial investors across multiple large firms within the same sector has raised concern about anti-competitive effects. When there are common owners across the large firms within a sector, as is the case with the dominant agricultural input firms, market concentration is often more pronounced than what traditional indicators suggest. Such ownership patterns can also encourage more consolidation, which further enhances market power of the top firms. Further, common ownership patterns can increase pressures to collude, tacitly or explicitly, to raise prices to serve shareholder demands for higher returns. Although the EU did take note of common ownership dynamics in its evaluation of some of the recent seed and chemical firm megamergers, this factor did not play a key role in its decisions on those cases. Competition law expert Ioannis Lianos and colleagues have argued that better legal tools need to be developed by competition authorities to tackle the anticompetitive effects of financial ownership patterns, especially in the agrifood sector where these dynamics are prevalent.[12] Such measures can help to push back against the primacy of shareholder value in driving corporate decisions.

Competition policies could also pay closer attention to innovation impacts of consolidation. Although current merger enforcement guidelines include some consideration of investment spending, it is important to examine firms' behaviors regarding defensive innovation spending versus transformative research. Such an approach would help guide decisions on whether mergers are likely to dampen or encourage innovations that support the public good over private interests. This wider approach to innovation impacts, combined with support for market structures that encourage smaller and medium-sized enterprises in the sector, can create openings for the kinds of innovations that are more accessible and that can better respond to farmers' needs, increase production, reduce inequalities, and promote environmental sustainability.

There is also a need for better coordination between competition policies in the agricultural sector and public policies and regulations in other areas, including environmental, social, labor, and health regulations. For example, stricter regulations on the introduction of new products such as pesticides and gene edited seeds and an end to subsidies that encourage fossil energy dependent industrial agriculture are important to pair with strong rules on competition. Such an approach would help prevent large firms from exploiting their access to market power in ways that can undermine broader social goals, such as by externalizing the costs of the technologies that they sell.[13]

Because the agricultural inputs firms are truly global in scope, as the analysis in this book makes clear, it is important to coordinate competition policies across countries and jurisdictions. Without such coordination, firms can exploit the differences in domestic regulations in ways that serve their interests and externalize costs in other countries. By working more closely together through coordination and possibly considering an international treaty on competition policy, governments can more effectively rein in the power of the dominant global agribusiness firms and hold them accountable in all of the jurisdictions in which they operate.

There is growing political support for a shift in antitrust policies within some countries and regions to tackle corporate concentration across the economy, including in the agricultural sector. As merger deals reached near record levels by the mid-2010s, there were growing calls to strengthen antitrust policies along the lines detailed above. A growing movement of antitrust scholars and activists in the United States, for example, began to argue that US antitrust policies should return to their roots, building on the original ideas behind such policies as articulated by US Supreme Court Justice Louis Brandeis in the early 1900s, which focused on market structure and opportunities for entrepreneurship.

Those calling for a return of antitrust enforcement to focus on ensuring competitive market structures see themselves as part of a New Brandeis movement.[14] The New Brandeisians draw on Brandeis's observation (and, indeed, warning) that market power can beget political power and therefore should be closely monitored because this kind of influence can threaten democracy. The New Brandeisians thus call for a strong role for the state to ensure policies—competition policies especially, but not exclusively—that work toward building competitive markets. Much of the focus of the New Brandeisians has been on the ways in which merger guidelines miss important dimensions of corporate power, especially as exemplified by today's Big Tech firms. As these digital goliaths have grown ever larger, they have gained extraordinary power because they control critical infrastructure that their rivals must also use, enabling them to gain from network effects and platform power. As such, they are gatekeepers who are able to collect data from others that advance their business interests, including in ways that can undermine their rivals.[15] These ideas are highly relevant for the agricultural sector, which, as this book shows, has become deeply enmeshed in the digital economy in recent decades.

As these ideas about the need for antitrust reform gained wider approval, in 2021, the newly elected Biden administration put the leading thinkers of the movement—Lina Khan, Jonathan Kanter, and Tim Wu—into key positions in his government, with Khan as the chair of the Federal Trade Commission, Kanter as the head of the antitrust division of the Department of Justice, and Wu as a key presidential adviser on antitrust policy. It was under the guidance of New Brandeisian advocates that President Biden issued his executive order on the promotion of competition in the US economy within six months of taking office. The executive order mentions the need to address market power not just of Big Tech, but also that of Big Ag, including the agricultural inputs industry: "Consolidation in the agricultural industry is making it too hard for small family farms to survive. Farmers are squeezed between concentrated market power in the agricultural input industries—seed, fertilizer, feed, and equipment suppliers—and concentrated market power in the channels for selling agricultural products."[16]

Progressive farmers' organizations—including both the US and Canadian National Farmers Unions—are also calling for policy changes along similar lines to push back against corporate monopolies. They have been among the most vocal critics of corporate mergers in the sector, which they see as a direct threat to the livelihoods of their members. They have also called for more territorialized agrifood markets grounded in more local and regional market structures as a way to push back against corporate market power in the sector.

Major policy change is already taking place along these lines in some countries. In 2022, the USDA opened consultations on how corporate concentration has caused harm in food systems and embarked on drawing up a strategy to address it. While much of the focus of this initiative thus far has been on concentration in the livestock sector, growing attention is also being directed to fertilizers and seeds.[17] At a broader level, stronger merger guidelines in both Canada and the United States were adopted in late 2023 in ways that broadened the authority of regulators to challenge and prevent mergers that are likely to dampen competition, which are highly relevant to the agrifood sector. Canada, for example, dispensed with exemptions that allowed merging firms to gain significant market share provided they could prove that the deal would result in efficiencies that outweighed potential anticompetitive effects.[18] The United States tightened its rules in ways that better address platform power and network effects from proposed mergers involving digital technologies. The revised US merger guidelines also put closer scrutiny on common ownership, mergers resulting in vertical integration, and the impact of buyer power on workers and producers.[19]

STRONGER MEASURES TO CURB CORPORATE POLITICAL INFLUENCE AND ENSURE ACCOUNTABILITY

Countering the political power of firms in the policy process will require stronger measures to reduce corporate influence over regulatory decisions, scientific research, and public discourse. These kinds of policy measures also go beyond the food system but are deeply important for determining outcomes. Some governments already have rules in place for the disclosure of lobbying expenditures and activities, which is a step in the right direction. But certainly much more can be done to ensure that dominant firms with deep pockets cannot simply pay to gain privileged access to policymakers. Chapter 12 noted that many countries lack any sort of disclosure rules on corporate lobbying, especially in the Global South, where there is little publicly available information about the amounts spent by large firms and the scale of their activities.

More stringent requirements for transparency in scientific research—including funding sources—would expose the extent of corporate influence over the broader research agenda regarding agricultural inputs and their potential risks. Greater transparency and rules to reduce conflicts of interest in government regulatory contexts is also important. Stronger rules, for example, on the time that must elapse for individuals who alternate positions between government and industry, and regarding disclosure of research funding and authorship, could go a long way toward helping reduce conflicts of interest. Rules that prioritize independent scientific studies in policy and regulatory decisions would also go some way to reducing corporate influence over how scientific research informs policymaking, as was made clear by the case of Monsanto's attempts to influence regulations on glyphosate.

In addition to stronger rules to curb corporate influence over policy and regulatory processes, it is important to foster more diversity in these contexts by opening up spaces for greater public participation. The creation of more equitable and democratic policy and governance spaces would support the prioritization of goals that serve the public good over private interests, such as policies that encourage more sustainable food systems and uphold the right to food. Such an approach would mean creating and supporting dedicated governance spaces—at all scales from local to global—in which citizens, food producers, food system workers, and social movements play a leading role. These kinds of governance settings can counter corporate influence by prioritizing the voices of marginalized populations and enhance their agency within food systems.

Participatory governance settings also create opportunities for noncorporate actors to engage in a meaningful way with policymakers.[20] Food policy councils and stronger science-policy interface bodies are important governance structures that can facilitate greater participation of all citizens in food system policymaking. The establishment and enforcement of rights frameworks for farmers and food system workers, alongside more robust commitment by states to uphold the right to food for all citizens, is also important to provide a set of principles by which such policies should be guided.[21]

Civil society and Indigenous peoples' groups and food systems social movements have been highlighting the role of corporate power in influencing governance settings and outcomes for decades. They see corporate power and dominance in the sector as a major barrier to the transformation of food systems toward more equitable and sustainable means of food provisioning. These groups have called for a number of the kinds of measures outlined above, with particular focus on curtailing conflicts of interest and the capture of governance spaces by corporations, including in food-related UN bodies. Specifically, as noted in chapter 12, they have called for ending partnerships between the FAO and private corporations and their lobby groups. They have also called for more transparency and disclosure of lobby activities, rules to end conflicts of interest in food systems governance, and for more open and democratic governance spaces for food systems.[22] It should not be up to these movements alone to act as watchdogs to enforce norms of transparency and good practice, however, since this drains their limited resources. Rather, it is important for governments and international institutions to step up and put stronger rules in place to prevent corporate influence in the first place.

These groups are also calling for more concrete policies and frameworks to hold firms accountable to address harms that have already occurred and prevent new harms from taking place. At the international level, these groups have supported the development of a legally binding treaty on transnational corporations and human rights, which would place regulations on transnational corporations and their supply chains to ensure accountability for any potential harms they cause. Negotiations on this treaty began under UN auspices in 2014, following the 2011 adoption by the UN Human Rights Council of Guiding Principles on Business and Human Rights, which set out guidelines for both states and global firms to prevent and respond to human rights abuses that arise from business operations. While important, these guidelines are only voluntary, which prompted civil society organizations—including those working on food and agriculture systems—to push for a binding treaty alongside a group of developing country governments. Negotiations on a binding treaty are ongoing, and civil society groups have advocated for stronger liability mechanisms to address human rights violations by transnational firms.[23] Such an agreement would ensure that large firms are held accountable in cases such as the 1984 Bhopal disaster, discussed in chapter 6.

GREATER PUBLIC SECTOR SUPPORT FOR ALTERNATIVE AGRICULTURAL MODELS

The multifaceted power of the large agricultural input firms has meant that they are able to shape responses to the problems that their own technologies have introduced. In doing so, the solutions they put forward have consistently responded to their own profit needs. Because they are so vested in the industrial agricultural model, their "solutions" typically further entrench the industrial agricultural paradigm rather than facilitate a move away from it. The history outlined in this book shows that each corporate solution seemed at first to resolve a problem, only to introduce new problems, and the cycle was repeated. For this reason, most critical analysts promoting food systems transformation call for a complete break with the industrial agricultural model and advocate instead for agroecology alongside more equitable land distribution.[24]

In this context, governments can foster more diversity in production systems by supporting public sector agricultural research and development into alternative production systems outside of industrial agriculture. More public sector investment is needed to support accessible and sustainable production models that serve the public good rather than the corporate need for profits. It is also important for public research programs to follow participatory practices that include end users to ensure that they meet the needs of farmers rather than exclusively focusing on the needs of corporations. For example, publicly supported research into agroecological farming systems could dramatically expand awareness and uptake of natural farming methods. Only a fraction of public research spending in most countries, and only a tiny proportion of international agricultural assistance spending, for example, is dedicated to agroecological farming methods that do not rely on external inputs such as chemical herbicides, pesticides, and fertilizers.[25] Increased investment in public plant-breeding programs and nonprofit, open-source seed initiatives, could also go some way to expanding farmers' seed choices.[26]

The adoption of policies that redistribute farmland or facilitate access to farmland for marginalized populations through community and cooperative landholding initiatives is also important to reverse the trends that have systematically disadvantaged farmland access for some groups, such as Black, Indigenous, female, and new farmers. Policies that support land access and more diversified farm structures are needed to counter the inequalities associated with the expansion of the industrial agricultural model that led to farmland consolidation and land dispossession for many marginalized groups. Land reform that redistributes land and provides secure tenure for a diversity of small-scale farmers is widely seen to be mutually supportive with agroecological farming systems.[27] Some analysts show that adoption of agroecological farming methods in the Global North, for example, is slow largely because of the highly unequal landholding structure.[28]

Greater public investment in diverse food production and marketing systems that benefit small- and medium-sized enterprises is also important.[29] This might include, for example, investment in natural biological methods to fertilize plants, which would also help reduce the ecological footprint of the sector and open opportunities for smaller enterprises.[30] Alternative weed and pest control, for example, using renewable electricity, is another area where research could be supported that may favor smaller-scale firms and more competitive market structures.[31] It is important to recognize that these kinds of technologies could introduce new ecological risks as well as corporate capture. However, they could be potentially useful ways to reduce ecological problems in the sector if implemented in ways that support a broader transition to more sustainable agricultural production models.

Public support for open access data systems could also help to curtail the corporate lock on data and information in digital farming systems. For example, programs that provide public access to data on input prices as well as data on soil and climate conditions would enable greater transparency and accountability in food systems, while reducing the lock-ins that tie farmers to corporate controlled farm data analysis platforms. Policies along these lines could increase access to digital farming technologies for small-scale farmers and facilitate the development of more responsible models of digital agriculture.[32] They would also support what food system analyst Maywa Montenegro de Wit calls "technology sovereignty" within food systems—the right to appropriate technologies in food and agriculture, recognition of food producers as technology providers, local community control over technologies and data, and innovations that work with nature and build on local and Indigenous peoples' knowledge and skills.[33]

The calls for change along these lines are emanating from a number of quarters. Civil society and Indigenous peoples' organizations are increasingly calling for an end to the corporate capture of food systems, which they see as blocking the kind of food systems transformation that is needed. These groups are part of a broad international movement that in recent decades has called for more just, resilient, and diverse farming and food systems to support small-scale producers—often in a food sovereignty framework promoting principles of agroecology—that would see diverse communities and countries taking ownership of their own food systems.[34] Numerous groups are leading initiatives that promote food sovereignty, agroecology, and land redistribution. These include international groups such as La Via Campesina, FIAN, Focus on the Global South, the CSIPM, the ETC group, and IPES-Food. Progressive farmers' organizations and numerous other groups at national and local levels around the world are also promoting these ideas while also taking a strong stand against corporate monopolies.

These groups have different mandates, but they all advocate agroecology in one form or another as a viable food production model because it works within ecological boundaries. At the same time, agroecology is also a social movement that seeks to address inequities and improve the agency and voice of agricultural producers, especially when coupled with land reform. The groups advocating an agroecological transition explicitly resist the growing reliance on the giant agricultural input corporations that dominate the world food economy and instead envision a productive agriculture that does not require a reliance on those firms and seeks to break the lock-ins of industrial technologies.[35]

This movement has expressed concern about the large agricultural input corporations potentially co-opting agroecology for their own purposes. That is, there is worry that they are picking and choosing which aspects of agroecology to endorse—such as field practices—rather than the whole package, which also includes more democratic and participatory governance processes and the curtailment of corporate power.[36] These groups also recognize, however, that transition to agroecology on a wide scale faces many barriers, such as deeply entrenched technological lock-ins that will be difficult to overcome, especially if large agribusiness firms continue to shape research agendas.

Advocates of agroecology recognize that many policymakers and mainstream analysts see a possibility of transformation within the industrial model—for example, digital agriculture and efficiency gains from the latest technologies to fix problems with the older ones—and do not always problematize corporate power. As mentioned in chapter 12, there was a clash between this movement and the leadership of the UN Food Systems Summit in 2021, with the former making their participation in the summit contingent on the latter including corporate power as a topic for discussion. That call that went unheeded, resulting in those groups boycotting the process. Although civil society groups were able to highlight the problem of corporate power in their own messaging around the time of the UNFSS, the summit itself nonetheless welcomed corporate actors and prioritized digital technologies in its reports.

Despite the challenges, the broader movement promoting this alternative agricultural vision has made remarkable inroads into a variety of policymaking forums. Agroecology has been discussed as a viable model of food systems transformation at the Food and Agriculture Organization of the United Nations, the UN Committee on World Food Security and its High Level Panel of Experts on Food Security and Nutrition, as well as in scientific assessments of the Intergovernmental Panel on Climate Change and the International Science-Policy Platform on Biodiversity and Ecosystem Services. The in-depth consideration of this agricultural model in these forums has raised awareness of agroecology's multifaceted benefits. At the same time, the civil society groups and social movements promoting agroecology remain concerned that these international forums have paid more attention to the technical elements of agroecological practices while continuing to downplay the problem of corporate power.

FINAL THOUGHTS

As is clear from this overview of potential first steps toward policy change to address the problems associated with corporate bigness, concentration, and power in the agricultural inputs sector, the challenge is enormous and has long been entrenched. Strong and coordinated public policies are required to curtail the power of concentrated firms in the sector as part of a broader transformation of agri-food systems. Leaving this task to the market alone will not break the lock-ins that are gripping the global industrial food system. Indeed, leaving it to the market alone will only reinforce technological lock-ins and reliance on big corporations.

This is not to say that producers and consumers do not have a role to play or that corporations themselves do not have a role to play. But we cannot leave it to the corporations alone to propose "solutions" and assume that any failures in the form of hunger and unsustainable food systems are due to insufficient production and poor product choices by agricultural producers and consumers. If governments are serious about meeting the UN Sustainable Development Goals, they need to play a much more prominent role in shaping the transformation of food systems, much as they did in the nineteenth and early twentieth centuries. But instead of focusing on developing large-scale industrial inputs and then handing the reins over to large and dominant, powerful firms, governments today need to focus on more sustainable agricultural models such as agroecology and share that know-how directly with farmers and communities.

Finally, the analysis presented in this book has focused squarely on the large and powerful players in the agricultural inputs sector—farm machinery firms, fertilizer corporations, and the seed and agrochemical industry—which has served to illustrate how corporate size and power shape food systems in ways that undermine broader societal and environmental goals. In mapping out this story, I tried to follow political economist Susan George's advice: "Study the rich and powerful, not the poor and powerless. . . . not nearly enough work is being done on those who hold the power and pull the strings. As their tactics become more subtle and their public pronouncements more guarded, the need for better spade-work becomes crucial."[37] Because I chose an in-depth and historical approach, I was able to cover only the inputs industries. Even that was a large task that took more time and energy than I had anticipated. Much work remains to be done. Many of the same kinds of problems as I outlined in earlier chapters are also prevalent in other parts of the global industrial food system where just a few large players dominate: the processed food companies, the meat and livestock sector, the large commodity trading firms, and food retail. My hope is that this book has provided a useful framework for continued work that examines corporate dominance and power in these other parts of food systems, and indeed across a wider set of industries as well.[38]

NOTES

CHAPTER 1

1. Quoted in Barboza 1999.
2. See, for example, Bork 1978; Cowen 2019; Atkinson and Lind 2018, 63.
3. Quoted in DuPont 2015.
4. For a detailed analysis of bigness in these sectors, see Adams and Brock 2007.
5. Quoted in Bayer and Monsanto 2016.
6. Stone 2022a.
7. Clapp et al. 2021; Canfield et al. 2021.
8. McMichael 2013; Clapp 2021a.
9. Foroohar 2019; Khan 2017; Klobuchar 2021.
10. Brandeis 1914.
11. Quoted in Lonergan 1941.
12. Brandeis 1934, 115.
13. See Wu 2018 on corporate bigness.
14. Law 2016. The Herfindahl-Herschman Index (HHI) is a more precise measure of market concentration that some economists use. The HHI is the sum of the squares of each firm's share in a given market and can range from 0 (a perfectly competitive market) to 10,000 (a single player dominating the entire market). An HHI of 2500 and higher is typically considered concentrated.
15. Chandler 1959.
16. Wu 2018; Brandeis 1934.

17. Brandeis 1914; Adams and Brock 2007.
18. Jones and Nisbett 2011; Isakson 2014.
19. Lieberman and Montgomery 1988.
20. Makri et al. 2010.
21. Weis 2010.
22. Cecere et al. 2014; Dosi 1982, 158.
23. Schwartz 2016.
24. Kloppenburg 2004.
25. US Federal Trade Commission website: https://www.ftc.gov/advice-guidance/competition-guidance/guide-antitrust-laws/antitrust-laws; for the original text, see US Congress 2004.
26. US Federal Trade Commission website: https://www.justice.gov/atr/antitrust-laws-and-you.
27. On the weakening of antitrust and competition policies in the United States and globally, see Khan 2017; Wu 2018; Stoller 2019; Klobuchar 2021; Damro and Guay 2012; Ergen and Kohl 2019. On the Webb Pomerene Act, see Taylor and Moss 2011.
28. Landes and Posner 1981.
29. Adams and Brock 2007, 119.
30. Falkner 2008.
31. Strange 1988.
32. Schumpeter 1942; Arrow 1962; Gilbert 2006, 190.
33. MacDonald 2017a; IPES-Food 2017, 56.
34. Kurz 2023, 4.
35. Schimmelpfennig 2004.
36. For example, Clapp and Fuchs 2009; Clapp and Scrinis 2017; IPES-Food 2023b.
37. On lobbying, see Clapp and Fuchs 2009; on revolving door, see Nestle 2007; on PPPs, see Kaan and Liese, 2010.
38. Strange 1988; Fuchs 2005; Gill and Law 1989.
39. Clapp and Fuchs 2009; Falkner 2008.
40. Anderson et al. 2021; Wezel et al. 2020.
41. Strange 1996.
42. Levy and Newell 2005; Falkner 2008; Clapp and Helleiner 2012.
43. Arthur 1989; Seto et al. 2019; Dosi 1982.
44. Klobuchar 2021; Stoller 2019; Foroohar 2019.
45. For example, Kloppenburg 2004; Stone 2022a; Fitzgerald 1990, 2003; Bosso 1988; Markham 1958.
46. Canfield et al. 2021.
47. McMichael 2005, 2013; Friedmann and McMichael 1989.

CHAPTER 2

1. Phillips 1956, 3.
2. Ott 2014.
3. The information in this and the following paragraph draws from a biography of Cyrus H. McCormick, written by his grandson: McCormick 1931.
4. Phillips 1956.
5. McCormick 1931, 58.
6. Phillips 1956, 5.
7. Winder 1995.
8. Chandler 1959.
9. Kramer 1964, 284.
10. *New York Times* 1861.
11. Kramer 1964, 284; Phillips 1956.
12. Schwartzman 1970.
13. The information in this and the following paragraph draw from Broehl 1984.
14. On the Grange movement, see Buck 1913; Martin 1873.
15. Broehl 1984.
16. Buck 1913, 34–38.
17. Martin 1873, 6.
18. Broehl 1984, 165.
19. On these offers and arrangements, see Martin 1873; Broehl 1984, 165; Buck 1913, 266.
20. Buck 1913, 266.
21. Broehl 1984, 192.
22. Buck 1913, 269.
23. Buck 1913.
24. On these dynamics, see Kramer 1964 and Ozanne 1967.
25. Kramer 1964, 285.
26. Phillips 1956.
27. Ozanne 1967, 45; Kramer 1964, 288.
28. US Bureau on Corporations 1913.
29. Kramer 1964, 297.
30. US Bureau on Corporations 1913, 336; Phillips 1956, 14.
31. Townsend 1911, 833.
32. Ozanne 1967, 71.
33. Phillips 1956, 14; Clarke 2021.
34. US Bureau on Corporations 1913.

35. Wu 2018.
36. Kramer 1964.
37. Broehl 1984; Phillips 1956.
38. J. D. Woods and Gordon Ltd. 1956, 39.
39. Ewart and Melanson 2010.
40. J. D. Woods and Gordon Ltd. 1956, 39; Ewart and Melanson 2010, 66–67.
41. Eward and Melanson 2010, 73–75.
42. Conant 1953, 28.
43. Phillips 1956; Schwartzman 1970, 20.
44. Phillips 1956, 25.
45. Broehl 1984, 351.
46. Marsh 1985, 419.
47. Phillips 1956, 32.
48. Wik 1964.
49. Phillips 1956, 26–29.
50. Conant 1953, 27, 35.
51. Olmstead and Rhode 2001, 23.
52. Conant 1953, 27.
53. Phillips 1956.
54. Tavenner 1912.
55. Townsend 1911, 835.
56. Rosenberg 2019, 81.
57. Bittlingmayer 1996.
58. US Bureau of Corporations 1913, 70.
59. US Bureau of Corporations 1913, 243.
60. Phillips 1956, 20; US Bureau of Corporations 1913.
61. Ott 2014.
62. US Department of Justice 1918.
63. United States v. International Harvester Co., 274 U.S. 693 (1927), https://supreme.justia.com/cases/federal/us/274/693/.
64. Jasny 1935; Ellenberg 2000.
65. Nourse 1930, 125.
66. McCormick 1931, 215–216.
67. Fitzgerald 2003, 99.
68. Quoted in Ellenberg 2000, 552.
69. Fitzgerald 2003, 94.

70. Nourse 1930; Jasny 1935; Gaines and Crowe 1950; Ellenberg 2000.

71. Nourse 1930; Berardi 1984.

72. Rochester 1940, 10.

73. Beale 1991.

74. Rochester 1940, 171; Fitzgerald 2003, 93; Olmstead and Rhode 2001; Berardi 1984, 11.

75. Nourse 1930, 124.

76. McMillan 1949, 24.

77. Taylor 2018; Olmstead and Rhode 2001, 670.

78. Hamilton 1939; US Department of Agriculture (USDA) 1940; Berardi 1984.

79. USDA 1940, 83.

80. McMillan 1949, 26.

81. Quoted in Ellenberg, 2000, 562.

82. Lal et al. 2007.

83. Holleman 2017.

84. Lal et al. 2007, 4.

85. Sears 1935; Faulkner 1945; Lal 2007.

86. Faulkner 1943.

87. Schofield 1944.

CHAPTER 3

1. On the early history of fertilizers, see Russel and Williams 1977; Wines 1985; Ron 2023.

2. Wines 1985, 6.

3. Ciceri et al. 2015.

4. Ron 2023, 100.

5. Quoted in Pollard 2021, 101.

6. Wines 1985, 23.

7. Liebig 1840.

8. Crop residues, however, were often left on the field, but were not significant forms of nutrient-rich biomass.

9. Warde 2018.

10. Goldberg 2018, 135.

11. Melillo 2012, 1031–37.

12. Marchesi 2020, 205–206.

13. Goldberg 2018, 135.

14. On the history of guano production and trade, and working conditions, see Melillo 2012; Wines 1985; Clark and Foster 2009; Mann 2011.

15. *New York Times* 1855.

16. Wines 1985, 45–46; Vizcarra 2009, 375.

17. Wines 1985, 46.

18. Skaggs 1994, 9.

19. See Melillo 2012; Skaggs 1994, 10; Wines 1985.

20. On the Guano Islands act, see Skaggs 1994; Goldberg 2018.

21. On the South American nitrate investment arrangements in this era, see Clark and Foster 2009; Mayo 1980; Greenhill and Miller 1973.

22. Clark and Foster 2009; Mayo 1980.

23. Melillo 2012, 1045.

24. Monteón 2003, 76.

25. Rippy 1948.

26. Lamer 1957, 164.

27. Brown 1963.

28. Pallister 2022.

29. Wines 1985, 100.

30. See Shick and Doyle 1985; Dixon 2018.

31. Information from this and the subsequent paragraph are drawn from Ceceri et al. 2015.

32. Tosdal 1913.

33. On these various mergers and consolidation in the sector in this period, see Chandler 1959, 18; Tosdal 1913, 174; Markham 1958, 70, 42.

34. Markham 1958, 71–72.

35. Markham 1958, 163–164.

36. Tosdal 1913.

37. With respect to the United States, see National Potash Producers Association and National Borax Producers Association 1933. With respect to other countries, see Ciceri et al. 2015.

38. Wills 2022.

39. National Potash Producers Association and National Borax Producers Association 1933.

40. On these episodes, see Ciceri et al. 2015 and Markham 1958, 85–86.

41. Taylor and Moss 2013.

42. Markham 1958, 39–45.

43. Travis 2017, 2018.

44. Johnson 2016, 215.
45. Lie 2008.
46. Russel and Williams 1977.
47. Szöllösi-Janze 2017; Smil 2001.
48. Travis 2017.
49. Lamer 1957, 169; Johnson 2016.
50. Brand 1945, 105.
51. Johnson 2016 details this fascinating history.
52. Wengert 1949.
53. On this history, see Travis 2017, 2021.
54. Johnson 2016.
55. Henry Ford bid on the Muscle Shoals plants in 1921, promising to build new towns and factories to produce cheap fertilizer as well as automobile parts (though it is unclear how this effort was potentially linked to his promotion of Fordson tractors, which were hugely popular at the time, as noted in the previous chapter). On the history of the Muscle Shoals operations, see Johnson 2016.
56. Markham 1958, 100.
57. Travis 2021.
58. Lamer 1957; Travis 2017.
59. Pettigrew 1985.
60. Coleman 2006.
61. Lamer 1957; Travis 2017; Pettigrew 1985.
62. Norsk Hydro website, 1930: Cooperation and market shares during the depression: https://www.hydro.com/en-LT/about-hydro/company-history/1929–1945/1930-cooperation-and-market-shares-during-the-depression/.
63. Travis 2017, 13; Lamer 1957.
64. Markham 1958, 101–105.
65. Yamamura 1964.
66. On the Zaibatsu firms in the fertilizer sector, see Lamer 1957, 175.
67. Markham 1958, 68.
68. Agricultural and Food Chemistry 1957; Wengert 1949.
69. Lamer 1957, 627.
70. Jenny 2012.
71. Molot and Laux 1979, 229–230.
72. Conford 2002.
73. These quotes are from Sears 1935, 29, 128, 67.
74. Balfour 1943, 64.

75. Howard 1947, 71.
76. Howard 1947, 76.
77. Howard 1946, quoted in Heckman 2006, 145.
78. Vogt 2007, 15; Balfour 1943.
79. Heckman 2006, 146.

CHAPTER 4

1. Fowler 1994; Kloppenburg 2004.
2. Carney 2013.
3. Kloppenburg 2004.
4. Fowler 1994; Mann 2011.
5. M.M.B. 1906.
6. Fowler 1994.
7. Gayon and Zallen 1998.
8. Fowler 1994, 17.
9. On the history of free seed distribution in the United States, see Kloppenburg 2004; Cooke 2002.
10. Kloppenburg 2004, 63–64.
11. Hightower 1973.
12. Cooke 2002, 531.
13. Fowler 1994, 21; Cooke 2002, 532.
14. Cooke 2002, 541.
15. Fowler 1994, 45.
16. Walters 1997, 67.
17. Steele 1982.
18. Duvick 1998, 193.
19. Fowler 1994, 40.
20. Fitzgerald 1990; Bogue 1983.
21. Culver and Hyde 2000, 13.
22. Crabb 1947.
23. Kingsbury 2009.
24. See Fitzgerald 1990, 29; Kloppenburg 2004; Duvick 1998.
25. Crabb 1947.
26. Kloppenburg 2004.
27. Quoted in Kloppenburg 2004, 99.
28. Fitzgerald 1990131; Walters 1997.

29. See Crabb 1947, 25, 67.
30. On Holbert's role in the hybridization story, see Crabb 1947; Fitzgerald 1990.
31. Fitzgerald 1990, 165.
32. Crabb 1947, 123.
33. Crabb 1947.
34. Duvick 1998.
35. Crabb 1947.
36. Duvick 1998.
37. Crabb 1947.
38. Fitzgerald 1990.
39. Crabb 1947, 98–99.
40. Crabb 1947; Kloppenburg 2004.
41. Fernandez-Cornejo 2004.
42. Duvick 1998; Fitzgerald 1990.
43. Fernandez Cornejo 2004, 25.
44. Bogue 1983, 22; Fitzgerald 1990, 189.
45. Fitzgerald 1990, 126; on yield consequences of hybrids; see also Fitzgerald 1993.
46. Fitzgerald, 1993, 339.
47. Bogue 1983, 9–10; Weber 2018, 387.
48. Culver and Hyde 2000; Sutch 2008, 15.
49. Weber 2018.
50. Fitzgerald 1990, 162.
51. Steele 1982.
52. Duvick 1998; Fitzgerald 1990.
53. Bogue 1983; Fitzgerald 1990.
54. Fitzgerald 1990.
55. Fitzgerald 1990; Bosso 1988.
56. Duvick 1998, 202–203.
57. US Department of Agriculture (USDA), 1936.
58. Wallace, in USDA, 1936.
59. Sutch 2008, 16.
60. Pegg 1988, 109.
61. Byerlee 2020, 116–118.
62. See Duvick 1999; Fernandez-Cornejo 2004.
63. Crabb 1947.

64. Kloppenburg 2004, 108–110.
65. Kloppenburg 2004, 110.
66. Mt. Pleasant and Burt 2010.
67. Fitzgerald 1993, 338.
68. Fitzgerald 1990, 189.
69. Fowler 1994, 61–62.
70. Fitzgerald 1993, 325; Stone 2007.
71. Fitzgerald 1993, 338.
72. Harland and Martini 1936; Landauer 1945.
73. Curry 2017b.
74. Clark 1954; Curry 2017a.
75. Clark 1954, 78.
76. Mangelsdorf, 1951, 44.
77. Clark 1954, 79.
78. Clark 1956, 194. See also Curry 2017a.
79. Curry 2017b, 3.
80. Kloppenburg 2004; Fitzgerald 1990.

CHAPTER 5

1. On this early history of pest control, see Bozzini 2017; Smith and Secoy 1975; Boardman 1986; Davies et al. 2007.
2. Johnson 1935; Achilladelis et al 1987.
3. Watson 2018, 9.
4. Boardman 1986, 30.
5. Dunlap 1981.
6. Bosso 1988, 28.
7. León Araya 2023.
8. Whorton 1974, 6; Dunlap 1981, 18.
9. Gachelin et al. 2018.
10. Whitaker 1974; Boardman 1986.
11. Whorton 1974, 22–24.
12. Timmons 2005.
13. Achilladelis et al. 1987.
14. MacIntyre 1987, 546; Johnson 1935.
15. Whorton 1974, 16.
16. Russell 1993, 60.
17. Whitaker 1974.

18. MacIntyre 1987; Dunlap 1981, 20.
19. Dunlap 1981.
20. See McWilliams 2008; Russell 1993.
21. See also Dunlap 1981; Russell 1993; McWilliams 2008.
22. See Russell 2001, 20; Dunlap 1981; McWilliams 2008.
23. Bosso 1988, 32.
24. Whorton 1974, 71–72.
25. Whittaker 1974, 64; Elmore 2021.
26. Russell 1993, 61–62.
27. Bosso 1988, 48.
28. Whitaker 1974, 66; Bosso 1988.
29. See Whitaker 1974, 80; Perkins 1982, 3; MacIntyre 1987.
30. Bosso 1988, 28; Whorton 1974, 29–31.
31. McWilliams 2008, 483.
32. Russell 1993; Palladino 1996; McWilliams 2008.
33. Russell 1993.
34. Dunlap 1981, 36–37.
35. Perkins 1982, 5.
36. Elmore 2021, 71.
37. Bosso 1988; Shattuck 2021.
38. Boardman 1986, 30.
39. Achilladelis et al. 1987, 181; Jarman and Ballschmiter 2012.
40. Chandler 1962, 81.
41. Cerveaux 2013.
42. Corteva Agricscience website, 2023, Our History, https://www.corteva.com/who-we-are/our-history.html; E.I. du Pont de Nemours & Company 1956.
43. Lamphere and East 2017, 79.
44. Russell 1993, 209.
45. Chandler 1962, 393; Perkins 1982, 13.
46. Achilladelis et al. 1987, 181; Russell 2001, 82. Rohm and Haas was purchased by Dow Chemical in 2008.
47. Whitaker 1974.
48. Achilladelis et al. 1987, 181.
49. Russell 1993, 240–241.
50. Quoted in Russell 2001, 83.
51. Berry-Cabán 2011; Dunlap 1981.
52. Jarman and Ballschmiter 2012.

53. Russell 1993, 373–374; Dunlap 1981, 61.
54. Perkins 1982, 13; Dunlap 1981, 73.
55. Russell 2001; Achilladelis et al. 1987.
56. Elmore 2021, 72; Eichers and Szmedra 1990.
57. Perkins 1978, 185–186; Bosso 1988.
58. Elmore 2021, 52.
59. MacIntyre 1987.
60. Perkins 1982, 13.
61. Gay 2012; Achilladelis et al. 1987.
62. Perkins 1982, 14; Lamphere and East 2017, 79.
63. Braunholtz 1982, 484.
64. Bosso 1988, 31, 63.
65. Bosso 1988, 53–54; Whitaker 1974, 423.
66. Bosso 1988, 58–60.
67. Gunter and Harris 1998.
68. Dunlap 1978.
69. Cottam and Higgins 1946.
70. Dunlap 1981, 64–66.
71. Dunlap 1981, 71–74.
72. Vandeman 1995.
73. Vandeman 1995, 55; Flint and Van den Bosch 1981, 70.
74. Lindquist and Wilson 1948.
75. MacIntyre 1987, 22; Perkins 1982, 11.
76. Flint and Van den Bosch 1981, 74.
77. Perkins 1982, 21.
78. Flint and Van den Bosch 1981, 76.
79. MacIntyre 1987, 552.
80. Bosso 1988, 31; Perkins 1982, 22.

CHAPTER 6

1. Magrini et al. 2016; Dosi 1982, 158.
2. Arthur 1989.
3. Cesere at al. 2014.
4. Dosi et al. 1982.
5. Magrini et al. 2016; Gowdy et al. 2016; Berkhout 2005.
6. Valorinta et al. 2011.

7. Cecere et al. 2014; Seto et al. 2016, 428.
8. Dosi 1982, 158; Cecere et al. 2014.
9. On pesticides, see Cowan and Gunby 1996; Hüesker and Lepenies 2022; Hammond Wagner et al. 2016. On machinery, see Sutherland et al. 2012. On fertilizer, see Struckman 2020; Secchi 2020. On alternative agriculture, see Vanloquerin and Baret 2009; Gowdy and Baveye 2019; Magrini et al. 2019.
10. Fitzgerald 2003, 99.
11. Bogue 1983, 6.
12. Bogue 1983, 11; Fitzgerald 1990.
13. Duvick 1998, 203; Sutch 2008, 20.
14. Kloppenburg 2004, 118.
15. Fitzgerald 2003, 14.
16. Kloppenburg 2004, 119.
17. Hamilton 2014.
18. Huffman and Evenson 2001.
19. Lacy et al. 2021.
20. Clapp 2012; Friedmann 1993; Friedmann and McMichael 1989.
21. USDA 1940, 4.
22. USDA 1940, 82.
23. Broehl 1984; Leibenluft 1981.
24. Gilpin 1975, 17.
25. Broehl 1984, 597, 627–628.
26. Steele 1982.
27. Bugow 2020.
28. See Perkins 1997, 106; Kinkela 2011, 64; Cullather 2010.
29. Perkins 1997, 106; Curry 2022, 56.
30. Perkins 1997; Kinkela 2011, 64.
31. Kinkela 2011, 68.
32. See Cullather 2010.
33. Cullather 2010; Shiva 1991; Perkins 1997.
34. Turner 1972, 14.
35. Shiva 1991, 40–42.
36. Danaher 1989, 30–31.
37. Brown, 1970, 59.
38. Melo and Yost, 1970, 10.
39. Dahlberg 1979, 120.

40. Cleaver 1972, 180.
41. Faust 2020, 6.
42. Dahlberg 1979, 110.
43. Cleaver 1972; Dahlberg 1979, 114–115.
44. Ahmed, 1987, 67.
45. Melo and Yost 1970.
46. Cleaver 1972, 80; Bugow 2020.
47. FAO Archives.
48. Turner 1972, 1973.
49. Jacoby, 1975, 96.
50. Melo and Yost 1970, 10; Turner 1973, 149.
51. Bugow 2020, 119.
52. Ahmed 1975, 19.
53. Hendra 1987.
54. Turner 1972, 18.
55. Bugow 2020, 94.
56. Pray and Nagarajan 2014, 147; Brown 1970, 58.
57. Turner 1972.
58. Bugow 2020, 47.
59. FAO Archives.
60. Brown 1970, 60.
61. Kinkela 2011, 77–78.
62. FAO Archives.
63. Turner 1972, 18.
64. Faust 2020, 10–13.
65. Morehouse 1993.
66. UN 1974, 4.
67. UN 1974.
68. Markham 1958.
69. Lamer 1957, which filled over seven hundred pages.
70. Schwartzman 1970.
71. Barber 1971.
72. Palmer 1972, 65–66.
73. Broehl 1984.
74. Barber 1971; Schwartzman 1970.
75. Barber 1971.

NOTES

76. Broehl 1984, 810.
77. Markham 1958.
78. Markham 1958, 72; Paul et al. 1977, 7; Lyden 1978.
79. Paul et al. 1977, 4.
80. Duvick 1998.
81. Braunholtz 1982, 480.
82. For this wider history, see e.g., Shiva 1991; Dahlberg 1979; Jacoby 1975; Cleaver 1972; Patel 2013.
83. Wharton 1969, 467.
84. Shiva 1991; Wharton 1969; Cleaver 1972, 185.
85. Cleaver 1972.
86. Jacoby 1975, 95.
87. Shiva 1991, 58; Cleaver 1972, 184; Wharton 1969, 468; Palmer 1972, 59.
88. Dinham 1993.
89. Cleaver 1972, 184; Franke 1974, 45.
90. Davis 2019.
91. Carson 1962.
92. Borlaug 1972, 21.
93. Kinkela 2005.
94. Morehouse 1993.
95. Broughton 2005.

CHAPTER 7

1. Rothschild 1976; Clapp 2020.
2. Mah 1971; Dong et al. 1995.
3. Barnett 2000, 370; Clapp 2012.
4. Clapp 2020.
5. Barnett 2000, 371.
6. Quoted in Thompson 2010.
7. Lovec 2018.
8. Henderson et al. 2011.
9. Greenhouse 1984a.
10. Barnett 2000, 374.
11. Estenson 1987, 621.
12. Barnett 2000, 375.
13. Henderson et al. 2011; Stam and Dixon 2004.

14. Leibenluft 1981, 117.
15. Armour 1963.
16. Armour 1963; Thomas 1972.
17. Broehl 1984.
18. Potts 1987.
19. Greenhouse 1984a.
20. Charlier 1984.
21. Quoted in Greenhouse 1984b.
22. O'Connor 1984.
23. Phillips 1986.
24. Kotlowitz et al. 1985.
25. Quoted in Bertin 1985.
26. Marsh 1985.
27. Charlier 1984.
28. Marsh 1985.
29. *Wall Street Journal* 1984a, 1984b.
30. Moskal 1985.
31. Nag 1985.
32. O'Connor 1984.
33. Kubota Virtual Museum website: https://www.kubota.com/museum/history/1973_1985.html.
34. Waddell 1985.
35. Roger 1985; Fusaro 1989.
36. US Senate 2001.
37. Potts 1987.
38. Rufo 1980, 4.
39. Leibenluft 1981, 11.
40. Larson 1970; Crittenden 1975.
41. Reed 1974.
42. Lie 2008.
43. Freedman 1996.
44. Terra Industries 2002.
45. Rufo 1980, 4.
46. Laurenson 1990.
47. Freedman 1996.
48. Yara website: Our History: https://www.yara.com/this-is-yara/our-history/.
49. Milmo 1996.

50. De la Merced 2011.

51. Molot and Laux 1979.

52. Potash Corporation of Saskatchewan 1996.

53. Busse 2016.

54. Firn 2004.

55. Quoted in Laurenson 1990.

56. See Broehl 1984 for the 1980 figure; Kulick and Card 2022, 19, for the 2002 figure; and MacDonald 2017a for the 2012 figure.

57. US Senate 2001.

58. Fuglie et al. 2011.

59. Freedman 1996.

60. Barboza 1999; USDA 1998; Reed 1975.

61. Reed 1974.

62. *New York Times* 1977.

63. Gowers 1984.

64. USDA 1996, 18.

65. Barboza 1999; Schwartz and Gurwitz 2018.

66. Bork 1978.

67. Wu 2018, 89.

68. Oreskes and Conway 2023, 258.

69. Khan 2017; Wu 2018.

70. MacDonald et al. 2013.

71. Huffman and Evenson 2001.

72. MacDonald et al. 2013, 23.

73. Quoted in Blumenthal 1977.

74. Ferguson 2021.

75. Taylor 2018, 53.

76. Hamza and Anderson 2005.

77. Smil 2011, 12–13.

78. IATP and GRAIN 2022.

79. Browne 1988.

80. Constance 2010, 51.

81. Kemesiz 1990, 6.

82. Open Secrets website: Agribusiness Lobbying, 2022, https://www.opensecrets.org/industries/lobbying.php?ind=A.

83. See Browne 1988; Clapp and Fuchs 2009.

CHAPTER 8

1. Kimle and Hayenga 1993, 19.
2. Lesser 1999, 56; see also Leibenluft 1981.
3. Juma 1989, 83; Rufo 1980; Mooney 1980.
4. Fowler and Mooney 1990.
5. Kimle and Hayenga 1993, 19.
6. See US Congress 1991; Juma 1989, 83 3.
7. Davis 2019.
8. Webster 1969.
9. Mooney 1980.
10. Achilladelis et al. 1987, 185; Rufo 1980, 21.
11. Rufo 1980, 21.
12. ICF 1980, 67; Leibenluft 1981, 52.
13. Juma 1989, 82.
14. Rufo 1980, 21; Achilladelis 1987, 185.
15. ICF 1980, 48–49.
16. Moretti 2006, 9.
17. Fowler and Mooney 1990, 128–129.
18. Sanderson 2017.
19. Kloppenburg 2004, 11.
20. US Congress 1991, 110; Fernandez Cornejo 2004, 26.
21. Schenkelaars et al. 2011, 16; Leibenluft 1981, 99.
22. Leibenluft 1981, 100.
23. Fowler and Mooney 1990, 129.
24. Mooney 1980, 56; Fowler and Mooney 1990, 118.
25. Mooney 1980, 56–57.
26. Hamilton and D'Ippolito 2022.
27. Kilman and Warren 1999; Kilman 1999.
28. Reuters 2007.
29. Howard 2009.
30. Fuglie et al. 2011, 16. Industry began to refer to these chemicals as "crop protection" in this period.
31. Schenkelaars et al., 2011, 17.
32. Kloppenburg 2004.
33. Schenkelaars et al. 2011, 25; Mooney 2017, 5.
34. Schenkelaars et al. 2011, 17.

35. Clapp 2021b.
36. ISAAA 2004.
37. ISAAA 2004.
38. Ollinger and Pope 1995, 56.
39. Clapp 2021b.
40. Fernandez-Cornejo and Just 2007.
41. Howard 2015, 2.
42. Wield et al. 2010; Howard 2016.
43. Elmore 2021, 177.
44. Dupraz 2012, 223.
45. Howard 2016, 84.
46. Grushkin 2013.
47. Howard 2015, 2009.
48. Clapp 2021b.
49. Leibenluft 1981, 112.
50. US Senate 2001; Cornejo-Fernandez 2004, 30.
51. See Leibenluft 1981, 64; ICF 1980, 16; Leibenluft, 1981, 69; US Department of Commerce 2006, 33.
52. Friends of the Earth 2017; Howard 2009.
53. Howard 2009.
54. Bryant et al. 2016, 12; Maisashvili et al. 2016; On patent thickets, see Schimmelpfennig 2004.
55. Barboza 2003; Barboza 2004a.
56. Barboza 2004b.
57. Barboza 2001.
58. Gillam 2017; Khan 2013.
59. King 2001.
60. Robertson 2000.
61. Fuglie et al. 2011, 13.
62. Shi et al. 2010, 2011; Stiegert et al 2010; Torshizi and Clapp 2021.
63. Howard 2009, 2015.
64. Luby and Goldman 2016.
65. Howard 2016, 85.
66. Elmore 2021, 224.
67. ETC Group 2013.
68. ISAAA 2014.

69. Benbrook 2016.
70. Shattuck et al. 2023.
71. Leguizamón 2016.
72. Clapp 2021.
73. Richmond 2018.
74. Brown et al. 2016.
75. Fuglie 2016, 2011; Schimmelpfennig 2004.
76. Fuglie et al. 2018.
77. Ollinger and Fernandez-Cornejo 1998, 141.
78. Dayan 2019.
79. Fuglie et al. 2011, 49.
80. Rüegg et al. 2006, 272.
81. Duke 2012.
82. Fuglie et al. 2011.
83. Stone 2007, 20.
84. Marskak et al. 2021.
85. Glover 2010; Khan 2013.
86. Newell and Mackenzie 2004; Sell 2009.
87. Food and Water Watch 2010.
88. Newell 2003, 62.
89. Khan 2013.
90. Clapp 2018.
91. Jansen 2017; Griesse 2007.
92. Glover 2007, 855.
93. Quoted in Lamphere and East 2017, 81.
94. Krimsky and Gillam 2018; McHenry 2018.

CHAPTER 9

1. Ecklecamp 2012.
2. Terazono et al. 2015.
3. See Philpott 2015; Enoch 2015.
4. Dow 2016.
5. Matthews et al. 2016.
6. On this deal, see Fontanella-Khan and Massoudi 2016; Cookson 2016a.
7. Quoted in Chazan 2016a.

8. BASF. BASF Signs Agreement to Acquire Significant Parts of Bayer's Seed and Non-Selective Herbicide Businesses. News release, October 13, 2017, https://www.basf.com/global/en/media/news-releases/2017/10/p-17-336.html.
9. ETC Group 2015.
10. Wiggerthale 2021.
11. McMichael 2009.
12. McMichael 2020.
13. Clapp 2014.
14. Bunge 2019.
15. ETC Group 2015.
16. Bunge 2016.
17. Clapp 2018.
18. Fontanella-Khan and Wilson 2016.
19. See Terazono 2013; Wilson 2013
20. Clapp and Isakson 2018.
21. Ferreira et al. 2009; Froud et al. 2000.
22. Noel 2016.
23. Mordock 2016.
24. Terazono et al. 2016.
25. George and Lorsch 2014.
26. Ferreira et al. 2009.
27. Crooks 2015.
28. Benoit 2015.
29. Quoted in Gandel 2016.
30. Massoudi and Fontanella-Khan 2015.
31. Terazono 2015.
32. Koven 2015.
33. Chazan 2016b.
34. Fontanella-Khan and Massoudi 2015.
35. On the financing of these deals, see Kynge et al. 2016; Massoudi, Fontanella-Khan and Chazan 2016; Massoudi, Weinland, Atkins, Donnan, and Jopson 2016.
36. Fichtner et al. 2017; Azar et al. 2016; Schmalz 2018.
37. Schmalz 2018; Azar et al. 2016; Lianos et al. 2020.
38. Brooks et al. 2018; Schmalz 2018.
39. Clapp 2019; Torshizi and Clapp 2021.
40. S&P Capital IQ data, at https://www.capitaliq.com.

41. Clapp 2018.
42. ETC Group 2016.
43. ETC Group 2016.
44. Mitchell et al. 2016.
45. Kynge et al. 2016.
46. McCullough 2020.
47. Maisashvili et al. 2016; ETC Group 2015.
48. Howard 2009.
49. Hayley 2016.
50. Zhang et al. 2018; Bartkowski et al. 2018. CRISPR is the commonly used term for the genome editing technique clustered regularly interspaced short palindromic repeats sequences and associated enzymes. Another method known as TALEN refers to transcription activator-like effector nucleases.
51. IHS Markit 2019, 13; Montenegro de Wit 2020; Clapp and Ruder 2020.
52. Brinegar et al. 2017; Cotter and Perls 2018.
53. Canadian Biotechnology Action Network 2022.
54. Cohen 2019; Sender 2019.
55. Phillips 2020.
56. Tita and Bunge 2022.
57. CNH 2020. CNH Industrial Acquires a Minority Stake in Zasso Group AG. CNH Industrial Newsroom: https://media.cnhindustrial.com/EMEA/CNH-INDUSTRIAL-CORPORATE/cnh-industrial-acquires-a-minority-stake-in-zasso-group-ag/s/cd9fa2f1-cabc-4633-be07-48d085583815.
58. AGCO 2022. AGCO Acquires JCA Industries. May 2, https://news.agcocorp.com/news/agco-acquires-jca-industries.
59. Accenture 2022. Kubota and Accenture Establish Joint Venture for a More Sustainable Society, August 30, https://newsroom.accenture.com/news/kubota-and-accenture-establish-joint-venture-for-a-more-sustainable-society.htm.
60. Clapp and Ruder 2020; Bronson 2022.
61. Bayer 2016. Bayer and Monsanto to Create a Global Leader in Agriculture. September 14, https://www.bayer.com/sites/default/files/2020-11/Ad-hoc_2016-09-14_e.pdf; Chazan 2016a.
62. Burwood-Taylor 2016.
63. Khan 2017; Wu 2018.
64. Kwoka 2017.
65. Khan 2017.
66. Abbott and Weinstein 2010.
67. Damro and Guay 2012.

CHAPTER 10

1. Biden 2021; USDA 2022a.
2. Blake, Cassels, and Graydon 2021.
3. See Eeckhout 2021.
4. De Loecker et al. 2021.
5. Naldi and Flamini 2014.
6. MacDonald 2017b.
7. IPES-Food 2017; ETC Group 2015, 2019; OECD 2018.
8. On pesticides, see Statista 2019 *Market Share of Five Largest Agricultural Chemical Companies Worldwide as of 2018*, https://www.statista.com/statistics/950490/market-share-largest-agrochemical-companies-worldwide/; ETC Group 2022. On seeds, see IHS Markit 2019; IHS Markit 2021 and 2021; ETC Group 2022.
9. Fuglie et al. 2012, 2.
10. Bekkerman et al. 2020, 1; Kreisle 2020; Farm Action 2022, 2; Open Markets Institute 2022.
11. ETC Group 2022, 69.
12. Tita and Bunge 2022.
13. Shoham 2020; Fuglie et al. 2011. See also Malhotra 2022.
14. MacDonald, Dong, and Fuglie 2023,11.
15. MacDonald, Dong, and Fugile 2023, 14.
16. OECD 2018, 120–123.
17. OECD 2018, 124.
18. Azar et al. 2016.
19. Clapp 2019; Torshizi and Clapp 2021; Lianos et al. 2020; Wood et al. 2021; ETC Group 2022.
20. De Loecker and Eeckhout 2021. See also De Loecker et al. 2020.
21. Eeckhout 2021.
22. American Antitrust Institute 2022, 4.
23. USDA 2023a, 43.
24. Canadian Competition Bureau 2018.
25. USDA 2023a, 47.
26. AAI 2022, 5.
27. Bryant et al. 2016.
28. Stiegert et al. 2010; Shi et al. 2010; Torshizi and Clapp 2021.
29. OECD 2018.
30. American Antitrust Institute 2022, 9.
31. USDA 2023a, 48.

32. Cape Law Firm PLC 2022, 3.
33. Montenegro de Wit 2020.
34. Contreras and Sherkow 2017, 700.
35. Egelie et al. 2016.
36. Canadian Biotechnology Action Network 2022, 6.
37. Robinson 2021, 43.
38. Fatka 2021; Kelloway 2021a.
39. Guenther 2018.
40. Reported in Fatka 2021.
41. AgNews 2021.
42. Canadian Competition Bureau, 2022.
43. Thomas 2022.
44. Kelloway 2022.
45. Quoted in FTC 2022.
46. Montello 2020.
47. Mirr 2020, 2397.
48. Mirr 2020.
49. Larew 2023.
50. Stone 2022b; Fitzgerald 1993.
51. Abraham 2023.
52. Neely 2022.
53. Abraham 2023.
54. USDA 2022d.
55. Quoted in USDA 2022e.
56. Wilson et al. 2013.
57. Taylor and Moss 2013, 9.
58. Buthelezi et al. 2023.
59. USDA 2022c.
60. IATP and GRAIN 2023.
61. Quinn 2022; Farm Action et al. 2022.
62. USDA 2022c.
63. Farm Action et al. 2022, 4.
64. Farm Action et al. 2022, 5.
65. See Nutrien 2021, 2022, 2023.
66. Cordero 2022.
67. Cited in Farm Action et al. 2022, 5.

68. Farm Action et al. 2022, 4–5.
69. Nutrien 2021.
70. Bayer 2023.
71. Bayer 2023.
72. S&P data; Syngenta 2023.
73. Corteva Agriscience 2023.
74. Deere 2023.
75. USDA 2023b.
76. IPES-Food, 2017, 49.
77. Taylor and Moss 2013, 68.
78. Buthelezi et al. 2023; Malpass 2022; IPES-Food 2023a.
79. Bogmans et al. 2022.
80. Emont 2022; USDA 2022b.
81. FAO et al. 2022.
82. Kelloway 2019.
83. Montenegro de Wit 2020.
84. Taylor and Moss 2013.
85. Ennis et al. 2019; Kurz 2023.
86. Eeckhout 2021, 74.

CHAPTER 11

1. Bayer and Monsanto 2016.
2. Clancey et al. 2016.
3. Pardey et al. 2016, 301.
4. Chai et al. 2019, 1.
5. Fuglie et al. 2018, 44.
6. King et al. 2012; Anderson et al. 2017.
7. IPES-Food 2017.
8. Schumpeter 1942.
9. Baker 2007; Gilbert 2006.
10. Schumpeter 1942, 82.
11. Arrow 1962.
12. Gilbert 2006, 165.
13. Gilbert 2006, 190.
14. Fuglie et al. 2011, 15.
15. Quoted in Bunge 2019.

16. Grant 2016.
17. Casey and Milford 2015.
18. Buck 2019.
19. *Financial Times* 2016.
20. Fuglie et al. 2017, 539.
21. Powell 2016.
22. AAI 2022, 10.
23. Bonny 2016.
24. Vieira et al. 2020.
25. Benbrook 2016; Clapp 2021b; Shattuck 2021.
26. AAI et al. 2016, 7.
27. Appleby 2005; Duke 2012; Dayan 2019.
28. Duke 2012.
29. Dow 2016.
30. Phillips McDougall 2013.
31. AAI 2022.
32. Quoted in Cookson 2016b.
33. Fuglie et al. 2017, 540.
34. Pham and Stack 2018, 128.
35. John Deere Operations Center website: https://www.deere.com/en/technology-products/precision-ag-technology/operations-center/features/.
36. John Deere Announces Strategic Partnership with SpaceX to Expand Rural Connectivity to Farmers through Satellite Communications, January 16, 2024, https://www.deere.ca/en/news/all-news/john-deere-partnership-with-spacex/.
37. On platform power, see Fox 2019; Khan 2017.
38. See Vincent 2022; Knight 2022.
39. McCormick 1931, 224–225.
40. Clapp and Ruder 2020. See also Rotz et al. 2019.
41. Tita and Bunge 2022.
42. Lajoie-O'Malley et al. 2020; Clapp and Ruder 2020; Carolan 2020; Prause et al. 2021.
43. Rotz et al. 2019; Klerkx et al. 2019; Bronson 2022.
44. On these various issues, see, for example, Clapp and Ruder 2020; Baldé et al. 2017; Gupta et al. 2024; Saenko 2023.
45. Carolan 2020, 1048.
46. Hackfort 2021, 11; Stone 2022b.
47. Quoted in Buck 2019.

48. Bronson 2022; Fraser 2019.
49. Pham and Stack 2018; Rotz et al. 2019, 8–10.
50. Carbonell 2016; Bronson 2019; Rose and Chilvers 2018.
51. Duncan et al. 2022; Fraser 2019.
52. Tita and Bunge 2022.
53. Deere 2023, 3.
54. Bayer Highlights Advancements of Agriculture Industry's Most Prolific R&D Pipeline, February 16, 2022. https://www.bayer.com/media/en-us/bayer-highlights-advancements-of-agriculture-industrys-most-prolific-rd-pipeline/.
55. Abdulai 2022.
56. Tsan et al. 2019.
57. Montenegro de Wit 2020.
58. Henry 2020; Zhang et al. 2018; Pixley et al. 2019.
59. Cotter and Perls 2018.
60. Steinwand and Ronald 2020; Karavolias et al. 2021.
61. Davis and Frisvold 2017; Bain et al. 2017; Bonny 2016.
62. Cotter and Perls 2018; Mooney 2018.
63. Neve 2018; ETC Group and Heinrich Böll Foundation 2018.
64. Berry 2012.
65. Sun et al. 2022.
66. Illies 2016, 100.
67. See Kelloway 2021b; Everhart 2023, 34.
68. Plume and Nickel 2021.
69. Quoted in Gullickson 2021.
70. Plume and Nickel 2021.
71. National Farmers Union (Canada) 2021, 1.
72. Quoted in Plume and Nickel 2021.
73. Open Markets Institute and Friends of the Earth 2022, 2.
74. Bayer website: https://www.bayer.com/en/agriculture/carbon-program-united-states.
75. Corteva Agriscience website: https://www.corteva.us/products-and-solutions/digital-solutions/carbon.html.
76. Open Markets Institute and Friends of the Earth 2023, 12.
77. Quoted in Plume and Nickel 2021.
78. Gullickson 2021.
79. Newell and Taylor 2018, 118; Thomas 2020.
80. Clapp 2021b; Benbrook 2016; Shattuck 2021.

81. Kelloway 2021b.
82. Duncan et al. 2022.
83. Plume 2022.
84. Rotz et al. 2019; Bronson 2022.
85. Friends of the Earth 2022, 1.
86. Open Markets Institute and Friends of the Earth 2023, 11.
87. Torretta et al. 2018.
88. Myers et al. 2016; Xu et al. 2019; Noori et al. 2018.
89. CFIA 2017.
90. Solomon 2020; Grau et al. 2022; Gillam 2022.
91. Schütte et al. 2017.
92. Hébert et al. 2019.
93. For the 2017 figure, see S&P Global: https://www.spglobal.com/commodityinsights/en/ci/research-analysis/the-glyphosate-market-in-2018.html; for the 2022 figure, see Research Nester: https://www.globenewswire.com/en/news-release/2023/07/06/2700311/0/en/Glyphosate-Market-revenue-to-cross-USD-18-Billion-by-2035-says-Research-Nester.html.
94. Vanloqueren and Baret 2009.

CHAPTER 12

1. Lacy-Nichols et al. 2022.
2. Nestle 2007.
3. Kaan and Liese, 2010.
4. Fuchs 2005.
5. Fuchs 2005; Strange 1988.
6. Falkner 2008; Nestle 2007. Fuchs 2005; Clapp and Fuchs 2009.
7. Data at Open Secrets website: Agribusiness: Lobbying, 2022: https://www.opensecrets.org/industries/lobbying.php?ind=A.
8. Data at LobbyFacts website: https://www.lobbyfacts.eu/.
9. Data at Office of the Commissioner of Lobbying of Canada, Registry of Lobbyists: https://lobbycanada.gc.ca/app/secure/ocl/lrs/do/guest.
10. Gerbet 2023.
11. Sharratt 2023.
12. Friends of the Earth Europe 2022.
13. Bollmohr and Haffmans 2022.
14. Lerner 2021.
15. Data at Open Secrets website: https://www.opensecrets.org.
16. Wilson 2018.

17. Herrera 2023.
18. Quoted in Malkin 2018.
19. WHO 2015.
20. Gillam 2019.
21. Monsanto 2017
22. Quoted in Foucart and Horel 2017.
23. International Agency for Research on Cancer 2018.
24. Foucart and Horel 2017.
25. Shochat and Fournier 2019.
26. Krimsky and Gillam 2018.
27. Quoted in Shochat and Fournier 2019.
28. See Krimsky and Gillam 2018.
29. Bayer 2018.
30. Tosun et al. 2019.
31. Benbrook 2019.
32. Shochat and Fournier 2019.
33. Nelson 2019.
34. Brzeziński 2024.
35. For a complete and updated list of jurisdictions with restrictions on glyphosate, see https://www.baumhedlundlaw.com/toxic-tort-law/monsanto-roundup-lawsuit/where-is-glyphosate-banned/.
36. Tanakasempipat 2020.
37. Gillam 2021.
38. Gillam 2023a.
39. See Wise 2023; Lawder 2023; Gillam and Hettinger 2024.
40. Cohen 2020.
41. Temple-West and Storbeck 2024.
42. Gillam 2023b.
43. European Union 2020.
44. Bremmer et al. 2021, 5.
45. Bremmer et al. 2021, 6
46. Quoted in Corporate Europe Observatory, 2022, 6.
47. Tremblay 2020.
48. CropLife documents, cited in Corporate Europe Observatory, 2022, 18–20.
49. Swissinfo 2022.
50. European Commission, Expert Group on the European Food Security Crisis Preparedness and Response Mechanism: https://ec.europa.eu/transparency/expert-groups

-register/screen/expert-groups/consult?lang=en&groupId=3829&fromMeetings=true&meetingId=38594. See also Carlile and Healy 2022.

51. Canada 2020.

52. Fawcett-Atkinson 2022.

53. See Fertilizer Canada, Stewardship, https://nutrientstewardship.org/4rs/.

54. Data at Office of the Commissioner of Lobbying of Canada, Registry of Lobbyists, https://lobbycanada.gc.ca/app/secure/ocl/lrs/do/guest.

55. Beer 2021.

56. Fawcett-Atkinson 2022.

57. Data at Open Secrets, https://www.opensecrets.org.

58. Fang 2022.

59. See Fang 2022; Quinn 2021; Open Markets 2022.

60. Mosaic 2021.

61. Hamann 2022.

62. Harris 2022.

63. Clayton 2022.

64. Swanson 2023.

65. Dogget 2021.

66. Fang 2022; Pratt 2023.

67. Corporate Europe Observatory 2019.

68. Tups and Dannenberg 2023.

69. Murray 2023.

70. Mirr 2020, 2395.

71. Montello 2020, 171.

72. PIRG Right to Repair website: https://pirg.org/campaigns/right-to-repair/. Repair Association website: https://www.repair.org/.

73. AEM 2018; Mirr 2020.

74. Quoted in Mirr, 2020, 14.

75. Biden 2021.

76. Gray 2022; Tester 2022.

77. AFBF and Deere 2023.

78. Glenna 2023.

79. AFBF 2023; AFBF and Deere 2023.

80. Quoted in Flowers 2023.

81. EU 2013.

82. EU 2022; Sajn 2022.

83. Government of India 2022.

84. Heppner 2022.
85. McKeon 2014; Prášková and Novotný 2021.
86. FAO 2020.
87. FAO and CropLife International 2020.
88. FAO 2020.
89. Quoted in Hruska 2021.
90. Alliance for Food Sovereignty in Africa et al. 2021; Pesticide Action Network et al. 2022.
91. Corporate Accountability and FIAN 2022, 11.
92. Pesticide Action Network North America 2022; Pesticide Action Network International et al. 2024.
93. Qu 2020.
94. Hruska 2021.
95. Pesticide Action Network et al. 2024.
96. Corporate Accountability and FIAN 2022.
97. Agrievolution Alliance website: https://www.agrievolution.com/about.
98. McMichael 2021; Canfield et al. 2021, 184; Gleckman 2023.
99. World Economic Forum website, Our Mission, https://www.weforum.org/about/world-economic-forum/.
100. IPES-Food 2023b.
101. CSIPM 2021.
102. Kalibata 2021.
103. Fakhri 2022; Fakhri et al. 2021; Clapp et al. 2021.
104. UNFSS 2021.
105. Cited in Clapp et al. 2021.
106. FAO 2022.
107. IPES-Food 2023b; Corporate Accountability and FIAN 2022.
108. Guttal 2021.
109. Clapp et al. 2022.

CHAPTER 13

1. IPES-Food 2021.
2. LeBaron 2020; Bartley 2021.
3. Pucker and King 2022.
4. Ruggie and Middleton 2019; Bryan 2023.
5. Stoller 2019, 456.
6. Clapp and Moseley 2020; Clapp 2022a; IPES-Food 2022a.

7. Canadian Competition Bureau 2023.
8. For example, Buthelezi et al. 2023.
9. Buthelezi et al. 2023.
10. Wu 2018; Meagher 2020; Kurz 2023.
11. Isakson 2014.
12. Lianos et al. 2020.
13. Khan 2018.
14. Khan 2018; Schlesinger 2021.
15. Khan 2017.
16. Biden 2021.
17. USDA 2023a.
18. See Canadian Competition Bureau, https://ised-isde.canada.ca/site/competition-bureau-canada/en/how-we-foster-competition/education-and-outreach/guide-december-2023-amendments-competition-act.
19. See US Federal Trade Commission, https://www.justice.gov/opa/pr/justice-department-and-federal-trade-commission-release-2023-merger-guidelines.
20. Barrett et al. 2020; Swinburn et al. 2019; IPES-Food 2023b.
21. Anderson 2008.
22. Corporate Accountability and FIAN 2022; IPES-Food 2023b.
23. Hamm 2021; Mares 2022; IPES Food 2023b.
24. Anderson et al. 2021; Wezel et al. 2020.
25. DeLonge et al. 2016; IPES-Food 2020.
26. Luby and Goldman 2016.
27. Wittman and James 2022; Anderson et al. 2021.
28. Calo et al. 2023.
29. Springmann et al. 2018.
30. Comer et al. 2019; Soumare et al. 2020.
31. Toyoda 2020.
32. Bronson 2022; Mehrabi et al. 2021.
33. Montenegro de Wit 2022.
34. Rosset 2008; Wittman et al. 2010; Anderson et al. 2021.
35. HLPE 2019; Wezel et al. 2020; Anderson et al. 2021.
36. IPES-Food 2022b.
37. George 1976, 289.
38. For a review and research agenda, see Clapp 2022b. Excellent work on these themes include Grabs and Carodenuto 2021; Grabs and Ponte 2019; Hendrickson et al. 2020; Howard 2016, 2019; Wood et al. 2001; and Stuckler and Nestle 2012.

REFERENCES

Abbott, Alden F., and Samuel N. Weinstein. 2010. The New U.S. Horizontal Merger Guidelines and International Competition Policy Convergence. *Antitrust* 25:39.

Abdulai, A. 2022. A New Green Revolution (GR) or Neoliberal Entrenchment in Agri-Food Systems? Exploring Narratives around Digital Agriculture (DA), Food Systems, and Development in Sub-Sahara Africa. *Journal of Development Studies* 58(8): 1588–1904.

Abraham, Roshan. 2023. Justice Department Says John Deere Should Let Farmers Repair Their Tractors. *Vice*, February 15. https://www.vice.com/en/article/n7zayb/doj-john-deere-right-to-repair-lawsuit.

Achilladelis, Basil, Albert Schwarzkopf, and Martin Cines. 1987. A Study of Innovation in the Pesticide Industry: Analysis of the Innovation Record of an Industrial Sector. *Research Policy* 16 (2–4): 175–212.

Adams, Walter, and James W. Brock. 2004. *The Bigness Complex: Industry, Labor and Government in the American Economy* (2nd ed.). Stanford: Stanford University Press.

AgNews. 2021. US: Lawsuit Alleges Crop Input Suppliers Collude in Pricing. January 21. https://news.agropages.com/News/NewsDetail—37857.htm.

Agricultural and Food Chemistry. 1957. TVA and the Fertilizer Industry. A Staff Report. *Journal of Agricultural and Food Chemistry* 5(8): 570–573.

Ahmed, Raisuddin. 1987. Structure and Dynamics of Fertilizer Subsidy: The Case of Bangladesh. *Food Policy* 12(1): 63–75.

Alliance for Food Sovereignty in Africa et al. 2021. Letter to FAO Director General Dongyu Qu. February 25. https://pan-international.org/wp-content/uploads/Latter-to-FAO-2021-February-25-en.pdf.

American Antitrust Institute (AAI). 2022. Comments of the American Antitrust Institute. Comments to USDA. https://www.antitrustinstitute.org/wp-content/uploads/2022/05/USDA-Comment-Agbiotech-6-10-22-REVISED-FINAL-FOR-AAI-WEBSITE.pdf.

American Antitrust Institute, Food & Water Watch, and National Farmers Union. 2016. Letter to U.S. Department of Justice Re: The Proposed Dow-DuPont Merger. May 31. https://www.antitrustinstitute.org/wp-content/uploads/2018/08/AAI-FWW-NFU_Dow-Dupont_5.31.16_0.pdf.

American Farm Bureau Federation. 2023. AFBF Signs Right to Repair Memorandum of Understanding with John Deere. January 8. https://www.fb.org/news-release/afbf-signs-right-to-repair-memorandum-of-understanding-with-john-deere.

American Farm Bureau Federation and John Deere. 2023. Memorandum of Understanding. https://www.fb.org/files/AFBF_John_Deere_MOU.pdf.

Anderson, C. Leigh, Travis W. Reynolds, Pierre Biscaye, and Matthew Fowle. 2017. Policy and Economic Considerations for Global Public Goods Provision: Agricultural and Health R&D Funding from the Funding from the Private, Public, and Philanthropic Sectors. Paper prepared for presentation at the 21st ICABR Conference "Bioeconomy in Transition: New Players and New Tools," University of California, Berkeley, May 31–June 2.

Anderson, Colin Ray, Janneke Bruil, M. Jahi Chappell, Csilla Kiss, and Michel Patrick Pimbert. 2021. *Agroecology Now!: Transformations towards More Just and Sustainable Food Systems*. Cham: Springer.

Anderson, Molly. 2008. Rights-Based Food Systems and the Goals of Food Systems Reform. *Agriculture and Human Values* 25(4): 593–608.

Appleby, Arnold P. 2005. A History of Weed Control in the United States and Canada—A Sequel. *Weed Science* 53(6): 762–768.

Armour, Lawrence A. 1963. Two Fat Years in a Row: That's the Cheery Prospect for Makers of Farm Equipment. *Barron's National Business and Financial Weekly* 43(7), February 18.

Arrow, Kenneth. 1962. "Economic Welfare and the Allocation of Resources to Invention." In *The Rate and Direction of Inventive Activity: Economic and Social Factors*, edited by National Bureau of Economic Research, 609–626. Princeton, NJ: Universities-National Bureau Committee.

Arthur, W. Brian. 1989. Competing Technologies, Increasing Returns, and Lock-In by Historical Events. *Economic Journal* 99(394): 116–131.

Association of Equipment Manufacturers. 2018. AEM, EDA Announce Statement of Principles on "Right to Repair." February 1. https://www.aem.org/news/aem-eda-announce-statement-of-principles-on-right-to-repair.

Atkinson, Robert D., and Michael Lind. 2018. Is Big Business Really That Bad? *Atlantic*, March 9. https://www.theatlantic.com/magazine/archive/2018/04/learning-to-love-big-business/554096/.

Azar, José, Martin Schmalz, and Isabel Tecu. 2016. *Anti-Competitive Effects of Common Ownership*. Ross School of Business paper 1235. https://papers.ssrn.com/sol3/papers2.cfm?abstract_id=2427345.

Bain, Carmen, Theresa Selfa, Tamera Dandachi, and Sara Velardi. 2017. "'Superweeds" or "Survivors"? Framing the Problem of Glyphosate Resistant Weeds and Genetically Engineered Crops. *Journal of Rural Studies* 51: 211–221.

Baker, Jonathan. 2007. Beyond Schumpeter vs. Arrow: How Antitrust Fosters Innovation. *Antitrust Law Journal* 74.

Baldé, Cornelis P., Vanessa Forti, Vanessa Gray, Ruediger Kuehr, and Paul Stegmann. 2017. *The Global E-Waste Monitor 2017: Quantities, Flows, and Resources*. http://collections.unu.edu/view/UNU:6341.

Balfour, Eve. 1943. *The Living Soil*. London: Faber and Faber.

Barber, Clarence. 1971. *Report of the Royal Commission on Farm Machinery*. Ottawa: Information Canada.

Barboza, David. 1999. Is the Sun Setting on Farmers? *New York Times*, November 28. https://www.nytimes.com/1999/11/28/business/is-the-sun-setting-on-farmers.html.

Barboza, David. 2001. The Power of Roundup; A Weed Killer Is a Block for Monsanto Build On, *New York Times*, August 2.

Barboza, David. 2003. Judge Rejects Class Action against Seed Producers. *New York Times*, October 2.

Barboza, David. 2004a. Bias Issue Arises for Monsanto Case Judge. *New York Times*, January 9.

Barboza, David. 2004b. Questions Seen on Seed Prices Set in the 90's. *New York Times*, January 6.

Barnett, Barry J. 2000. The U.S. Farm Financial Crisis of the 1980s. *Agricultural History* 74(2): 366–380.

Barrett, Christopher B., Tim G. Benton, Karen A. Cooper, Jessica Fanzo, Rikin Gandhi, Mario Herrero, and Steven James. 2020. Bundling Innovations to Transform Agri-Food Systems. *Nature Sustainability* 3(12): 974–976.

Bartkowski, Bartosz, Insa Theesfeld, Frauke Pirscher, and Johannes Timaeus. 2018. Snipping Around for Food: Economic, Ethical and Policy Implications of CRISPR/Cas Genome Editing. *Geoforum* 96: 172–180.

Bartley, Tim. 2021. Power and the Practice of Transnational Private Regulation. *New Political Economy* 27(2): 188–202.

Bayer. 2018. Global Leaders Reiterate Importance of Glyphosate. https://www.bayer.com/sites/default/files/bayer-global-glyphosate-leaders-comments_0.pdf.

Bayer. 2023. Bayer: Significant Growth in Sales and Earnings. February 28. https://www.bayer.com/media/en-us/bayer-significant-growth-in-sales-and-earnings/.

Bayer and Monsanto. 2016. Bayer and Monsanto Merger Press Conference. SEC Filing 14A. September 14. https://www.sec.gov/Archives/edgar/data/1110783/0001 19312516712356/d243622ddefa14a.htm.

Beale, Calvin. 1991. Black Farmers: Why Such a Severe and Continuing Decline? *Rural Development Perspectives* 7(2): 12–14.

Beer, Mitchell. 2021. Fertilizer Lobby "Trying to Scare Farmers" to Head Off Reductions in Climate Super-Pollutant. *Energy Mix Climate News Network*, October 19. https://www.theenergymix.com/2021/10/19/exclusive-fertilizer-lobby-trying-to-scare-farmers-to-head-off-reductions-in-climate-super-pollutant/.

Bekkerman, Anton, Gary W. Brester, and David Ripplinger. 2020. The History, Consolidation, and Future of the U.S. Nitrogen Fertilizer Production Industry. *Choices*, quarter 2. https://www.choicesmagazine.org/choices-magazine/submitted-articles/the-history-consolidation-and-future-of-the-us-nitrogen-fertilizer-production-industry.

Benbrook, Charles M. 2016. Trends in Glyphosate Herbicide Use in the United States and Globally. *Environmental Sciences Europe* 28: 3.

Benbrook, Charles M. 2019. How Did the US EPA and IARC Reach Diametrically Opposed Conclusions on the Genotoxicity of Glyphosate-Based Herbicides? *Environmental Sciences Europe* 31: 2.

Benoit, David. 2015. Dow, DuPont Deal Underscores Rise of Activists. *Wall Street Journal*, December 14.

Berardi, Gigi M. 1984. Socio-Economic Consequences of Agricultural Mechanization in the United States: Needed Redirections for Mechanization Research. In *The Social Consequences and Challenges of New Agricultural Technologies*, edited by Gigi M. Berardi and Charles Geisler. Boulder, CO: Westview Press.

Berkhout, Frans. 2022. Technological Regimes, Path Dependency and the Environment. *Global Environmental Change* 12(1): 1–4.

Berry, Ian. 2012. Monsanto to Buy Planting Technology Company. *Wall Street Journal*, May 24.

Berry-Cabán, Cristóbal S. 2011. DDT and Silent Spring: Fifty Years After. *Journal of Military and Veterans' Health* 19(4): 19–24.

Bertin, Oliver. 1985. Japanese Tractors Invade Quietly. *Globe and Mail*, April 22.

Biden, Joseph R. 2021. Executive Order on Promoting Competition in the American Economy. https://www.whitehouse.gov/briefing-room/presidential-actions/2021/07/09/executive-order-on-promoting-competition-in-the-american-economy/.

Bittlingmayer, George. 1996. Antitrust and Business Activity: The First Quarter Century. *Business History Review* 70(3): 363–401.

Blake, Cassels and Graydon LLP. 2021. Agricultural Industry Competition Law in Canada. https://www.blakes.com/insights/agricultural-industry-and-competition-law-in-canada.

REFERENCES

Blumenthal, Ralph. 1977. TV-Equipped Tractors Lighten Long Hours. *New York Times*, June 28.

Boardman, Robert. 1986. *Pesticides in World Agriculture*. London: Palgrave Macmillan.

Bogmans, Christian, Andrea Pescatori, and Ervin Prifti. 2022. Global Food Prices to Remain Elevated amid War, Costly Energy, La Niña. December 9. https://www.imf.org/en/Blogs/Articles/2022/12/09/global-food-prices-to-remain-elevated-amid-war-costly-energy-la-nina.

Bogue, Allan G. 1983. Changes in Mechanical and Plant Technology: The Corn Belt, 1910–1940. *Journal of Economic History* 43(1): 1–25.

Bollmohr, Silke, and Susan Haffmans. 2022. Imports and Exports: Banned But Sold Anyway. In *Pesticide Atlas*, 40–41. Brussels: Heinrich Boll Siftung. https://eu.boell.org/sites/default/files/2023-04/pesticideatlas2022_ii_web_20230331.pdf.

Bonny, Sylvie. 2016. Genetically Modified Herbicide-Tolerant Crops, Weeds, and Herbicides: Overview and Impact. *Environmental Management* 57(1): 31–48.

Bork, Robert. 1978. *The Antitrust Paradox*. New York: Basic Books.

Borlaug, Norman. 1972. Ecology Fever. *Ceres* 5(1): 21–25.

Bosso, Christopher. 1988. *Pesticides and Politics: The Life Cycle of a Public Issue*. Pittsburgh: University of Pittsburgh Press.

Bozzini, Emanuela. 2017. *Pesticide Policy and Politics in the European Union: Regulatory Assessment, Implementation and Enforcement*. New York: Springer.

Brand, Charles J. 1945. Some Fertilizer History Connected with World War I. *Agricultural History* 19(2): 104–113.

Brandeis, Louis D. 1914. *Other People's Money and How the Bankers Use It*. New York: Frederick A. Stokes.

Brandeis, Louis D. 1934. *The Curse of Bigness: Miscellaneous Papers of Louis Brandeis*. New York: Viking Press.

Braunholtz, John T. 1982. Crop Protection: The Evolution of a Chemical Industry. In *The Chemical Industry*, edited by D. H. Sharp and T. F. West, 474–490. Chichester, UK: Ellis Horwood.

Bremmer, Johan, Ana Gonzalez-Martinez, Roel Jongeneel, Hilfred Huiting, Rob Stokkers, and Marc Ruijs. 2021. *Impact Assessment of EC 2030 Green Deal Targets for Sustainable Crop Production*. No. 2021-150. Wageningen, Netherlands: Wageningen Economic Research.

Brinegar, Katelyn, Ali K. Yetisen, Sun Choi, Emily Vallillo, Guillermo U. Ruiz-Esparza, Anand M. Prabhakar, Ali Khademhosseini, and Seok Hyun Yun. 2017. The Commercialization of Genome-Editing Technologies. *Critical Reviews in Biotechnology* 37(7): 924–932.

Broehl, Wayne G. Jr. 1984. *John Deere's Company: A History of Deere and Company and Its Times*. New York: Doubleday.

Bronson, Kelly. 2019. Looking through a Responsible Innovation Lens at Uneven Engagements with Digital Farming. *NJAS—Wageningen Journal of Life Sciences* 90–91: 100294.

Bronson, Kelly. 2022. *The Immaculate Conception of Data: Agribusiness, Activists, and Their Shared Politics of the Future*. Montreal: McGill Queens Press.

Brooks, Chris, Zhong Chen, and Yeqin Zeng. 2018. Institutional Cross-Ownership and Corporate Strategy: The Case of Mergers and Acquisitions. *Journal of Corporate Finance* 48: 187–216.

Broughton, Edward. 2005. The Bhopal Disaster and Its Aftermath: A Review. *Environmental Health* 4: 1–6.

Brown, J. R. 1963. Nitrate Crises, Combinations, and the Chilean Government in the Nitrate Age. *Hispanic American Historical Review* 43(2): 230–246.

Brown, Lester. 1970. *Seeds of Change: The Green Revolution and Development in the 1970's*. New York: Praeger.

Brown, Mark J. F., Lynn V. Dicks, Robert J. Paxton, Katherine C. R. Baldock, Andrew B. Barron, Marie-Pierre Chauzat, Breno M. Freitas, et al. 2016. A Horizon Scan of Future Threats and Opportunities for Pollinators and Pollination. *PeerJ* 4: e2249.

Browne, William 1988. *Private Interests, Public Policy, and American Agriculture*. Lawrence: University Press of Kansas.

Bryan, Kenza. 2023. US Investors Ditch Green Funds as "Woke Capitalism" Backlash Bites. *Financial Times*, April 28.

Bryant, Henry, Aleksandre Maisashvili, Joe Outlaw, and James Richardson. 2016. *Effects of Proposed Mergers and Acquisitions among Biotechnology Firms on Seed Prices*. College Station: Agricultural and Food Policy Center, and Texas A&M University. https://www.afpc.tamu.edu/pubs/0/675/WP_16-2.pdf.

Brzeziński, Bartosz. 2024. Glyphosate: Raft of Legal Challenges Launched Against EU Approval. *Politico*. January 25. https://www.politico.eu/article/glyphosate-legal-launched-against-eu-approval-pan-europe/.

Buck, Solon Justus. 1913. *The Granger Movement: A Study of Agricultural Organization and Its Political, Economic and Social Manifestations*. Cambridge, MA: Harvard University Press.

Buck, Tobias. 2019. Bayer Promotes Tech Vision to Counter Monsanto Woe. *Financial Times*, January 29.

Bugow, Karin. 2020. *The Role of Multinational Corporations in the Green Revolution, 1960s and 1970s*. PhD diss., Jacobs University.

REFERENCES

Bunge, Jacob. 2016. Farmers Reconsider GMO Revolution. *Wall Street Journal*, September 15.

Bunge, Jacob. 2019. Corteva Debut Caps Years of Seed Company Consolidation; Farmers and Politicians Have Raised Concerns about Lack of Competition in Agricultural Economy. *Wall Street Journal*, June 4.

Burwood-Taylor, Louisa. 2016. Why Bayer Invested in 5 Agtech Funds and Big Data Is So Exciting. *Agfunder News*, November 1.

Busse, Meghan. 2016. CF Industries. https://www.emerald.com/insight/content/doi/10.1108/case.kellogg.2021.000054/full/html.

Buthelezi, Thembalethu, Myriam Hammadi, Simon Roberts, and Carin Smaller. 2023. *Empowering African Producers and Agricultural Enterprises Through Stronger Competition Law and Policy*. Shamba Centre for Food and Climate. https://www.shambacentre.org/s/Shamba-Centre_report_Competition-Law-and-Policy_231220_v15.pdf.

Byerlee, Derek. 2020. The Globalization of Hybrid Maize, 1921–70. *Journal of Global History* 15(1): 101–122.

Calo, Adam, Kirsteen Shields, and Alastair Iles. 2023. Using Property Law to Expand Agroecology: Scotland's Land Reforms Based on Human Rights. *Journal of Peasant Studies* 50(5): 2075–2111.

Canada. 2020. Canada's Fertilizer Emissions Reduction Target. https://agriculture.canada.ca/en/department/transparency/public-opinion-research-consultations/share-ideas-fertilizer-emissions-reduction-target/canadas-fertilizer-emissions-reduction-target.

Canadian Biotechnology Action Network (CBAN). 2022. Patents on Genome Editing in Canada. https://cban.ca/wp-content/uploads/Patents-on-Genome-Editing-cban-March-2022.pdf.

Canadian Competition Bureau. 2018. Bayer AG's acquisition of Monsanto Company. https://ised-isde.canada.ca/site/competition-bureau-canada/en/how-we-foster-competition/education-and-outreach/position-statements/bayer-ags-acquisition-monsanto-company.

Canadian Competition Bureau. 2022. Competition Bureau Statement Regarding Its Investigation into Alleged Anti-Competitive Conduct of Wholesalers and Manufacturers of Crop Inputs in Western Canada. March 15. https://ised-isde.canada.ca/site/competition-bureau-canada/en/how-we-foster-competition/education-and-outreach/position-statements/competition-bureau-statement-regarding-its-investigation-alleged-anti-competitive-conduct.

Canadian Competition Bureau. 2023. Canada Needs More Grocery Competition. https://ised-isde.canada.ca/site/competition-bureau-canada/sites/default/files/attachments/2023/CB-Retail-Grocery-Market-Study-Report-EN-2023-06-23.pdf.

Canadian Food Inspection Agency (CFIA). 2017. Safeguarding with Science: Glyphosate Testing in 2015–2016. *CFIA-Science Branch Survey Report, Food Safety Science Directorate*. https://inspection.canada.ca/DAM/DAM-food-aliments/STAGING/text-texte/chem_testing_report_2015-2016_glyphosate_srvy_rprt_1491855525292_eng.pdf.

Canfield, Matthew, Molly D. Anderson, and Philip McMichael. 2021. UN Food Systems Summit 2021: Dismantling Democracy and Resetting Corporate Control of Food Systems. *Frontiers in Sustainable Food Systems* 5: 661552.

Cape Law Firm PLC. 2022. Comments to USDA. https://www.regulations.gov/comment/AMS-AMS-22-0025-0062.

Carbonell, Isabelle M. 2016. The Ethics of Big Data in Big Agriculture. *Internet Policy Review* 5(1): 1–13.

Carlile, Clare, and Hazel Healy. 2022. Flagship EU Green Farming Reforms in Peril as Lobbyists Exploit Ukraine War. *DeSmog*, December 9. https://www.desmog.com/2022/12/09/eu-farming-reforms-pesticides-targets-in-peril-lobbyists-exploit-ukraine-war/.

Carney, Judith. 2013. Seeds of Memory: Botanical Legacies of the African Diaspora. In *African Ethnobotany in the Americas*, edited by Robert Voeks and John Rashford, 13–33. New York: Springer.

Carolan, Michael. 2020. Digitization as Politics: Smart Farming through the Lens of Weak and Strong Data. *Journal of Rural Studies* 91: 208–216.

Carson, Rachel. 1962. *Silent Spring*. Boston: Houghton Mifflin.

Casey, Simon, and Phil Milford. 2015. DuPont to Cut 1,700 Delaware Jobs before Dow Chemical Merger. *Bloomberg*, December 30. https://www.bloomberg.com/news/articles/2015-12-29/dupont-to-cut-1-700-delaware-based-jobs-ahead-of-dow-merger?leadSource=uverify percent20wall.

Cecere, Grazia, Nicoletta Corrocher, Cédric Gossart, and Muge Ozman. 2014. Lock-In and Path Dependence: An Evolutionary Approach to Eco-Innovations. *Journal of Evolutionary Economics; Heidelberg* 24(5): 1037–1065.

Cerveaux, Augustin. 2013. Taming the Microworld: DuPont and the Interwar Rise of Fundamental Industrial Research. *Technology and Culture* 54(2): 262–288.

Chai, Yuan, Philip Pardey, Connie Chan-Kang, Jikun Huang, Kyuseon Lee, and Wanlu Dong. 2019. Passing the Food and Agricultural R&D Buck? The United States and China. *Food Policy* 86: 101729.

Chandler, Alfred D. 1959. The Beginnings of "Big Business" in American Industry. *Business History Review* 33(1): 1–31.

Chandler, Alfred D. 1962. *Strategy and Structure: Chapters in the History of the Industrial Enterprise*. Cambridge, MA: MIT Press.

REFERENCES

Charlier, Marj. 1984. Farm-Gear Makers' Sever Price Cutting Is Set to Intensify; More Mergers Are Seen. *Wall Street Journal*, December 10.

Chazan, Guy. 2016a. Bayer Targets One-Stop Shop with Monsanto. *Financial Times*, September 14.

Chazan, Guy. 2016b. Scepticism Swirls around Bayer's Megadeal. *Financial Times*, September 15.

Chynoweth, Emma. 1990. Kemira Outlines Plans for U.K. Fertilizers. *Chemical Week*, August 8.

Ciceri, Davide, David A. C. Manning, and Antoine Allanore. 2015. Historical and Technical Developments of Potassium Resources. *Science of the Total Environment* 502: 590–601.

Civil Society and Indigenous Peoples Mechanism (CSIPM) of the Committee on World Food Security. 2021. Letter to the CFS Chair on Food Systems Summit. http://www.csm4cfs.org/letter-csm-coordination-committee-cfs-chair/.

Clancey, Matthew, Keith Fuglie, and Paul Heisey. 2016. U.S. Agricultural R&D in an Era of Falling Public Funding. *Amber Waves*, November 10. https://www.ers.usda.gov/amber-waves/2016/november/us-agricultural-r-d-in-an-era-of-falling-public-funding/.

Clapp, Jennifer. 2012. *Hunger in the Balance: The New Politics of International Food Aid*. Ithaca, NY: Cornell University Press.

Clapp, Jennifer. 2014. Financialization, Distance and Global Food Politics. *Journal of Peasant Studies* 41(5): 797–814.

Clapp, Jennifer. 2018. Mega-Mergers on the Menu: Corporate Concentration and the Politics of Sustainability in the Global Food System. *Global Environmental Politics* 18(2): 12–33.

Clapp, Jennifer. 2019. The Rise of Financial Investment and Common Ownership in Global Agrifood Firms. *Review of International Political Economy* 26(4): 604–629.

Clapp, Jennifer. 2020. *Food*. 3rd edition. Cambridge: Polity Press.

Clapp, Jennifer. 2021a. The Problem with Growing Corporate Concentration and Power in the Global Food System. *Nature Food* 2(6): 404–408.

Clapp, Jennifer. 2021b. Explaining Growing Glyphosate Use: The Political Economy of Herbicide-Dependent Agriculture. *Global Environmental Change* 67: 102239.

Clapp, Jennifer. 2022a. Concentration and Crises: Exploring the Deep Roots of Vulnerability in the Global Industrial Food System. *Journal of Peasant Studies* 50(1): 1–25.

Clapp, Jennifer. 2022b. The Rise of Big Food and Agriculture: Corporate Influence in the Food System. In *A Research Agenda for Food Systems*, edited by Colin Sage, 45–66. Cheltenham: Edward Elgar.

Clapp, Jennifer, and Doris A. Fuchs, eds. 2009. *Corporate Power in Global Agrifood Governance.* Cambridge, MA: MIT Press.

Clapp, Jennifer, and Eric Helleiner. 2012. International Political Economy and the Environment: Back to the Basics? *International Affairs* 88(3): 485–501.

Clapp, Jennifer, and S. Ryan Isakson. 2018. *Speculative Harvests: Financialization, Food and Agriculture.* Halifax: Fernwood.

Clapp, Jennifer, and William G. Moseley. 2020. This Food Crisis Is Different: COVID-19 and the Fragility of the Neoliberal Food Security Order. *Journal of Peasant Studies* 47(7): 1393–1417.

Clapp, Jennifer, William G. Moseley, Barbara Burlingame, and Paola Termine. 2022. The Case for a Six-Dimensional Food Security Framework. *Food Policy* 106: 102164.

Clapp, Jennifer, Indra Noyes, and Zachary Grant. 2021. The Food Systems Summit's Failure to Address Corporate Power. *Development* 64(3): 192–198.

Clapp, Jennifer, and Sarah-Louise Ruder. 2020. Precision Technologies for Agriculture: Digital Farming, Gene-Edited Crops, and the Politics of Sustainability. *Global Environmental Politics* 20(3): 49–69.

Clapp, Jennifer, and Gyorgy Scrinis. 2017. Big Food, Nutritionism, and Corporate Power. *Globalizations* 14(4): 578–595.

Clark, Brett, and John Bellamy Foster. 2009. Ecological Imperialism and the Global Metabolic Rift: Unequal Exchange and the Guano/Nitrates Trade. *International Journal of Comparative Sociology* 50(3–4): 311–334.

Clark, J. Allen. 1954. Preventing Extinction of Original Strains of Corn. *News Report, National Academy of Sciences National Research Council* 4(5): 78–81.

Clark, J. Allen. 1956. Collection, Preservation and Utilization of Indigenous Strains of Maize. *Economic Botany* 10(2): 194–200.

Clarke, Sally H. 2021. Stress and Struggle inside International Harvester. *Enterprise and Society* 22(3): 663–695.

Clayton, Chris. 2022. Import Fertilizer Victory for Farmers. *Progressive Farmer,* July 18. https://www.dtnpf.com/agriculture/web/ag/crops/article/2022/07/18/itc-rules-import-tariffs-uan-russia.

Cleaver, Harry M. 1972. The Contradictions of the Green Revolution. *American Economic Review* 62(1/2): 177–186.

Cohen, Jon. 2019. Fields of Dreams: China Bets Big on Genome Editing of Crops. *Science* 365(6452): 422–425.

Cohen, Patricia. 2020. Roundup Maker to Pay $10 Billion to Settle Cancer Suits. *New York Times,* June 24. https://www.nytimes.com/2020/06/24/business/roundup-settlement-lawsuits.html.

Coleman, Kim. 2006. *IG Farben and ICI, 1925–53: Strategies for Growth and Survival*. London: Palgrave Macmillan.

Comer, Benjamin M., Porfirio Fuentes, Christian O. Dimkpa, Yu-Hsuan Liu, Carlos A. Fernandez, Pratham Arora, Matthew Realff, Upendra Singh, Marta C. Hatzell and Andrew J. Medford. 2019. Prospects and Challenges for Solar Fertilizers. *Joule* 3(7): 1578–1605.

Conant, Michael. 1953. Competition in the Farm-Machinery Industry. *Journal of Business of the University of Chicago* 26(1): 26–36.

Conford, Philip. 2002. The Myth of Neglect: Responses to the Early Organic Movement, 1930–1950. *Agricultural History Review* 50(1): 89–106.

Constance, Douglas H. 2010. Sustainable Agriculture in the United States: A Critical Examination of a Contested Process. *Sustainability* 2(1): 48–72.

Contreras, Jorge L., and Jacob S. Sherkow. 2017. CRISPR, Surrogate Licensing, and Scientific Discovery. *Science* 355(6326): 698–700.

Cooke, Kathy J. 2002. Expertise, Book Farming, and Government Agriculture: The Origins of Agricultural Seed Certification in the United States. *Agricultural History* 76(3): 524–545.

Cookson, Clive. 2016a. Bayer-Monsanto Deal Is a Bet on GM Crop Expansion. *Financial Times*, November 27.

Cookson, Clive. 2016b. GM Crops Hold Key to Bayer's Global Growth; Agribusiness Sector Suffers First Decline in Modified Seeds Market for Two Decades But Long-Term Prospects Look Better. *Financial Times*, November 28.

Cordero, Mónica. 2022. Farmers Endured a Rough Year, But Fertilizer Companies Cashed In. *Investigate Midwest*, December 22. https://investigatemidwest.org/2022/12/22/farmers-endured-a-rough-year-but-fertilizer-companies-cashed-in/.

Corporate Accountability and FIAN International. 2022. *Corporate Capture of FAO: Industry's Deepening Influence on Global Food Governance*. https://www.fian.org/files/files/CorporateCaptureoftheFAO-EN.pdf.

Corporate Europe Observatory. 2019. Yara: Poisoning Our Soils, Burning Our Planet. https://corporateeurope.org/en/2019/09/yara-poisoning-our-soils-burning-our-planet.

Corporate Europe Observatory. 2022. *A Loud Lobby for a Silent Spring: The Pesticide Industry's Toxic Lobbying Tactics against Farm to Fork*. https://corporateeurope.org/en/2022/03/loud-lobby-silent-spring.

Corteva Agriscience. 2023. Cocrteva Reports Fourth Quarter and Full-Year 2022 Results, Provides 2023 Guidance. News release Q4 2022, February 1. https://www.corteva.com/content/dam/dpagco/corteva/global/corporate/files/press-releases/02.01.2022_4Q_2022_Earnings_Release_Graphic_Version_Final.pdf.

Cottam, Clarence, and Elmer Higgins. 1946. *DDT: Its Effect on Fish and Wildlife.* US Department of the Interior, Fish and Wildlife Service. Washington DC: US Government Printing Office.

Cotter, Janet, and Dana Perls. 2018. *Gene-Edited Organisms in Agriculture: Risks and Unintended Consequences.* Friends of the Earth US, September 12. https://foe.org/news/new-report-gene-editing-agriculture-poses-new-risks-health-environment/.

Cowan, Robin, and Philip Gunby. 1996. Sprayed to Death: Path Dependence, Lock-In and Pest Control Strategies. *Economic Journal* 106: 521–542.

Cowen, Tyler. 2019. *Big Business: A Love Letter to an American Anti-Hero.* New York: St. Martin's Press.

Crabb, Richard A. 1947. *The Hybrid-Corn Makers: Prophets of Plenty.* New Brunswick, NJ: Rutgers University Press.

Crittenden, Ann. 1975. Phosphate: Taking a Leaf from Oil's Book. *New York Times.* November 9.

Crooks, Ed. 2015. Dow and DuPont Aim to Pre-Empt Activists with Megadeal. *Financial Times,* December 9.

Cullather, Nick. 2010. *The Hungry World: America's Cold War Battle against Poverty in Asia.* Cambridge, MA: Harvard University Press.

Culver, John C., and John Hyde. 2000. *American Dreamer: The Life and Times of Henry A. Wallace.* New York: Norton.

Curry, Helen Anne. 2017a. Breeding Uniformity and Banking Diversity: The Genescapes of Industrial Agriculture, 1935–1970. *Global Environment* 10(1): 83–114.

Curry, Helen Anne. 2017b. From Working Collections to the World Germplasm Project: Agricultural Modernization and Genetic Conservation at the Rockefeller Foundation. *History and Philosophy of the Life Sciences* 39(5): 1–20.

Curry, Helen Anne. 2022. *Endangered Maize: Industrial Agriculture and the Crisis of Extinction.* Oakland: University of California Press.

Dahlberg, Kenneth. 1979. *Beyond the Green Revolution: The Ecology and Politics of Global Agricultural Development.* New York: Plenum Press.

Damro, Chad, and Terrence Guay. 2012. Transatlantic Merger Relations: The Pursuit of Cooperation and Convergence. *Journal of European Integration* 34(6): 643–661.

Danaher, Kevin. 1989. US Food Power in the 1990s. *Race and Class* 30(3): 31–46.

Davies, T. G. E., L. M. Field, P. N. R. Usherwood, and M. S. Williamson. 2007. DDT, Pyrethrins, Pyrethroids and Insect Sodium Channels. *IUBMB Life* 59(3): 151–162.

Davis, Adam S., and George B. Frisvold. 2017. Are Herbicides a Once in a Century Method of Weed Control? *Pest Management Science* 73(11): 2209–2220.

Davis, Frederick Rowe. 2019. Pesticides and the Perils of Synecdoche in the History of Science and Environmental History. *History of Science* 57(4): 469–492.

Dayan, Franck E. 2019. Current Status and Future Prospects in Herbicide Discovery. *Plants* 8(9): 341.

De La Merced, Michael. 2011. Cargill to Split off Mosaic Unit in Complex Deal. *New York Times*, January 18.

De Loecker, Jan, and Jan Eeckhout. 2021. Global Market Power. National Bureau of Economic Research working paper 24768. https://www.janeeckhout.com/wp-content/uploads/Global.pdf.

De Loecker, Jan, Jan Eeckhout, and Simon Mongey. 2021. Quantifying Market Power and Business Dynamism in the Macroeconomy. National Bureau of Economic Research working paper28761. https://www.nber.org/system/files/working_papers/w28761/w28761.pdf.

De Loecker, Jan, Jan Eeckhout, and Gabriel Unger. 2020. The Rise of Market Power and the Macroeconomic Implications. *Quarterly Journal of Economics* 135(2): 561–644.

Deere & Co. 2022. Deere Reports Net Income of $2.246 Billion for Fourth Quarter, $7.131 Billion for Fiscal Year. https://s22.q4cdn.com/253594569/files/doc_financials/2022/q4/DE-4Q22-News-Release-and-Financials.pdf.

Deere & Co. 2023. *2023 Annual Report*. https://s22.q4cdn.com/253594569/files/doc_financials/2023/ar/2023-deere-company-annual-report.pdf.

DeLonge, M., A. Miles, and L. Carlisle. 2016. Investing in the Transition to Sustainable Agriculture. *Environmental Science and Policy* 55: 266–273.

Dinham, Barbara. 1993. *The Pesticide Hazard*. London: Zed Books.

Dixon, Marion W. 2018. Chemical Fertilizer in Transformations in World Agriculture and the State System, 1870 to Interwar Period. *Journal of Agrarian Change* 18(4): 768–786.

Doggett, Jon. 2021. American Farmers Face Crippling Prices at the Hands of a Fertilizer Oligopoly. National Corn Growers Association. November 19. https://www.ncga.com/stay-informed/media/in-the-news/article/2021/11/op-ed-american-farmers-face-crippling-prices-at-the-hands-of-fertilizer-oligopoly.

Dong, Xiao-Yuan, Terrence S. Veeman, and Michele M. Veeman. 1995. China's Grain Imports: An Empirical Study. *Food Policy* 20(4): 323–338.

Dosi, Giovanni. 1982. Technological Paradigms and Technological Trajectories: A Suggested Interpretation of the Determinants and Directions of Technical Change. *Research Policy* 11(3): 147–162.

Dow. 2016. DowDupont Merger of Equals Update. https://www.sec.gov/Archives/edgar/data/29915/000119312516623676/d151726d425.htm.

Duke, Stephen O. 2012. Why Have No New Herbicide Modes of Action Appeared in Recent Years? *Pest Management Science* 68(4): 505–512.

Duncan, Emily, Sarah Rotz, André Magnan, and Kelly Bronson. 2022. Disciplining Land through Data: The Role of Agricultural Technologies in Farmland Assetisation. *Sociologia Ruralis* 62(2): 231–249.

Dunlap, Thomas R. 1978. Science as a Guide in Regulating Technology: The Case of DDT in the United States. *Social Studies of Science* 8(3): 265–285.

Dunlap, Thomas R. 1981. *DDT: Scientists, Citizens, and Public Policy*. Princeton: Princeton University Press.

DuPont. 2015. DuPont and Dow to Combine in Merger of Equals. https://www.investors.dupont.com/news-and-media/press-release-details/2015/Dupont-And-Dow-To-Combine-In-Merger-Of-Equals/default.aspx.

Dupraz, Emily. 2012. Monsanto and the Quasi-Per Se Illegal Rule for Bundled Discounts. *Vermont Law Review* 37: 203–237.

Duvick, Donald. 1998. The United States. In *Maize Seed Industries in Developing Countries*, edited by Michael Morris, 193–211. Boulder, CO: Lynne Rienner.

E. I. du Pont de Nemours & Company. 1956. The Story of Grasselli. Hagley Digital Archives. https://digital.hagley.org/08025062_story_of_grasselli.

Ecklecamp, Margy. 2012. Monsanto Plans to Acquire Precision Planting. *AgWeb: Farm Journal*, May 23. https://www.agweb.com/news/machinery/new-machinery/monsanto-plans-acquire-precision-planting.

Eekhout, Jan. 2021. *The Profit Paradox: How Thriving Firms Threaten the Future of Work*. Princeton: Princeton University Press.

Egelie, Knut J., Gregory D. Graff, Sabina P. Strand, and Berit Johansen. 2016. The Emerging Patent Landscape of CRISPR–Cas Gene Editing Technology. *Nature Biotechnology* 34(10): 1025–1031.

Eichers, Theodore, and Philip Szmedra. 1990. Pesticides. In *Seven Farm Input Industries*, edited by Joseph Barse. ERS Agricultural Economic Report 635: 30–45.

Ellenberg, George B. 2000. Debating Farm Power: Draft Animals, Tractors, and the United States Department of Agriculture. *Agricultural History* 74(2): 545–568.

Elmore, Bartow J. 2021. *Seed Money: Monsanto's Past and Our Food Future*. New York: Norton.

Emont, Jon. 2022. "Farms Are Failing" as Fertilizer Prices Drive Up Cost of Food. *Wall Street Journal*, January 21. https://www.wsj.com/articles/farms-are-failing-as-fertilizer-prices-drive-up-cost-of-food-11642770182.

Ennis, Sean, Pedro Gonzaga, and Chris Pike. Inequality: A Hidden Cost of Market Power. *Oxford Review of Economic Policy* 35(3): 518–549.

Enoch, Daniel. 2015. Monsanto Earnings Fall; Company Announces Job Cuts. *AgriPulse*, October 7. https://www.agri-pulse.com/articles/6085-monsanto-earnings-fall-company-announces-job-cuts.

Ergen, Timur, and Sebastian Kohl. 2019. Varieties of Economization in Competition Policy: Institutional Change in German and American Antitrust, 1960–2000. *Review of International Political Economy* 26(2): 256–286.

Estenson, Paul. 1987. Farm Debt and Financial Instability. *Journal of Economic Issues* 21(2): 617–627.

ETC Group. 2013. *Gene Giants Seek "Philanthrogopoly."* Communiqué issue 110. http://www.etcgroup.org/sites/www.etcgroup.org/files/ETCCommCharityCartel_March2013_final.pdf.

ETC Group. 2015. *Breaking Bad: Big Ag Mega-Mergers in Play; Dow+Dupont in the Pocket? Next: Demonsanto?* https://www.etcgroup.org/content/breaking-bad-big-ag-mega-mergers-play.

ETC Group. 2016. *Merge-Santo: New Threat to Food Sovereignty.* Briefing note. March 23. http://www.etcgroup.org/content/merge-santo-new-threat-food-sovereignty.

ETC Group. 2019. *Plate Tech-Tonics.* https://www.etcgroup.org/content/plate-tech-tonics.

ETC Group. 2022. *Food Barons 2022: Crisis Profiteering, Digitalization and Shifting Power.* https://www.etcgroup.org/content/food-barons-2022.

ETC Group and Heinrich Böll Foundation. 2018. *Forcing the Farm: How Gene Drive Organisms Could Entrench Industrial Agriculture and Threaten Food Sovereignty.* https://www.etcgroup.org/content/forcing-farm

European Union. 2013. Regulation (EU) No. 167/2013 of the European Parliament and of the Council of 5 February 2013 on the Approval and Market Surveillance of Agricultural and Forestry Vehicles.

European Union. 2020. Farm to Fork Strategy. https://food.ec.europa.eu/system/files/2020-05/f2f_action-plan_2020_strategy-info_en.pdf.

European Union. 2022. Proposal for a Directive on Common Rules Promoting the Repair of Goods. European Commission. https://commission.europa.eu/document/afb20917-5a6c-4d87-9d89-666b2b775aa1_en.

Everhart, Sarah. 2023. Growing Carbon Credits: Strengthening the Agricultural Sector's Participation in Voluntary Carbon Markets through Law and Policy. *New York University Environmental Law Journal* 31(1): 65–116.

Ewart, John, and Stewart Melanson. 2010. Canada's First Great Manufacturing Enterprise: The Story of Massey-Harris. In *Relentless Change: A Casebook for the Study of Canadian Business History*, edited by Joe Martin, 60–78. Toronto: University of Toronto Press.

Fakhri, Michael. 2022. The Food System Summit's Disconnection from People's Real Needs. *Journal of Agricultural and Environmental Ethics* 35: 16.

Fakhri, Michael, Hilal Elver, and Olivier de Schutter. 2021. The UN Food Systems Summit: How Not to Respond to the Urgency of Reform. Inter Press Services. March 22. http://www.ipsnews.net/2021/03/un-food-systems-summit-not-respond-urgency-reform/.

Falkner, Robert. 2008. *Business Power and Conflict in International Environmental Politics*. London: Palgrave McMillan.

Fang, Lee. 2022. Lobbying Blitz Pushed Fertilizer Prices Higher, Fueling Food Inflation. *Intercept*. https://theintercept.com/2022/08/03/fertilizer-prices-food-inflation-mosaic/.

FAO 2020. FAO and CropLife International Strengthen Commitment to Promote Agri-Food Systems Transformation. October 2. https://www.fao.org/newsroom/detail/FAO-and-CropLife-International-strengthen-commitment-to-promote-agri-food-systems-transformation/.

FAO. 2022. FAO and World Economic Forum Bolster Collaboration to Transform Agrifood Systems. September 19. https://www.fao.org/newsroom/detail/fao-and-world-economic-forum-bolster-collaboration-to-transform-agrifood-systems/en.

FAO and CropLife International. 2020. Letter of Intent between the Food and Agriculture Organization of the United Nations and CropLife International. October 2. https://www.fao.org/fileadmin/user_upload/newsroom/docs/CropLife.pdf.

FAO, IFAD, UNICEF, WFP and WHO. 2022. *The State of Food Security and Nutrition in the World 2022. Repurposing Food and Agricultural Policies to Make Healthy Diets More Affordable*. Rome: FAO.

Farm Action. 2022. Farm Action Comments on Access to Fertilizer Competition and Supply Chain Concerns. Comments to USDA. https://www.regulations.gov/comment/AMS-AMS-22-0027-1407.

Farm Action et al. 2022. Comments on Access to Fertilizer: Competition and Supply Chain Concerns. Submitted to USDA. https://farmaction.us/wp-content/uploads/2022/06/Farm-Action-Fertilizer-Competition-Comments-6.10.22.pdf.

Fatka, Jacqui. 2021. Farmers File Antitrust Lawsuit against Crop Input Suppliers. *Farm Progress*. https://www.farmprogress.com/corn/farmers-file-antitrust-lawsuit-against-crop-input-suppliers.

Faulkner, Edward H. 1943. *Plowman's Folly*. Norman: University of Oklahoma Press.

Faust, Julian. 2020. Filling a Colonial Void? German Business Strategies and Development Assistance in India, 1947–1974. *Business History* 64(9): 1684–1708.

Fawcett-Atkinson, Marc. 2022. Dog Photos and Veiled Threats: How Canada's Fertilizer Lobby Is Fighting against Climate Laws. *National Observer*, July 4. https://www.nationalobserver.com/2022/07/04/investigations/how-canadas-fertilizer-lobby-fighting-climate-laws.

Federal Trade Commission (FTC). 2022. FTC and State Partners Sue Pesticide Giants Syngenta and Corteva for Using Illegal Pay-to-Block Scheme to Inflate Prices for Farmers. September 29. https://www.ftc.gov/news-events/news/press-releases/2022/09/ftc-state-partners-sue-pesticide-giants-syngenta-corteva-using-illegal-pay-block-scheme-inflate.

Ferguson, Rafter. 2021. *Losing Ground: Farmland Consolidation and Threats to New Farmers, Black Farmers, and the Future of Farming.* Cambridge, MA: Union of Concerned Scientists. https://www.ucsusa.org/resources/losing-ground.

Fernandez-Cornejo, Jorge. 2004. *The Seed Industry in U.S. Agriculture: An Exploration of Data and Information on Crop Seed Markets, Regulation, Industry Structure, and Research and Development.* Agriculture Information Bulletin no. 786. US Department of Agriculture, Economic Research Service. https://www.ers.usda.gov/publications/pub-details/?pubid=42531.

Fernandez-Cornejo, Jorge, and Richard E. Just. 2007. Researchability of Modern Agricultural Input Markets and Growing Concentration. *American Journal of Agricultural Economics* 89(5): 1269–1275.

Ferreira, Miguel, Massimo Massa, and Pedro Matos. 2009. Shareholders at the Gate? Cross-Country Evidence on the Role of Institutional Investors in Mergers and Acquisitions. *Review of Financial Studies* 23(2): 601–644.

Fichtner, Jan, Eelke M. Heemskerk, and Javier Garcia-Bernardo. 2017. Hidden Power of the Big Three? Passive Index Funds, Re-Concentration of Corporate Ownership, and New Financial Risk. *Business and Politics* 19(2): 298–326.

Financial Times (Lex). 2016. Bayer/Monsanto: Tipping the Scales. *Financial Times*, September 7.

Firn, David. 2004. Norsk Hydro to Price Yara at NKr25bn: Fertiliser Spin-Off. *Financial Times*, March 8.

Fitzgerald, Deborah. 1990. *The Business of Breeding: Hybrid Corn in Illinois, 1890 to 1940.* Ithaca, NY: Cornell University Press.

Fitzgerald, Deborah. 1993. Farmers Deskilled: Hybrid Corn and Farmers' Work. *Technology and Culture* 34(2): 324–343.

Fitzgerald, Deborah. 2003. *Every Farm a Factory: The Industrial Ideal in American Agriculture.* New Haven: Yale University Press.

Flint, Mary Louise, and Robert van den Bosch. 1981. A History of Pest Control. In *Introduction to Integrated Pest Management*, edited by Mary Louise Flint and Robert van den Bosch, 51–81. Boston: Springer US.

Flowers, Bianca. Colorado Passes First US Right to Repair Legislation for Farmers. *US News and World Report*, April 12. https://money.usnews.com/investing/news/articles/2023-04-12/colorado-passes-first-us-right-to-repair-legislation-for-farmers.

Fontanella-Khan, James, and Arash Massoudi. 2015. Maths, Not History, Drives Mergers and Acquisitions. *Financial Times*, June 29.

Fontanella-Khan, James, and Arash Massoudi. 2016. Bayer Closes in on $66bn Deal with Monsanto. *Financial Times*, September 13.

Fontanella-Khan, James, and James Wilson. 2016. PotashCorp and Agrium in Talks to Form $30bn Group. *Financial Times*, August 30. https://www.ft.com/content/4e2f692a-6ec5-11e6-a0c9-1365ce54b926.

Food and Water Watch. 2010. Food and Agriculture Biotechnology Industry Spends More Than Half a Billion Dollars to Influence Congress. Issue brief. November.

Foroohar, Rana. 2019. *Don't Be Evil: The Case against Big Tech*. London: Penguin Books.

Foucart, Stephane, and Horel Stephane. 2017. The Monsanto Papers, Part 1—Operation: Intoxication. *Le Monde*, June 2. https://www.europeanpressprize.com/article/monsanto-papers/.

Fowler, Cary. 1994. *Unnatural Selection: Technology, Politics, and Plant Evolution*. Yverdon, Switzerland: Gordon and Breach Science Publishers.

Fowler, Cary, and Pat Mooney. 1990. *The Threatened Gene: Food, Politics, and the Loss of Genetic Diversity*. Cambridge: Lutterworth Press.

Fox, Eleanor M. 2019. Platforms, Power, and the Antitrust Challenge: A Modest Proposal to Narrow the U.S.-Europe Divide. *Nebraska Law Review* 98(2): 297–318.

Franke, Richard W. 1974. Miracle Seeds and Shattered Dreams in Java. *Challenge* 17(3): 41–47.

Fraser, Alistair. 2019. Land Grab/Data Grab: Precision Agriculture and Its New Horizons. *Journal of Peasant Studies* 46(5): 893–912.

Freedman, William. 1996. Fertilizer Mergers: The Field Narrows. *Chemical Week*, October 16: 10.

Friedmann, Harriet. 1993. The Political Economy of Food: A Global Crisis. *New Left Review* 1(197): 29–57.

Friedmann, Harriet, and Philip McMichael. 1989. Agriculture and the State System: The Rise and Decline of National Agricultures, 1870 to the Present. *Sociologia Ruralis* 29(2): 93–117.

Friends of the Earth. 2017. Sign-on Letter on Agrochemical and Seed Industry Mergers. On file with author.

Friends of the Earth. 2022. Comments Submitted to USDA Consultation on Corporate Concentration. Friends of the Earth, Comment on "Competition," 1. https://www.regulations.gov/comment/AMS-AMS-22-0025-0057.

Friends of the Earth Europe. 2022. *The Powers Pushing for the Planet-Wrecking EU-Mercosur Trade Deal . . . and Using It as a License to Greenwash.* https://friendsoftheearth.eu/wp-content/uploads/2022/03/The-powers-pushing-for-the-planet-wrecking-EU-Mercosur-deal.pdf.

Froud, Julie, Colin Haslam, Sukhdev Johal, and Karel Williams. 2000. Shareholder Value and Financialization: Consultancy Promises, Management Moves. *Economy and Society* 29(1): 80–110.

Fuchs, Doris. 2005. Commanding Heights? The Strength and Fragility of Business Power in Global Politics. *Millennium* 33(3): 771–801.

Fuglie, Keith. 2016. The Growing Role of the Private Sector in Agricultural Research and Development World-Wide. *Global Food Security* 10: 29–38.

Fuglie, Keith O., Matthew Clancy, and Paul W. Heisey. 2018. Private Sector Research and Development. In *From Agriscience to Agribusiness: Theories, Policies and Practices in Technology Transfer and Commercialization, Innovation, Technology, and Knowledge Management*, edited by Nicholas Kalaitzandonakes, Elias G. Carayannis, Evangelos Grigoroudis, and Stelios Rozakis, 41–73. Cham: Springer.

Fuglie, Keith O., Matthew Clancy, Paul Heisey, and James MacDonald. 2017. Research, Productivity, and Output Growth in U.S. Agriculture. *Journal of Agricultural and Applied Economics* 49(4): 514–554.

Fuglie, Keith O., Paul W. Heisey, John L. King, Carl E. Pray, Kelly Day-Rubenstein, David Schimmelpfennig, Sun Ling Wang, and Rupa Karmarkar-Deshmukh. 2011. *Research Investments and Market Structure in the Food Processing, Agricultural Input, and Biofuel Industries Worldwide*. US Department of Agriculture, Economic Research Service ERR-130.

Fuglie, Keith O., John L. King, Paul W. Heisey, and David E. Schimmelpfennig. 2012. Rising Concentration in Agricultural Input Industries Influences New Farm Technologies. *Amber Waves*. https://ageconsearch.umn.edu/record/142404.

Fusaro, Dave. 1989. First US Manufacturing Plant for Kubota Opens in Georgia. *Metalworking News*, August 28.

Gachelin, Gabriel, Paul Garner, Eliana Ferroni, Jan Peter Verhave, and Annick Opinel. 2018. Evidence and Strategies for Malaria Prevention and Control: A Historical Analysis. *Malaria Journal* 17: 96.

Gaines, James P., and Grady B. Crowe. 1950. Workstock vs. Tractors in the Yazoo-Mississippi Delta. *MAFES Technical Bulletins*, March 1.

Gandel, Stephen. 2016. DuPont's Former CEO Just Took a Major Swipe at Dow Chemical Deal. *Fortune*, October 18. http://fortune.com/2016/10/18/ellen-kullman-dupont-dow-deal/.

Gay, Hannah. 2012. Before and after Silent Spring: From Chemical Pesticides to Biological Control and Integrated Pest Management—Britain, 1945–1980. *Ambix* 59(2): 88–108.

Gayon, Jean, and Doris T. Zallen. 1998. The Role of the Vilmorin Company in the Promotion and Diffusion of the Experimental Science of Heredity in France. *Journal of the History of Biology* 31: 241–262.

George, Bill, and Jay W. Lorsch. 2014. How to Outsmart Activist Investors. *Harvard Business Review* 92(5): 88–95.

George, Susan. 1976. *How the Other Half Dies: The Real Reasons for World Hunger.* Harmondsworth: Penguin.

Gerbet, Thomas. "Tiger Team": When Civil Servants and Lobbyists Cooperate in the Shadows. *Radio Canada.* September 26. https://ici.radio-canada.ca/nouvelle/2012358/tiger-team-fonctionnaires-lobbyistes-croplife-canada-federal.

Gilbert, Richard. 2006. Looking for Mr. Schumpeter: Where Are We in the Competition-Innovation Debate? In *Innovation Policy and the Economy*, edited by Adam B. Jaffe, Josh Lerner, and Scott Stern, 160–215. Cambridge, MA: MIT Press.

Gillam, Carey. 2017. *Whitewash: The Story of a Weed Killer, Cancer, and the Corruption of Science.* Washington, DC: Island Press.

Gillam, Carey. 2019. Monsanto Exec Reveals $17 Million Budget for Anti-IARC, Pro-Glyphosate Efforts. *US Right to Know.* https://usrtk.org/monsanto-roundup-trial-tacker/monsanto-executive-reveals-17-million-for-anti-iarc-pro-glyphosate-efforts.

Gillam, Carey. 2021. Revealed: Monsanto Owner and US Officials Pressured Mexico to Drop Glyphosate Ban. *Guardian,* February 16. https://www.theguardian.com/business/2021/feb/16/revealed-monsanto-mexico-us-glyphosate-ban.

Gillam, Carey. 2022. "Disturbing": Weedkiller Ingredient Tied to Cancer Found in 80% of US Urine Samples. *Guardian,* July 9. https://www.theguardian.com/us-news/2022/jul/09/weedkiller-glyphosate-cdc-study-urine-samples.

Gillam, Carey. 2023a. As Trade Dispute Heats Up, Mexico Further Slashes Glyphosate Imports. *New Lede,* April 5. https://www.thenewlede.org/2023/04/as-trade-dispute-heats-up-mexico-further-slashes-glyphosate-imports/.

Gillam, Carey. 2023b. Revealed: The Secret Push to Bury a Weedkiller's Link to Parkinson's Disease. *Guardian,* June 2. https://www.theguardian.com/us-news/2023/jun/02/paraquat-parkinsons-disease-research-syngenta-weedkiller.

Gillam, Carey and Jonathan Hettinger. 2024. Mexico Delays Planned April 1 Glyphosate Ban. New Lede. April 1. https://www.thenewlede.org/2024/04/mexico-delays-planned-april-1-glyphosate-ban/.

Gilpin, Robert. 1975. *U.S. Power and the Multinational Corporation: The Political Economy of Foreign Direct Investment.* New York: Basic Books.

Gleckman, Harris. 2023. *Multi-Stakeholderism: A Corporate Push for a New Form of Global Governance.* Amsterdam: Transnational Institute. https://www.tni.org/en/publication/multi-stakeholderism-a-corporate-push-for-a-new-form-of-global-governance.

REFERENCES

Glenna, Leland. 2023. Farmers Have Been Fighting for "Right-to-Repair" Laws for Years and Supporters Say a Toothless New Agreement Doesn't Go Far Enough. *Fortune*, February 22. https://fortune.com/2023/02/22/right-to-repair-farming-agriculture-tech-rural-america/.

Glover, Dominic. 2007. Monsanto and Smallholder Farmers: A Case Study in CSR. *Third World Quarterly* 28(4): 851–867.

Glover, Dominic. 2010. The Corporate Shaping of GM Crops as a Technology for the Poor. *Journal of Peasant Studies* 37(1): 67–90.

Goldberg, Walter M. 2018. *The Geography, Nature and History of the Tropical Pacific and Its Islands*. Cham: Springer.

Government of India. 2022. Department of Consumer Affairs Sets Up Committee to Develop Comprehensive Framework on the Right to Repair. July 14. https://pib.gov.in/PressReleasePage.aspx?PRID=1841403.

Gowdy, John, and Philippe Baveye. 2019. An Evolutionary Perspective on Industrial and Sustainable Agriculture. In *Agroecosystem Diversity*, edited by Gilles Lemaire, Paulo César De Faccio Carvalho, Scott Kronberg, and Sylvie Recous, 425–433. London: Academic Press.

Gowdy, John, Mariana Mazzucato, Jeroen C. J. M. van den Bergh, Sander E. van der Leeuw, and David S. Wilson. 2016. Shaping the Evolution of Complex Societies. In *Complexity and Evolution: Toward a New Synthesis for Economics*, edited by David S. Wilson and Alan Kirman, 327–350. Cambridge, MA: MIT Press.

Gowers, Andrew. 1984. John Deere Is Fined ECU 2m. *Financial Times*, December 18.

Grabs, J., and S. L. Carodenuto. 2021. Traders as Sustainability Governance Actors in Global Food Supply Chains: A Research Agenda. *Business Strategy and the Environment* 30(2): 1314–1332.

Grabs, J., and S. Ponte. 2019. The Evolution of Power in the Global Coffee Value Chain and Production Network. *Journal of Economic Geography* 19(4): 803–828.

Grant, Hugh. 2016. Comments at Joint Investor Conference Call. https://www.sec.gov/Archives/edgar/data/1110783/000119312516711104/d250543ddefa14a.htm.

Grau, Daniel, Nicole Grau, Quentin Gascuel, Christian Paroissin, Cecile Stratonovitch, Denis Lairon, Damien Devault and Julie Di Cristofaro. 2022. Quantifiable Urine Glyphosate Levels Detected in 99% of the French Population, with Higher Values in Men, in Younger people, and in Farmers. *Environmental Science and Pollution Research* 29: 32882–32893.

Gray, Alex. 2022. The Debate over Right to Repair in 2022. *Successful Farming*, September 9. https://www.agriculture.com/machinery/repair-maintenance/the-debate-for-right-to-repair-in-2022-joe-biden-jon-tester-john-deere.

Greenhill, Robert G., and Rory M. Miller. 1973. The Peruvian Government and the Nitrate Trade, 1873–1879. *Journal of Latin American Studies* 5(1): 107–131.

Greenhouse, Steven. 1984a. Farm Equipment Hits a Trough. *New York Times*, November 11.

Greenhouse, Steven. 1984b. A Harvester-Tenneco Deal? *New York Times*, November 22.

Griesse, Margaret Ann. 2007. Developing Social Responsibility: Biotechnology and the Case of DuPont in Brazil. *Journal of Business Ethics* 73(1): 103–118.

Grushkin, Daniel. 2013. Threat to Global GM Soybean Access as Patent Nears Expiry. *Nature Biotechnology* 31(1): 10–11.

Guenther, Lisa. 2018. From Silicon Valley to Yorkton, Sask.: Farmers Business Network Is a New Grower Network That Connects Farmers Digitally. *Grainews*, December 3.

Gullickson, Gil. 2021. Carbon Markets Galore. *Successful Farming*, June 22. https://www.agriculture.com/crops/conservation/carbon-markets-galore.

Gunter, Valerie J., and Craig K. Harris. 1998. Noisy Winter: The DDT Controversy in the Years before Silent Spring. *Rural Sociology* 63(2): 179–198.

Gupta, Joyeeta, Hilmer Bosch and Luc van Vilet. 2024. AI's Excessive Water Consumption Threatens to Drown Out its Environmental Contributions. *The Conversation*. https://theconversation.com/ais-excessive-water-consumption-threatens-to-drown-out-its-environmental-contributions-225854.

Guttal, Shalmali. 2021. Re-Imagining the UN Committee on World Food Security. *Development* 64(3): 227–235.

Hackfort, Sarah. 2021. Patterns of Inequalities in Digital Agriculture: A Systematic Literature Review. *Sustainability* 13(22): 12345.

Hamann, Jasper. 2022. Morocco World. Mosaic Reduces Production Despite Calls to Boost Fertilizer Supply. *Morocco World News*, September 3. https://www.moroccoworldnews.com/2022/09/351146/mosaic-reduces-production-despite-calls-to-boost-fertilizer-supply.

Hamilton, Horace. 1939. The Social Effects of Recent Trends in the Mechanization of Agriculture. *Rural Sociology* 4(1): 3–19.

Hamilton, Shane. 2014. Agribusiness, the Family Farm, and the Politics of Technological Determinism in the Post–World War II United States. *Technology and Culture* 55(3): 560–590.

Hamilton, Shane, and Beatrice D'Ippolito. 2022. From Monsanto to "Monsatan": Ownership and Control of History as a Strategic Resource. *Business History* 64(6): 1040–1070.

Hamm, Brigitte. 2022. The Struggle for Legitimacy in Business and Human Rights Regulation—a Consideration of the Processes Leading to the UN Guiding Principles and an International Treaty. *Human Rights Review* 23(1): 103–125.

Hammond Wagner, Courtney, Michael Cox, and José Luis Bazo Robles. 2016. Pesticide Lock-In in Small Scale Peruvian Agriculture. *Ecological Economics* 129: 72–81.

Hamza M. A., and Anderson WK. 2005. Soil Compaction in Cropping Systems. *Soil and Tillage Research* 82(2): 121–45.

Harland, H. V., and M. L. Martini 1936. Problems and Results in Barley Breeding. In *USDA Yearbook of Agriculture*, 303–346. Washington DC: US Government Printing Office.

Harris, Lee. 2022. Fertilizer Firms Spread Wealth to Shareholders as Farmers Weather Extreme Prices. *American Prospect*, March 23. https://prospect.org/economy/fertilizer-firms-spread-wealth-to-shareholders-farmers-weather-extreme-prices/.

Hayley, Andrea. 2016. New Technology Spurs Consolidation in Seed Industry. *Epoch Times*, September 27. http://www.theepochtimes.com/n3/2162211-why-crispr-is-key-to-massive-agribusiness-consolidations/.

Hébert, Marie-Pier, Vincent Fugère, and Andrew Gonzalez. 2019. The Overlooked Impact of Rising Glyphosate Use on Phosphorus Loading in Agricultural Watersheds. *Frontiers in Ecology and the Environment* 17(1): 48–56.

Heckman, Joseph. 2006. A History of Organic Farming: Transitions from Sir Albert Howard's "War in the Soil" to USDA National Organic Program. *Renewable Agriculture and Food Systems* 21(3): 143–150.

Henderson, Jason, Brent Gloy, and Michael Boehlje. 2011. Agriculture's Boom-Bust Cycles: Is This Time Different? *Economic Review*, Federal Reserve Bank of Kansas City.

Hendra, John. 1987. Only "Fit to Be Tied": A Comparison of the Canadian Tied Aid Policy with the Tied Aid Policies of Sweden, Norway and Denmark. *Canadian Journal of Development Studies/Revue Canadienne d'études du Développement* 8(2): 261–81.

Hendrickson, Mary, Philip Howard, Emily Miller, and Douglas Constance. 2020. *Food System Concentration and Its Impacts*. Family Farm Action Alliance. https://farmaction.us/wp-content/uploads/2021/05/Hendrickson-et-al.-2020.-Concentration-and-Its-Impacts_FINAL_Addended.pdf.

Henry, Robert J. 2020. Innovations in Plant Genetics Adapting Agriculture to Climate Change. *Current Opinion in Plant Biology* 56: 168–173.

Heppner, Kelvin. 2022. Machinery Dealers Ask for Farm Equipment to Be Exempt from Proposed Right-to-Repair Law. November 17. https://www.realagriculture.com/2022/11/machinery-dealers-ask-for-farm-equipment-to-be-exempt-from-proposed-right-to-repair-law/.

Herrera, Lucía Cholakian. 2023. Environmental Activists Protest Ex-Syngenta CEO's Appointment as Advisor. *Buenos Aires Herald*, January 11. https://buenosairesherald

.com/society/environmental-activists-protest-ex-syngenta-ceos-appointment-as-advisor.

High Level Panel of Experts on Food Security and Nutrition. 2019. *Agroecological and Other Innovative Approaches for Sustainable Agriculture and Food Systems That Enhance Food Security and Nutrition.* Report by the High Level Panel of Experts on Food Security and Nutrition of the Committee on World Food Security. Rome.

Hightower, Jim. 1973. *Hard Tomatoes, Hard Times: A Report of the Agribusiness Accountability Project on the Failure of America's Land Grant College Complex.* Cambridge: Schenkman.

Holleman, Hannah. 2017. De-Naturalizing Ecological Disaster: Colonialism, Racism and the Global Dust Bowl of the 1930s. *Journal of Peasant Studies* 44(1): 234–260.

Howard, A. 1946. *The War in the Soil.* Emmaus, PA: Rodale Press.

Howard, Albert. 1947. *The Soil and Health: A Study of Organic Agriculture.* London: Faber and Faber.

Howard, Philip H. 2009. Visualizing Consolidation in the Global Seed Industry: 1996–2008. *Sustainability* 1(4): 1266–1287.

Howard, Philip H. 2015. Intellectual Property and Consolidation in the Seed Industry. *Crop Science* 55(6): 2489.

Howard, Philip H. 2016. *Concentration and Power in the Food System.* New York: Bloomsbury.

Howard, Philip H. 2019. Corporate Concentration in Global Meat Processing: The Role of Feed and Finance Subsidies. In *Global Meat: Social and Environmental Consequences of the Expanding Meat Industry,* edited by Bill Winders and Elizabeth Ransom, 1–53. Cambridge, MA: MIT Press.

Hruska, Allan. 2021. What the Global Battle against the Fall Armyworm Reveals about How the US and China See the Future of Global Food Production. *Issues in Science and Technology,* May 6. https://issues.org/fall-armyworm-us-china-global-food-production-hruska/.

Hüesker, Frank, and Robert Lepenies. 2022. Why Does Pesticide Pollution in Water Persist? *Environmental Science and Policy* 128: 185–193.

Huffman, Wallace E., and Robert E. Evenson. 2001. Structural and Productivity Change in US Agriculture, 1950–1982. *Agricultural Economics* 24(2): 127–147.

IATP and GRAIN. 2022. *The Fertilizer Trap.* https://www.iatp.org/the-fertiliser-trap.

IATP and GRAIN. 2023. *A Corporate Cartel Fertilizes Food Inflation.* https://www.iatp.org/corporate-cartel-fertilises-food-inflation.

ICF Incorporated. 1980. *Economic Profile of the Pesticide Industry.* Prepared for the US Environmental Protection Agency.

IHS Markit. 2019. *Analysis of Sales and Profitability within the Seed Sector.* http://www.fao.org/3/ca6929en/ca6929en.pdf.

IHS Markit. 2021. *Featured Insight: The Global Seed Market in 2020.* https://cdn.ihsmarkit.com/www/pdf/1221/IHS-Markit-Seed-Market-Data-Featured-Insight.pdf.

Illies, Christian. 2016. New Debates in Old Ethical Skins. In *Synthetic Biology Analyzed: Tools for Discussion and Evaluation*, edited by Margret Englehard, 89–126. Cham: Springer.

International Agency for Research on Cancer (IARC). 2018. *IARC Response to Criticisms of the Monographs and the Glyphosate Evaluation.* https://www.iarc.fr/wp-content/uploads/2018/07/IARC_response_to_criticisms_of_the_Monographs_and_the_glyphosate_evaluation.pdf.

IPES-Food 2022a. *Another Perfect Storm?* International Panel of Experts on Sustainable Food Systems. https://ipes-food.org/_img/upload/files/AnotherPerfectStorm.pdf.

IPES-Food 2022b. *Smoke and Mirrors: Examining Competing Framings of Food System Sustainability.* http://www.ipes-food.org/pages/smokeandmirrors.

IPES-Food. 2017. *Too Big to Feed: Exploring the Impacts of Mega-Mergers, Consolidation and Concentration of Power in the Agri-Food Sector.* International Panel of Experts on Sustainable Food Systems. https://www.ipes-food.org/_img/upload/files/Concentration_FullReport.pdf.

IPES-Food. 2020. *Money Flows: What Is Holding Back Investment in Agroecological Research for Africa?* https://www.ipes-food.org/_img/upload/files/Money%20Flows_Full%20report.pdf.

IPES-Food. 2021. *The Long Food Movement: Transforming Food Systems by 2045.* http://www.ipes-food.org/_img/upload/files/LongFoodMovementEN.pdf.

IPES-Food. 2023a. *Breaking the Cycle of Unsustainable Food Systems, Hunger and Debt.* http://www.ipes-food.org/pages/debtfoodcrisis.

IPES-Food. 2023b. *Who's Tipping the Scales? The Growing Influence of Corporations on the Governance of Food Systems, and How to Counter It.* http://www.ipes-food.org/pages/tippingthescales.

ISAAA. 2004. *Global Status of Commercialized Biotech/GM Crops: 2004.* ISAAA briefs 33. Ithaca, NY: International Service for the Acquisition of Agribiotech Applications.

ISAAA. 2014. *Global Status of Commercialized Biotech/GM Crops: 2014.* ISAAA briefs 49. Ithaca, NY: International Service for the Acquisition of Agri-biotech Applications.

Isakson, S. Ryan. 2014. Food and Finance: The Financial Transformation of Agro-Food Supply Chains. *Journal of Peasant Studies* 41(5): 749–775.

J. D. Woods and Gordon, Limited. 1956. *The Canadian Agricultural Machinery Industry.* Ottawa: Royal Commission on Canada's Economic Prospects. https://publications.gc.ca/site/eng/9.893513/publication.html.

Jacoby, Erich H. 1975. Transnational Corporations and Third World Agriculture. *Development and Change* 6(3): 90–97.

Jansen, Kees. 2017. Business Conflict and Risk Regulation: Understanding the Influence of the Pesticide Industry. *Global Environmental Politics* 17(4): 48–66.

Jarman, Walter M., and Karlheinz Ballschmiter. 2012. From Coal to DDT: The History of the Development of the Pesticide DDT from Synthetic Dyes till Silent Spring. *Endeavour, Silent Spring after Fifty Years* 36(4): 131–142.

Jasny, Naum. 1935. Tractor versus Horse as a Source of Farm Power. *American Economic Review* 25(4): 708–723.

Jenny, Frédéric. 2012. Export Cartels in Primary Products: The Potash Case in Perspective. In *Trade, Competition, and the Pricing of Commodities*, edited by Simon Evenett and Frédéric Jenny, 99–132. London: Centre for Economic Policy Research.

Johnson, George Fiske. 1935. The Early History of Copper Fungicides. *Agricultural History* 9(2): 67–79.

Johnson, Timothy. 2016. Nitrogen Nation: The Legacy of World War I and the Politics of Chemical Agriculture in the United States, 1916–1933. *Agricultural History* 90(2): 209–229.

Jones, Bryn, and Peter Nisbet. 2011. Shareholder Value Versus Stakeholder Values: CSR and Financialization in Global Food Firms. *Socio-Economic Review* 9(2): 287–314.

Juma, Calestous. 1989. *The Gene Hungers: Biotechnology and the Scramble for Seeds*. London: Zed Books.

Kaan, Christopher, and Andrea Liese. 2010. Public Private Partnerships in Global Food Governance: Business Engagement and Legitimacy in the Global Fight Against Hunger and Malnutrition. *Agriculture and Human Values* 28(3): 385–399.

Karavolias, Nicholas G., Wilson Horner, Modesta N. Abugu, and Sarah N. Evanega. 2021. Application of Gene Editing for Climate Change in Agriculture. *Frontiers in Sustainable Food Systems* 5. https://www.frontiersin.org/articles/10.3389/fsufs.2021.685801.

Kelloway, Claire. 2019. At FTC Workshop, Advocates and Business Owners Say Manufacturers Monopolize Repair. *Food and Power*, August 1. https://www.foodandpower.net/latest/2019/08/01/at-ftc-workshop-advocates-and-business-owners-say-manufacturers-monopolize-repair.

Kelloway, Claire. 2021a. Farmers Sue Big Ag for Allegedly Sidelining E-Commerce Startups. *Food and Power*, March 4. https://www.foodandpower.net/latest/crop-inputs-retail-antitrust-suit.

Kelloway, Claire. 2021b. The Tricky New Way That Big Ag Is Getting Farm Data. *Washington Monthly*, October 5. http://washingtonmonthly.com/2021/10/05/the-tricky-new-way-that-big-ag-is-getting-farm-data/.

Kelloway, Claire. 2022. FTC Says Pesticide Companies Paid to Block Cheaper Competitors, Raising Prices. *Food and Power*, October 13. https://www.foodandpower.net/latest/10-13-2022-ftc-pesticide-loyalty-rebates-suit.

Kemesiz, Paul. 1990. Fertilizers: A Growing Role in 1990. *Chemical Week*, February 21: 6–7.

Khan, Lina M. 2013. How Monsanto Outfoxed the Obama Administration. *Salon*, March 15.

Khan, Lina M. 2017. Amazon's Antitrust Paradox. *Yale Law Journal* 126: 710–805.

Khan, Lina M. 2018. The New Brandeis Movement: America's Antimonopoly Debate. *Journal of European Competition Law and Practice* 9(3): 131–132.

Khan, Lina, and Sandeep Vaheesan. 2017. Market Power and Inequality: The Antitrust Counterrevolution and Its Discontents. *Harvard Law and Policy Review* 11: 235–294.

Kilman, Scott. 1999. Monsanto Avoids Gene Controversy by Quitting Bid. *Wall Street Journal*, December 22.

Kilman, Scott, and Susan Warren. 1999. Monsanto Has Held Talks with DuPont and Others about Merger or Alliance. *Wall Street Journal*, March 4.

Kimle, Kevin L., and Marvin L. Hayenga. 1993. Structural Change among Agricultural Input Industries. *Agribusiness* 9(1): 15–27.

King, John L. 2001. *Concentration and Technology in Agricultural Input Industries*. USDA Economic Research Service, Agriculture Information Bulletin 763. March. https://www.researchgate.net/profile/John_King15/publication/23516824_Concentration_and_Technology_in_Agricultural_Input_Industries/links/0c96051ddba4f06fa4000000.pdf.

King, John, Andrew Toole, and Keith Fuglie. 2012. The Complementary Roles of the Public and Private Sectors in U.S. Agricultural Research. USDA economic brief 19. September.

Kingsbury, Noel. 2009. *Hybrid: The History and Science of Plant Breeding*. Chicago: University of Chicago Press.

Kinkela, David. 2005. The Question of Success and Environmental Ethics: Revisiting the DDT Controversy from a Transnational Perspective, 1967–72. *Ethics, Place and Environment* 8(2): 159–179.

Kinkela, David. 2011. *DDT and the American Century: Global Health, Environmental Politics, and the Pesticide That Changed the World*. Chapel Hill: University of North Carolina Press.

Klerkx, Laurens, Emma Jakku, and Pierre Labarthe. 2019. A Review of Social Science on Digital Agriculture, Smart Farming and Agriculture 4.0: New Contributions and a Future Research Agenda. *NJAS—Wageningen Journal of Life Sciences* 90–91: 100315.

Klobuchar, Amy. 2021. *Antitrust: Taking on Monopoly Power from the Gilded Age to the Digital Age*. New York: Knopf.

Kloppenburg, Jack R. 2004. *First the Seed: The Political Economy of Plant Biotechnology*, 2nd ed. Madison: University of Wisconsin Press.

Knight, Will. 2022. John Deere's Self-Driving Tractor Stirs Debate on AI in Farming. *Wired*, January 4. https://www.wired.com/story/john-deere-self-driving-tractor-stirs-debate-ai-farming/.

Kotlowitz, Alex, Damon Darlin, and Bill Abrams. 1985. Ford to Purchase Sperry's New Holland Farm-Equipment Unit for $330 Million. *Wall Street Journal*, October 11.

Koven, Peter. 2015. Agrium Inc Activist Investor ValueAct Happy to Keep Hands Off and Enjoy Profits. *Financial Post*, March 12. https://financialpost.com/investing/agrium-inc-activist-investor-valueact-happy-to-keep-hands-off-and-enjoy-profits.

Kramer, Helen M. 1964. Harvesters and High Finance: Formation of the International Harvester Company. *Business History Review* 38(3): 283–301.

Kreisle, Nicholas. 2020. Price Effects from the Merger of Agricultural Fertilizer Manufacturers Agrium and PotashCorp. Bureau of Economics, Federal Trade Commission working paper 345.

Krimsky, Sheldon, and Carey Gillam. 2018. Roundup Litigation Discovery Documents: Implications for Public Health and Journal Ethics. *Journal of Public Health Policy, Basingstoke* 39(3): 318–326.

Kulick, Robert, and Andrew Card. 2022. *Industrial Concentration in the United States 2002–2017*. NERA Economic Consulting and US Chamber of Commerce.

Kurz, Mordecai. 2023. *The Market Power of Technology: Understanding the Second Gilded Age*. New York: Columbia University Press.

Kwoka, J. 2017. U.S. Antitrust and Competition Policy amid the New Merger Wave. Washington Center for Equitable Growth. https://equitablegrowth.org/wp-content/uploads/2017/07/072717-kwoka-antitrust-report.pdf.

Kynge, James, Tom Mitchell, and Arash Massoudi. 2016. M&A: China's World of Debt. *Financial Times*, February 11.

Lacy, Katherine, Peter F. Orazem, and Skyler Schneekloth. 2023. Measuring the American Farm Size Distribution. *American Journal of Agricultural Economics* 105(1): 219–242.

Lacy-Nichols, Jennifer, Robert Marten, Eric Crosbie, and Rob Moodie. 2022. The Public Health Playbook: Ideas for Challenging the Corporate Playbook. *Lancet Global Health* 10(7): e1067–e1072.

Lajoie-O'Malley, Alana, Kelly Bronson, Simone van der Burg, and Laurens Klerkx. 2020. The Future(s) of Digital Agriculture and Sustainable Food Systems: An Analysis of High-Level Policy Documents. *Ecosystem Services* 45: 101183.

Lal, R., D. C. Reicosky, and J. D. Hanson. 2007. Evolution of the Plow over 10,000 Years and the Rationale for No-Till Farming. *Soil and Tillage Research* 93(1): 1–12.

REFERENCES

Lamer, Mirko. 1957. *The World Fertilizer Economy*. Stanford: Stanford University Press.

Lamphere, Jenna A., and Elizabeth A. East. 2017. Monsanto's Biotechnology Politics: Discourses of Legitimation. *Environmental Communication* 11(1): 75–89.

Landauer, Walter. 1945. Shall We Lose or Keep Our Plant and Animal Stocks? *Science* 101(2629): 497–499.

Landes, William M., and Richard A. Posner. 1981. Market Power in Antitrust Cases. *Harvard Law Review* 94(5): 937–996.

Larew, Rob. 2023. Testimony of Rob Larew, President (NFU). Submitted to the U.S. House of Representatives Committee on Agriculture: Uncertainty, Inflation, Regulations: Challenges for American Agriculture, February 28. https://agriculture.house.gov/uploadedfiles/larew_testimony_package.pdf.

Larson, David. 1970. An Economic Analysis of the Webb-Pomerene Act. *Journal of Law and Economics* 13(2): 461–500.

Laurenson, John. 1990. New Era in Europe? *Chemical Week* 146(20): 26.

Law, Jonathan. 2016. Oligopoly. In *A Dictionary of Business and Management*, edited by Jonathan Law. Oxford: Oxford University Press.

Lawder, David. 2023. U.S. Demands Mexico Explain Science behind GMO Corn Ban. Reuters, February 9. https://www.reuters.com/markets/commodities/us-demands-mexico-explain-science-behind-gmo-corn-ban-2023-02-10/.

LeBaron, G. 2020. *Combatting Modern Slavery: Why Labour Governance Is Failing and What We Can Do about It*. Cambridge: Polity Press.

Leguizamón, Amalia. 2016. Environmental Injustice in Argentina: Struggles against Genetically Modified Soy. *Journal of Agrarian Change* 16(4): 684–692.

Leibenluft, Robert. 1981. *Competition in Farm Inputs: An Examination of Four Industries*. Policy Planning Issues paper. Washington DC: Federal Trade Commission.

León Araya, Andrés. 2023. Monocrops. *Journal of Peasant Studies* 50(3): 797–808.

Lerner, Sharon. 2021. The Department of Yes: How Pesticide Companies Corrupted the EPA and Poisoned America. *Intercept*. https://theintercept.com/2021/06/30/epa-pesticides-exposure-opp/.

Lesser, William. 1999. Intellectual Property Rights and Concentration in Agricultural Biotechnology. http://www.agbioforum.org/v1n2/v1n2a03-lesser.htm.

Levy, David, and Peter Newell, eds. 2005. *The Business of Global Environmental Governance*. Cambridge, MA: MIT Press.

Lianos, Ioannis, Alina Velias, Dmitry Katalevsky, and George Ovchinnikov. 2020. Financialization of the Food Value Chain, Common Ownership and Competition Law. *European Competition Journal* 16(1): 149–220.

Lie, Einar. 2008. Market Power and Market Failure: The Decline of the European Fertilizer Industry and the Expansion of Norsk Hydro. *Enterprise and Society* 9(1): 70–95.

Lieberman, Marvin B., and David B. Montgomery. 1987. First-Mover Advantages. *Strategic Management Journal* 9: 41–58.

Liebig, Justus von. 1840. *Organic Chemistry in Its Application to Agriculture and Physiology*. London: Taylor and Walton.

Lindquist, Arthur, and H. G. Wilson. 1948. Development of a Strain of Houseflies Resistant to DDT. *Science* 107(2776): 276.

Lonergan, Raymond. 1941. Labor, Organ of the 15 Recognized Standard Railroad Labor Organizations. In *Mr. Justice Brandeis, Great American*, edited by Irving Dilliard. Modern View Press.

Lovec, M. 2018. The Common Agricultural Policy Crisis of the 1970s/1980s: Accommodating the Logics of Appropriateness and Consequences. *Journal of European Integration History* 23(2): 245–262.

Luby, Claire H., and Irwin L. Goldman. 2016. Freeing Crop Genetics through the Open Source Seed Initiative. *PLoS Biology* 14(4): e1002441.

Lyden, O. 1978. *Growth of Cooperatives in Seven Industries*. Cooperative Management Division, Economics, Statistics, and Cooperatives Service, US Department of Agriculture.

M.M.B. 1906. The Jardin des Plantes before and during the Revolution. *Plant World* 9(8): 196–199.

MacDonald, James. 2017a. Consolidation, Concentration, and Competition in the Food System. *Economic Review*, Federal Reserve Bank of Kansas City, 85–105.

MacDonald, James. 2017b. *Mergers and Competition in Seed and Agricultural Chemical Markets*. Economic Research Service, US Department of Agriculture. https://www.ers.usda.gov/amber-waves/2017/april/mergers-and-competition-in-seed-and-agricultural-chemical-markets/.

MacDonald, James, Xiao Dong, and Keith Fuglie. 2023. Concentration and Competition in U.S. Agribusiness. Economic Information bulletin 256. USDA Economic Research Service. https://www.ers.usda.gov/webdocs/publications/106795/eib-256.pdf?v=352.7

MacDonald, James M., Penni Korb, and Robert A. Hoppe. 2013. Farm Size and the Organization of U.S. Crop Farming. Economic Research Service, US Department of Agriculture. US Department of Agriculture. https://www.ers.usda.gov/webdocs/publications/45108/39359_err152.pdf.

MacIntyre, Angus A. 1987. Why Pesticides Received Extensive Use in America: A Political Economy of Agricultural Pest Management of 1970. *Natural Resources Journal* 27(3): 533–578.

Magrini, Marie-Benoit, Marc Anton, Célia Cholez, Guenaelle Corre-Hellou, Gérard Duc, Marie-Hélène Jeuffroy, Jean-Marc Meynard, Elise Pelzer, Anne-Sophie Voisin, and Stéphane Walrand. 2016. Why Are Grain-Legumes Rarely Present in Cropping Systems Despite Their Environmental and Nutritional Benefits? Analyzing Lock-In in the French Agrifood System. *Ecological Economics* 126: 152–162.

Magrini, Marie-Benoit, Nicolas Berfort, and Martino Nieddu. 2019. Technological Lock-In and Pathways for Crop Diversification in the Bio-Economy. In *Agroecosystem Diversity*, edited by Gilles Lemaire, Paulo César De Faccio Carvalho, Scott Kronberg, and Sylvie Recous, 375–388. London: Academic Press.

Mah, Feng-Hwa. 1971. Why China Imports Wheat. *China Quarterly* 45: 116–128.

Maisashvili, Aleksandre, Henry Bryant, J. Marc Raulston, George Knapek, Joe Outlaw, and James Richardson. 2016. Seed Prices, Proposed Mergers and Acquisitions among Biotech Firms. *Choices* 31(4). http://www.choicesmagazine.org/choices-magazine/submitted-articles/seed-prices-proposed-mergers-and-acquisitions-among-biotech-firms.

Makri, Marianna, Michael A. Hitt, and Peter J. Lane. 2010. Complementary Technologies, Knowledge Relatedness, and Invention Outcomes in High Technology Mergers and Acquisitions. *Strategic Management Journal* 31(6): 601–628.

Malhotra, Bharti. 2022. Featured Insight: Seed Market Performance in 2021. https://cdn.ihsmarkit.com/www/pdf/0922/SeedMarketPerformance2021.pdf.

Malkin, Stacy. 2018. Secret Documents Expose Monsanto's War on Cancer Scientists. *Truthout*, July 16. https://truthout.org/articles/secret-documents-expose-monsantos-war-on-cancer-scientists/.

Malpass, David. 2022. A Transformed Fertilizer Market is Needed in Response to the Food Crisis in Africa. *Voices, World Bank Blogs*. https://blogs.worldbank.org/voices/transformed-fertilizer-market-needed-response-food-crisis-africa.

Mangelsdorf, Paul C. 1951. Hybrid Corn. *Scientific American* 185(2): 39–47.

Mann, Charles. 2011. *1493: Uncovering the New World Columbus Created*. New York: Knopf.

Marchesi, Greta. 2020. Justus von Liebig Makes the World: Soil Properties and Social Change in the Nineteenth Century. *Environmental Humanities* 12(1): 205–226.

Mares, Radu. 2022. Regulating Transnational Corporations at the United Nations—the Negotiations of a Treaty on Business and Human Rights. *International Journal of Human Rights* 26(9): 1522–1546.

Markham, Jesse. 1958. *The Fertilizer Industry: Study of an Imperfect Market*. Nashville, TN: Vanderbilt University Press.

Marsh, Barbara. 1985. *A Corporate Tragedy: The Agony of International Harvester Company*. New York: Doubleday.

Marshak, Maya, Fern Wickson, Amaranta Herrero, and Rachel Wynberg. 2021. Losing Practices, Relationships and Agency: Ecological Deskilling as a Consequence of the Uptake of Modern Seed Varieties among South African Smallholders. *Agroecology and Sustainable Food Systems* 45(8): 1189–1212.

Martin, Edward Winslow. 1873. *History of the Grange Movement or, the Farmer's War against Monopolies Being a Full and Authentic Account of the Struggles of the American Farmers against the Extortions of the Railroad Companies*. Reprinted 1967: New York: Burt Franklin.

Massoudi, Arash, and James Fontanella-Khan. 2015. Monsanto Gives Up on $46bn Syngenta Deal. *Financial Times*, August 26.

Massoudi, Arash, James Fontanella-Khan, and Guy Chazan. 2016. Bayer Braced for Tough Scrutiny over $66bn Monsanto Deal. *Financial Times*, September 14.

Massoudi, Arash, Don Weinland, Ralph Atkins, Shawn Donnan, and Barney Jopson. 2016. ChemChina Plays Down Alarm over $44bn Syngenta Bid. *Financial Times*, February 3.

Matthews, Sheenagh, Dinesh Nair, and Ruth David. 2016. July 13. Monsanto Revives Talks with BASF over Bayer Alternative. *Bloomberg*. https://www.bloomberg.com/news/articles/2016-07-13/monsanto-said-to-revive-talks-with-basf-over-bayer-alternative#xj4y7vzkg.

Mayo, John. 1980. A "Company" War? The Antofagasta Nitrate Company and the Outbreak of the War of the Pacific. *Boletín de Estudios Latinoamericanos y del Caribe* 28: 3–11

McCormick, Cyrus. 1931. *The Century of the Reaper*. Boston: Houghton Mifflin.

McCullough, Michael. 2020. What Investors Still Don't Understand about Nutrien. *Globe and Mail*, October 27.

McHenry, Leemon B. 2018. The Monsanto Papers: Poisoning the Scientific Well. *International Journal of Risk and Safety in Medicine* 29(3–4): 193–205.

McKeon, Nora. 2014. *The New Alliance for Food Security and Nutrition: A Coup for Corporate Capital*. Amsterdam: Transnational Institute. https://www.tni.org/en/publication/the-new-alliance-for-food-security-and-nutrition.

McMichael, Philip. 2005. Global Development and the Corporate Food Regime. In *New Directions in the Sociology of Global Development*, edited by F. H. Buttel and P. McMichael, eds., 265–299. Leeds: Emerald.

McMichael, Philip. 2009. A Food Regime Analysis of the "World Food Crisis." *Agriculture and Human Values* 26(4): 281.

McMichael, Philip. 2013. *Food Regimes and Agrarian Questions*. Halifax: Fernwood Publishing.

McMichael, Philip. 2020. Does China's "Going Out" Strategy Prefigure a New Food Regime? *Journal of Peasant Studies* 47(1): 116–154.

McMichael, Philip. 2021. Shock and Awe in the UNFSS. *Development* 64(3): 162–171.

McMillan, Robert T. 1949. Effects of Mechanization on American Agriculture. *Scientific Monthly* 69(1): 23–28.

McWilliams, James E. 2008. "The Horizon Opened Up Very Greatly": Leland O. Howard and the Transition to Chemical Insecticides in the United States, 1894–1927. *Agricultural History* 82(4): 468–495.

Meagher, M. 2020. *Competition Is Killing Us: How Big Business Is Harming Our Society and Plant—and What to Do about It*. London: Penguin.

Mehrabi, Zia, Mollie J. McDowell, Vincent Ricciardi, Christian Levers, Juan Diego Martinez, Natascha Mehrabi, Hannah Wittman, Navin Ramankutty and Andy Jarvis. 2021. The Global Divide in Data-Driven Farming. *Nature Sustainability* 4(2): 154–160.

Melillo, Edward D. 2012. The First Green Revolution: Debt Peonage and the Making of the Nitrogen Fertilizer Trade, 1840–1930. *American Historical Review* 117(4): 1028–1060.

Melo, Hector, and Israel Yost. 1970. Funding the Empire: Us Foreign Aid—Part 1. *NACLA Newsletter* 4(2): 1–13.

Milmo, Sean. 1996. BASF Selling Potash Stake to PCS. *Chemical Marketing Reporter*, August 19, 9.

Mirr, Nicholas A. 2020. Defending the Right to Repair: An Argument for Federal Legislation Guaranteeing the Right to Repair Notes. *Iowa Law Review* 105(5): 2393–2428.

Mitchell, Tom, Christian Shepherd, and Ralph Atkins. 2016. Syngenta Offers ChemChina Seeds of GM Growth. *Financial Times*, February 3.

Molot, Maureen Appel, and Jeanne Kirk Laux. 1979. The Politics of Nationalization. *Canadian Journal of Political Science/Revue canadienne de science politique* 12(2): 227–258.

Monsanto. 2017. IARC's Report on Glyphosate, April 21. https://monsanto.com/company/media/statements/glyphosate-report-response/.

Montello, S. Kyle. 2020. The Right to Repair and the Corporate Stranglehold over the Consumer: Profits over People Comments. *Tulane Journal of Technology and Intellectual Property* 22: 165–184.

Montenegro de Wit, Maywa. 2020. Democratizing CRISPR? Stories, Practices, and Politics of Science and Governance on the Agricultural Gene Editing Frontier. *Elementa: Science of the Anthropocene* 8: 9.

Montenegro de Wit, Maywa. 2022. Can Agroecology and CRISPR Mix? The Politics of Complementarity and Moving Toward Technology Sovereignty. *Agriculture and Human Values* 39(2): 733–755.

Monteón, Michael. 2003. John T. North, the Nitrate King, and Chile's Lost Future. *Latin American Perspectives* 30(6): 69–90.

Mooney, Pat. 2018. What's Cooking for Climate Change? Techno-Fixing Dinner for 10 Billion. *Bulletin of the Atomic Scientists* 74(6): 390–396.

Mooney, Pat Roy. 1980. *Seeds of the Earth: A Private or Public Resource?* Ottawa: Inter Pares, for the International Coalition for Development Action and Canadian Council for International Cooperation.

Mordock, Jeff. 2016. A Wildly Different DuPont a Year after Peltz Defeat. *News Journal*, Delaware Online, April 29. http://www.delawareonline.com/story/money/2016/04/29/duponts-wild-ride/83650956/.

Morehouse, Ward. 1993. The Ethics of Industrial Disasters in a Transnational World: The Elusive Quest for Justice and Accountability in Bhopal. *Alternatives: Global, Local, Political* 18(4): 475–504.

Moretti, Irene Musselli. 2006. Tracking the Trend toward Market Concentration: The Case of the Agricultural Input Industry, UNCTAD. UNCTAD/DITC/COM/2005/16.

Morris, Gregory. 1989. Shell's Seeds Seek Growth. *Chemical Week*, December 13: 9.

Morris, Gregory. 1996. Norsk Hydro Buys Nutrite Outright. *Chemical Week* 158(3): 20

Mosaic. 2021. Morocco and Russia Subject to Phosphate Fertilizer Import Duties, March 11. https://investors.mosaicco.com/press-releases/news-details/2021/Morocco-and-Russia-Subject-to-Phosphate-Fertilizer-Import-Duties/default.aspx.

Moskal, Brian S. 1985. Tenneco's Big Gamble *Industry Week* 224(5): 20.

Mt. Pleasant, Jane, and Robert F. Burt. 2010. Estimating Productivity of Traditional Iroquoian Cropping Systems from Field Experiments and Historical Literature. *Journal of Ethnobiology* 30(1): 52–79.

Murray, David. 2023. Justice Department Sides with Farmers in Right-to-Repair Case. *High Plains Journal*, March 1. https://www.hpj.com/ag_news/justice-department-sides-with-farmers-in-right-to-repair-case/article_1068884c-b3a1-11ed-bd27-bb778edd5a1b.html.

Myers, John Peterson, Michael Antoniou, Bruce Blumberg, Lynn Carroll, Theo Colburn, Lorne G. Everett, Michael Hansen, et al. 2016. Concerns over Use of Glyphosate-Based Herbicides and Risks Associated with Exposures: A Consensus Statement. *Environmental Health; London* 15: 19.

Nag, Amal. 1985. Ford Will Move Production to Europe of Large Farm Tractors by End of Year. *Wall Street Journal*, February 15.

Naldi, Maurizio, and Marta Flamini. 2014. *The CR4 Index and the Interval Estimation of the Herfindahl-Hirschman Index: An Empirical Comparison.* https://papers.ssrn.com/sol3/papers.cfm?abstract_id=2448656.

National Farmers Union (Canada). 2021. NFU Comments on Draft Greenhouse Gas Offset Credit System Regulations. Fedl-Regulations-for-Offset-Protocols-NFU-submission-May-2021-Final(1).pdf.

National Potash Producers Association and National Borax Producers Association. 1933. Proposed Code of Fair Competition for the Potash and Borax Industry. National Recovery Administration. Washington DC: US Government Printing Office.

Neely, Todd. 2022. John Deere Right-to-Repair Lawsuit: Consolidated Class Action Lawsuit Underway in Federal Court. *DTN Progressive Farmer*, November 4. https://www.dtnpf.com/agriculture/web/ag/equipment/article/2022/11/04/john-deere-right-repair-lawsuit.

Nelson, Arthur. 2019. EU Glyphosate Approval was based on Plagiarised Monsanto Text, Report Finds. *Guardian*, January 16.

Nestle, Marion. 2007. *Food Politics: How the Food Industry Influences Nutrition and Health*. Berkeley: University of California Press.

Neve, Paul. 2018. Gene Drive Systems: Do They Have a Place in Agricultural Weed Management?: Gene Drive and Weed Management. *Pest Management Science* 74(12): 2671–2679.

Newell, Peter. 2003. Globalization and the Governance of Biotechnology. *Global Environmental Politics* 3(2): 56–71.

Newell, Peter, and Ruth Mackenzie. 2004. Whose Rules Rule? Development and the Global Governance of Biotechnology. *IDS Bulletin* 35(1): 82–91.

Newell, Peter, and Olivia Taylor. 2018. Contested Landscapes: The Global Political Economy of Climate-Smart Agriculture. *Journal of Peasant Studies* 45(1): 108–129.

New York Times. 1855. Peru and Its Relations, April 16.

New York Times. 1861. Agriculture and the Patent Office, January 30.

New York Times. 1977. 5 Major Potash Producers Acquitted on Price Fixing, May 7, 13.

Noel, Andrew Marc. 2016. Syngenta Says U.S. Talks over ChemChina Bid "Constructive." *Bloomberg*, July 22. http://www.bloomberg.com/news/articles/2016-07-22/syngenta-says-regulatory-talks-over-chemchina-bid-constructive.

Noori, Jafar, Maria Dimaki, John Mortensen, and Winnie Svendsen. 2018. Detection of Glyphosate in Drinking Water: A Fast and Direct Detection Method without Sample Pretreatment. *Sensors* 18(9): 2961.

Nourse, E. G. 1930. Some Economic and Social Accompaniments of the Mechanization of Agriculture. *American Economic Review* 20(1): 114–132.

Nutrien. 2021. Annual Report 2021. https://www.nutrien.com/investors/financial-reporting.

Nutrien. 2022. Annual Report 2022. https://www.nutrien.com/investors/financial-reporting.

O'Connor, Matt. 1984. Farm-Equipment Makers Find Times Are More Harrowing Than Expected. *Wall Street Journal*, October 12.

OECD. 2018. *Concentration in Seed Markets: Potential Effects and Policy Responses.* OECD. https://www.oecd-ilibrary.org/agriculture-and-food/concentration-in-seed-markets_9789264308367-en.

Ollinger, Michael, and Jorge Fernandez-Cornejo. 1995. *Regulation, Innovation, and Market Structure in the U.S. Pesticide Industry.* USDA Economic Research Service, Agricultural Economic Report 719.

Ollinger, Michael, and Jorge Fernandez-Cornejo. 1998. Sunk Costs and Regulation in the U.S. Pesticide Industry. *International Journal of Industrial Organization* 16(2): 139–168.

Ollinger, Michael, and Leslie Pope. 1995. Strategic Research Interests, Organizational Behavior, and the Emerging Market for the Products of Plant Biotechnology. *Technological Forecasting and Social Change, Biotechnology and the Future of Agriculture and Natural Resources* 50(1): 55–68.

Olmstead, Alan L., and Paul W. Rhode. 2001. Reshaping the Landscape: The Impact and Diffusion of the Tractor in American Agriculture, 1910–1960. *Journal of Economic History* 61(3): 663–698.

Open Markets Institute. 2022. Comment from Open Markets Institute. Comments to USDA. https://www.regulations.gov/comment/AMS-AMS-22-0027-1411.

Open Markets Institute and Friends of the Earth. 2023. *Agricultural Carbon Markets, Payments, and Data: Big Ag's Latest Power Grab.* https://foe.org/resources/ag-carbon-markets-report/.

Ott, Daniel. 2014. Producing a Past: McCormick Harvester and Producer Populists in the 1890s. *Agricultural History* 88(1): 87–119.

Ozanne, Robert. 1967. *A Century of Labor-Management Relations at McCormick and International Harvester.* Madison: University of Wisconsin Press.

Palladino, Paolo. 1996. *Entomology, Ecology and Agriculture: The Making of Scientific Careers in North America, 1885–1985.* Amsterdam: Harwood Academic.

Pallister, Casey. 2022. The Bone Hunters: New Visions of an Ossified Past. *Great Plains Quarterly* 42(3): 191–209.

Palmer, Ingrid. 1972. *Food and the New Agricultural Technology.* Geneva, Switzerland: United Nations Research Institute for Social Development.

Pardey, Philip G., Connie Chan-Kang, Steven P. Dehmer, and Jason M. Beddow. 2016. Agricultural R&D Is on the Move. *Nature* 537(7620): 301–303.

Patel, Raj. 2013. The Long Green Revolution. *Journal of Peasant Studies* 40(1): 1–63.

Paul, Duane, Richard Kilmer, Marilyn Altobello, and David Harrington. 1977. *The Changing U.S. Fertilizer Industry.* Agricultural Economic Report 378. National Economic Analysis Division, Economic Research Service, US Department of Agriculture.

Pegg, Leonard. 1988. *Pulling Tassels: A History of Seed Corn in Ontario.* Blenheim, Ontario: Blenheim.

Perkins, John. 1982. *Insects, Experts, and the Insecticide Crisis: The Quest for New Management Strategies.* New York: Plenum Press.

Perkins, John. 1997. *Geopolitics and the Green Revolution: Wheat, Genes and the Cold War.* New York: Oxford University Press.

Pesticide Action Network et al. 2022. Addressing the Conflict of Interest and Incompatibility of FAO's Partnership with CropLife International. https://pan-international.org/wp-content/uploads/CropLife-Conflict-of-Interest-Briefing-to-FAO-Member-States-PAN-and-Partners.pdf.

Pesticide Action Network North America. 2022. Nearly 200k Strong against FAO's #ToxicAlliance. December 20. https://www.panna.org/news/nearly-200k-strong-against-fao-toxicalliance/.

Pesticide Action Network, et al. 2024. Statement of Civil Society and Indigenous Peoples on the end of the FAO partnership with CropLife International. June 10. https://pan-international.org/wp-content/uploads/Statement-on-end-of-ToxicAlliance-061024-EN.pdf.

Pettigrew, Andrew. 1985. *The Awakening Giant: Continuity and Change in Imperial Chemical Industries.* London: Blackwell.

Pham, Xuan, and Martin Stack. 2018. How Data Analytics Is Transforming Agriculture. *Business Horizons* 61(1): 125–133.

Phillips McDougall. 2013. *R&D Trends for Chemical Crop Protection Products and the Position of the European Market.* September 30. https://issuu.com/cropprotection/docs/r_and_d_study_2013_v1.8_webversion_.

Phillips McDougall. 2016. *The Cost of New Agrochemical Product Discovery, Development and Registration in 1995, 2000, 2005–8 and 2010–2014.* http://www.seedquest.com/News/pdf/2016/PMcD.pdf.

Phillips, Matthew, and William Archer. 2020. Agrochemical Industry Development, Trends in R&D and the Impact of Regulation. *Pest Management Science* 76(10): 3348–3356.

Phillips, Stephen. 1986. Tractor Slump Seen Ending. *New York Times*, August 14.

Phillips, William Gregory. 1956. *The Agricultural Implement Industry in Canada: A Study in Competition.* Toronto: University of Toronto Press.

Philpott, Tom. 2015. Monsanto's Stock Is Tanking. Is the Company's Own Excitement about GMOs Backfiring? *Mother Jones*, October 9. https://www.motherjones.com/food/2015/10/monsanto-stock-decline-layoffs/.

Pixley, Kevin V., Jose Falck-Zepeda, Ken Giller, Leland Glenna, Fred Gould, Carol Mallory-Smith, David Stelly, and C. NMeal Stewart Jr. 2019. Genome Editing, Gene

Drives, and Synthetic Biology: Will They Contribute to Disease-Resistant Crops, and Who Will Benefit? *Annual Review of Phytopathology* 57(1): 165–188.

Plume, Karl. 2022. Bayer Launches Sustainable Agriculture Hub to Connect U.S. Farmers, Food and Fuel Makers. Reuters, August 15. https://www.reuters.com/business/sustainable-business/bayer-launches-sustainable-ag-hub-connect-us-farmers-food-fuel-makers-2022-08-15/.

Plume, Karl, and Nickel, Rod. 2021. Dollars in the Dirt: Big Ag Pays Farmers for Control of their Soil-Bound Carbon. *Western Producer*, October 25. https://www.producer.com/news/dollars-in-the-dirt-big-ag-pays-farmers-for-control-of-their-soil-bound-carbon/.

Pollard, Tony. 2021. These Spots of Excavation Tell: Using Early Visitor Accounts to Map the Missing Graves of Waterloo. *Journal of Conflict Archaeology* 16(2): 75–113.

Potash Corporation of Saskatchewan. 1996. Form 10-K US Securities and Exchange Commission. https://www.sec.gov/Archives/edgar/data/855931/0000950150-97-000407.txt.

Potts, Mark. 1987. Farm Equipment Makers Plowing Rougher Fields; Farmers' Continuing Hard Times Cause Wide Industry Shakeout. *Washington Post*, July 12.

Powell, Joy. 2016. Going Deeper on Deere, Monsanto Disagreement with DOJ. *Farm Industry News*, September 14. https://www.farmprogress.com/farming-equipment/going-deeper-on-deere-monsanto-disagreement-with-doj.

Prášková, Dagmar Milerová, and Josef Novotný. 2021. The Rise and Fall of the New Alliance for Food Security and Nutrition: A Tale of Two Discourses. *Third World Quarterly* 42(8): 1751–1769.

Pratt, Sean. 2023. Phosphate Supply to Remain Tight. *Western Producer*. November 15. https://www.producer.com/news/phosphate-supply-to-remain-tight/.

Prause, Louisa, Sarah Hackfort, and Margit Lindgren. 2021. Digitalization and the Third Food Regime. *Agriculture and Human Values* 38(3): 641–55.

Pray, Carl E., and Latha Nagarajan. 2014. The Transformation of the Indian Agricultural Input Industry: Has It Increased Agricultural R&D? *Agricultural Economics* 45(S1): 145–156.

Pucker, Kenneth, and Andrew King. 2022. ESG Isn't Designed to Save the Planet. *Harvard Business Review*, August 1. https://hbr.org/2022/08/esg-investing-isnt-designed-to-save-the-planet.

Qu, Dongyu. 2020. FAO Director General. 2020. Letter to Civil Society and Indigenous Peoples Organizations. November 27. https://www.fao.org/fileadmin/user_upload/newsroom/docs/DG%20to%20Civil%20Society[2].pdf.

Quinn, Russ. 2021. USITC Orders Duties on P Imports. *Progressive Farmer*, March 11. https://www.dtnpf.com/agriculture/web/ag/crops/article/2021/03/11/us-imports-phosphate-fertilizer-will.

Quinn, Russ. 2022. Ag Groups: End Fertilizer "Cartels." *Progressive Farmer*, June 17. https://www.dtnpf.com/agriculture/web/ag/crops/article/2022/06/17/farm-groups-accuse-fertilizer-price.

Reed, Roy. 1974. U.S. Fertilizer Shortage Expected to Be Damaging to Many Poorer Nations. *New York Times*, April 4.

Reed, Roy. 1975. Farmers Angry over Doubling of Machinery Costs. *New York Times*, August 28.

Reuters. 2007. U.S. Permits Monsanto Acquisition of Delta and Pine Land, May 31. https://www.cnbc.com/id/18967652.

Richmond, Martha. 2018. Glyphosate: A Review of Its Global Use, Environmental Impact, and Potential Health Effects on Humans and Other Species. *Journal of Environmental Studies and Sciences* 8: 416–434.

Rippy, J. Fred. 1948. Economic Enterprises of the "Nitrate King" and His Associates in Chile. *Pacific Historical Review* 17(4): 457–465.

Robertson, Robert. 2000. Biotechnology: Information on Prices of Genetically Modified Seeds in the United States and Argentina. Statement of Robert E. Robertson, Associate Director, Food and Agriculture Issues, Resources, Community, and Economic Development Division, US General Accounting Office. GAO/T-RCED/NSIAD-00-228.

Robinson, Claire. 2021. *Gene Editing Myths and Reality: A Guide through the Smokescreen*. European Greens. https://www.greens-efa.eu/files/assets/docs/geneeditingmyths_report_a4_v4_web_reduced.pdf.

Rochester, Anna. 1940. *Why Farmers Are Poor: The Agricultural Crisis in the United States*. New York: International Publishers.

Roger, Ian. 1985. World Trade News: Kubota Plans Tractor Sales Drive in US/Japanese Farm Equipment Maker to Sell Medium Sized Tractors in US. *Financial Times*, November 19.

Ron, Ariel. 2023. *Grassroots Leviathan: Agricultural Reform and the Rural North in the Slaveholding Republic*. Baltimore: Johns Hopkins University Press.

Rose, David Christian, and Jason Chilvers. 2018. Agriculture 4.0: Broadening Responsible Innovation in an Era of Smart Farming. *Frontiers in Sustainable Food Systems* 2 (November 21, 2019). https://www.frontiersin.org/articles/10.3389/fsufs.2018.00087/full

Rosenberg, Chaim. 2019. *International Harvester Company: A History of the Founding Families and their Machines*. Jefferson, NC: McFarland.

Rosset, Peter. 2008. Food Sovereignty and the Contemporary Food Crisis. *Development* 51(4): 460–463.

Rothschild, Emma. 1976. Food Politics. *Foreign Affairs* 54(2): 285–307.

Rotz, Sarah, Emily Duncan, Matthew Small, Janos Botschner, Rozita Dara, Ian Mosby, Mark Reed, and Evan Fraser. 2019. The Politics of Digital Agricultural Technologies: A Preliminary Review. *Sociologia Ruralis* 59(2): 203–229.

Rüegg, W. T., M. Quadranti, and A. Zoschke. 2007. Herbicide Research and Development: Challenges and Opportunities. *Weed Research* 47(4): 271–375.

Rufo, Giovanni. 1980. *Technical Change and Economic Policy: Science and Technology in the New Economic and Social Context.* Paris: OECD.

Ruggie, J. G., and E. Middleton, 2019. Money, Millennials and Human Rights: Sustaining "Sustainable Investing." *Global Policy* 10(1): 144–150.

Russel, Darrell, and Gerald Williams. 1977. History of Chemical Fertilizer Development. *Soil Science Society of America Journal* 41(2): 260–265.

Russell, Edmund. 1993. *War on Insects: Warfare, Insecticides, and Environmental Change in the United States, 1870–1945.* PhD diss., University of Michigan.

Russell, Edmund. 2001. *War and Nature: Fighting Humans and Insects with Chemicals from World War I to Silent Spring.* Cambridge: Cambridge University Press.

Saenko, Kate. 2023. Is Generative AI Bad for the Environment? A Computer Scientists Explains the Carbon Footprint of ChatGPT and its Cousins. *The Conversation.* https://theconversation.com/is-generative-ai-bad-for-the-environment-a-computer-scientist-explains-the-carbon-footprint-of-chatgpt-and-its-cousins-204096.

Şajn, Nikolina. 2022. Right to Repair. European Parliamentary Research Service. January. https://www.europarl.europa.eu/RegData/etudes/BRIE/2022/698869/EPRS_BRI(2022)698869_EN.pdf.

Sanderson, Jay. 2017. *Plants, People and Practices: The Nature and History of the UPOV Convention.* Cambridge: Cambridge University Press.

Schenkelaars, Piet, Huib de Vriend, and Nicholas Kalaitzandonakes. 2011. Drivers of Consolidation in the Seed Industry and its Consequences for Innovation. Report commissioned by COGEM. Netherlands. https://cogem.net/app/uploads/2019/07/CGM-2011-01-drivers-of-consolidation-in-the-seed-industry-and-its-consequences-for-innovation-1.pdf.

Schimmelpfennig, David. 2004. Agricultural Patents: Are They Developing Bad Habits? *Choices* 19(1). https://www.choicesmagazine.org/2004-1/2004-1-04.htm.

Schlesinger, Jacob M. 2021. The Return of the Trustbusters—A New Generation of Regulators Inspired by Louis Brandeis Hopes to Overturn the Light-Touch Approach to Antitrust Shaped by Robert Bork. *Wall Street Journal,* August 27.

Schmalz, Martin C. 2018. Common Ownership, Concentration and Corporate Conduct. CESIFO working papers, February.

Schofield, R. 1944. Plowman's Folly. *Nature* 153: 391.

REFERENCES

Schumpeter, Joseph. 1942. *Capitalism, Socialism and Democracy*. New York: Harper.

Schütte, Gesine, Michael Eckerstorfer, Valentina Rastelli, Wolfram Reichenbecher, Sara Restrepo-Vassalli, Marja Ruohonen-Lehto, Anne-Gabrielle Wuest Saucy, and Martha Mertens. 2017. Herbicide Resistance and Biodiversity: Agronomic and Environmental Aspects of Genetically Modified Herbicide-Resistant Plants. *Environmental Sciences Europe* 29(1): 5.

Schwartz, Andrew, and Ethan Gurwitz. 2018. Big Business Rules American Agriculture—and Congress Doesn't Seem to Care. Center for American Progress. https://www.americanprogress.org/article/big-business-rules-american-agriculture-congress-doesnt-seem-care/.

Schwartz, H. M. 2016. Wealth and Secular Stagnation: The Role of Industrial Organization and Intellectual Property Rights. *RSF: The Russell Sage Foundation Journal of the Social Sciences* 2(6): 226–249.

Schwartzman, David. 1970. *Oligopoly in the Farm Machinery Industry*. Ottawa: Information Canada.

Sears, Paul B. 1935. *Deserts on the March*. Norman: University of Oklahoma Press.

Secchi, Silvia. 2020. The Political Economy of Unsustainable Lock-Ins in North American Commodity Agriculture: A Path Forward—Response to Struckman. *Nordia Geographical Publications* 49(5): 107–111.

Sell, Susan. 2009. Corporations, Seeds, and Intellectual Property Rights Governance. In *Corporate Power in Global Agrifood Governance*, edited by Jennifer Clapp and Doris Fuchs, 187–223. Cambridge, MA: MIT Press.

Sender, Henny. 2019. Changing the Image of the Agrochemicals Industry. *Financial Times*, July 29.

Seto, Karen C., Steven J. Davis, Ronald B. Mitchell, Eleanor C. Stokes, Gregory Unruh, and Diana Ürge-Vorsatz. 2016. Carbon Lock-In: Types, Causes, and Policy Implications. *Annual Review of Environment and Resources* 41: 425–452.

Sharratt, Lucy. 2023. Corporate-Government "Tiger Team" Gutted GMO Regulations. *Watershed Sentinel*. November 28. https://watershedsentinel.ca/articles/corporate-government-tiger-team-gutted-gmo-regulations/.

Shattuck, Annie et al. 2023. Global Pesticide Use and Trade Database (GloPUT): New Estimates Show Pesticide Use Trends in Low-Income Countries Substantially Underestimated. *Global Environmental Change* 81: 102693.

Shattuck, Annie. 2021. Generic, Growing, Green?: The Changing Political Economy of the Global Pesticide Complex. *Journal of Peasant Studies* 48(2): 231–253.

Shi, Guanming, Jean-Paul Chavas and Kyle Stiegert. 2010. An Analysis of the Pricing of Traits in the U.S. Corn Seed Market. *American Journal of Agricultural Economics* 92(5): 1324–1338.

Shi, Guanming, Kyle W. Stiegert, and Jean P. Chavas. 2011. An Analysis of Bundle Pricing in Horizontal and Vertical Markets: The Case of the U.S. Cottonseed Market. *Agricultural Economics* 42(s1): 77–88.

Shick, Tom W., and Don H. Doyle. 1985. The South Carolina Phosphate Boom and the Stillbirth of the New South, 1867–1920. *South Carolina Historical Magazine* 86(1): 1–12, 14–15, 17–31.

Shiva, Vandana. 1991. *The Violence of the Green Revolution: Third World Agriculture, Ecology, and Politics*. Lexington: University Press of Kentucky.

Shochat, Gil, and Sylvie Fournier. 2019. Court Documents Reveal Monsanto's Efforts to Fight Glyphosate's "Severe Stigma." *CBC News*, March 12. https://www.cbc.ca/news/health/glyphosate-monsanto-intertek-studies-1.4902229

Shoham, Jonathan. 2020. Impact of COVID-19 on the Global Seed Market. FAO. https://ssl.fao.org/glis/ITPGRFA/COVID19/8-Shoham_FAO.pdf.

Skaggs, Jimmy M. 1994. *The Great Guano Rush: Entrepreneurs and American Overseas Expansion*. New York: St. Martin's Press.

Smil, Vaclav. 2001. *Enriching the Earth: Fritz Haber, Carl Bosch, and the Transformation of World Food Production*. Cambridge, MA: MIT Press.

Smil, Vaclav. 2011. Nitrogen Cycle and World Food Production. *World Agriculture* 2: 9–13.

Smith, Allan E., and Diane M. Secoy. 1975. Forerunners of Pesticides in Classical Greece and Rome. *Journal of Agricultural and Food Chemistry* 23(6): 1050–1055.

Solomon, Keith R. 2020. Estimated Exposure to Glyphosate in Humans via Environmental, Occupational, and Dietary Pathways: An Updated Review of the Scientific Literature. *Pest Management Science* 76(9): 2878–2885.

Soumare, Abdoulaye Abdala G. Diedhiou, Moses Thuita, Mohamed Hafidi, Yedir Ouhdouch, Subramaniam Gopalakrishnan, and Lamfeddal Kouisni. 2020. Exploiting Biological Nitrogen Fixation: A Route towards a Sustainable Agriculture. *Plants* 9(8): 1011.

Springmann, M., Michael Clark, Daniel Mason-D'Croz, Keith Wiebe, Benjamin Leon Bodirsky, Luis Lassaletta, Wim de Vries, et al. 2018. Options for Keeping the Food System within Environmental Limits. *Nature* 562 (7728): 519–525.

Stam, Jerome M., and Bruce L. Dixon. 2004. Farmer Bankruptcies and Farm Exits in the United States, 1899–2002. Agriculture Information Bulletin 788, Economic Research Service, US Department of Agriculture.

Steele, Leon. 1982. *The Founding of Funk Seeds*. Pamphlet.

Steinwand, Michael A., and Pamela C. Ronald. 2020. Crop Biotechnology and the Future of Food. *Nature Food* 1(5): 273–283.

REFERENCES

Stiegert, Kyle W., Guanming Shi, and Jean Paul Chavas. 2010. Innovation, Integration, and the Biotechnology Revolution in U.S. Seed Markets. *Choices* 25(2).

Stoller, Matt. 2019. *Goliath: The 100-Year War between Monopoly Power and Democracy.* New York: Simon and Schuster.

Stone, Glenn Davis. 2007. Agricultural Deskilling and the Spread of Genetically Modified Cotton in Warangal. *Current Anthropology* 48(1): 67–103.

Stone, Glenn Davis. 2022b. Surveillance Agriculture and Peasant Autonomy. *Journal of Agrarian Change* 22(3): 608–631.

Stone, Glenn. 2022a. *The Agricultural Dilemma: How Not to Feed the World.* London: Routledge.

Strange, Susan. 1988. *States and Markets.* London: Pinter.

Strange, Susan. 1996. *The Retreat of the State: The Diffusion of Power in the World Economy.* Cambridge: Cambridge University press.

Struckman, Luke. 2020. Technological and Institutional Lock-in and Excessive Synthetic Nitrogen Fertilizer Use on North American Grain and Oilseed Farms. *Nordia Geographical Publications* 49(5): 93–101.

Stuckler, David, and Marion Nestle. 2012. Big Food, Food Systems, and Global Health. *PLoS Medicine* 9(6): e1001242.

Sun, Tao, Jie Song, Meng Wang, Chao Zhao, and Weiwen Zhang. 2022. Challenges and Recent Progress in the Governance of Biosecurity Risks in the Era of Synthetic Biology. *Journal of Biosafety and Biosecurity* 4(1): 59–67.

Sutch, Richard. 2008. *Henry Agard Wallace, the Iowa Corn Yield Tests, and the Adoption of Hybrid Corn.* Cambridge, MA: National Bureau of Economic Research.

Sutherland, Lee-Ann et al. 2012. Triggering Change: Towards a Conceptualisation of Major Change Processes in Farm Decision-Making. *Journal of Environmental Management* 104: 142–151.

Swanson, Krista. 2023. Phosphate Farm Prices Remain Elevated, It's Time for Action on Import Tariffs. National Corn Growers Association. https://www.ncga.com/stay-informed/media/editorials/article/2023/03/phosphate-farm-prices-remain-elevated-it-s-time-for-action-on-import-tariffs.

Swinburn, Boyd A, Vivica I Kraak, Steven Allender, Vincent J Atkins, Phillip I Baker, Jessica R Bogard, Hannah Brinsden. 2019. The Global Syndemic of Obesity, Undernutrition, and Climate Change: The Lancet Commission Report. *Lancet* 39 (10173): 791–846.

Swissinfo.ch. 2022. Stop Organic Farming to Help Future Food Crisis, Says Syngenta Boss. May 8. https://www.swissinfo.ch/eng/business/stop-organic-farming-to-help-future-food-crisis—says-syngenta-boss/47576514

Syngenta 2023. *Financial Report 2022.* https://www.syngenta.com/sites/syngenta/files/bond-investor-information/financial-results/financial-report-2022.pdf.

Szöllösi-Janze, Margit. 2017. The Scientist as Expert: Fritz Haber and German Chemical Warfare during the First World War and Beyond. In *One Hundred Years of Chemical Warfare: Research, Deployment, Consequences,* edited by Bretislav Friedrich, Dieter Hoffmann, Jürgen Renn, Florian Schmaltz, and Martin Wolf, 11–23. Cham: Springer.

Tanakasempipat, Patpicha. 2020. In the Weeds: How Bayer, U.S. Govt Teamed Up against Thailand's Glyphosate Ban. Reuters, September 17. https://www.reuters.com/article/thailand-usa-trade-idCNL4N2GE3OM.

Tavenner, C. H. 1912. Harvester Trust Report Suppressed by Roosevelt. *Steamboat Pilot,* May 15. (Accessed from Colorado Historic Newspapers Collection).

Taylor, C. Robert, and Diana L. Moss. 2013. *The Fertilizer Oligopoly: The Case for Global Antitrust Enforcement.* Washington DC: American Antitrust Institute.

Taylor, Dorceta E. 2018. Black Farmers in the USA and Michigan: Longevity, Empowerment, and Food Sovereignty. *Journal of African American Studies* 22(1): 49–76.

Temple-West, Patrick and Olaf Storbeck. 2024. Bayer Turns to State Lobbying in Battle over Roundup Weedkiller. *Financial Times.* March 4. https://www.ft.com/content/37658602-dd17-4411-a451-cbb3de1b06e5.

Terazono, Emiko. 2013. Cartel Break-Up Reshapes Fertiliser Market. *Financial Times,* October 2.

Terazono, Emiko. 2015. Syngenta Plans $2bn Share Buyback. *Financial Times,* September 3.

Terazono, Emiko. 2016. Monsanto Operating Chief Sees a Crop of Seed and Chemical Deals. *Financial Times,* March 15.

Terazono, Emiko, James Fontanella-Khan, and Gregory Meyer. 2016. PotashCorp and Agrium Agree Near-$30bn Fertilisers Merger. *Financial Times,* September 12.

Terazono, Emiko, Arash Massoudi, and James Fontanella-Khan. 2015. Monsanto Targets Tax Inversion Strategy with Syngenta Offer. *Financial Times,* June 8.

Terra Industries. 2002. Form 10-K, Securities and Exchange Commission. http://getfilings.com/o0000950131-03-001254.html.

Tester, Jon. 2022. S.3549—Agricultural Right to Repair Act. https://www.congress.gov/bill/117th-congress/senate-bill/3549.

Thomas, Dana L. 1972. While the Sun Shines: Farm Equipment Manufacturers Are Busily Making Hay. *Barron's National Business and Financial Weekly* 52(5), January 31.

Thomas, Jim. 2020. The Biodigital Power Grab: Data as Industrial Input and Resource for the Next Agribusiness Assault. In *Agroecology and Digitalisation: Traps and Opportunities to Transform the Food System,* by IFOAM Organics Europe. Brussels: IFOAM Organics Europe.

Thomas, Patrick. 2022. Regulators Accuse Pesticide Makers of Inflating Prices for Farmers. *Wall Street Journal*, September 30.

Thompson, Paul B. 2010. *The Agrarian Vision: Sustainability and Environmental Ethics*. Lexington: University Press of Kentucky.

Timmons, F. L. 2005. A History of Weed Control in the United States and Canada. *Weed Science* 53(6): 748–761.

Tita, Bob, and Jacob Bunge. 2022. Deere Invests in Software to Boost Machinery. *Wall Street Journal*, September 12.

Torretta, Vincenzo, Ioannis A. Katsoyiannis, Paolo Viotti, and Elena Cristina Rada. 2018. Critical Review of the Effects of Glyphosate Exposure to the Environment and Humans through the Food Supply Chain. *Sustainability* 10(4): 950.

Torshizi, Mohammad, and Jennifer Clapp. 2021. Price Effects of Common Ownership in the Seed Sector. *Antitrust Bulletin* 66(1): 39–67.

Tosdal, H. R. 1913. The Kartell Movement in the German Potash Industry. *Quarterly Journal of Economics* 28(1): 140–190.

Tosun, Jale, Herman Lelieveldt, and Trevelyan S. Wing. 2019. A Case of "Muddling Through"? The Politics of Renewing Glyphosate Authorization in the European Union. *Sustainability* 11(2): 440.

Townsend, Burdette D. 1911. Appendix. In *United States Steel Corporation, Hearings before the Committee on Investigation of United States Steel Corporation*. House of Representatives. Washington DC: US Government Printing Office.

Toyoda, Hideyoshi. 2020. Insect Physical Control: Electric Field-Based Pest Management Approach. *Insects* 11(8): 480.

Travis, Anthony. 2017. Globalising Synthetic Nitrogen: The Interwar Inauguration of a New Industry. *Ambix* 64(1): 1–28.

Travis, Anthony. 2018. *Nitrogen Capture: The Growth of an International Industry (1900–1940)*. Cham: Springer.

Travis, Anthony. 2021. First Steps: Synthetic Ammonia in the United States. *Substantia* 5(2): 55–77.

Tremblay, Bruno. 2020. Smart and Sustainable Food Systems: Creating More Resilience in Europe's Farm-to-Fork Supply Chains. *Politico*, December 9. https://www.politico.eu/sponsored-content/smart-and-sustainable-food-systems/.

Tsan, Michael; Totapally, Swetha; Hailu, Michael; Addom, Benjamin K. 2019. The Digitalisation of African Agriculture Report 2018–2019. Wageningen, The Netherlands: CTA/Dalberg Advisers. https://hdl.handle.net/10568/101498.

Tups, Gideon, and Peter Dannenberg. 2023. Supplying Lead Firms, Intangible Assets and Power in Global Value Chains: Explaining Governance in the Fertilizer Chain. *Global Networks* (January 9): 1–20.

Turner, Louis. 1972. Multinationals, the United Nations and Development. *Columbia Journal of World Business* 7(5): 13–22.

Turner, Louis. 1973. *Multinational Companies and the Third World*. New York: Hill and Wang.

United Nations. 1974. Consultation with Agro Industrial Leaders. 10–11 September. World Food Conference. Toronto, Canada. DDI:G/74/89.

United Nations Food Systems Summit. 2021. Private Sector Engagement Guidelines. https://www.un.org/sites/un2.un.org/files/unfss_private_sector_guidelines_feb2021.pdf.

US Bureau of Corporations. 1913. The International Harvester Company. March 3. Reprinted in *Trusts, Pools and Corporations*, rev. ed. 1916, edited by William Z. Ripley, 324–355. Boston: Ginn.

US Congress. 2004. Sherman Act. Chapter 647 of the 51st Congress; Enacted 1890; 26 Stat. 209. As Amended 2004.

US Congress, Office of Technology Assessment. 1991. *Biotechnology in a Global Economy*, OTA-BA-494. Washington DC: US Government Printing Office.

US Department of Agriculture. 1940. *Technology on the Farm*. Washington DC: US Government Printing Office.

US Department of Commerce. 2006. *Concentration Ratios: 2002*. 2002 Economic Census: Manufacturing EC02-31SR-1. https://www2.census.gov/library/publications/economic-census/2002/manufacturing-reports/subject-series/ec0231sr1.pdf.

US Department of Justice 1918. United States District Court, District of Minnesota, Third Division. The United States of America, Petitioner, vs. International Harvester Company, et al., Defendants. Final Decree of November 2nd 1918. At https://www.justice.gov/atr/page/file/1436371/download.

US Senate. 2001. Agriculture Market Concentration. Hearing before a Subcommittee of the Committee on Appropriations. Washington, DC: US Government Printing Office. https://www.govinfo.gov/content/pkg/CHRG-107shrg76970/html/CHRG-107shrg76970.htm.

USDA. 1936. *Yearbook of Agriculture*. Washington DC: US Government Printing Office.

USDA. 1940. *Technology on the Farm*. A special report by an Inter-Bureau Committee and the Bureau of Economics of the United States Department of Agriculture. Washington, DC.

USDA. 1996. *Concentration in Agriculture: A Report of the USDA Advisory Committee on Concentration in Agriculture*. Advisory Committee on Agricultural Concentration, USDA.

USDA. 1998. *A Time to Act: A Report on the USDA National Commission on Small Farms*. National Commission on Small Farms, USDA.

USDA. 2022a. *Agricultural Competition: A Plan in Support of Fair and Competitive Markets*. USDA's Report to the White House Competition Council. May. https://www.ams.usda.gov/sites/default/files/media/USDAPlan_EO_COMPETITION.pdf.

USDA. 2022b. Impacts and Repercussions of Price Increases on the Global Fertilizer Market. June. https://www.fas.usda.gov/data/impacts-and-repercussions-price-increases-global-fertilizer-market.

USDA. 2022c. Access to Fertilizer: Competition and Supply Chain Concerns. Federal Register. https://www.federalregister.gov/documents/2022/03/17/2022-05670/access-to-fertilizer-competition-and-supply-chain-concerns.

USDA. 2022d. Impacts and Repercussions of Price Increases on the Global Fertilizer Market. 2022. *USDA* Foreign Agricultural Service. June 30. https://www.fas.usda.gov/data/impacts-and-repercussions-price-increases-global-fertilizer-market.

USDA. 2022e. USDA Announces Plans for $250 Million Investment to Support Innovative American-made Fertilizer to Give US Farmers More Choices in the Marketplace. March 11. https://www.usda.gov/media/press-releases/2022/03/11/usda-announces-plans-250-million-investment-support-innovative.

USDA. 2023a. *More and Better Choices for Farmers: Promoting Fair Competition and Innovation in Seeds and Other Agricultural Inputs*. A report directed by President Biden's Executive Order Number 14036: Promoting Competition in America's Economy. March. https://www.ams.usda.gov/sites/default/files/media/SeedsReport.pdf.

USDA. 2023b. U.S. Department of Agriculture, Economic Research Service. *Farm Sector Income and Finances: Assets, Debt, and Wealth*. February 7. https://www.ers.usda.gov/topics/farm-economy/farm-sector-income-finances/assets-debt-and-wealth/.

Valorinta, Mikko, Henri Schildt, and Juha-Antti Lamberg. 2011. Path Dependence of Power Relations, Path-Breaking Change and Technological Adaptation. *Industry and Innovation* 18(8): 765–790.

Vandeman, Ann. 1995. Management in a Bottle: Pesticides and the Deskilling of Agriculture. *Review of Radical Political Economics* 27(3): 49–59.

Vanloqueren, Gaetan, and Philippe V. Baret. 2009. How Agricultural Research Systems Shape a Technological Regime That Develops Genetic Engineering But Locks Out Agroecological Innovations. *Research Policy* 38(6): 971–983.

Vieira, Bruno C., Joe D. Luck, Keenan L. Amundsen, Rodrigo Werld, Todd A. Gaines, and Greg R. Kruger. 2020. Herbicide Drift Exposure Leads to Reduced Herbicide Sensitivity in *Amaranthus* Spp. *Scientific Reports* 10(1): 2146.

Vincent, James. 2022. John Deere's Self-Driving Tractor Lets Farmers Leave the Cab—and the Field. *The Verge*. January 4. https://www.theverge.com/2022/1/4/22866699/john-deere-autonomous-farming-ai-machine-vision-kit.

Vizcarra, Catalina. 2009. Guano, Credible Commitments, and Sovereign Debt Repayment in Nineteenth-Century Peru. *Journal of Economic History* 69(2): 358–387.

Vogt, Gunter. 2007. The Origins of Organic Farming. In *Organic Farming—An International History*, edited by W. Lockeretz, 9–30. Wallingford: CABI.

Waddell, Christopher. 1985. Farm Machinery Makers Face Shakeout. *Globe and Mail*, January 19.

Wall Street Journal. 1984a. Tenneco Files to Offer $300 Million of Debt amid Acquisition Talk, November 20.

Wall Street Journal. 1984b. Tenneco to Reduce Total Dealers 15 percent In Harvester Pact. November 28.

Walters, William D., Jr. 1997. *The Heart of the Cornbelt: An Illustrated History of Corn Farming in McLean County*. Bloomington, IL: McLean County Historical Society.

Warde, Paul. 2018. *The Invention of Sustainability: Nature and Destiny, c. 1500–1870*. Cambridge: Cambridge University Press.

Watson, Dave. 2018. *Pesticides and Agriculture: Profits, Politics and Policy*. Cambridge: Burleigh Dodds Science Publishing.

Weber, Margaret. 2018. The American Way of Farming: Pioneer Hi-Bred and Power in Postwar America. *Agricultural History* 92(3): 380–403.

Webster, Bayard. 1969. Effect of DDT Ban Worries Farmers. *New York Times*, November 15.

Weis, Tony. 2010. The Accelerating Biophysical Contradictions of Industrial Capitalist Agriculture. *Journal of Agrarian Change* 10(3): 315–341.

Wengert, Norman. 1949. The Land—TVA—and the Fertilizer Industry. *Land Economics* 25(1): 11–21.

Wezel, Alexander, Barbara Gemmill Herren, Rachel Bezner Kerr, Edmundo Barrios, André Luiz Rodrigues Gonçalves and Fergus Sinclair. 2020. Agroecological Principles and Elements and their Implications for Transitioning to Sustainable Food Systems. A Review. *Agronomy for Sustainable Development* 40: 1–13.

Wharton, Clifton R. 1969. The Green Revolution: Cornucopia or Pandora's Box? *Foreign Affairs* 47(3): 464–476.

Whitaker, Adelynne Hiller. 1974. *A History of Federal Pesticide Regulation in the United States to 1947*. PhD diss., Emory University.

Whorton, James. 1974. *Before Silent Spring: Pesticides and Public Health in Pre-DDT America*. Princeton: Princeton University Press.

Wield, David, Joanna Chataway, and Maurice Bolo. 2010. Issues in the Political Economy of Agricultural Biotechnology. *Journal of Agrarian Change* 10(3): 342–366.

Wiggerthale, Marita. 2021. Corporate Power in the Food System Facts and Figures on Market Concentration in the Agri-food Sector. https://marita-wiggerthale.de/wp-content/uploads/2023/03/Corporate_power_food_system_Jan_2021_1_.pdf.

Wik, Reynold M. 1964. Henry Ford's Tractors and American Agriculture. *Agricultural History* 38(2): 79–86.

Wills, Matthew. 2022. Burning Kelp for War. *JSTOR Daily*, January 13. https://daily.jstor.org/burning-kelp-for-war/.

Wilson, James. 2013. PotashCorp to Cut Production and Shed 1 in 5 Jobs. *Financial Times* December 2. https://www.ft.com/content/954814c0-5c11-11e3-b4f3-00144feabdc0.

Wilson, James, Courtney Weaver, and Emiko Terazono. 2013. Global Fertiliser Shake-Up after Cartel Falls Apart. *Financial Times*, July 30. https://www.ft.com/content/a39e7e1c-f8f5-11e2-a6ef-00144feabdc0.

Wilson, Megan. 2018. EPA Pesticide Settlement Comes under Scrutiny, *The Hill*, May 8. https://thehill.com/business-a-lobbying/386610-epa-pesticide-settlement-comes-under-scrutiny.

Winder, Gordon M. 1995. Before the Corporation and Mass Production: The Licensing Regime in the Manufacture of North American Harvesting Machinery, 1830–1910. *Annals of the Association of American Geographers* 85(3): 521–552.

Wines, Richard. 1985. *Fertilizer in America: From Waste Recycling to Resource Exploitation*. Philadelphia: Temple University Press.

Wise, Timothy A. 2023. Mexico Calls U.S. Bluff on Science of GMO Corn Restrictions. *Food Tank*. https://foodtank.com/news/2023/03/mexico-calls-us-bluff-on-science-of-gmo-corn-restrictions/.

Wittman, Hannah, Annette Desmarais, and Nettie Wiebe. 2010. The Origins and Potential of Food Sovereignty. In *Food Sovereignty: Reconnecting Food, Nature and Community*, 1–14. Oakland, CA: Food First.

Wittman, Hannah, and Dana James. 2022. Land Governance for Agroecology. *Elementa: Science of the Anthropocene* 10(1): 00100.

Wood, Benjamin, Owain Williams, Phil Baker, Vijaya Nagarajan, and Gary Sacks. 2021. The Influence of Corporate Market Power on Health: Exploring the Structure-Conduct-Performance Model from a Public Health Perspective. *Globalization and Health* 17(1): 41.

World Health Organization (WHO). 2015. *Evaluation of Five Organophosphate Insecticides and Herbicides*. Lyon: International Agency for Research on Cancer.

Wu, Tim. 2018. *The Curse of Bigness: Antitrust in the New Gilded Age*. New York: Columbia Global Reports.

Xu, Jingwen, Shayna Smith, Gordon Smith, Weiqun Wang, and Yonghui Li. 2019. Glyphosate Contamination in Grains and Foods: An Overview. *Food Control* 106: 106710.

Yamamura, Kozo. 1964. Zaibatsu, Prewar and Zaibatsu, Postwar. *Journal of Asian Studies* 23(4): 539–554.

Zhang, Yi, Karen Massel, Ian D. Godwin, and Caixia Gao. 2018. Applications and Potential of Genome Editing in Crop Improvement. *Genome Biology* 19(1): 210.

INDEX

Note: Italicized page numbers refer to figures; tables are noted with a *t*.

Accountability, ensuring, 334–335, 336. *See also* Transparency
Acid rain, 187
Acquisitions. *See* Mergers and acquisitions
Activist investors, recent agribusiness megamergers and, 229–232, 243
Advisory Committee on Agricultural Concentration, 183
Afghanistan, Russian invasion of, 167
African fertilizer markets, cartels in, 260
AGCO, x, 1, 172–173, *174*, 226, 248
　business activities, 2023, 279*t*
　CEMA membership, 314
　MOU signed with AFBF, 310
　opposition to right-to-repair movement, 309
　recent digital acquisitions of, *240*
Agent Orange, 199
Agfa, 78
AgrEvo, 201
Agribusiness firms. *See also* Agricultural input industries
　dominant, long historical trajectory of, 21, 22
　shaping of policy and governance by, 15–16
Agribusiness megamergers, drivers of, 221–243
　broad economic context of, 243
　common ownership's influence on corporate incentives, 232–234
　financialization and activist investors, 221–222, 229–232, 243
　intensification of consolidation, 221, 222–224, 226–227, 243
　mergers of distress and of opportunity, 243
　new forms of genetic engineering, 236–238
　pressures of the boom-bust farm cycle, 221, 227–229
　product complementarity and technological integration, 234–236
　rise of digital agriculture, 238–239, 241, 243

Agribusiness megamergers, drivers of (cont.)
  unwinding of antitrust, culmination of, 241–243
Agribusiness multinationals, global governance forums and, 151–155
Agricultural Adjustment Act (AAA), 103, 122, 144
Agricultural biotechnology, 2, 192, 201–207, 210, 215, 217, 218, 237, 243
Agricultural deskilling, 108, 111, 133, 215, 258, 281–282, 292
Agricultural experiment stations, 90, 91, 95, 117, 125
Agricultural industrial sectors, investments between, 145
Agricultural input firms
  defining term "big " in relation to, 6–7
  market and financial dynamics and, 7, 8–9
  policy context and, 7, 11–12
  recent digital and biological acquisitions of, 238, *240*
  technological change and, 7, 9–11
  unequal dynamics of industrial capitalism and, 7
Agricultural input industries, 339, 340. *See also* Agribusiness megamergers, drivers of; Farm machinery input industry; Fertilizer input industry; Pesticide input industry; Seed input industry
  as big business, 1
  "bigger is always better" narrative and, 3, 4, 16
  broader costs of corporate concentration in, 16–19
  calls for reform of, 23–24
  carbon credit programs and, 286–287
  common ownership in, 233–234
  consolidation of agrochemical and seed industries, 191–192, 217–218
  digital farming software products/services and, 278, 279*t*
  digital technologies and, 239
  farm crisis of 1980s and strain on, 167
  global food crisis of 1970s and, 164–167
  globalization of, 145–147
  global scope of, 330
  Green Revolution and, 147–151, 153–155
  increasing integration among, 139, 142, 145, 162
  integrative approach to historical time frame of, 21–22
  inverted U-shaped relationship to innovation and, 273
  lock-ins and dominance of, 139, 140
  major, business activities, 2023, 279*t*
  repeated restructuring within, 2, 3
Agricultural Insecticide and Fungicide Association, 131, 145
Agricultural R&D, growing private sector share of, 270–271
Agriculture boom-and-bust cycle, 163–167, 221, 222, 227–229
Agrievolution Alliance, 314
Agrifood markets, territorialized, 332
Agrigenetics, 202
Agrium, 177, 179, *181*, 226, 229, 234
Agrium-Potash Corporation merger, 228, 231, 235, 256
Agrochemical firms
  allure of seeds for, 197–199
  globalization of, 147
  regulatory and time frame hurdles faced by, 195–196, 204
  seed company acquisitions and promise of, 201, 202
Agrochemical industry, 339, *see also* Pesticides input industry
  attack on Farm to Fork initiative and, 302–304
  biological products and, 238

INDEX

conjoining of seed industry and, 191–192, 217–218
corporate consolidation, R&D, and, 214–215
farm crisis of 1980s and, 196
financial and intellectual property incentives for, 204–207
large conglomerates set their eyes on seeds, 192–193
Agrochemicals, 23. *See also* Pesticides
Carson's work and critique of, 195
corporate concentration in, 157–158
corporate profiteering in, 263
protection of intellectual property and development of, 10
Agroecology, 23, 142, 339
advocating for, 335, 337, 338
co-opting of, concerns about, 337–338
FAO-CropLife alliance impact on, 313
transitioning to, obstacles related to, 291
Agronomic Tech Corp., *240*
AgVend, 254, 255
AI. *See* Artificial intelligence (AI)
Aldrin, 128, 195
Alibaba, 284
Alliance for Food Sovereignty in Africa, 312
Allied Chemical, 78, 79, 129, *181*, *225*
Allied-Signal, *181*
Allis-Chalmers Company, 47, 48, 168, 169, 170, *174*
Allis & Co., *174*
Allis-Gleaner Corporation. *See* AGCO
Alternative agriculture, 335–338, 353n9. *See also* Agroecology
Amazon, 284
American Agribusiness Council (ABC), 152–153
American Agricultural Chemical Company, 71
American Antitrust Institute, 253, 260

American Association of Economic Entomologists, 119
American Chemical Paint Company, 158, *225*
American Cyanamid, 74, 149
American Farm Bureau Foundation (AFBF), 310
American Guano Company, 66
American Harvester Company, 40
American Oversight, 307
American Plow Company, 42
American Seed Trade Association, 90
American War Industries Board, 76
Ammonia, 75, 175, 177–178
Anderson, Jo, 29
Anti-Combines Act of 1889 (Canada), 12
Antitrust cases. *See also* Mergers and acquisitions; Monopolies
against fertilizer companies, 72
International Harvester, 49–51
Antitrust law and policy
culmination of unwinding of, 241–243
Deere & Co. and breaching of, 258–259
potash corporations indicted for violation of, 182–183
US and enforcement of, 11–12
support for shift in, 330–332
weakened implementation of, 184–185, 209–210
Antitrust reformers, growing movement of, 23–24
Antofagasta Nitrate and Railroad Company, 67
Antony Gibbs, 65, 66, 76
Appleby, John, 37
Aquatic ecosystems, glyphosate-based herbicides and, 290
Archer Daniels Midland, 216
Argentina, 212, 228
Armour, 69, 72, 76, *181*
Arrow, Kenneth, 272, 274
Arsenic-based pesticides, 115, 120
Arthur, W. Brian, 140

Artificial intelligence (AI) in farming, 238, 278–281
Asgrow, 192
Assetization of farmland, data collection and, 283
Asset management firms, 232, 233, *233*
Association of Equipment Manufacturers, 309
Astra-Zeneca, *194*, 200, 208, *225*
Atlas Powder Company, 123
Aventis, 201, *225*

Bankruptcies
　farm crisis of 1980s and, 167, 169, 170
　fertilizer companies and, 176, 177
Barclays, 286
Barrett Company, 75, 76, 77, 78, 79
BASF (Badische Anilin & Soda-Fabrik), 1, 78, 81, 84, 122, 129, 154, 158, 178, *181*, *194*, 200, 224, *225*, 238, 296, 312, 361n8
　boycotting of online sellers and, 255
　business activities, 2023, 279*t*
　carbon farming and, 286
　concentration ratio of, 248
　digital software platform investments, 241
　EU-Mercosur trade agreement and, 297
　4R approach and, 305
　Haber-Bosch process of ammonia synthesis and, 75, 76, 77
　IFDC membership, 313
　lobbying expenditures by, 295
　moves into seed market, 235, 251
　recent digital acquisitions of, *240*
　removal of LibertyLink seed traits from public domain, 253, 276
Baumann, Werner, 4
Bayer, 1, 78, 81, 122, 129, 149, 154, 155, 158, *194*, 200, 208, 224, *225*, 229, 296, 304, 312, 315, 367n54
　battle over glyphosate and, 298, 299, 301, 302
　boycotting of online sellers and, 255
　business activities, 2023, 279*t*
　carbon credit program, 287
　carbon farming and, 286
　concentration ratio of, 248
　digital services charges, 289
　EU-Mercosur trade agreement and, 297
　4R approach and, 305
　investments in plant breeding programs, 237
　Liberty brand, 211, 224, 251
　lobbying expenditures by, 295
　New Alliance for Food Security and Nutrition and, 311
　operating profit margin, 2022, 263
　on pesticide regulation, 304
　recent digital and biological acquisitions of, 238, *240*, 241
Bayer CropScience, 282
Bayer-Monsanto merger, 4, 224, 231, 232, 235, 236, 239, 241, 252, 269, 273, 274, 282, 285, 298, 299, 301, 362n61
Behavioral factors, lock-ins and, 141
Belarussian Potash Company cartel, collapse of, 228
Bell, Patrick, 28
Benbrook, Charles, 211
Benzene hexachloride, 128
Bhopal disaster (1984), 160, 161, 335
Biden, Joe, 246, 309
Biden administration, promotion of competition and, 327, 331
Big data, digital farming and, 280, 281, 282
Big Tech firms
　concentrated power of, 5
　New Brandeis movement and, 331
　stepped up oversight of, 245–246
Bioaccumulation, synthetic pesticides and, 135, 160
Biodiversity
　glyphosate-based herbicides and, 290

Green Revolution and loss of, 160
  hybrids and loss of, 108–110
Biofuels, 227
Bio-herbicides, 284, 285
Biological products, 238
Bio-pesticides, 284
Biotech crops, global area of, 211, *212*
Biotechnica International, 202
Biotechnology Industry Organization (BIO), 216
Birkeland, Kristian, 75
Birkeland Eyde process, 75, 79
Birmingham Works (UK), 79
Bison bones, superphosphates production and, 68
Black farmers
  digital agriculture and, 289, 290
  disenfranchisement of, 186
  farmland consolidation process and, 18
  tractor ownership and decline in number of, 54, 57
Black freedmen, phosphorus mining and, 69
BlackRock, 233, *233*, 234, 249, 286
Bogue, Allan, 142
Bolivia, Nitrate War and, 67
Boll weevils, control of, 116
Bone products (as fertilizer), 61–62, 68, 69
Boom-and-bust cycle. *See* Agriculture boom-and-bust cycle
Bork, Robert, 184
Borlaug, Norman, 148, 161
Bosch, Carl, 75
Bosso, Christopher, 131
Botanical pest control formulations, 116
Branch houses, Deere & Company, 34
Brandeis, Louis, 5, 6, 7, 49, 331
Braunholtz, John, 129
Brazil
  agrochemicals lobbying in, 297
  carbon sequestration programs in, 287

commodity bust in, 2014, 228
expanded herbicide use in, 212
seed centers in, 109
Breeding, quest for corn improvement through, 93–96
Breen, Ed, 3
Bretton Woods institutions, 146
British Petroleum, 202
Broughton, Edward, 161
Brown, Lester, 150
Brunner, Mond and Company, 77, 78
Bt (*Bacillus thuringiensis*) (Bt), 203
Bureau of Entomology, 118
Butz, Earl, 166

Calcium arsenate, 115, 116
Calcium cyanamide, 75, 76, 80
Calgene, 202
Camacho, Ávila, 147
Canada
  carbon sequestration programs in, 287
  farm machinery sector concentration in, 43–45
  fertilizer emissions reduction target in, 305, 306
  glyphosate's re-registration process and, 298, 300
  hybrid seed production in, 98, 102, 104
  lobbying in, 296
  potash production in, 81
  regulatory decisions on glyphosate in, 300
  R2R legislation in, 311
  stepped up competition policy in, 246
  stronger merger guidelines in, 332, 372n18
Canadian-American Reciprocity Treaty, 43–44
Canadian Competition Bureau, 251, 255, 327, 372n18
Canadian Food Inspection Agency, 290
Canadian International Development Agency, 153

Canadian National Farmers Union, 287
Canola, 203, 251
Canpotex, 80
Capital, privileged access to, 8–9
Capital Group, 233, *233*, 234
Carbon accounting, 239
Carbon credit programs, 291
  environmental problems related to, 288–289
  farm management software integrated with, 280
  marginalized populations and, 290
  product bundling and, 288
Carbon farming, technology lock-ins and, 286–289
Carbon-offset programs, 269
Carbon sequestration programs, critique of, 287–288, 292
Cargill, 179, *181*, 201
Caribou Biosciences, 254
Caro, Nikoderm, 74
Carolan, Michael, 281
Carson, Rachel, 18, 161, 195
Cartels, 9, 173, 179
  Belarussian Potash Company, 228
  Canadian potash firms, 80
  Chilean nitrate producers, 68
  in commercial fertilizer industry, 60, 78–81, 84, 175, 260
  DEN cartel, 79
  German potash syndicate, 70–71
  PhosChem, 228
  phosphate producers, 74
  potash, 73
  zaibatsu firms, 80, 81
Carver, George Washington, 93
Case, Jerome I., 34
Castor bean, 121
CEMA (Comité Européen des Groupements de Constructeurs du Machinisme Agricole; European Agricultural Machinery Association), 145

Center for Biological Diversity, 301
Central Farmers Fertilizer Company, 179–180, *181*. *See also* CF Industries
Certification of seeds, 91
CF Industries Holdings, Inc., 1, 179, 180, *181*, 248
  business activities, 2023, 279*t*
  IFDC membership, 313
  net income of, 2017–2022, 262, *262*
  net profit margin for, 2020–2022, *263*
  urea ammonium nitrate petition, 307
CFS. *See* Committee on World Food Security (CFS)
CGIAR. *See* Consultative Group on International Agricultural Research (CGIAR)
Charleston Mining and Manufacturing Company, 69
ChemChina, *194*, 223–224, *225*, 231, 232, 235
Chemical industry, , 193, 197, 195–197, 233, 192
Chemical revolution, of eighteenth century, 114
Chemical runoff, 18
Chile
  monopoly on sodium nitrate, 74, 75
  nitrates from, 68, 121
  Nitrate War and, 67
  Rockefeller Foundation initiatives in, 148
Chile saltpeter (sodium nitrate), 66
China
  ancient, pest control in, 113
  fertilizer sector consolidation dynamics and, 178
  food self-sufficiency policies in, 227
  GM crops market in, 235
  private sector share of agricultural R&D in, 270
  reenters global grain market, 165
Chincha Islands of Peru, guano deposits on, 63–64, 66

Chinese indentured laborers, international guano trade and, 64
Chlordane, 128
Ciba-Geigy, 126, 127, 129, 149, 152, 154, 193, *194*, 197, 200, 207, 208, *225*
CIMMYT. *See* International Maize and Wheat Improvement Centre (CIMMYT)
Civil Society and Indigenous Peoples' Mechanism (CSIPM), 314, 336
Civil War (US), 34, 35
Clark, J. Allen, 109
Clayton Act (1914), 12
Climate Corp, 222
Climate FieldView, *240*, 241, 282, 283, 287
Closed pedigree hybrid varieties, 100
Cloud-based digital farm management tools, 239
CNH Industrial, 1, 173, *174*, 226, 239, 248, 362n57
  business activities, 2023, 279*t*
  CEMA membership, 314
  lobbying expenditures by, 295
  MOU signed with AFBF by, 310
  opposition to right-to-repair movement, 309
  recent digital acquisitions of, *240*
Cold War, Green Revolution and, 149
Colombia, 109, 148
Colorado, R2R law in, 310
Colorado potato beetle, 115, 116, 126
Columbus, Christopher, 88
Combine harvesters, 45–46, 49
Cominco Fertilizer, 80, 177, *181*
Commercial seed salesmen, farmers, false claims, and, 91
Committee on World Food Security (CFS), 314, 338
Commodity crop production, expanded, commercial fertilizer industry and, 60

Commodity prices, volatile, farming patterns and, 55
Common ownership, 249, 329
Competition
  International Harvester and suppression of, 50
  investment in innovation and, 272
  lack of, consolidation in farm machinery and fertilizer sectors and, 182–185
  market power and reduction in, 13
  policies, more robust, 327–332
Competition law, 12, 242. *See also* Antitrust law and policy
Concentrated Phosphate Export Association, 175
Concentration ratios, 7, 248–250, 251
Condon, Liam, 282, 312
Consolidated Mining and Smelting Company of Canada, 80
Consolidation. *See also* Agribusiness megamergers, drivers of; Corporate concentration; Mergers and acquisitions
  of agrochemical and seed industries, 191–192, 217–218
  in Canadian farm machinery sector, 44–45
  in chemical pesticides industry, 113
  corporate bigness in context of, 321
  development of seed industry and, 92
  encouragement of, factors behind, 3–4
  farmland, 143–144, 185, 186, 283, 289–290
  farm machinery manufacturers and, 38, 40–43
  of farm machinery sector, 1980s-1990s, 167–173, 189
  in fertilizer industry, 59, 71–74, 78–81, 176–180, *181*, 189
  global food crisis of 1970s and, 164
  of industrial agricultural model, 139

Consolidation (cont.)
  industrial production systems and, 2–3
  innovation and impact of, 271–274
  investor pressure for, 9
  of market position in new global age, 155–158
  in plow industry, 42–43
  political power and, 293
  recent drivers of, 23
  seed and chemical, second wave of, 200–201
  seed industry, first wave of, 192–193, 197
  tractors, rivalry, and, 45–49
Consultative Group on International Agricultural Research (CGIAR), 149, 153
Consumer welfare standard, 184
Conway, Erik, 184
Cooperatives
  fertilizer plants operated by, 157
  privatization of fertilizer companies, 179
Copa Cogeca, 303
Copper arsenate, 115
Copper sulfate, 115
Corn, 60, 227. *See also* Maize
  hybridization of, research on, 96–99
  hybrid *vs.* open-pollinated varieties of, 109
  livestock industry and high demand for, 92
  ownership of IP for, 251
  quest for improvement of, through breeding, 93–96
Corn herbicide market, corporate concentration in, 207–208
Corn Laws, Britain's repeal of, 92
Corn seeds, price of, 210
Corn shows, 93, 94
Corporate bigness. *See also* Consolidation; Corporate concentration; Future policy shifts, priority areas for
  defining, 6–7
  exploring origins of, 321
  market and financial dynamics and, 7, 8–9
  policy context and, 7, 11–12
  technological change and, 7, 9–11
Corporate concentration, 245. *See also* Agribusiness megamergers, drivers of; Consolidation; Mergers and acquisitions
  food system and broader costs of, 16–19, *20*
  historical look at drivers behind, 3–4
  innovation and impact of, 271–274
  market power and, 246–250, 363n8
  in seed markets, 251–254
  seeds-chemicals mergers and, 207–208
  wide-ranging costs of, 323
Corporate dominance within industrial agriculture. *See also* Corporate bigness
  appreciating history behind, xi
  economic dominance, public critique of, 246
  taking long view on, importance of, 5
Corporate Europe Observatory, 303
Corporate food regime, 22
Corporate incentives, common ownership and, 232–234, *233*
Corporate power
  analyzing, study of rich and powerful in, 339–340
  examining in other parts of food systems, 340, 372n38
  to shape markets, 12, 13–14, 19, 23, 245–267
  to shape policy and governance, 13, 15–16, 19, 23, 293–317
  to shape technology, 12, 14–15, 19, 23, 269–292
Corporate social responsibility (CSR), 295, 325

Corteva Agriscience, 1, 3, *194*, 223, 235, 236, 237, 238, 249, 284, 296, 304, 312
   boycotting of online sellers and, 255
   business activities, 2023, 279*t*
   carbon farming and, 286
   concentration ratio of, 248
   CRISPR patents for agriculture and, 254
   digital software platform investments, 241
   4R approach and, 305
   Granular software app, 287–288
   lobbying expenditures by, 295
   Mexico's glyphosate ban and, 301
   operating profit margin, 2022, 264
   rebates scheme lawsuit, 255, 256
   recent digital and biological acquisitions of, *240*
Cotton, 60, 203, 211, 251, 271
Cover-cropping practices, 286
COVID-19 pandemic, 252, 259, 261, 267, 326
Crabb, Richard, 97
"Creative destruction," 271
Credit
   Deere & Company and use of, 34
   Grange movement and, 37
   guano trade and, 65
   McCormick's distribution and sales model and, 31, 32
CR4. *See* Four-firm concentration ratio (CR4)
CRISPR, 237, 253, 254, 284, 362n50
Crop damage, global trade, pest infestations, and, 115
Crop improvement, seed selection and, 87
CropLife, 295, 303, 304
CropLife America, 131, 217, 255
CropLife Brasil, 297
CropLife Canada, lobbying over gene editing legislation by, 296
CropLife International (CLI), 216, 311–314

Cross-licensing agreements, 206–208, 236, 253
CSIPM. *See* Civil Society and Indigenous Peoples' Mechanism (CSIPM)
CSR. *See* Corporate social responsibility (CSR)
Cultural practices, chemical pesticides and abandonment of, 118, 134
Curry, Helen, 110Dahlberg, Kenneth, 150

Danaher, Kevin, 149
Data privacy, 288, 292
DDT, 135, 154, 157, 195, 326
   banning of, 131, 161, 195
   civilian use and marketing of, 127
   concerns about human safety of, 132–133, 160–161
   discovery of pesticidal qualities in, 113, 126–127
   farmers' dependence on, 130
   impact studies on wildlife and, 132
   licenses for production of, 129
   pest resistance to, 134
   social and ecological costs of, 131–133
   World War II and use of, 126–127
Debt. *See also* Bankruptcies
   Farm debt, quadrupling of, in 1970s, 166
   food crisis of 1970s and, 166–167, 186
   higher fertilizer prices and, 265
   tractor adoption and, 54–55, 57
Deere, Charles, 33, 45
Deere, John, 33
Deere & Co., 36, 42, 45, 145, 147, 152, 156, 168, 169, 172, *174*, 183, 226, 234, 238, 248, 274, 284
   business activities, 2023, 279*t*
   carbon farming and, 286
   CEMA membership, 314
   emergence of and tactics used by, 33–34
   equipment repair lawsuits, 258–259
   farm machinery repairs and, 257

Deere & Co. (cont.)
  4R approach and, 305
  lobbying expenditures by, 295
  MOU signed with AFBF by, 310
  net income, 2020–2023, 264
  recent digital acquisitions of, *240*
  right-to-repair legislation opposed by, 308, 309
  SpaceX partnership with, 278, 366n36
  on "technology stack," 283
  tractor production and, 46, 48
Deering, William, 37, 40
Deering Harvester Co., 37–38, 40, 41
Defensive innovation spending, transformative research *vs.*, 330
Defensive R&D, 14, 274–277
DeKalb, 97–99, 153, 157, 192, 193, *194*, 202, 207, *225*
De Loecker, Jan, 250
Delta and Pineland, 200
DEN cartel, 79
Denmark, seed sector concentration in, 249
Deserts on the March (Sears), 82–83
Deskilling. *See* Agricultural deskilling
Deutz-Allis, 170, 172, *174*
Diamond v. Chakrabarty, 205
Dicamba, drifting of, to adjacent fields, 275
Dieldrin, 128, 195
Digital agricultural software and hardware, 269, 277, 278–279, 280–284, 291
Digital agriculture, 23, 269, 270, 273, 329, 336–337, 338
  carbon credit initiatives and, 287–288
  digital subscription services and, 289
  ecological critiques of, 281
  equity issues and, 289–290, 292
  more responsible models of, 336–337
  ownership of data concerns and, 282–283
  rise of, 222, 238–239, 241, 277–284
  user agreements and, 283
Digital economy, agricultural sector and, 331
Digital farming. *See* Digital agriculture
Digital subscription services, 289
Diseconomies of scale, 8
Diverse market structures, supporting, 328, 330
Diversity on multiple fronts, fostering, 325–326
Doggett, Jon, 307
DOJ. *See* US Department of Justice (DOJ)
Double cross hybridization, 95, 98
Dow Agrosciences, 201, 206
Dow Chemical Corporation, 3, 128, 129, 149, 154, *194*, 195, 200, 201, 223, *225*, 230, 234, 236, 275
Dow-DuPont merger, 3, 230, 234, 273–274, 275
Dreyfus Frères & Cie, guano trade and, 65
Droughts, 103, 227
Duke, Stephen, 276
Dunlap, Thomas, 121
DuPont, 75, 76, 77, 78, 79, 129, 145, 154, 161, *181*, *194*, 200, 201, 223, *225*, 229, 236, 254
  DDT manufacture during World War II, 127
  Dow-DuPont merger, 3, 230, 234, 273–274, 275
  synthetic pesticides development and, 123–124
Dust Bowl, 56, 82
Dyestuffs Corporation, 78
Dyestuffs sector, 123

East, Edward, 94, 95, 98
Economic entomology field, emergence of, 117
Economies of scale, 8
  farm machinery firms and, 57

fertilizer sector and, 60, 84
pesticide industry and, 136
specialized farms and, 163
Eeckhout, Jan, 250, 266
Eli Lilly, 201
Elmore, Bartow, 129
Enclosure of farmland, soil productivity and, 60
End-user license agreements (EULAS), 257, 259
Environment, corporate concentration, food systems, and, 18–19, *20*
Environmental, social, and governance (ESG) performance, 325
EPA. *See* US Environmental Protection Agency (EPA)
Equipment Dealers Association, 309
Equity, digital agriculture and, 289–290, 292
ETC Group, 324, 336
EU-Mercosur trade agreement, 297
EuropaBio, 217
Europe
  carbon sequestration programs in, 287
  farm machinery sector mergers and sales from, 173, *174*
European Agricultural Machinery Association (CEMA), FAO partnership with, 313, 314
European Commission, 300
  Expert Group on the European Food Security Crisis Preparedness and Response Mechanism, 304, 369–370n50
European Community Common Agricultural Policy, 166
European corn borer infestations, 103, 115
European Union (EU)
  Framework Regulation 167/2013 in, 310
  glyphosate regulation in, 300
  lobbying expenditures in, disclosure of, 295, 297

Eutrophication, 187
Eyde, Sam, 75

Falkner, Robert, 14
FAO. *See* Food and Agriculture Organization of the United Nations (FAO)
Farm Action, 262
Farm economy, agriculture boom-and-bust cycle and, 163–167, 221, 222, 227–229
Farm Equipment Manufacturers Association, 145
Farmer agency and choice, enhanced market power and, 265, 267
Farmers
  chemical pesticides use and individualist ethos of, 118–119
  consolidation of industrial production systems and, 2–3
  dependence on synthetic chemical pesticides by, 130
  in developing countries, rising fertilizer prices and, 265
  digital farming and revenue streams of, 282
  ecological deskilling among, 215
  interwar years and precarity of, 101
  livelihoods of, growing corporate concentration and, 17, *20*
  multiyear carbon sequestration contracts and, 288
  "pesticides treadmill" and, 122, 136
  price-cost squeeze and, 329
  private seed companies and, 91
  right-to-repair movement and, 258
  seed breeding role of, 107–108
  synthetic pesticides, "deskilling," and, 133, 136
  technological determinism and, 143–144
  World War I and demand for pesticides from, 121

Farmers Business Network (FBN), 254, 255
Farm incomes, food crisis of 1970s and decline in, 166–167
Farmland
  consolidation of, 143–144, 185, 186
  redistributing, adoption of policies for, 336
Farm machinery, 23
  harvester wars and megamergers, 37–38, 40–43
  mechanical reapers, 28–32
  plows, 33–34
Farm machinery input industry, 339
  asset management ownership in, 234
  Canadian concentration in, 43–45
  corporate concentration in, 156
  digital agriculture and, 238–239
  FAO partnership with CEMA and, 314
  farm crisis of 1980s and, 167
  full-line approach in, 45–46
  globalization and, 145, 146
  Green Revolution and, 153
  International Harvester antitrust case and, 49–51
  lack of market competition and increased concentration in, 182–185
  lock-in dynamics and, 139, 142, 162
  major mergers and acquisitions in, since the 1830s, *174*
  oil crisis of 1973 and, 165
  opposition to right-to-repair legislation, 308–311, 317
  rapid transformation of, 27–28
  reconfigurations in, early 2000s, 226
  restructuring and consolidation of, 1980s-1990s, 167–173
  social and ecological consequences of growth in, 51–56, 57
  technological lock-ins and, 10
  tractors and consolidation in, 45–49

Farm machinery repairs. *See also* Right-to-repair (R2R) movement
  enhanced market power and, 265
  market dominance and, 257–259
Farms and farm size, 17, 53–54, 143–144, 168, 185
Farm to Fork (F2F) initiative (EU), sustained attack on by industry, 302–304, 305, 306
Faulkner, Edward H., 56
Federal Insecticide, Fungicide, and Rodenticide Act (FIFRA), 130–131
Federal Insecticide Act of 1910, 119, 130, 131
Federal Trade Commission (FTC), 11, 216, 255, 256, 309
Felix, Herbert, 151
Female farmers, digital agriculture and, 289
Ferguson Company, *174*
Fernandez-Cornejo, Jorge, 101
Fertilizer Canada, 305, 306
Fertilizer firms
  enhanced market power and, 266
  major, net income of, 2017–2022, 261, *262*
  major, net profit margin for, 2020–2022, 261, *263*
Fertilizer input industry, 17, 59, 60, 339
  asset management ownership in, 234
  biological products and, 238
  commercial, emergence of, 60–63
  commercial, guano trade and, 63–66
  commercial, rise of, 59–60
  corporate concentration/consolidation in, 71–74, 78–81, 84, 157, 248
  digital technologies and, 239
  expansion of, into retailing, 256–257
  farm crisis of 1980s and, 167
  4R narrative promoted by, 305–306
  globalization and, 145

Green Revolution and, 153
influence on policy, multipronged approach to, 304–308
lack of market competition and increased concentration in, 182–185
lock-in dynamics and, 139, 142, 162
major restructuring in, after 2015, 226
mergers in, late 20th century, 173, 175–180, *181*
N, P, K standard mixing practice in, 71
national security and, 76
nitrogen synthesis and, 74–78
oil crisis of 1973 and, 165
overproduction in, 175
phosphorus, potassium, and the German potash syndicate, 68–71
profiteering complaints about, 260–263, *262, 263*
sodium nitrate trade, 66–68
technological change and, 10
Fertilizer Institute (FI), 188, 295, 306
Fertilizers, 23, 323
commercial, social and ecological concerns with, 81–84
cumulative global use of, 1961–2021, 187, *187*
Green Revolution and, 151
natural biological methods, investing in, 336
protection of intellectual property and development of, 10
soil quality and, 18
synthetic, critiques of, 82–84
FIAN International, 312, 336
Fiat, 173, *174*
Fidelity, 233, *233*
FIFRA. *See* Federal Insecticide, Fungicide, and Rodenticide Act (FIFRA)
Financial capital, preferential access to, 3
Financial crisis of 2008, wave of megamergers and, 227–228
Financialization, 221–222, 229–232, 329, 361n35
Fitzgerald, Deborah, 101, 107, 108
Fixed Nitrogen Research Laboratory (FNRL), 77, 78
Focus on the Global South, 336
Food and Agriculture Organization of the United Nations (FAO), 151, 152, 153, 154
agroecology discussions at, 338
collaboration with World Economic Forum, 315
corporate influence within, 311–314, 317, 334
Food commodities, unaffordability of fertilizer and, 265
Food crisis of 1970s, 152, 163–167, 199
Food price inflation, calls for policy reform and, 326–327
Food surpluses, government policies and, 144
Food systems
broader costs of corporate concentration in, 16–19, *20*
examining corporate power in other parts of, 340, 372n38
governments and transformation of, 339
greater transparency and accountability in, 336
rise of corporate power and future of, 4–5
sustainable and just, calls for, 326
technology sovereignty in, supporting, 337
transformation agenda of, debates over, 22
wider costs of corporate political power in, 315–317
Ford, Henry, bid on Muscle Shoals plants, 347n55
Ford Foundation, 153

Ford Motor Company, 152, 153, 156, 172, *174*
　Fordson tractor launched by, 47, 347n55
Ford-New Holland Inc., 170, *174*
Foreign direct investment (FDI), for agricultural input companies, 146–147, 162
ForGround, *240*, 241
Fosdick, Raymond, 148
Fossil energy, industrialization of agriculture and, 10
4R method, fertilizer industry and promotion of, 305–306
Four-firm concentration ratio (CR4), 7, 248–250, 273
Fowler, Carey, 92, 107, 198
Frank, Adolph, 74
Frank-Caro cyanamide process, 74
Fraud and deception
　in chemical pesticides sector, 117, 119
　in fertilizer sector, 65
Friends of the Earth, 289
Fruits, arsenic residues on, 120, 125
FTC. *See* Federal Trade Commission (FTC)
F2F initiative. *See* Farm to Fork (F2F) initiative (EU)
Fuglie, Keith, 214
Fungicides, 196
Fungus infestations, monocultures and, 115
Funk, Eugene, 91, 92, 96, 97
Funk Brothers Seed Company, 91–92, 96–97, 102, 105, 125, 147, 157, 192, 193, *194*, 200, 207, *225*
Funk Farms, USDA experimental research station at, 97, 98, 105
Future policy shifts, priority areas for alternative agricultural models, greater support for, 335–338
　curbing corporate political influence, 332–333
　ensuring stronger accountability measures, 334–335
　final thoughts on, 339–340
　more robust competition policies, 327–332
　participatory governance settings and, 333–334
　transparency in scientific research, need for greater, 333
　turning point for?, 324–327
　uncertain path ahead, 321–341
Fyrwald, Erik, 304

Gajaria, Rajan, 273
Galvani, 226
Gene editing. *See* Genome editing
General Agreement on Tariffs and Trade, 146
General Chemical, 78
Genetically modified seed-herbicide technological packages, 192
Genetically modified (GM) seeds
　concentration ratios and, 248–249
　defensive R&D and, 275
　development of, 10
　Monsanto and development of, 203
　"stacked traits" and, 236
　technological lock-in of, 211
Genetic engineering
　new forms of, 236–238
　technological lock-ins and, 291
Genetic narrowing, Green Revolution and, 160
Genome editing, 13, 23, 222, 237, 243, 269, 270, 279*t*, 284–286, 291, 296–297, 330
George, Bill, 230
George, Susan, 339
German Potash Law, 72–73
German potash syndicate, 70–71, 72–73
Germany, glyphosate ban and, 300
Gesarol (DDT), 126

INDEX

Gilded age, corporate consolidation during, 42
Gilpin, Robert, 146
Glickman, Dan, 3, 183
Global governance forums, agribusiness working together in, 151–155
Global Industry Coalition, 217
Globalization
　consolidation in fertilizer sector and, 178
　industrial agricultural model and, 139, 140, 145–147, 158–161, 162
　of agribusiness, 145–147, 155
　power of big players and, 1
Global North
　agricultural deskilling in, 215
　agroecological farming methods in, 336
　digital farming apps in, 283
　increased glyphosate use in, 212
Global South, 162
　agricultural deskilling in, 215
　corporate influence at FAO and, 313
　digital farming apps in, 283–284
　fertilizer industry lobbying in, 308
　food assistance policies and, 144
　glyphosate use in, 212
　lobbying in, lack of transparency for, 297, 333
　toxic pesticides use in, 160, 161
　transnational agribusiness firms and, 152
Global trade, pest infestations and, 115
Glyphosate, 158, 203, 209, 211, 275, 285, 289
　bans on, 300–301, 369n35
　battle over, 298–302
　ecological and health costs related to, 290
　global use of, 1990–2014, 212, *213*
　glyphosate-based herbicides, 15, 209
　herbicide resistance and, 203, 211
　safety concerns about, 212–213
　value of global market for, 290, 368n93

GM seeds. *See* Genetically modified (GM) seeds
Goldberg, Walter, 63
Gordon, Ben, 286
Gorham, Marquis L., 31
Governance. *See* Political power; Policy
Governments, 3
　fertilizer sector and support of, 60
　seed acquisition, distribution, and research by, 88–90
Grain markets
　China's reentry into, 165
　Soviet Union's entry into (1970s), 164–165
Grange movement, 34–37, 51
　cooperative efforts of, 36–37
　formation of, 34
　popular support for, 35
　strategies of, 35–36
Grant, Hugh, 223, 273
Granular, *240*, 288
Grasselli Chemical Company, 124
Great Britain, plant collection and colonial initiatives of, 88
Great Chinese Famine, 165
Great Depression, ix, 54, 80, 101, 157, 167
Greece (ancient), pest control in, 113
Greenhouse gas emissions, 84, 323
　agrochemicals and, 302
　chemical fertilizer industry and, 187–188
　4R approach and, 305–306
　industrial model of agriculture and, 18–19
　machinery in industrial agriculture and, 186
Green Revolution, 11, 23, 140, 161, 290, 323
　capitalizing on, 147–151, 153, 162
　consequences of shipping out the model and, 158–161

Greenhouse gas emissions (cont.)
  farm mechanization and displaced labor in, 159
  important drivers behind, 149
  multinational firms and, role of, 149–150
  tractor manufacturers and, 153
Grenadines, glyphosate ban and, 300
Guano, 63, 65, 68
  fraud in, 65
  in Peru, 63–66
  price volatility and uncertain supply in, 65–66
  working conditions in, 64, 81, 346n14
Guano Islands Act, 65–66, 346n20
Gulf Cooperation council, glyphosate ban and, 300
Gunn, Charlie, 97, 98, 99
Gunter, Valerie, 132

Haber, Fritz, 75
Haber-Bosch process, 75, 76, 77, 78, 79, 80, 85
Hardware, digital farming and, 278–280
Harris, A., Son and Company Limited, 43
Harris, Craig, 132
Hartley, C. P., 100
"Harvester Wars," 38, 40
Harvesting machine industry, harvester wars and megamergers, 37–38, 40–43
Harvesting machines
  mechanical reapers, 28–32
  repairs of, market dominance in, 257
Hatch Act, 90, 117
Hayes, Wayland J., Jr., 132
Hello Tractor, 284
Heptachlor, 128
Herbicide resistance, glyphosate and, 203, 211. *See also* Roundup
Herbicide-resistant weeds, 275, 285

Herbicides, 10, 157, 192, 201, 203, 204, 211, 215, 236, 323. *See also* Glyphosate; Roundup
  Carson's work and critique of, 195
  dearth of new R&D into, 276
  decline in registered patents for, 214
  expanded use of, costs related to, 192, 218
  gene editing and, 237
  glyphosate-based, 15
  network effects and use of, 143
  no-till farming and, 289
  rapid growth in market for, 196
  synthetic, early, 128
Herbicide-tolerant crop traits, 203
Hercules Powder Company (Hercules Inc.), 123, 125, 127, *225*
Herfindahl-Herschman Index (HHI), market concentration and, 341n14
Hi-Bred Corn Company (Pioneer), 94, 97, 98
High-yield varieties (HYVs), 156, 157
  Green Revolution and, 148, 149
  narrowing of genetic base of food production and, 160
Hindman, Jahmy, 278
Hindustan Organic Chemicals, 154
Hoechst, 78, 81, 122, 129, 152, 154, 158, *225*
Holbert, Jim, 96, 97, 98, 99, 100, 105
Honeybees, pest resurgence and, 134
Horizontal consolidation, in fertilizer sector, 177, 189
Horizontal integration, 328, 329
Horses over tractors, advocates of, 52–53
Household and Commercial Products Association, 131
Howard, Leland O., 118, 121
Howard, Philip, 208
Howard, Sir Albert, 83
Humus theory, 61, 62, 83
Hussey, Obey, 28, 29

INDEX 439

H. V. McKay Company, ix, x
Hybrid corn, Mendel's work and development of, 94
Hybrid corn seed R&D, public to private shift in, 105–106, 110
Hybridization
  early work in, 94
  intellectual property protection and, 95–96
  seed industry and advent of, 87–88
  US seed industry and impact of, 96–99
Hybrid seed companies, fate of, after the 1970s, *194*
Hybrid seeds
  built-in intellectual property protection for, 197
  marketing campaigns for, 102
  network effects, tractor adoption, and, 142–143
  promotion and adoption of, 101–105
Hybrid seeds industry
  corporate concentration in, 157
  US public sector research initiatives, 100
HYVs. *See* High-yield varieties (HYVs)

IARC. *See* International Agency for Research on Cancer (IARC)
IBM, 284, 286
ICI. *See* Imperial Chemical Industries (ICI)
ICP. *See* Industry Cooperative Program (ICP)
IFDC. *See* International Fertilizer Development Center (IFDC)
IG Farben, 78, 79, 81, 84, 123, 124, 126, 128, 129, 158, *225*
Illies, Christian, 286
IMC Global, 177, 178–179, 182
Imperial Chemical Industries (ICI), 78, 79, 84, 123, 124, 128, 129, 145, 149, 161, 177, *181*, 193, 197, *225*
India
  Bhopal disaster in, 160, 161, 335
  carbon sequestration programs in, 287
  fertilizer sector consolidation dynamics and, 178
  Green Revolution in, 140, 151, 153, 154–155, 160, 290
  Rockefeller Foundation initiatives in, 148
  R2R legislation in, 311
  Warangal District, deskilling in, 215
Indigenous farmers, digital agriculture and, 289
Indigenous peoples
  building on knowledge and skills of, 337
  Columbus and maize seeds acquired from, 88
  corporate dominance in food policy and, 317
  growth of farm machinery sector and displacement of, 55, 57
  maize cultivation in, 106–107
Indigo Agriculture, 286
Indonesia, Green Revolution in, 140, 148, 151
Industrial agricultural inputs
  government policymaking and, 144–145
  "technological treadmill" and, 143
Industrial agricultural model, 335
  corporate concentration and wide-ranging costs of, 323
  ecological and health costs of, 17–19
  endurance of, 22
  fragility of, 326–327
  globalization of, 145–147
  greenhouse gases and, 18–19
  lock-in of, 139, 140–145, 155, 158, 162, 163, 164, 192
  postwar consolidation of, 139
  shaping policy in support of, 188–189

Industrial agricultural model (cont.)
  shipping out of: consequences related to, 158–161, 162
  significance of glyphosate in, 298
  social costs of, 17–18, *20*
  technology power and wider costs of, 290–291, 292
Industrial capitalism, neoliberalism and, 7
Industrial farming
  enormous ecological problems with, 323
  farmland consolidation and, 289–290
  improvements in, digital agriculture and, 280–281
Industrial Revolution, in North America, 28
Industry associations, formation of, 145
Industry Cooperative Program (ICP), 151–152, 154
Inequality
  digital agriculture and, 289–290, 292
  market power and increase in, 266
Inflation, 252, 265
  COVID-19 pandemic and, 259
  food price, calls for policy reform and, 326–327
  1970s global food crisis and, 164, 165, 166
Innovation. *See also* Patents; Research and development (R&D)
  agricultural, seed and chemical mergers and, 214
  chemical industry and downturn in, 196
  competition policies and, 329–330
  digital farming, early, 277–278
  influence of hyper-concentration on, 271–274
  intellectual property protection and, 11
  knowledge power and, 14
  profit-oriented, rewarding, 322–323

Insect control, World War I and, 120–122
Insecticides
  chemical industry and sales of, 196
  pyrethrum-based powders, 116
Insecticides Manufacturers Association, 131
Insect infestations, monocultures and, 115
Institute for Agriculture and Trade Policy, 312
Institutional investors, 232
Integrated farming solutions, 273
Intellectual property (IP), seed markets and ownership of, 251
Intellectual property protection, 28. *See also* Innovation; Patents
  advent of hybrids and, 95–96
  corporate bigness and, 322
  first movers and, 9, 10
  for genetically modified seed varieties, 205–206
  hybrid seeds and, 88, 197
  innovation and, 11
  for large chemical firms, 129, 135
  market dominance in seed industry and, 198–199
  market power and, 247
  rise of organic chemistry and, 114
  seeds and agrochemicals merger clusters and, 236
  for sexually reproducing plants, 198
  strengthening of, seed company acquisitions and, 198
  TRIPS agreement and, 216
Intercropping, 1, 113
Interest rates, 166, 231
Intergovernmental Panel on Climate Change, discussions about agroecology and, 338
Interlocking directorships, 12
Internal combustion engine, gasoline tractors and, 46

INDEX

International Agency for Research on Cancer (IARC), 298–299, 300
International Agricultural Corporation, 71, 72, *181*
International Competition Network, 242
International Fertilizer Association (IFA), 305, 313
International Fertilizer Development Center (IFDC), 313
International Harvester Company, ix–x, 45, 48, 153, 156, 168, *174*, 256
  antitrust case, 49–51
  collapse of, 170–171
  farm crisis of 1980s and, 169
  megamerger deal and creation of, 41–42
  Tenneco acquisition, 171, 172
  tractor production and, 46
International Maize and Wheat Improvement Centre (CIMMYT), 149
International Minerals and Chemicals Corporation, 177, *181*
International Monetary Fund, 146
International organizations, Green Revolution and, 149
International Panel of Experts on Sustainable Food Systems (IPES-Food), 324
International Plant Nutrition Institute, 305
International Rice Research Institute (IRRI), 149
International Science-Policy Platform on Biodiversity and Ecosystem Services
  discussions about agroecology and, 338
International Trade Commission (ITC), 307
IPES-Food, 336
Iroquois women farmers, disruption of, 107
IRRI. *See* International Rice Research Institute (IRRI)
Italy, seed sector concentration in, 249
ITC. *See* International Trade Commission (ITC)

Jacoby, Erich, 152, 159
Jana Partners, 231
Japan
  farm machinery sector mergers and sales from, 173, *174*
  nitrogen synthesis in, 80, 81, 84
  soga sosha trading houses in, 172
  zaibatsu firms of, 80, 81
Jardin des Plantes (Paris), 88, 89
J. I. Case, 168, 171, 172, 173, *174*
J. I. Case Plow Works, 34
J. I. Case Threshing Machine Company, 34, 46
Jochum, Gunter, 287
John Deere, 1, 153. *See also* Deere & Co.
Jones, Donald, 94, 95, 98
JP Morgan Chase, 40–41, 50, 286
J. R. Geigy, 123, *225*

Kanter, Jonathan, 331
Kawasaki, 80
Kelloway, Claire, 289
Kern County Land Company, 168
Kew Gardens, 88
Khan, Lina, 216, 256, 331
Klockner-Humboldt Deutz, 170, 172
Kloppenburg, Jack, 90, 106, 143
Knowledge power, 14
Koch Industries, 178, 248
Kodak, 259
Kramer, Helen, 38
Krug, George, 99
Krug Corn, 99
K+S, 178, *181*
Kubota, 1, 172, *174*, 226, 239, 248, 356n33, 362n59
  business activities, 2023, 279t
  CEMA membership, 314

441

Kubota (cont.)
  opposition to right-to-repair movement, 309
  recent digital acquisitions of, *240*
Kullman, Ellen, 230
Kurz, Mordecai, 14

Labor displacement
  Green Revolution and, 159
  industrial farming and, 323
  tractor adoption and, 53
Labor unions, farm machinery firms and, 38
Lal, Rattan, 56
Land-grant colleges, agricultural experiment stations at, 90, 125
Land redistribution, marginalized populations and, 336
Land use
  access to, equity issues and, 289–290
  assetization of, 283
  digital data storage/processing and, 281
  diversity of small-scale farmers, land reform, and, 336
  equitable, 335
Larew, Rob, 258
Latin America, Climate FieldView software marketed in, 283
Latin American Business Development Corporation, 152
La Via Campesina, 336
Lead arsenate, 115, 116, 120
Leibenluft, Robert, 198
Lennox, Donald D., 169
Lianos, Ioannis, 329
LibertyLink seed traits, BASF and removal of, from public domain, 253, 276
Liebig, Justus von, 62–64, 68, 83
Limagrain, 193
Lindane, 128
Linde Air Products Company, 124

Livestock industry, 61, 92
Loan repayment, tractor adoption and, 54–55. *See also* Debt
Lobbying, 293, 294, 317, 322
  by agribusiness firms, 15, 16
  agricultural biotechnology firms and, 215–217
  spending on, 295–296
  in support of industrial agricultural model, 188
  transparency and disclosure of, need for, 334
Lobby registries, 293
Lock-ins, 158. *See also* Technological lock-ins
  carbon credit initiatives and, 288
  corporate concentration and power and, 141–142
  dynamics among four industrial agricultural inputs and, 139, 162
  institutional, 141
  of herbicide-genetically modified seed technological package, 276–277
  of industrial agricultural model, 139, 140–145, 155, 158, 163, 164, 192
  oligopolistic market structures and, 162
  reasons behind occurrence of, 140–141
Loeb, Daniel, 230
London purple, 116
Lorsch, Jay, 230
Low-input sustainable agriculture (LISA), 188
Luxembourg, glyphosate ban and, 300
Lymphoma cancers, glyphosate and, 213, 290, 298

Macdonald, James, 247
Machinery manufacturers, blocking of R2R movement by, 308–311
MacIntyre, Angus, 134

Maize, 24, 211. *See also* Corn
  biodiversity loss and impact on, 109–110
  hybrid, network effects, tractor adoption, and, 143
  Indigenous societies and cultivation of, 106–107
  pest-resistant, 203
  private sector R&D and, 271
  seeds, Columbus and trade in, 88
Maize Committee, 109
Malaria, DDT and fight against, 127
Malathion, 128
Manglesdorf, Paul, 109
Manning, William, 28
Manufacturing Chemists' Association, 132
Marginalized populations
  corporate dominance in food policy and, 317
  farmland redistribution policies and, 336
Market and financial dynamics
  agricultural input firms and, 7, 8–9
  weakened market competition, titans of industrial agriculture, and, 4
Market concentration, measuring, 7, 341n14. *See also* Concentration Ratios
Market power. *See also* Political power; Technology power
  accusations of corporate profiteering, 246, 259–264, 267
  compounding of, by dominant firms, 247
  concentration and, 246–250, 363n8
  corporate bigness and, 322–323
  corporate concentration, food systems, and, *20*
  definition of, 13, 246
  digital farming and, 280
  digital subscriptions and, 283
  innovation and, debate on, 272–273
  market dominance for farm machinery repairs, 257–259
  New Brandeis movement and, 331
  new retailers crowded out by input suppliers, 254–257, 266
  ownership patterns and, 329
  in post-2015 merger context, 245, 266
  seed market and, 251–254
  shaping of, 12, 13–14, 19, 23, 245–267
  wider costs of, 264–266
Marshall Plan, 105
Marsh Harvester, 37
Martin, Edward, 35
Marubeni Corporation, 172
Massey, Daniel, Jr., 43
Massey, Hart, 43
Massey-Ferguson, x, 147, 152, 153, 156, 168, 169–170, 172, 173, *174*
Massey-Harris, x, 43, 44, 46, 48
Massey Manufacturing Company, 43
McArdle, Archie, 170
McCormick, Cyrus (grandson), 52, 279
McCormick, Cyrus, Jr., 38
McCormick, Cyrus H., 52
  Deering Harvester Co. and, 37–38, 40
  distribution and sales model of, 31, 32
  establishes dominance in harvester industry, 30–31
  failed bid for currency plan, 50
  Grangers and, 35–36
  mass production at Chicago plant of, 30
  origin story of mechanical reapers and, 28–29
  secures patent for reaper design, 29
McCormick, Edith (Rockefeller), 41
McCormick, Harold, 41
McCormick Harvesting Machine Company, 29, 30, 33, 38
  factory view, 1896, *39*
  Harvester Wars and, 40
McCormick Reaper Company, *174*
McWilliams, James, 120

Meat-packing plants, fertilizer division within, 69
Mechanical reapers, 28–32
  invention of, 38
  McCormick and origin story of, 28–29
Melo, Hector, 150
Memorandum of understanding (MOU), signed with American Farm Bureau Foundation, 310
Mendel, Gregor, hybrid corn and influence of, 94
Merck, 127, *225*
Mergers and acquisitions, 3, 12, 23. *See also* Agribusiness megamergers, drivers of; Consolidation; Corporate concentration; Monopolies
  Canadian farm machinery sector, 44–45
  in chemical pesticide industry, since late 1800s, *225*
  conjoining of agrochemical and seed industries, 191–192, 217–218
  corporate bigness in context of, 321–322
  between farm equipment firms, ix, x
  in farm machinery sector, 1980s-1990s, 167–173
  in fertilizer sector, 71–73, 173, 175–180, *181*
  financial dynamics behind, 8–9
  first wave of seed industry consolidation, 192–193, 197
  harvester firms, 38, 40–43
  major, in farm machinery sector since the 1830s, *174*
  mergers of distress and/or opportunity 163, 189, 191, 218, 221, 243
  most recent, seed and agrochemical industry, 3
  second wave of seed and chemical consolidation, 200–201
  stronger guidelines for, emergence of, 332

synthetic chemicals firms and, 129
synthetic nitrogen production firms, 78–79
in synthetic pesticides industry, 123–124
technological change and, 10
tractor market, 48
weakening of antitrust laws and, 12
Mexican Agricultural Program (MAP), launch of, 148
Mexico
  Deere's sales in, 147
  glyphosate ban and, 300, 301
  Green Revolution in, 140, 148, 151
  pesticide use in, 154
  Rockefeller Foundation's corn improvement program in, 108–109
  seed centers in, 109
Microsoft, 284
Mineral-based pesticides, 115, 125
Mineral resource extraction, digital technologies and, 281
Minneapolis-Moline, 48, 168, *174*
"Miracle seeds," 148
Mitsubishi, 80, 152
Mitsui, 80
MNCs. *See* Multinational corporations (MNCs)
Mobil Oil, *181*
Moline Plow Company, 34, 48, *174*
Monocultures, 107
  biodiversity concerns and, 18
  commodity crop production and, 60
  Green Revolution and, 160
  network effects and, 143
  simple ecological systems in, 115
Monopolies. *See also* Corporate concentration, Mergers and acquisitions
  Brandeis on, 6, 7, 49
  German potash syndicate, 70–71, 72
  Grange movement and push back against, 34–37

INDEX

McCormick's mechanical reapers and, 29–32
Peruvian guano production, 64–65
sodium nitrate production and trade, 67
Monsanto, 124, 125, 127, 128, 129, 145, 149, 158, 193, *194*, 197, 199, 200, 201, 206, 211, 224, *225*, 226, 229, 231, 232, 235, 236, 251
  acquisitions of seed and biotechnology firms, 202–203
  agribusiness policy lobbying by, 216
  anticompetitive practices of, 208, 209
  battle over glyphosate and, 298–300, 301, 333
  Bayer-Monsanto merger, 4, 224, 231, 232, 235, 236, 269, 273, 274, 282, 285, 298, 299, 301
  Climate Corp platform, 239
  expiration of glyphosate patent, 214
  inroads into digital farming, 222–223
  New Alliance for Food Security and Nutrition and, 311
  scientific studies and papers influenced by, 217
Monsanto Papers, 299
Montenegro de Wit, Maywa, 337
Mooney, Pat, 198, 276
Morgan Stanley, 168
Morrill Acts, 89, 90
Morton, J. Sterling, 90
Mosaic Company, 1, 179, *181*, 226, 228, 248, 306
  business activities, 2023, 279t
  control over US phosphate fertilizer market, 306–307
  4R approach and, 305
  IFDC membership, 313
  net income of, 2017–2022, 262, *262*
  net profit margin for, 2020–2022, *263*
  recent biological acquisitions of, *240*

Moss, Diana L., 264
MOU. *See* Memorandum of understanding (MOU)
Müller, Paul, 126, 127
Multinational corporations (MNCs), 146–147, 149–150
Muscle Shoals, Alabama, nitrogen synthesis plants in, 76, 80 347n55
Musk, Elon, 278
Mycogen, 201, 202

National Agricultural Chemical Association, 132
National Association of Insecticide and Disinfectant Manufacturers, 131
National Borax Producers Association, 346n37
National Carbon Company, 124
National Corn Growers Association (NCGA), 307
National Defense Act of 1916, 76
National Farmers Unions, 332
National Fertilizer Association, 77
National Policy (Canada), 44
National Potash Producers Association, 346n37
Natural farming methods, expanding awareness about, 335
Natural pest control approaches, shift to chemical pest control approach, 114, 117–122, 135
Navistar, 171
NCGA. *See* National Corn Growers Association (NCGA)
Neoliberalism
  capital accumulation and rise of, 7
  consolidation in fertilizer sector and, 178, 179
  new interpretation of antitrust laws and, 12, 242
  rise of, 164
  state governance and, 294

Neoliberalism (cont.)
  weakened competition policies and, 327
  weakening of antitrust legislation and, 184, 189
Nerve gas, 128
Network effects, 332
  corporate bigness and, 322
  digital farming services and, 239
  industrial agricultural inputs and, 141, 142
New Alliance for Food Security and Nutrition, 311
New Brandeis movement, focus of, 331
New Deal, 103
New Holland, 173, *174*
New retailers, crowded out by input suppliers, 254–257
New York Stock Exchange, 41
NGOs. *See* Nongovernmental organizations (NGOs)
Nickerson Seeds, 193, 202
"Night soil," 61
Nitrate War, 67
Nitric acid, 75
Nitrogen, 3, 63, 173, 176, 177, 178
  cumulative global use of, 1961–2021, *187*
  from South America: guano and sodium nitrate, 63–68
Nitrogen, phosphorus, and potassium (NPK), 63, 83, 235
Nitrogen-fixing microbes, 284
Nitrogen pollution, 84, 187
Nitrogen synthesis, 10, 74–78, 82, 124, 177–178, 180
  consolidation and cartels and, 78–81
  importance of, reasons for, 75–76
  mastering, US government and, 76–77
  new techniques for, 163
  overproduction and, 175
  processes for, 74–75, 85

Nitrous oxide, nitrogen runoff and emissions of, 187
Nixon administration, price controls and, 176
Nobel Industries, 78
Nongovernmental organizations (NGOs), 245, 304
Non-Hodgkin's lymphoma, glyphosate and, 290, 298
Norges Bank Investment Management, 233
Norsk Hydro, 75, 79, 84, 178, 180, *181*, 347n62
North, Thomas ("Nitrate King"), 67, 68
North America
  commercial seed market development in, 89–90
  intensive settler cultivation and landscapes of, 114–115
Northwestern Plow Manufacturers Association, 36
No-till farming, 286, 289
Novartis, *194*, 200, 208, *225*
Nutrien, 1, *181*, 226, 231, 235, 248, 256, 262
  boycotting of online sellers and, 255
  business activities, 2023, 279t
  carbon credit initiative, 288
  carbon farming and, 286
  digital software platform investments, 241
  4R approach and, 305, 306
  IFDC membership, 313
  lobbying by, 295, 296
  net income of, 2017–2022, *262*
  net profit margin for, 2020–2022, *263*
  recent digital acquisitions of, *240*
Nutrient Stewardship, 305

Occidental Petroleum, 202
Oceanic Phosphate Company of San Francisco, 66

INDEX

OECD, proprietary cross-country seed price data, 252
Oil companies, allure of seeds for, 197
Oil price shocks of 1970s, 165, 199
Oligopolistic markets, 7, 162
Oliver, James, 34
Oliver Chilled Plow Works, 34, 48, *174*
Oliver Farm Equipment Company, 48, 168
Open access data systems, public support for, 336
Open pedigree hybrid varieties, 100
Open Secrets website, 357n82
Open-source seed initiatives, 336
Order of the Patrons of Husbandry. *See* Grange movement
Oreskes, Naomi, 184
Organic chemistry, 114, 122–125
Organic farming, 84
Organization of Petroleum Exporting Countries (OPEC), oil crisis in 1973, 165
Organochlorines, 125–126, 195
  DDT, 126
  lindane, 128
Organophosphates, 125–126, 128, 160
Ozanne, Robert, 41

Panic of 1873, 34–35
Paraquat, 302
Parathion, 128
Paribas, 75
Paris green, 115–116, 117, 120, 122
Parke, Davis and Company, 124
Participatory governance settings, creating, 333–334
Passive investors, 232
Patent Office Division of Agriculture, 89
"Patent pools," rise of, 30–31
Patents, 9, 10, 11, 13, 28, 56, 140. *See also* Innovation
  agrochemicals, 197, 204
  concentration levels and, 249

CRISPR and, 237, 253–254
  for DDT use, 126
  defensive R&D and, 275
  early pesticide industry and, 116–117
  expiry of, removal of LibertyLink seed traits from public domain prior to, 253, 276
  for genetically engineered microorganisms, 205, 206
  information technology platforms and, 241
  market concentration and, 236
  for mechanical reaper industry, 28, 29, 30, 31, 32
  for plow sector, 34
  protection for large chemical firms, 129–130, 135
  seed company acquisitions and, 198
"Patent thickets," 208
Paulson and Co., 231
PCBs, 199
PCS. *See* Potash Corporation of Saskatchewan (PCS)
PEA. *See* Phosphate Export Association (PEA)
Peltz, Nelson, 230
Pension funds, 232
Perkins, George, 40–41, 50
Persia, pest control in, 113
Peru, 64–66, 67
Pest control
  early history of, 113–114, 350n1
  World War I and, 120–122
Pesticide Action Network (PAN), 312
Pesticide input industry, 113–136, 191
  commercial, early history of, 114–117, 135
  corporate concentration in, 157–158
  DDT and new era for, 113
  DDT and other early synthetic pesticides, 125–131
  dominant companies in, 129
  Green Revolution and, 154–155

Pesticide input industry (cont.)
  growth of, social and ecological costs of, 131–135, 136
  lock-in dynamics and, 139, 142, 162
  major mergers and acquisitions in, since late 1800s, 225
  organic chemistry and rise of synthetic pesticides, 122–125, 135
  salesmen and fraud in, 117
  shift to chemical pesticides in, 117–122, 135–136
Pesticide paradigm, continuation of, 135
Pesticides, 204, 323. *See also* Agrochemicals
  attack on Farm to Fork initiative and, 302, 304
  competition policies and, 330
  concentration ratios and market control of, 248, 363n8
  conjoining of seed industry and, 191–193, 195–97, 217–218
  ecological and health concerns about, 213, 218
  FAO CropLife partnership and use of, 312–313
  market-distorting practices and sales of, 255–256
  network effects and use of, 143
  new to market, rising costs and time to develop for, 1975–2014, 204, *205*
  regulations on, 195
  screening of, 196–197
  synthetic, development of, 10
  synthetic, organic chemistry and rise of, 122–125
Pest resistance, to synthetic pesticides, 133–134
Pest resurgence, synthetic pesticide use and, 134
Petroleum companies, seed breeding and sales and, 192
Pfister, Lester, 97, 99
Pfister Hybrid Corn Company, 97, 99

Pfister Seeds, 157, 192, *194, 225*
Pfizer, 200, 207
Pharmaceutical companies
  allure of seeds for, 197
  seed breeding and sales and, 192
  seed company acquisitions, agricultural biotechnology, and, 201, 202
Pharmacia-Upjohn, 200, *225*
Philanthropic foundations, Green Revolution and, 149
Philippines, Green Revolution in, 140, 148, 151
PhosChem, 175, 228
Phosphate, 3, 72, 80, 82, 178
  cumulative global use of, 1961–2021, *187*
  rock deposits, discoveries of, 69, 72
Phosphate Export Association (PEA), 74, 145, 175
Phosphorus, 63, 173, 175, 176
Phosphorus mines, racialized labor regimes in, 69
Pioneer Hi-Bred Corn Company, 98, 102, 104, 109, 153, 157, 192, 193, *194,* 200, 207, 208, 209, *225,* 234, 251
PL480 food aid program (US), 151, 154
Plant-breeding programs, 237, 336
Plant genetic acquisitions, global nature of, 88–89
Plant genetic diversity, hybrids and implications for, 108
Plant Variety Protection Act (PVPA), 198, 199, 205
Platform power, digital farming services and, 239
Plow industry, consolidation in, 42–43
Plow manufacturers, Grangers and, 36
Plows, 27
  development of modern plow business, 33–34
  soil degradation and, 55–56, 57

Plow technologies, development of seed industry and, 92
Policy
  governance and, 13, 15–16, 19, 23
  reform, growing calls for, 326–327
  in support of industrial agriculture, shaping, 188–189
Political power. *See also* Market power; Technology power
  agribusiness influence at UN Food Systems Summit, 314–315, 317
  battle over glyphosate, 298–302
  corporate bigness and, 322–323
  corporate concentration, food systems, and, *20*
  corporate influence at the FAO, 311–314, 317
  corporate power and shaping of, 13, 15–16, 19, 23, 293–317
  efforts to block right-to-repair legislation, 308–311, 317
  food systems and wider costs of, 315–317
  influence campaigns of the agribusiness titans, 295–297
  multipronged offensive of fertilizer industry, 304–308
  New Brandeis movement and, 331
  sustained attack on EU's Farm to Fork strategy, 302–304
Potash, 3, 80, 82, 121, 175, 176, 177, 178, 179, 248
  cumulative global use of, 1961–2021, *187*
  description of, 69–70
  postwar discoveries of, 81
Potash Company of America, 73, 182
PotashCorp, *181*, 226, 228, 229, 234, 235, 256
Potash Corporation of Saskatchewan (PCS), 177, 178, 179, *181*
Potash salts, 70
Potassium, 63, 173

"Poudrette," 61
Poverty, tractors and growth in, 53
"Powder trust," 79
Precision agriculture, rise of, 222
Precision Planting, 222, 223, 226, 238, *240*, 274
Precision spraying equipment, 280
Predatory pricing, 12
Prest-O-Lite Company, 124
Price
  disruptions, adoption of hybrid seeds and, 107, 111
  markups, market power and, 250
  price-cost squeeze, farmers and, 329
Private sector R&D expenditure, growth of, 270–271
Product complementarity, technological integration and, among dominant firms, 234–236
Production systems, fostering more diversity in, 335
Profiteering complaints, 259–264
  COVID-19 pandemic and, 259
  farm machinery sector and, 264
  fertilizer industry and, 260–263, *262*, *263*
  seed and agrochemical markets and, 263–264
Profits
  of chemical companies, regulatory context for, 196
  lock-ins of industrial agriculture and, 291
  market power and, 13, 250
  maximized, corporate bigness and, 322
  seed industry, food crisis of 1970s, and, 199
Public-private partnerships (PPPs), 15, 294, 311
Public sector, seed industry and role of, 99–101
Pyrethrum, 113, 116, 121, 126

Racial discrimination, fertilizer sector and, 17
Railway expansion, 28, 31, 43, 92
Replacement effect, 272
Research and development (R&D)
  agricultural in China, private sector share of, 270
  agrochemicals, corporate consolidation, and, 214–215
  defensive, 274–277
  herbicide-related, dearth of new, 276
  hybrid corn seed, public to private shift in, 105–106, 110
  private sector, cotton and, 271
  private sector expenditures on, growth of, 270–271
  seed hybridization, 11
  state-sponsored funding of, 11
Revolving doors, 294, 297, 316, 317, 322
Rhône-Poulenc, 193, 197, *225*
Rice, 227
Richey, F. D., 100
Right-to-repair (R2R) movement, 258
  blocking of legislation, machinery manufacturers and, 308–311, 317
  PIRG Right to Repair website, 370n72
Riley, Charles, 117–118
Rochester, Anna, 53
Rockefeller, John D., 41, 42, 49, 50
Rockefeller, Nelson, 148
Rockefeller Foundation, 108–109, 148, 153, 154
Rohm and Haas, 124, 201, *225*, 351n46
Rome (ancient), pest control in, 113
Roosevelt, Franklin D., 93, 103
Roosevelt, Theodore, 49–50
Rotenode, 121
Roundup, 202, 203, 206, 209, 211, 213, 216, 223, 224, 229, 285
  battle over glyphosate and, 298, 302
  Roundup Ready soybeans, 211
Royal Bank of Canada, 234

Royal Commission on Farm Machinery (Canada), 155–156
Royal Dutch Shell, 193, 202
Royster Guano Company, 82
R2R movement. *See* Right-to-repair (R2R) movement
Russia
  hybrid seed experimentation in, 105
  invasion of Ukraine, 252, 261, 262, 267, 304, 307, 326
  revoked plans for duties against UAN imports from, 307

Sandoz, 193, 197, 200, *225*
Schumpeter, Joseph, 271, 272
Scientific studies, corporate influence on, 295, 299, 303, 317, 322
SDGs. *See* United Nations Sustainable Development Goals (SDGs)
Sears, Paul, 82–83
Secondary pest outbreaks, synthetic pesticide use and, 134
Seed firms; *See also* Seed input industry
  global CR4 in, 248
  ownership of, by large asset management firms, 233, *233*
Seed-herbicide technological packages, genetically modified, 192
Seed hybridization, state-funded R&D and, 11
Seed input industry, 87–111, 339
  biological products and, 238
  commercial, emergence of, 91–92
  commercial, hybridization and, 87–88
  commercial, social and ecological consequences of, 106–111
  conjoining of pesticide industry and, 191–193, 217–218
  corporate concentration in, 156
  corporate profiteering in, 263
  digital technologies and, 239
  government seed acquisition, distribution, and research, 88–90

INDEX 451

Green Revolution and, 153–154
lock-in dynamics and, 139, 162
role of the public sector in, 99–101
shift from public to private seed R&D, 105–106, 110
US, impact of hybridization on, 96–99
Seed markets, market power and, 251–254, 363n8
Seeds, 23
  certified, 91
  free, provided by US government, 89–90, 107
  genetically engineered, 10, 203–204, 211, 236, 275
  hybridization of, 10
  natural reproducibility of, 87
  selecting for pest-resistant varieties, 113
Seeds-chemicals mergers, consequences of, 207–217
  heightened market influence, 207–210
  intensified policy influence, 215–217
  new technological landscape, 210–215
Settler colonialism, expansion of, 60
Shapiro, Robert, 217
Sharecroppers, tractor adoption and displacement of, 53, 54
Shareholder activism, definition of, 230
Shareholder value, 9, 229
Sharpe and Dohme, 124
Shattuck, Annie, 212
Shell Chemicals, 149, 152, 153, 154, 208, *225*
Sherman Antitrust Act of 1890, 11–12, 40, 41, 50, 123, 184, 259
Sherwin-Williams, 124
Shull, George, 94, 96
SinoChem, *194*, 224
Slave labor, international guano trade and, 64
SmartStax corn seeds, 206
Societal inequalities, corporate concentration, food systems, and, 17, 18, *20*

Sodium nitrate
  Chile's monopoly on, 74, 75
  fertilizer and military applications with, 66
  trade, British corporate dominance in, 67, 68
Sodium nitrate mines, South America, 66–67
Soil degradation
  industrial farming and, 323
  polished iron and steel moldboard plows and, 55–56, 57
Soil fertility, 18
  declining, early responses to, 61–62
  dominant humus theory and, 61
Soil productivity, urbanization and, 60–61
Soil storms, Dust Bowl of the 1930s and, 56
Solvay Process, 78
South Africa
  Climate FieldView software marketed in, 283
  concentration in seed sector in, 249
South America
  nitrate investment arrangements in, 67, 346n14
  nitrogen from: guano and sodium nitrate, 63–68
  sodium nitrate mines of, 66–67
Soviet Union, former
  fall of, fertilizer production resources and, 178
  potash industry in, 81
Soy, 24, 203, 227, 210, 211, 251, 271
SpaceX, Deere's strategic partnership with, 278, 366n36
Sperry Corporation, 170
Sprayers, AI-assisted, 239
Stacked traits, 236, 275
Standard Oil Company, 12, 41, 46, 242
Starlink satellite network (SpaceX), 278

State-run fertilizer companies,
	privatization of, 179
State Street, 233, *233*, 234, 249
State support
	agricultural input industries and, 11
	industrial agricultural model and, 139, 162
Stauffer chemicals, 193, 208
Stickstoff-Syndikat, 79
Stoller, Matt, 325
Stone, Glenn, 215
Strange, Susan, 14, 19
St. Vincent, glyphosate ban and, 300
Subsidies, hybrid adoption and, 103
Sulfur compounds, mineral-based pesticides and, 115, 116
Sulfuric acid production, 124
Sulfur lime, 115
Sumimoto, 80
Sunshine Waterloo, ix, x, *xii*
Superphosphates, 68, 69
Sustainable production models, supporting, 335
Sutch, Richard, 104
Swift & Company, 69, 72, *181*
Syngenta, 200, 201, 223, *225*, 229, 231, 232, 235, 237, 238, 249, 296, 304, 312
	boycotting of online sellers and, 255
	business activities, 2023, 279*t*
	concentration ratio of, 248
	defense of paraquat, 302
	digital software platform investments, 241
	4R approach and, 305
	lobbying expenditures by, 295
	New Alliance for Food Security and Nutrition and, 311
	rebates scheme lawsuit, 255, 256
	recent digital and biological acquisitions of, *240*
	UNFSS and influence of, 315
Syngenta Group, 1, *194*, 224, *225*

FAO partnership with, 313
	operating profit margin, 2022, 263
Synthetic biology techniques, 284
Synthetic pesticides
	farmers, "deskilling," and, 133, 136
	organic chemistry and rise of, 122–125
	pest resistance to, 133–134
	two main types of, 125–126

TALEN, 362n50
Tarapacá Nitrate Company, 66
Tariffs, on Canadian farm machinery, 43–44
Taylor, C. Robert, 264
Technological change, agricultural input firms and, 7, 9–11
Technological integration, product complementarity and, among dominant firms, 234–236
Technological lock-ins, 3, 191. *See also* Lock-ins
	barriers to agroecology transition and, 338
	carbon farming and, 286–289
	corporate bigness and, 322
	corporate concentration, food systems, and, 20, *20*
	deepening, farm machinery and fertilizer consolidation and, 185–188, 189
	dynamics among four industrial agricultural inputs, 139, 162
	farmers' adoption of hybrid corn and, 103
	of genetically modified seeds, 211
	increasing returns to adoption and, 140, 141
	larger firms and, 10
	precision technologies and, 281
Technology licensing fees, 252
Technology power. *See also* Market power; Political power
	agribusiness, wider costs of, 289–291

INDEX

carbon farming, 269, 286–289, 291
corporate bigness and, 322–323
corporate concentration, food systems, and, *20*
defensive R&D, focus on, 274–277
genome editing, 269, 270, 284–286, 291
growing private sector share of agricultural R&D, 270–271
hyper-concentration on innovation, influence of, 271–274
rise of digital farming, 269, 270, 277–284
shaping of, 12, 14–15, 19, 23, 269–292
Technology sovereignty in food systems, supporting, 337
Technology stack, 283
Tenneco, 168, 171, 172
Tennessee Valley Authority (TVA), 80, 179
Terra Industries, 177, 179, *181*
Thailand, 249, 300, 301
Third Point hedge fund, 230
Third World Network, 312
Tied aid regimes, Green Revolution and, 151
Tillage, excessive, soil degradation and, 56
Titans of industrial agriculture. *See also* Agribusiness firms; Agribusiness megamergers, drivers of; Agricultural input industries; Consolidation; Corporate bigness
arguments advanced about rise of, 321–324
influence campaigns of, 295–297
market shaping and power of, 4–5
Tobago, revoked plans for duties against UAN imports from, 307
Townsend, Burdette, International Harvester investigative report, 49, 50
Tractors
advent of and expanded use of, 17–18

advocates of, 52
AI-guided, 278–279
Deere and sensors on, 277
displacement of farm labor, 53
Fordson, 47–48, 347n55
gasoline-powered, 27, 45, 46, 142
luxuries added to, 186
network effects and adoption of, 142–143
repairs of, market dominance in, 257, 308–309
rivalry and consolidation prompted by, 45–49
sales of, corporate concentration and, 156
steam, 46
Trade associations, lobbying activities and, 216
Trade Related Intellectual Property Rights (TRIPS) agreement, 216
Trade secrets, 9, 10
Transparency. *See also* Accountability
in food systems, enabling, 336
in scientific research, needed requirements for, 333
Transportation technologies, 8
Trian hedge fund, 230
Trinidad, revoked plans for duties against UAN imports from, 307
TRIPS agreement. *See* Trade Related Intellectual Property Rights (TRIPS) agreement
Trojan, 207
Trump administration, lobbying by Mosaic and, 306–307
Turkey, seed sector concentration in, 249
Turner, Louis, 152
TVA. *See* Tennessee Valley Authority (TVA)
Twine binders, 37
2,4-D, 128, 158, 275
2,4,5-T, 128

Tying or bundling of related products, 12
Typhus, DDT and fight against, 127

UAN. *See* Urea ammonium nitrate (UAN)
UCC. *See* Union Carbide Corporation (UCC)
Ukraine, Russian invasion of, 252, 261, 262, 267, 304, 307, 326
UN Conference on the Human Environment (1972), 154
UN Food Systems Summit (UNFSS), 22, 316
  agribusiness influence at, 314–315, 317, 338
  lack of attention to corporate dominance at, 2021, 4
UN Human Rights Council of Guiding Principles on Business and Human Rights, 334
Union Carbide, 124, 129, 149, 155, 161, 225
Union Carbide India Limited, Bhopal disaster, 161
Union for the Protection of New Plant Varieties (UPOV), 197–198, 205
United Alkali Company, 78
United Kingdom, seed sector concentration in, 249
United Nations Sustainable Development Goals (SDGs), 327, 339
United States
  antitrust and competition policies in, 11–12, 342n27
  carbon sequestration programs in, 287
  collection of foreign seeds sent back to, 89
  glyphosate's re-registration process and, 298, 300
  regulatory decisions on glyphosate in, 300
  spending on lobbying in, disclosure of, 295, 297
  stronger merger guidelines in, 332, 372n19
  total private sector agricultural R&D in, 270
University endowment funds, 232
University research labs
  gene editing technologies and, 237
  pesticide industry relationship with, 125
  seed industry relationship with, 96
UN Relief and Reconstruction Agency, 104–105
Upjohn, 192, 202, *225*
UPOV. *See* Union for the Protection of New Plant Varieties (UPOV)
Uralkali, 81
Urbanization, 60–61, 92
Urea ammonium nitrate (UAN), CF Industries petition on production of, 307
Uruguay, seed sector concentration in, 249
US Agency for International Development, 152
US Army, 126, 127
US Bureau of Corporations, 41, 50
US Department of Agriculture (USDA), 77, 89, 97, 105, 135, 173, 188, 210, 246, 248, 252, 253, 261, 264, 332
  Bureau of Entomology, 118, 121, 126
  certified seeds and, 91
  corn improvement research, 100
  Division of Entomology, 117, 118
  extension-agent model of, 102
  ownership of IP data, 251
  regional seed centers, 109–110
  synthetic herbicides promoted by, 128
US Department of Commerce, 307
US Department of Justice (DOJ), 172, 175, 200, 239, 274, 331
  farmers' right to repair statement, 259
  fertilizer industry investigations, 69, 72, 75, 76, 77, 78, 79

International Harvester antitrust case, 49, 50, 51
Monsanto investigation, 209
Tenneco-International Harvester merger, 171
US Environmental Protection Agency (EPA), 207, 297, 302
US government
  adoption of hybrids promoted by, 104
  agricultural sector and role of, 89–90
US Government Accountability Office, 210
US Guano Company, 66
US-Mexico, Canada Free Trade Agreement, 301
US Navy, 89
US Patent and Trademark Office, 30
US Steel Corporation, 40, 46, 49
US Tobacco, 46
US War Production Board, 127

ValueAct, 231
Vanguard Group, 233, *233*, 234, 249
Vegetables, arsenic residues on, 120, 125
Vertical integration, 328, 329, 332
  across inputs sectors, 13
  in fertilizer sector, 177, 182, 189, 256, 257
Vertical mergers, 242
Vietnam, glyphosate ban and, 300
Vilmorin, Henry de, 89
Vilmorin, Louis de, 89
Vilmorin & Cie, 89, 193
Vilmorin Seed Farm, 91, 96
Virginia-Carolina Chemical Company, 71, 72, *181*
Visser, Frans, 180

Wages, market power and reduction in, 266
Wallace, Henry A., 93, 94, 97, 98, 99, 100, 103, 104, 110, 122, 147–148
Wallace, Henry C., 93, 94, 98, 99

Wallace, Ilo, 98
Wallaces' Farmer, 93–94, 98
War of the Pacific, 67
Waterloo Gasoline Engine Company, 46, *174*
Waterloo Manufacturing Company, ix, x
Water use, digital data storage/processing and, 281
Wealth, Brandeis on concentration of, 5–6
Webb-Pomerene Act, 73, 175, 342n27
WEF. *See* World Economic Forum (WEF)
WeFarm, 284
Wheat, 24, 60, 227
Wheat seeds
  Mexican Agricultural Program and, 148
  price of, 210
White Motor Company, 168, *174*
White Tractor, 173
WHO. *See* World Health Organization (WHO)
William Gibbs and Company, 66–67
Wire binders, 37
Women
  corporate dominance in food policy and, 317
  Iroquois, farming and, 107
  tractor adoption and, 52, 53
World Bank, 146, 149, 151, 153
World Economic Forum (WEF), 314, 315
World Food Conference of 1974, 152, 166
World Health Organization (WHO), glyphosate concerns and, 298
World Trade Organization (WTO), TRIPS agreement of, 216
World War I, 50, 75, 76, 77, 79, 82, 116
  Chilean nitrates and munitions for, 68
  expanded chemical pesticide industry and, 120–122
  German potash monopoly broken after, 73

World War I (cont.)
  high commodity prices during, 101
  tractor adoption during, 53
World War II, 80, 104
  DDT use during, 126–127
  globalization of markets after, 8, 11
  rise of global corporations after, 146
  synthetic chemicals production and profits during, 128
W. R. Grace & Co., 76
W. S. Clark, *181*
WTO. *See* World Trade Organization (WTO)
Wu, Tim, 184, 331

Yara, 1, 75, 180, *181*, 226, 262, 284, 304
  business activities, 2023, 279*t*
  carbon farming and, 286
  digital software platform investments, 241
  4R approach and, 305
  IFDC membership, 313
  international lobbying activities, 308
  lobbying expenditures by, 295
  net income of, 2017–2022, *262*
  net profit margin for, 2020–2022, *263*
  New Alliance for Food Security and Nutrition and, 311
  recent digital acquisitions of, *240*
  UNFSS and influence of, 315
Yara-USA, 248
Yorkton Distributors, 255
Yost, Israel, 150

Zaibatsu firms (Japan), 80, 81
Zeidler, Othmar, 126